Bibliography of Canadian and Comparative Federalism, 1980-1985

Darrel R. Reid

Institute of
Intergovernmental
Relations

Queen's University
Kingston, Ontario
Copyright 1988

Canadian Cataloguing in Publication Data

Reid, Darrel R. (Darrel Robert), 1957-
  Bibliography of Canadian and comparative federalism, 1980-1985

Includes index.
ISBN 0-88911-451-X

1. Federal government - Canada - Bibliography.
2. Federal-provincial relations - Canada - Bibliography.* 3. Federal government -
Bibliography.
I. Queen's University (Kingston, Ont.). Institute of Intergovernmental Relations.
II. Title.

Z1387.F4R44 1987   016.32102'0971   C87-094974-8

The Institute of Intergovernmental Relations

The Institute, part of Queen's University, is the only organization in Canada whose mandate is solely to promote research and communication on the challenges facing the federal system.

Current research interests focus on the respective roles of federal and provincial governments in the economy, the place of Quebec in confederation, aboriginal self-government, and a wide range of policy issues affected by the structure and working of federalism.

The Institute pursues these objectives through research conducted by its own staff, and other scholars, at Queen's and elsewhere through an active and growing publications program and through seminars and conferences.

The Institute links academics and practitioners of federalism in federal and provincial governments and the private sector.

Contents

Preface

Scope

As its title suggests, this bibliography has primarily to do with Canadian federalism. It includes entries for books or relevant sections thereof, journal articles and government documents. As almost every bibliographic entity produced in Canada could fairly be said to relate in some manner or other to Canadian federalism, though, it has been necessary to limit entries in this bibliography to items that relate to the *interaction* of the various levels of government within the federation. Most of these have to do with federal-provincial or interprovincial matters, although there are selected references to federal-provincial-municipal matters and local government.

Although most of the entries in this bibliography document the Canadian federal experience, intergovernmental relations within this federation do not take place in a vacuum. They are informed, rather, by the experiences of other federations around the world. For this reason, selected references on federal theory, comparative federalism and intergovernmental relations in other federations have been included as well.

This bibliography covers the period from 1980-1985, and is intended to extend the bibliographic work of the Institute of Intergovernmental Relations which had previously covered the period 1967-1979. One exception to this five-year time frame has been made, however: in the case of the 1985 Royal Commission on the Economic Union and Development Prospects for Canada (Macdonald Commission), some of the seventy-one background *Research Studies* were published in 1986. As these constitute a major research resource on Canadian federalism and intergovernmental relations, I could see no good reason for dividing the corpus, and the contents of the 1986 publications within this series have been included in this volume. Submissions to the Royal Commissions have, for the most part, been excluded; in the case of the Macdonald Commission, those interested in the many submissions to that commission are referred to the seven-volume *Royal Commission on the Economic Union and Development Prospects for Canada Content Analysis* series (Ottawa: Supply and Services, 1985).

Organization

This bibliography has been organized into six sections: 1. **Federalism and Federal Countries** deals primarily with differing manifestations of federalism around the world, federal theory and comparative federalism; items treating Canadian federalism from the standpoint of federal theory are included here. 2. **Bases of**

Community: Territory and Ethnicity includes documents that examine the regional, ethnic and nationalistic components of federal states and movements and their relationship with federalism and intergovernmental relations. 3. **Courts and Constitutions** covers various legal approaches to federalism including the ways in which federal relationships have been encoded in law, and in which disputes are arbitrated through legal means. 4. **Intergovernmental Relations** focuses upon the mechanics of federal government and the administrative processes required for the implementation of policy within federations. 5. **Policy Issues and Roles** presents a broad view of the many policy areas in which the interests of different levels of government intersect and often collide. 6. **Politics and Government** reflects the differing ways federalism has worked itself out in the institutional arrangements of Canadian political life.

Each section is organized in alphabetical order by author. Each entry appears only once in the bibliography; in those cases - and there will, no doubt, be many - in which an item could have been placed in some or even all of the chapters, or if the reader's judgement on these matters differs with mine, access to a given item can be gained through the author, title and subject indexes at the back of the work. The subject index attempts to combine controlled-vocabulary and keyword approaches to the material. Major headings, a list of which may be found in the *Table of Contents,* are re-indexed for the users' convenience.

This work and its accompanying indexes were produced from a Procite bibliographic database. Citations are in ANSI (American National Standards Institute) format.

Due to the wide scope of the bibliography it is inevitable that some relevant documents will have been missed. The responsibility for such omissions is, of course, mine. Those users who identify relevant works left out are encouraged to contact the Institute so that these might be added to our federalism database and included in any possible reprints.

Darrel R. Reid

Acknowledgements

This bibliography has been a project in which all the staff of the Institute of Intergovernmental Relations have, to some extent, been involved. Some, like administrative secretary Patricia Candido, provided timely encouragement. Others rolled up their sleeves and dug into the task. Special recognition is due Valerie Jarus, who patiently endured the drudgery of turning cryptic printout sheets into a finished product. Anne Poels and Denis Robert kindly volunteered to proofread the text -- no mean task -- and Pat Probert spent long hours entering data into the computer.

Principal funding for the project, without which it could not have gone ahead, was generously provided by the Social Sciences and Humanities Research Council under its Canadian Research Tools Program. Valerie Mayman, Institute Librarian 1983-4, conceived the project and prepared the initial grant application to the SSHRC.

Darrel R. Reid, Bibliographer
Peter M. Leslie, Institute Director

1 Federalism and Federal Countries

1. Adams, E. Kathleen. *A changing federalism: the condition of the states*. Denver, Colo.: Education Finance Center, Education Programs Division, Education Commission of the States; [1982]; v, 63 p.

2. Advisory Commission on Intergovernmental Relations. *Agenda for American federalism: restoring confidence and competence: the federal role in the federal system: the dynamics of growth*. Washington, D.C.: ACIR; 1980. (US Advisory Commission on Intergovernmental Relations report A-86).

3. Advisory Commission on Intergovernmental Relations. *Condition of contemporary federalism: conflicting theories and collapsing constraints*. Washington, D.C.: ACIR; 1980; xii, 251 p. (Advisory Commission on Intergovernmental Relations report A-78).

4. Advisory Commission on Intergovernmental Relations. *Future of federalism in the 1980's: report and papers from the Conference on the Future of Federalism*, Alexandria, Virginia, July 25-26, 1980. Washington, D.C.: ACIR; 1981; vii, 135 p. (Advisory Commission on Intergovernmental Relations report M-126).

5. Advisory Commission on Intergovernmental Relations. *Regulatory federalism: policy, process, impact and reform*. [Washington, D.C.]: ACIR; 1984. (Advisory Commission on Intergovernmental Relations report A-95).

6. Advisory Commission on Intergovernmental Relations. *Studies in comparative federalism: Australia, Canada, the United States, and West Germany*, by Richard H. Leach. Washington, D.C.: Advisory Commission on Intergovernmental Relations; 1982; viii, 99 p.

7. Advisory Commission on Intergovernmental Relations. *Studies in comparative federalism: Australia*. [Washington, D.C.]: ACIR; 1981; vii, 60 p. (Advisory Commission on Intergovernmental Relations report M-129).

8. Advisory Commission on Intergovernmental Relations. *Studies in comparative federalism: Australia, Canada, the United States and West Germany*. [Washington, D.C.]: ACIR; 1981; viii, 99 p. (Advisory Commission on Intergovernmental Relations report M-130).

9. Advisory Commission on Intergovernmental Relations. *Studies on comparative federalism: Canada*. [Washington, D.C.]: ACIR; 1981; vii, 95 p. (Advisory Commission on Intergovernmental Relations report M-127).

10. Advisory Commission on Intergovernmental Relations. *Studies on comparative federalism: West Germany*. [Washington, D.C.]: ACIR; 1981; x, 89 p. (Advisory Commission on Intergovernmental Relations report M-128).

11. Advisory Council for Inter-Goverment Relations. *Federalism in West Germany: the functions and relations of the different levels of government*, by J. Rydon and H.A. Wolfsohn. Canberra: Advisory Council for Inter-Government Relations; 1980; vi, 116 p. (Relationships reference; information paper; v. 8).

12. Ahana, Daniel U. *The development of Nigerian federalism* [microfiche]: University of Waterloo; 1984; 3 fiches (209 fr.). Ottawa: National Library of Canada, 1985.

13. Aitken, Don. Australian politics in a federal context. In: Mathews, Russell, ed. *Public policies in two federal countries: Canada and Australia*. Canberra: Centre for Research on Federal Financial Relations, Australian National University; 1982; 47-50 p.

14. Armstrong, Christopher. Federalism, continentalism and economic development in Canada. *Czasopismo Prawno-Historyczne* (Poland); 1980; 32(1): 185-198.

15. Aspaturian, Vernon V. *The Union Republics in Soviet diplomacy : a study of Soviet federalism in the service of Soviet foreign policy*. Westport, Conn.: Greenwood Press; 1984; 228 p.

16. Bakvis, Herman. *Federalism and the organization of political life: Canada in comparative perspective*. Kingston: Institute of Intergovernmental Relations, Queen's University; c1981; ix, 98 p. (Queen's studies on the future of the Canadian communities; v. 2).

17. Bakvis, Herman. Structure and process in federal and consociational arrangements. *Publius*; 1985 Spring; 15(2): 57-69.

18. Ball, Howard. *Constitutional powers: cases on the separation of powers and federalism*. St. Paul: West Publishing Co.; 1980; xvi, 355 p.

19. Balmer, Colin. Criteria for the allocation of responsibilities: an interpretive discussion. In: Grewal, Bhajan Singh. *Towards adaptive federalism*. Canberra: Australian Government Publishing Service; Advisory Council for Inter-government Relations; 1981: 217-242; 243 p. (Relationships Reference; Information papers; v. 9).

20. Barnes, Nell D. *"New federalism" and the cities : a resource guide*. Chicago: CPL Bibliographies; c1985; ii, 7 p. (CPL bibliography; v. 161).

21. Bastien, Richard. *Federalism and decentralization, where do we stand?* [Ottawa]: Supply and Services Canada; c1981; vii, 56, 58, viii p.

22. Bastien, Richard. *Le fédéralisme canadien et ses problèmes*. Etudes (France); 1982; 357(6): 597-610.

23. Beam, David R. Forecasting the future of federalism: task and challenge. In: Advisory Commission on Intergovernmental Relations. *The future of federalism in the 1980's*. Washington D.C.: ACIR; 1981: 5-26; vii, 135 p. (Advisory Commission on Intergovernmental Relations report; v. M-126).

24. Becton, Clare; MacKay, A. Wayne, res. coords. *Recurring issues in Canadian federalism*. Toronto: University of Toronto Press; Royal Commission on the Economic Union and Development Prospects for Canada; 1986; xv, 187 p. (The collected research studies; v. 57).

25. Beer, Samuel H. [and others]. *Federalism: making the system work*. Washington D.C.: Centre for National Policy; 1982; 60 p.

26. Ben Dor, Gabriel. Federalism in the Arab world. In: Elazar, Daniel J, ed. *Federalism and political integration*. Latham, MD: University Press of America; 1984: 191-203; 231 p.

27. Bender, Lewis G.; Stever, James A., eds. *Administering the new federalism*. Boulder: Westview Press; 1985; p.

28. Bernier, Ivan; Roy, Nicolas; Pentland, Charles; Soberman, Daniel. The concept of economic union in international and constitutional law. In: Krasnick, Mark, res. coord. *Perspectives on the Canadian economic union*. Toronto: University of Toronto Press; Royal Commission on the Economic Union and Development Prospects for Canada; 1986: 35-153; xvi, 271 p. (The collected research studies; v. 60).

29. Blair, Philip M. *Federalism and judicial review in West Germany*. Oxford: Oxford University Press; 1981; xvii, 332 p.

30. Boily, Robert. Les Etats fédéralistes et pluralistes, le cas canadien: un processus de fédéralisation en éclatement. Czasopismo Prawno-Historyczne (Poland); 1980; 32(1): 199-221.

31. Boisvert, Michel. *Les implications économiques de la souveraineté-association: le Canada face à l'expérience des pays nordiques*. Montréal: Presses de l'Université de Montréal; 1980; 211 p.

32. Boogman, J. C.; van der Plaat, G. N. *Federalism: history and significance of a form of government*. The Hague: Martinus Nijhoff; 1980; 307 p.

33. Breton, Albert; Scott, Anthony. *The design of federations*. Montreal: Institute for Research on Public Policy; c1980; xxi, 60 p.

34. Brown, M. Paul. Responsiveness versus accountability in collaborative federalism: the Canadian experience. *Canadian Public Administration*; 1983 Winter; 26(4): 629-639.

35. Brunelle, Dorval. *L'état solide: sociologie du fédéralisme au Canada et au Québec*. Montréal: Editions Sélect; 1982; 174 p.

36. Brunet, Michel. Le fédéralisme canadien vu de Londres 1867-1980. *L'Action nationale*; 1981; 70(6): 451-462.

37. Burgess, Michael. Empire, Ireland and Europe: a century of British federal ideas. In: *idem*, ed. *Federalism and federation in western Europe*. London: Croom Helm; 1985: 127-152; 227 p.

38. Burgess, Michael. Federalism and federation in western Europe. In: *idem*, ed. *Federalism and federation in western Europe*. London: Croom Helm; 1985: 15-33; 227 p.

39. Burgess, Michael, ed. *Federalism and federation in western Europe*. London: Croom Helm; 1985; 227 p.

40. Burkett, Tony. The ambivalent role of the Bundesrat in the West German federation. In: Burgess, Michael, ed. *Federalism and federation in western Europe*. London: Croom Helm; 1985: 204-219; 227 p.

41. Burrows, Bernard; Denton, Geoffrey. *Devolution or federalism?: options for a United Kingdom. London*: Macmillan; 1980; xii, 94 p.

42. Cairns, Alan C. The embedded state: state-society relations in Canada. In: Banting, Keith, res. coord. *State and society: Canada in comparative perspective*. Toronto: University of Toronto Press; Royal Commission on the Economic Union and Development Prospects for Canada; 1986: 53-86; xiii, 131 p. (The collected research studies; v. 31).

43. Cairns, Alan C. *Political science 322 (text): Federalism in Canada*. Rev. ed. Vancouver: University of British Columbia; c1980; xiv, 50 p.

44. Canada. Canadian Unity Information Office. *Aspects of the flexibility of Canadian federalism*. [Ottawa]: Canadian Unity Information Office; 1982.

45. Canada. Canadian Unity Information Office. *Confederation, unitary system federation; federalism throughout the world; the common market and the Canadian experience; aspects of the flexibility of Canadian federalism*. Ottawa: Publications Canada; 1982; iv, 51, iv, 53 p.

46. Canada. Canadian Unity Information Office. *Notes on Canadian federalism*. [Ottawa]: Canadian Unity Information Office; 1982; 56, 60 p.

47. Cannon, Gordon E. Consociationalism versus control: Canada as a case study: *Western Political Quarterly*; 1982 January; 35(1): 50-64.

48. Carter, Richard. Séparation, annexion, et fédéralisme: au-delà des préceptes normatifs usuels. *L'Actualité économique*; 1983 September; 59(3): 596-619.

49. Chubb, John E. The political economy of federalism. *American Political Science Review*; 1985 December; 79(4): 994-1015.

50. Claeys, Paul H.; Loeb-Mayer Nicole. Le "para-fédéralisme" belge: une tentative de conciliation par le cloisonnement. *International Political Science Review*; 1984; 5(4): 473-490.

51. Cole, Richard L.; Taebel, Delbert A. The new federalism: promises, programs, and performance. *Publius*; 1986 Winter; 16: 3-10.

52. Collins, John. Federal ideas in contemporary Ireland. In: Burgess, Michael, ed. *Federalism and federation in western Europe*. London: Croom Helm; 1985: 99-126; 227 p.

53. Croisat, Maurice; Tournon, Jean. Centralisation et pluralisme: le paradoxe français. *International Political Science Review*; 1984; 5(4): 415-428.

54. Delmartino, Frank. Belgium: a regional state or a federal state in the making? In: Burgess, Michael, ed. *Federalism and federation in western Europe*. London: Croom Helm; 1985: 34-58; 227 p.

55. Dembkowski, Harry E. *The union of Lublin, Polish federalism in the golden age*. Boulder: East European Monographs; 1982; vii, 380 p. (East European monographs; v. 116).

56. Doerr, Audrey D. Public administration: federalism and intergovernmental relations. *Canadian Public Administration*; 1982; 25(4): 564-577.

57. Dua, B. D. India: a study in the pathology of a federal system. *Journal of Commonwealth and Comparative Politics*; 1981; 19(3): 257-275.

58. Duchacek, Ivo D. Consociational cradle of federalism. *Publius*; 1985 Spring; 15(2): 35-48.

59. Duchacek, Ivo D. Consociations of fatherlands: the revival of confederal principles and practices. *Publius*; 1982 Fall; 12(4): 129-177.

60. Duchacek, Ivo D. Federalist responses to ethnic demands. In: Elazar, Daniel J., ed. *Federalism and political integration*. Latham, MD.: University Press of America; 1984: 59-72; 321 p.

61. Dunn, Sheilagh M. Federalism, constitutional reform, and the economy: the Canadian experience. *Publius*; 1983 Spring; 13(2): 129-142.

62. Dupré, J. Stephan. Reflections on the workability of executive federalism. In: Simeon, Richard, res. coord. *Intergovernmental relations*. Toronto: University of Toronto Press; Royal Commission on the Economic Union and Development Prospects for Canada; 1985: 1-32; xiv, 263 p. (The collected research studies; v. 63).

63. Ehrlich, Stanislaw. Theoretical reflections on federations and federalism. *International Political Science Review*; 1984; 5(4): 359-368.

64. Elazar, Daniel J. Afterward: steps in the study of American political culture. *Publius*; 1980 Spring; 10(2): 127-139.

65. Elazar, Daniel J. *American federalism : a view from the States*. 3rd ed. New York: Harper & Row; c1984; v, 270 p.

66. Elazar, Daniel J. Confederation and federal liberty. *Publius*; 1982 Fall; 12(4): 1-14.

67. Elazar, Daniel J. Federalism and consociational regimes. *Publius*; 1985 Spring; 15(2): 17-35.

68. Elazar, Daniel J, ed. *Federalism and political integration*. Latham, MD: University Press of America; 1984; 231 p.

69. Elazar, Daniel J. The political theory of covenant: biblical origin and modern developments. *Publius*; 1980 Fall; 10(4): 3-30.

70. Elazar, Daniel J. The role of federalism in political integration. In: Elazar, Daniel J., ed. *Federalism and political integration*. Latham, MD.: University Press of America; 1984: 13-59; 231 p.

71. Elazar, Daniel J. The evolving federal system. *Proceedings of the Academy of Political Science*; 1981; 34(2): 5-19.

72. Engelmann, Frederick C.; Schwartz, Mildred A. Perceptions of Austrian federalism. *Publius*; 1981 Winter; 11(1): 81-93.

73. Epstein, Leon D. Party confederations and political nationalization. *Publius*; 1982 Fall; 12(4): 67-102.

74. Esman, Milton J. Federalism and modernization: Canada and the United States. *Publius*; 1984 Winter; 14(1): 21-38.

75. Esterbauer, Fried. Austrian experiences in utilizing federalism to conciliate ethnic minorities. In: Elazar, Daniel J., ed. *Federalism and political integration*. Latham, MD.: University Press of America; 1984: 145-154; 321 p.

76. Forsyth, Murray. *Union of states: the theory and practice of confederation*. New York: Homes and Meier Publishers; 1981; xii, 236 p.

77. Forsyth, Murray Greensmith. *Federalism and the future of South Africa*. Braamfontein: South African Institute of International Affairs; [1984]; 28 p. (Bradlow series; v. 2).

78. Freeman, Gordon M. The process of covenant. *Publius*; 1980 Fall; 10(4): 71-80.

79. Friedman, Murray. Religion and politics in an age of pluralism, 1945-1976: an ethnocultural view. *Publius*; 1980 Summer; 10(3): 45-76.

80. Gagnon, Alain G. *Fédéralisme en pays multicommunautaires: un cadre d'analyse théorique et comparatif*. [s.l.]: Association canadienne de science politique; 1982.

81. Gagnon, Alain G. *Politics in federal states: approaches to the study of comparative federalism* [Photocopy]. 13th World Congress of the International Political Science Association; July 15-20, 1985; Paris; [1985]; 25 p.

82. Galligan, Brian. Writing on Australian federalism: the current state of the art. *Australian Journal of Public Administration*; 1984 June; 43(2): 177-186.

83. Gaus, John M. Federalism and intergovernmental relations. In: Wright, Deil S.; White, Harvey L., eds. *Federalism and intergovernmental relations*. Washington: The American Society for Public Administration; 1984: 44-45; x, 333 p. (PAR classics).

84. Gibbins Roger; Knopff, Rainer; Morton, F.L. Canadian federalism, the Charter of Rights, and the 1984 election. *Publius*; 1985 Summer; 15(3): 155-169.

85. Gitelman, Zvi. Federalism and multiculturalism in socialist systems. In: Elazar, Daniel J., ed. *Federalism and political integration*. Latham, MD.: University Press of America; 1984: 157-169; 321 p.

86. Glendening, Parris N.; Reeves, Mavis Mann. *Pragmatic federalism: an intergovernmental view of American government*. 2nd ed. Pacific Palisades: Palisades Publishers; 1984; ix, 365 p.

87. Golembiewski, Robert T.; Wildavsky, Aaron B., eds. *The costs of federalism: in honor of James W. Fesler*. New Brunswick, N.J.: Transaction Books; 1984; viii, 132 p.

88. Graziano, Luigi; Girotti, Fiorenzo; Bonet, Luciano. Coalition politics at the regional level and center-periphery relationships: the case of Italy. *International Political Science Review*; 1984; 5(4): 429-442.

89. Greene, Jack P. The background of the Articles of Confederation. *Publius*; 1982 Fall; 12(4): 15-44.

90. Greilsammer, Ilan. Federalism and European integration. In: Elazar, Daniel J., ed. *Federalism and political integration*. Latham, MD.: University Press of America; 1984: 107-131; 321 p.

91. Grewal, Bhajan Singh. Economic criteria for the assignment of functions in a federal system. In: *idem.*, ed. *Towards adaptive federalism*. Canberra: Australian Government Publishing Service; Advisory Council for Inter-government Relations; 1981: 1-60; 243 p.

92. Grewal, Bhajan Singh. *Towards adaptive federalism: a search for criteria for responsibility sharing in a federal system*. Canberra: Australian Government Publishing Service; Advisory Council for Inter-government Relations; 1981; vii, 243 p. (Relationships Reference; Information papers; v. 9).

93. Grewal, Bhajan Singh; Brennan, H. Geoffrey; Mathews, Russell L, eds. *The economics of federalism*. Canberra: Australian National University Press; 1980; xiii, 432 p.

94. Haider, Donald H. The intergovernmental system. *Proceedings of the Academy of Political Science*; 1981; 34(2): 20-30.

95. Hanson, Russell. Political culture, interparty competition and political efficacy. *Publius*; 1980 Spring; 10(2): 17-36.

96. Hari, Ram. *Special status in Indian federalism, Jammu and Kashmir*. Delhi: Seema Publications; 1983; viii, 230 p.

97. Hartley, Trevor C. Federalism, courts and legal systems: the emerging constitution of the European community. *American Journal of Comparative Law*; 1986 Spring; (1): 229-247.

98. Hawkins, Robert B., Jr., ed. *American federalism, a new partnership for the Republic*. San Francisco: Institute for Contemporary Studies; 1982; xii, 281 p.

99. Herron, David R. *The ends of American federalism: a European perspective* [Photocopy]. Southwestern Political Science Association Annual Meeting; March 22, 1984; Fort Worth, Texas; [1984]; 44 p.

100. Hettich, W.; Winer, S. *Federalism, special interests and the exchange of policies for political resources*. Ottawa: Carleton University. Dept. of Economics; 1984. (Carleton Economics Papers; v. 84-16).

101. Hiemstra, John L. *Trudeau's political philosophy: its implication for liberty and progress* [M. Phil., Institute for Christian Studies]. Toronto: the author; 1983; 107 p.

102. Hiller, J.K. Canadian federalism and the Australian parallel. *Acadiensis*; 1980; 10(1): 154-158.

103. Hodge, William C. Federalism and the Soviet Constitution of 1977: commonwealth perspectives. *Washington Law Review*; 1980 June; 55(3): 505-542.

104. Homes, Jean. The Australian federalism system. *International Political Science Review*; 5; 4(397-414).

105. House, Peter W.; Steger, Wilbur A. *Modern federalism: an analytic approach*. Lexington, Mass.: Lexington Books; c1982; xvi, 301 p.

106. Howard, Lawrence C. Executive development: an intergovernmental perspective. In: Wright, Deil S.; White, Harvey L., eds. *Federalism and intergovernmental relations*. Washington: American Society for Public Administration; 1984: 244-260; 333 p.

107. Howitt, Arnold M. *Managing federalism: studies in intergovernmental relations*. Washington, D.C.: Congressional Quarterly Press; 1984; xiv, 321 p.

108. Hudon, Raymond. *Intégration et diversité: les dilemmes du fédéralisme canadien*. International Political Science Review; 1984; 5(4): 455-472.

109. Hueglin, Thomas O. Yet the age of anarchism. *Publius*; 1985 Spring; 15(2): 101-112.

110. Hueglin, Thomas O. *Federalism and fragmentation: a comparative view of political accommodation in Canada.* Kingston: Institute of Intergovernmental Relations, Queen's University; 1984; 19; iii, 58 p. (Discussion papers).

111. Huon de Kermadec, Jean-Michel. La persistence de la crise du fédéralisme canadien. Revue de droit public; 1982; 98(6): 1601-1626.

112. Hutcheson, John. Harold Innis and the unity and diversity of Confederation. *Journal of Canadian Studies;* 1982-83 Winter; 17(4): 57-73.

113. Irvine, Douglas McKinnon. South Africa: federal potentialities in current developments. *International Political Science Review;* 1984; 5(4): 491-506.

114. Jinadu, L. Adele. Federalism, the consociational state, and ethnic conflict in Nigeria. *Publius;* 1985 Spring; 15(2): 71-100.

115. Joslyn, Richard A. Manifestations of Elazar's political subcultures: state opinion and the content of political campaign advertising. *Publius;* 1980 Spring; 10(2): 37-58.

116. Kaden, Lewis B. Federalism in the courts: agenda for the 1990's. In: Advisory Commission on Intergovernmental Relations. *The future of federalism in the 1980's.* Washington D.C.: ACIR; 1981: 89-109; vii, 135 p. (Advisory Commission on Intergovernmental Relations report; v. M-126).

117. Kettl, Donald F. *Managing community development in the new federalism.* New York: Praeger; 1980; xi, 156 p.

118. Kettl, Donald F. *The regulation of American federalism.* Baton Rouge: Louisiana State University Press; 1983; xviii, 195 p. (Miller Center series on the American presidency).

119. Kettl, Donald F. The fourth face of federalism. In: Wright, Deil S.; White, Harvey L. *Federalism and intergovernmental relations.* Washington: American Society for Public Administration; 1984: 290-301; 333 p.

120. Kincaid, John. Influential models of political association in the western tradition. *Publius;* 1980 Fall; 10(4): 31-58.

121. Kincaid, John. Political culture and the quality of urban life. *Publius;* 1980 Spring; 10(2): 89-110.

122. Kincaid, John. Political cultures of the American compound republic. *Publius;* 1980 Spring; 10(2): 1-16.

123. King, Preston. *Federalism and federation.* Baltimore: The John Hopkins University Press; 1982; 159 p.

124. Kis, T. *Fédéralisme: ses perspectives historiques, théoriques et typologiques.* [Ottawa]: Université d'Ottawa. Département de science politique; 1980. (Université d'Ottawa Département de science politique. Notes de recherche; v. 9).

125. Kloti, Ulrich; Nussli, Kurt. Constitutional reform in Switzerland: task distribution, political ideas and financial interests. In: Burgess, Michael, ed. *Federalism and federation in western Europe*. London: Croom Helm; 1985: 187-203; 227 p.

126. Kornberg, Allan; Clarke, Harold D.; Stewart, Marianne C. Public support for community and regime in the regions of contemporary Canada. *American Review of Canadian Studies*; 1980 Spring; 10(1): 75-93.

127. Krishna Shetty, K. P. *The law of Union-state relations and Indian federalism*. Madras: Sai Naga Publications; 1981; viii, 530 p.

128. Landes, Ronald G. *The Canadian polity: a comparative introduction*. Scarborough: Prentice-Hall Canada; 1983; xii, 452 p.

129. Leach, Richard H. Canadian federalism revisited. *Publius*; 1984 Winter; 14(1): 9-20.

130. Legare, Anne. Towards a marxist theory of Canadian federalism: *Studies in Political Economy*; 1982 Summer; 8: 37-58.

131. Lemco, Jonathan; Regenstreif, Peter. The fusion of powers and the crisis of Canadian federalism. *Publius*; 1984 Winter; 14(1): 109-120.

132. Leonardi, Robert; Nanetti, Rafaella Y.; Putnam, Robert D. Devolution as a political process: the case of Italy. *Publius*; 1981 Winter; 11(1): 95-117.

133. Leslie, Peter M. Canada as a bicommunal polity. In: Becton, Clare; MacKay, A. Wayne, res. coords. *Recurring issues in Canadian federalism*. Toronto: University of Toronto Press; Royal Commission on the Economic Union and Development Prospects for Canada; 1986: 113-144; xv, 187 p. (The collected research studies; v. 57).

134. Levy, Claude. *Emancipation, sugar, and federalism : Barbados and the West Indies, 1833-1876*. Gainesville: University Presses of Florida; 1980; viii, 206 p. (Latin American monographs, 2nd series; v. 25).

135. Light, Alfred R. The Governors' push for emergency energy powers. *Publius*; 1980 Winter; 10(1): 57-68.

136. Lijphart, Arend. Non-majoritarian democracy: a comparison of federal and consociational theories. *Publius*; 1985 Spring; 15(2): 3-16.

137. Loughlin, John. Federalist and regionalist movements in France. In: Burgess, Michael, ed. *Federalism and federation in western Europe*. London: Croom Helm; 1985: 76-98; 227 p.

138. Lovrich, Nicholas P., Jr.; Daynes, Byron W.; Ginger, Laura. Public policy and the effects of historical-cultural phenomena: the case of Indiana. *Publius*; 1980 Spring; 10(2): 111-126.

139. Lowe, Carl, ed. *Reaganomics: the new federalism*. New York; H.W. Wilson Co; c1984. (The reference shelf; v. 55, 5).

140. Lowi, Theodore J. Why is there no socialism in the United States? A federal analysis. *International Political Science Review*; 1984; 5(4): 369-380.

141. Luther, Richard. The revitalization of federalism and federation in Austria. In: Burgess, Michael, ed. *Federalism and federation in western Europe*. London: Croom Helm; 1985: 154-186; 227 p.

142. Lutz, Donald S. From covenant to constitution in American political thought. *Publius*; 1980 Fall; 10(4): 101-134.

143. MacKay, A. Wayne; Becton, Clare. Institutional and constitutional arrangements: an overview. In: *idem.*, res. coords. *Recurring issues in Canadian federalism*. Toronto: University of Toronto Press; Royal Commission on the Economic Union and Development Prospects for Canada; 1986: 1-76; xv, 187 p. (The collected research studies; v. 57).

144. Martin, A.W. Australian federalism and nationalism: historical notes. In: Mathews, Russell, ed. *Public policies in two federal countries: Canada and Australia*. Canberra: Centre for Research on Federal Financial Relations, Australian National University; 1982; 27-46 p.

145. Mathews, Russell, ed. *Federalism in Australia and the Federal Republic of Germany: a comparative study*. Canberra: Australian National University Press, Centre for Research on Federal Financial Relations; 1980; xiii, 356 p.

146. Mathews, Russell. *Revenue sharing in federal systems*. Canberra: Centre for Research on Federal Financial Relations, Australian National University; 1980; viii, 89 p. (Research monograph; v. 31).

147. Mathews, Russell. Tax effectiveness and tax equity in federal countries. In: McLure, Charles E., Jr., ed. *Tax assignment in federal countries*. Canberra: ANU Press; 1983: 70-99; xix, 370 p.

148. Mawhood, Philip. The politics of survival: federal states in the third world. *International Political Science Review*; 1984; 5(4): 521-532.

149. McBeath, Gerald A.; Helms, Andrea R. C. Alternate routes to autonomy in federal and quasi-federal systems. *Publius*; 1983; 13(4): 21-41.

150. McLarty, R.A. *Federation in Canada and Australia: where might we go from here?* Canberra: Centre for Research on Federal Financial Relations, Australian National University; 1980; 10 p. (Reprint series; v. 35).

151. McRoberts, Kenneth. Unilateralism, bilateralism and multilateralism: approaches to Canadian federalism. In: Simeon, Richard, res. coord. *Intergovernmental relations*. Toronto: University of Toronto Press; Royal Commission on the Economic Union and Development Prospects for Canada; 1985: 71-130; xiv, 263 p. (The collected research studies; v. 63).

152. Miller, Robert F. *Federalism as a safety valve: the Yugoslav case.* Canberra: Centre for Research on Federal Financial Relations, Australian National University; 1981. (Occasional paper; v. 16).

153. Mintz, Jack M.; Simeon, Richard. *Conflict of taste and conflict of claim in federal countries.* Kingston: Institute of Intergovernmental Relations; 1982; ii, 41 p. (Discussion papers).

154. Monahan, Patrick J. At doctrine's twilight: the structure of Canadian federalism. *University of Toronto Law Journal*; 1984 Winter; 34(1): 47-99.

155. Monreal, Antoni. The new Spanish state structure. In: Burgess, Michael, ed. *Federalism and federation in western Europe.* London: Croom Helm; 1985: 59-75; 227 p.

156. Morley, Felix. *Freedom and federalism.* Indianapolis: Liberty Press; 1981; xxvi, 323 p.

157. Neuberger, Benjamin. Federalism and political integration in Africa. In: Elazar, Daniel J., ed. *Federalism and political integration.* Latham, MD.: University Press of America; 1984: 171-188.

158. Newton, Robert D. Administrative federalism. In: Wright, Deil S.; White, Harvey L., eds. *Federalism and intergovernmental relations.* Washington: American Society for Public Administration; 1984: 218-225; x, 333 p.

159. Norrie Kenneth H. Energy, Canadian federalism, and the West. *Publius*; 1984 Winter; 14(1): 79-91.

160. Norrie, Kenneth; Simeon, Richard; Krasnick, Mark. *Federalism and the economic union in Canada.* Toronto: University of Toronto Press; Royal Commission on the Economic Union and Development Prospects for Canada; 1986; xxiii, 349 p. (The collected research studies; v. 59).

161. Nuechterlein, Donald E. The demise of Canada's Confederation. *Political Science Quarterly*; 1981; 96(2): 225-240.

162. Orban, Edmond. *La dynamique de la centralisation dans l'état fédéral: un processus irréversible?* Montréal: Québec/Amérique; 1984; 526 p.

163. Ostrom, Vincent. Federal principles of organization and ethnic communities. In: Elazar, Daniel J., ed. *Federalism and political integration.* Latham, MD.: University Press of America; 1984: 73-88; 231 p.

164. Ostrom, Vincent. Hobbes, covenant and constitution. *Publius*; 1980 Fall; 10(4): 83-100.

165. Oyovbaire, S. Egite. *Federalism in Nigeria: a study in the development of the Nigerian state.* New York: St. Martin's Press; 1983; xx, 306 p.

166. Palmer, Kenneth T.; Pattakos, Alex N. *The state of American federalism*: 1984. Publius; 1985 Summer; 15(3): 1-18.

167. Patience, Allan; Scott, Jeffrey, eds. *Australian federalism, future tense*. New York: Oxford University Press; 1983; ix, 217 p.

168. Phukon, Girin. *Assam's attitude to federalism*. New Delhi: Sterling; 1984; xxvii, 172 p.

169. Prasad, Anirudh. *Centre and state powers under Indian federalism*. New Delhi: Deep & Deep; 1981.

170. Rakove, Jack. The legacy of the Articles of Confederation. *Publius*; 1982 Fall; 12(4): 45-66.

171. Ramet, Pedro. *Nationalism and federalism in Yugoslavia, 1963-1983*. Bloomington: Indiana University Press; 1984.

172. Rath, Sharada. *Federalism today: approaches, issues, and trends*. New Delhi: Sterling; 1984; cviii, 208 p.

173. Raynauld, André. The Canadian federation. *Canadian Journal of Economics*; 1984 November; 17(4): 635-53.

174. Reagan, Michael D.; Sanzone, John G. *The new federalism*. 2nd ed. New York: Oxford University Press; 1981; 196 p.

175. Rémillard, Gil. *Le fédéralisme canadien*. 2nd. ed. Montréal: Québec/Amérique; 1983; 734 p.

176. Rémillard, Gil. *Le fédéralisme canadien: éléments constitutionnels de formation et d'évolution*. Montréal: Québec/Amérique; 1980; 553 p.

177. Riemer, Neal. Covenant and the federal constitution. *Publius*; 1980 Fall; 10(4): 135-148.

178. Robertson, Gordon. A federation under strain: what is going on in Canada? In: Mathews, Russell, ed. *Public policies in two federal countries: Canada and Australia*. Canberra: Centre for Research on Federal Financial Relations, Australian National University; 1982; 273-280.

179. Robertson, Gordon. Northern political development within Canadian federalism. In: Whittington, Michael S., coord. *The north*. Toronto: University of Toronto Press; Royal Commission on the Economic Union and Development Prospects for Canada; 1985: 123-132; xvii, 183 p. (The collected research studies; v. 72).

180. Robinson, A. John. *Federalism and efficiency*. Canberra: Centre for Research on Federal Financial Relations, Australian National University; 1980; vii, 63 p. (Occasional paper; v. 14).

181. Romero, Migual Acosta. Mexican federalism: conception and reality. *Public Administration Review*; 1982 September-October; 42(5): 399-404.

182. Rose-Ackerman, Susan. Does federalism matter? Political choice in a federal republic. *Journal of Political Economy*; 1981 February; 89(1): 152-165.

183. Rothman, Rozann. The American Civil War and reconstruction: a crisis in national integration. In: Elazar, Daniel J. *Federalism and political integration.* Latham, MD: University Press of America; 1984: 89-106; 231 p.

184. Rothman, Rozann. The impact of covenant and contractual theories on conceptions of the U.S. Constitutions. *Publius*; 1980 Fall; 10(4): 149-164.

185. Rydon, Joan; Wolfson, H.A. *Federalism in West Germany.* Canberra: Australian Government Publishing Service; Advisory Council for Inter-government Relations; 1980; vi, 116 p. (Relationships Reference; Information papers; v. 8).

186. Sabetti, Filippo. *Covenant language in Canada: continuity and change in political discourse.* Philadelphia: Workshop on Covenant and Politics of the Center for the Study of Federalism, Temple University; 1980; 26 p. (Workshop on covenant and politics publications).

187. Sabetti, Filippo; Waller, Harold M. Crisis and continuity in Canadian federalism - introduction. *Publius*; 1984 Winter; 14(1): 1-8.

188. Sanguin, André-Louis. *La Suisse, essai de géographie politique.* Gap [France]: Editions Ophrys; 1983; 363 p.

189. Sanguin, André-Louis. Territorial aspects of federalism - a geography yet to be made. *Scottish Geographical Magazine*; 1983; 99(2): 66-76.

190. Scharpf, Fritz Wilhelm. *The joint-decision trap: lessons from German federalism and European integration.* Berlin: Wissenschaftszentrum Berlin; [1985]; 62 p.

191. Schechter, Stephen L. The founding of American local communities: a study of covenantal and other forms of associations. *Publius*; 1980 Fall; 10(4): 165-185.

192. Schechter, Stephen L. The state of American federalism: 1983. *Publius*; 1984 Summer; 14(3): 1-12.

193. Schechter, Stephen L. The state of American federalism: 1979. *Publius*; 1980 Winter; 10(1): 3-12.

194. Segre, Dan. Regionalism in Italy: an international conflict internalized. In: Elazar, Daniel J., ed. *Federalism and political integration.* Latham, MD.: University Press of America; 1984: 133-144; 321 p.

195. Sheer, Alain, ed. *North America--law, politics, and economics (symposium).* Durham, N.C: Duke University School of Law; 1981; 276 p.

196. Simeon, Richard. Criteria for choice in federal systems. *Queen's Law Journal*; 1983 Fall-Spring; 8(1-2): 131-157.

197. Smiley, Donald V. Public-sector politics, modernization, and federalism - the Canadian and American experiences. *Publius*; 1984 Winter; 14(1): 39-59.

198. Smiley, Donald V. *Canada in question: federalism in the eighties.* 3rd ed. Toronto: McGraw-Hill Ryerson; 1980; xii, 347 p. (McGraw-Hill Ryerson series in Canadian politics).

199. Smiley, Donald V. Federal states and federal societies, with special reference to Canada: *International Political Science Review*; 1984; 5(4): 443-454.

200. Smiley, Donald V. The structural problem of Canadian federalism. In: Fox, Paul W., ed. *Politics: Canada.* 5th ed. Toronto: McGraw-Hill Ryerson; 1982: 87-97; 693 p. (McGraw-Hill Ryerson series in Canadian politics).

201. Smiley, Donald V.; Watts, Ronald L. *Intrastate federalism in Canada.* Toronto: University of Toronto Press; Royal Commission on the Economic Union and Development Prospects for Canada; 1985; xix, 170 p. (The collected research studies; v.39).

202. Smith, James C. *Emerging conflicts in the doctrine of federalism: the intergovernmental predicament.* Lanham, MD: University Press of America; 1984.

203. Steiner, Jürg; Dorff, Robert H. Structure and process in consociationalism and federalism. *Publius*; 1985 Spring; 15(2): 49-56.

204. Stenburg, Carl W. Federalism in transition: 1959-1979. In: Advisory Commission on Intergovernmental Relations. *The future of federalism in the 1980's.* Washington D.C.: ACIR; 1981: 27-38; vii, 135 p. (Advisory Commission on Intergovernmental Relations reports; v. M-126).

205. Stevenson, Garth. Federalism and intergovernmental relations. In: Whittington, Michael J.; Williams, Glen, eds. *Canadian politics in the 1980's.* Toronto: Methuen; 1981: 275-291; xiv, 336 p.

206. Stevenson, Garth, ed. *Unfulfilled union: Canadian federalism and national unity.* Rev ed. Toronto: Gage Pub; 1982; x, 266 p. (Canadian controversies series).

207. Stewart, William H. *Concepts of federalism.* Lanham, MD: University Press of America; 1984; 239 p.

208. Stewart, William L. Metaphors, models, and the development of federal theory. *Publius*; 1982 Spring; 12(2): 5-24.

209. Subramaniam, V. *Some administrative aspects of federalism in India, Nigeria and Malaysia.* Canberra: Centre for Research on Federal Financial Relations, Australian National University; 1981; 18 p. (Reprint Series; v. 40).

210. Taylor, John F. A. Questions of path and questions of covenant. *Publius*; 1980 Fall; 10(4): 59-70.

211. Thorburn, Hugh G. *Interest groups in the Canadian federal system.* Toronto: University of Toronto Press; Royal Commission on the Economic Union and Development Prospects for Canada; 1985; xviii, 146 p. (The collected research studies; v. 69).

212. Trebilcock, Michael J.; Pritchard, J. R. S.; Courchene, Thomas J.; Whalley, J.; Wilkinson, B. W. *Federalism and the Canadian economic union*. Toronto: Ontario Economic Council; 1983; xiv, 560 p.

213. Trudeau, Pierre Elliot. In defence of federalism. In: Fox, Paul W., ed. *Politics: Canada*. 5th ed. Toronto: McGraw-Hill Ryerson; 1982: 203-206; 693 p.

214. Tupper, Allan. Federalism and the politics of industrial policy. In: Blais, André, res. coord. *Industrial policy*. Toronto: University of Toronto Press; Royal Commission on the Economic Union and Development Prospects for Canada; 1986: 347-378; xvii, 379 p. (The collected research studies; v. 44).

215. Verney, Douglas V. The reconciliation of parliamentary supremacy and federalism in Canada. *Journal of Commonwealth and Comparative Politics*; 1983; 21(1): 23-44.

216. von Beyme, Klaus. West Germany: federalism. *International Political Science Review*; 1984; 5(4): 381-396.

217. Walker, David B. Intergovernmental relations and dysfunctional federalism. In: Zimmerman, Diedre A.; Zimmerman, Joseph F., eds. *The politics of subnational governance*. New York: University Press of America; 1983: 40-51.

218. Walker, David B. *Toward a functioning federalism*. Cambridge, Mass.: Winthrop; 1981; xiv, 267 p. (Winthrop foundations of public management series).

219. Watts, Ronald L. The historical development of Canadian federalism. In: Mathews, Russell, ed. *Public policies in two federal countries: Canada and Australia*. Canberra: Centre for Research on Federal Financial Relations, Australian National University; 1982; 13-26 p.

220. Weissert, Carol S. The future of federalism: views of a roundtable. In: Advisory Commission on Intergovernmental Relations. *The future of federalism in the 1990's*. Washington D.C.: ACIR; 1981: 109-126; vii, 135 p. (Advisory Commission on Intergovernmental Relation report; v. M-126).

221. Welch, Susan; Peters, John G. State political culture and the attitudes of state senators toward social, economic welfare and corruption issues. *Publius*; 1980 Spring; 10(2): 59-68.

222. Whitaker, Reginald. *Federalism and democratic theory*. Kingston: Institute of Intergovernmental Relations, Queen's University; 1983; ii, 52 p. (Discussion papers; v. 17).

223. Whitlam, Gough. The cost of federation. In: Mathews, Russell, ed. *Public policies in two federal countries: Canada and Australia*. Canberra: Centre for Research on Federal Financial Relations, Australian National University; 1982; 281-293 p.

224. Wildavsky, Aaron. Bare bones: putting flesh on the skeleton of American federalism. In: Advisory Commission on Intergovernmental Relations. *The future*

of federalism in the 1980's. Washington D.C.: ACIR; 1981: 67-88; vii, 135 p. (Advisory Commission on Intergovernmental Relations report; v. M-126).

225. Wilson, John. On the dangers of bickering in a federal state: some reflections on the failure of the national party system. In: Kornberg, Allan; Clarke, Harold D., eds. *Political support in Canada: the crisis years.* Durham, N.C.: Duke University Press; 1983: 171-224; xvi, 463 p. (Duke University Centre for International Studies publications).

226. Wiltshire, Kenneth. Administrative criteria for the allocation of functions between levels of government in a federation. In: Grewal, Bhajan Singh. *Towards adaptive federalism.* Canberra: Australian Publishing Service; Advisory Council for Intergovernment Relations; 1981: 59-216; 243 p. (Relationships Reference; Information papers; v. 9).

227. Wirt, Frederick. Does control follow the dollar? Value analysis, school policy, and state-local linkages. *Publius;* 1980 Spring; 10(2): 69-88.

228. Woehrling, José. La conclusion et la mise en oeuvre des traités dans le fédéralisme allemand. *Revue juridique Thémis;* 1979-80; 14(1): 73-108.

229. Wright, Deil S.; White, Harvey L., eds. *Federalism and intergovernmental relations.* Washington: American Society for Public Administration; 1984. (PAR classics series; v. 5).

230. Wright, Deil S.; White, Harvey L. Federalism and intergovernmental relationships: evolving patterns and changing perspectives. In: *idem.,* eds. *Federalism and intergovernmental relations.* Washington: American Society for Public Administration; 1984: 1-30; x, 333 p. (PAR classics; v. 5).

2 Bases of Community: Territory and Ethnicity

231. Abele, Frances. Dene-government relations: the development of a new political minority. In: Nevitte, Neil; Kornberg, Allan, eds. *Minorities and the Canadian state*. Oakville: Mosaic Press; 1985: 239-256; 324 p.

232. Aboriginal Rights and Constitutional Development Secretariat. *Discussion paper on the Denendeh government proposal*. Yellowknife: Northwest Territories Legislative Assembly, Special Committee on Constitutional Development; 1982; ii, 39, (6) p.

233. Adshead, Gordon; Desrosiers, Danielle. *Referendum*. [Ottawa]: Ottawa Public Library; [1980]; 39 p.

234. Alberta Federation of Metis Settlement Associations. *Metisism: a Canadian identity: statement on aboriginal rights in the Constitution of Canada*. Edmonton: Alberta Federation of Metis Settlement Associations; 1982; 65 p.

235. Alexander, David G. New notions of happiness: nationalism, regionalism and Atlantic Canada. *Journal of Canadian Studies*; 1980 Summer; 15(2): 29-42.

236. Alexander, David G. Old and new money ("Power shift west: myth or reality?"). *Canadian Journal of Sociology*; 1981 Spring; 6(2): 166-169.

237. Anderson, Ellen. The Saskatchewan Indians and Canada's new Constitution. *Journal of International Affairs*; 1982 Spring-Summer; 36(1): 125-148.

238. Angers, François-Albert. Notre référendum - 1: mesure de l'échec. *L'Action nationale*; 1980 September; 70(1): 13-29.

239. Angers, François-Albert. Notre référendum - 2: les dangers d'une opération référendaire mal engagée et mal conduite. *L'Action nationale*; 1980 October; 60(2): 91-109.

240. Angers, François-Albert. René Lévesque et l'évolution du nationalisme québécois. *L'Action nationale*; 1985 October; 75(2): 123-132.

241. Angers, François-Albert. Sur la nécessité de l'indépendance pour le Québec. *L'Action nationale*; 1985 April; 74(8): 793-800.

242. Arès Richard. *La réponse du Québec*. [Montréal]: Libre Expression; 1980; 410 p.

243. Arès, Richard. *La réponse du Québec. [Montréal]: Libre expression; c[1980]; 410 p.*

244. Armour, Leslie. *The idea of Canada: and the crisis of community.* Ottawa: Steel Rail; c1981; xvii, 180 p.

245. Arnopoulos, Sheila McLeod; Clift, Dominique. *The English fact in Quebec.* 2nd ed. Kingston: McGill-Queen's University Press; 1984; xvi, 247 p.

246. Arnopoulos, Sheila; Clift, Dominique. *The English fact in Quebec.* Montreal: McGill-Queen's University Press; c1980; xvi, 239.

247. Asch, Michael I. *Home and native land : aboriginal rights and the Canadian Constitution.* Toronto: Methuen; c1984; x, 156 p.

248. Assembly of First Nations. *The case for Indian self-government;* 1985; Ottawa. Ottawa: The Assembly; 1985; 4 p.

249. Assembly of First Nations. *La question de l'autonomie gouvernementale des Indiens;* 1985; Ottawa. Ottawa: L'Assemblée; 1985; 4 p.

250. Association canadienne des sociologues et anthropologues de langue française. *La transformation du pouvoir au Québec : actes du Colloque de l'- Association canadienne des sociologues et anthropologues de langue française /* textes publiés sous la direction de Nadia Assimopoulos ... [et al.]. Québec: Editions coopératives A. Saint-Martin; 1980; xiii, 378 p. (Collection Recherches et documents Laval).

251. Association for Canadian Studies. *Perspectives on regions and regionalism in Canada : proceedings of the Annual Conference of the Association for Canadian Studies, held at the University of Ottawa, June 8-10, 1982.* Ottawa: The Association; [1983]; 137 p. (Canadian issues; v. 5).

252. Atlantic Provinces Economic Union. Arguments for Maritime union. In: Fox, Paul W, ed. *Politics: Canada.* 5th ed. Toronto: McGraw-Hill Ryerson; 1982: 135-139; 693 p.

253. Balthazar, Louis. Quebec at the hour of choice. In: Carty, R. Kenneth; Ward, W. Peter, eds. *Entering the eighties: Canada in crisis.* Toronto: University of Toronto Press; 1980: 60-77; 160 p.

254. Bankes, Nigel. *Resource-leasing options and the settlement of aboriginal claims.* Ottawa: Canadian Arctic Resources Committee; 1983; x, 236 p.

255. Barberis, Robert; Drouilly, Pierre. *Les illusions du pouvoir: les erreurs stratégiques du gouvernement Lévesque.* Montréal: Editions Sélect; c1980; 238 p.

256. Barr, Brenton M. The economic geography of prairie Canada in regional perspective. In: Rasporich, A.W, ed. *The making of the modern West.* Calgary: University of Calgary Press; 1984: 79-88.

257. Bartlett, Richard H. *The Indian Act.* Saskatoon: University of Saskatchewan, Native Law Centre; 1980; 35 p.

258. Bauer, Julien. Jewish communities, Jewish education and Quebec nationalism: *Social Compass*; 1984; 31(4): 391-407.

259. Beaudoin, Gérald A. *La protection constitutionnelle des minorités*. Les cahiers de droit; 1986 March; (1): 31-52.

260. Beaujot, Roderic P. The decline of official language minorities in Quebec and English Canada: *Canadian Journal of Sociology*; 1982 Fall; 7(4): 367-389.

261. Beaupré, Viateur. L'homme nouveau, selon M. Ryan. *L'Action nationale*; 1980; 69(5): 384-389.

262. Beauregard, Ludger. Le Québec, vedette du régionalisme canadien. In: Westfall, William, ed. *Perspectives on regions and regionalism in Canada*. Ottawa: The Association for Canadian Studies; 1983; v: 54-58; 137 p.

263. Beck, Murray F. An Atlantic region political culture: a chimera. In: Bercuson, David Jay; Buckner, Phillip A, eds. *Eastern and western perspectives*. Toronto: University of Toronto Press; 1981: 147-168; xi, 227 p.

264. Behiels, Michael D. The Bloc populaire canadien and the origins of French-Canadian neo-nationalism, 1942-48. *Canadian Historical Review*; 1982; 63(4): 487-512.

265. Behiels, Michael D. *Prelude to Quebec's quiet revolution: liberalism versus neo-nationalism*, 1945-1960. Kingston: McGill-Queen's University Press; c1985; xii, 366 p.

266. Bélanger, Réal; Sévigny, Albert. *L'impossible défi: Albert Sévigny et les conservateurs fédéraux*, 1902-1918. Québec: Presses de l'Université Laval; 1983; 368 p. (Les cahiers d'histoire de l'Université Laval; v. 27).

267. Bell, David V.J. Regionalism in the Canadian community. In: Fox, Paul W, ed. *Politics: Canada*. 5th ed. Toronto: McGraw-Hill Ryerson; 1982: 126-134; 693 p.

268. Bellefeuille, Pierre de. *Sauf vot' respect*. Montréal: Québec/Amérique; c1984; 115 p.

269. Bercuson, David Jay. Regionalism and "unlimited identity" in western Canada. *Journal of Canadian Studies*; 1980 Summer; 15(2): 121-126.

270. Berger, Thomas R. Native history, native claims and self-determination. *BC Studies*; 1983 Spring; 57: 10-23.

271. Berger, Thomas R. Native rights and self-determination. *Canadian Journal of Native Studies*; 1983; 3(2): 363-375.

272. Bergeron, Gérard. *Notre miroir à deux faces : Trudeau, Lévesque ... et, forcément, avec bien d'autres, Joe Clark, Brian Mulroney, Jean Marchand, Gérard Pelletier, John Turner, Jean Chrétien, etc., ainsi que Robert Bourassa, Pierre Bour-*

gault, Claude Ryan, Jacques Parizeau, Pierre-Marc Johnson, Robert Bourassa II, etc. Montréal: Québec/Amérique; c1985; 340 p.

273. Bergeron, Gérard. *Pratique de l'Etat au Québec*. Montréal: Québec/Amérique; c1984; 442 p.

274. Bergeron, Gérard; Pelletier, Réjean. *L'Etat du Québec en devenir*. Montréal: Boréal Express; c1980; 409 p.

275. Bernier, Jacques. *Géographie et unité canadienne*. Cahiers de geógraphie du Québec; 1980 April; 24(61): 81-108.

276. Berton, Pierre. *Why we act like Canadians: a personal exploration of our national character*. Toronto: McClelland and Stewart; c1982; 113 p.

277. Bilodeau, Roger. *La judiciarisation des conflits linguistiques au Canada*. Les cahiers de droit; 1986 March; (1): 215-225.

278. Binette, Denis. *Plébiscite: essai*. Clarke-City [Québec]: The Author; c1982; [80] p.

279. Bird, Roland. An outsider's view of Canada. *Canadian Business Review*; 1980 Summer; 7(2): 31-34.

280. Blanchard, René. L'action de nos sociétés nationales face à une constitution antinationale. *L'Action nationale*; 1980 January; 69(5): 363-371.

281. Boismenu, Gérard. *Espace régional et nation: pour un nouveau débat sur le Québec*. Montréal: Boréal Express; [1983]; 217 p.

282. Boisvert, David. *Forms of aboriginal self-government*. Kingston: Institute of Intergovernmental Relations, Queen's University; 1985; 88 p. (Background Paper; v. 2).

283. Boldt, Menno; Long, J. A. Tribal philosophies and the Canadian Charter of Rights and Freedoms. *Racial and Ethnic Studies*; 1984; 4(4).

284. Boldt, Menno; Long, J. Anthony. *The quest for justice: aboriginal peoples and aboriginal rights*. Toronto: University of Toronto Press; 1985; viii, 406 p.

285. Boldt, Menno; Long, J. Anthony. Tribal philosophies and the Canadian Charter of Rights and Freedoms. In: Boldt, Menno; Long, J. Anthony, eds. *The quest for justice: aboriginal peoples and aboriginal rights*. Toronto: University of Toronto Press; 1985: 165-182; viii, 406 p.

286. Boldt, Menno; Little Bear, Leroy; Long, J. Anthony. *Pathways to self-determination: Canadian Indians and the Canadian state*. Toronto: University of Toronto; 1984.

287. Bourgault, Pierre. *Ecrits polémiques*. [Montréal]: Edition du Club Québec Loisirs; 1983; v.

288. Bourgault, Pierre; Lebel, Andrée. *Le plaisir de la liberté: entretiens*. [Montréal]: Nouvelle Optique; 1983; 235 p. (Collection traces et paroles).

289. Bourque, Gilles; Dostaler, Gilles. *Socialisme et indépendance*. Montréal: Boréal Express; 1980; 223 p.

290. Boutet, Odina. Deux questions au Parti libéral. *L'Action nationale*; 1980 May; 69(9): 677-689.

291. Boutet, Odina. *Reprendre notre Canada*. *L'Action nationale*; 1980; 69(6): 430-439.

292. Breton, Albert; Breton, Raymond. *Why disunity?: an analysis of linguistic and regional cleavages in Canada*. Montreal: Institute for Research on Public Policy; 1980; xxi, 83 p. (The 1978 Dal Grauer memorial lectures).

293. Breton, Raymond. Multiculturalism and Canadian nation-building. In: Cairns, Alan; Williams, Cynthia, res. coords. *The politics of gender, ethnicity and language in Canada*. Toronto: University of Toronto Press; Royal Commission on the Economic Union and Development Prospects for Canada; 1986: 27-66; xvi, 247 p. (The collected research studies; v. 34).

294. Breton, Raymond; Reitz, Jeffrey G.; Valentine, Victor F. *Cultural boundaries and the cohesion of Canada*. Montreal: Institute for Research on Public Policy; c1980; xx, 422 p.

295. British Columbia. Tripartite Local Government Committee. *Report of the Tripartite Local Government Committee Respecting Indian Local Government in British Columbia*. Victoria, B.C.: Supply and Services; August 1981; 30 p.

296. Brotz, Howard. Multiculturalism in Canada: a muddle. *Canadian Public Policy*; 1980 Winter; 6(1): 41-46.

297. Brown, Timothy Benjamin. *Canadian cultural nationalism: a historical study of economic and political protectionism* [microfiche]: (M.A.) American University; 1982; 2 fiche. Ann Arbor, Mich. University Microfilms International, 1983.

298. Buffie, Erna. *The Massey Report and the intellectuals tory cultural nationalism in Ontario in the 1950's* [microfiche]: (M.A.) University of Manitoba; 1982; 4 fiche (296 fr.). Ottawa: National Library of Canada, 1983.

299. Burcuson, David Jay; Buckner, Phillip A, eds. *Eastern and western perspectives*. Toronto: University of Toronto Press; 1981; xi, 227.

300. Burghardt, Andrew F. Nation, state and territorial unity: a trans-outaouais view. *Cahiers de geógraphie du Québec*; 1980 April; 24(61): 123-134.

301. Cairns, Alan C.; Williams, Cynthia, res. coords. *The politics of gender, ethnicity and language in Canada*. Toronto: University of Toronto Press; Royal Commission on the Economic Union and Development Prospects for Canada; 1986; xvi, 247 p. (The collected research studies; v. 34).

302. Caldwell, Gary. Anglo-Quebec: demographic realities and options for the future. In: Bourhis, Richard Y, ed. *Conflict and language planning in Quebec*. London: Multilingual Matters; 1984: 205-221; xvi, 304 p. (Multilingual Matters; v. 5).

303. Caldwell, Gary. Discovering and developing English-Canadian nationalism in Quebec. *Canadian Review of Studies in Nationalism*; 1984 Fall; 11: 245-256.

304. Cameron, David M, ed. *Regionalism and supranationalism : challenges and alternatives to the nation-state in Canada and Europe*. Montreal: Institute for Research on Public Policy; 1981; xxv, 138 p.

305. Canada. Canadian Unity Information Office. *Collected questionnaires and survey results concerning Quebec referendum*. Ottawa: Canadian Unity Information Office; [1980]; 13 pts.

306. Canada. Department of Fisheries and Oceans; Canada. Indian and Northern Affairs Canada. *The northern Quebec agreements: Government of Canada involvement*. Ottawa: Fisheries and Oceans; Indian and Northern Affairs Canada; 1985; 16, 16 p.

307. Canada. Department of Indian Affairs and Northern Development. *In all fairness: a native claims policy: comprehensive claims*. Ottawa: DIAND; 1981; 30, 32 p.

308. Canada. Department of Indian Affairs and Northern Development. *James Bay and Northern Quebec Agreement Implementation Review*. Ottawa: Department of Indian Affairs and Northern Development; 1982; 126 p.

309. Canada. Department of Indian Affairs and Northern Development. *North - overview of the land, the people, a guide to early history, recent constitutional and political developments* [Ottawa]: DIAND; 1985.

310. Canada. Department of Indian and Northern Affairs. *Federal government response on land claims policies and processes*. Ottawa: Indian and Northern Affairs Canada; 1984; 24 p.

311. Canada. Department of Justice. *What the Constitution says about aboriginal peoples* [Ottawa]: Department of Justice; 1985.

312. Canada. House of Commons. Special Committee on Indian Self-Government. *Government of aboriginal peoples: executive summary*. Ottawa: The Committee; 1982.

313. Canada. Indian and Inuit Affairs Program. *Canada's Indian reserves: the usufruct in our Constitution* [Ottawa]: Indian and Inuit Affairs Program; 1980.

314. Canada. Indian and Northern Affairs Canada. 1983 *Constitutional Accord on Aboriginal Rights*. Ottawa: Indian and Northern Affairs Canada; c1983; [4, 4] p.

315. Canada. Indian and Northern Affairs Canada. *Biennial report of activities, April 1982-April 1984: The James Bay and Northern Quebec Agreement (chapter 22): environmental quality act (chapter II)*. Sainte-Foy: The Review Committee; 1984; 58, 55 p.

316. Canada. Indian and Northern Affairs Canada. *James Bay and Northern Quebec Agreement: implementation review* [Ottawa]: DIAND [1982]; 126 p.

317. Canada. Indian and Northern Affairs Canada.; Committee for Original Peoples' Entitlement. *The Western Arctic Claim: the Inuvialuit final agreement*. Ottawa: Indian and Northern Affairs Canada; c1984; 114 p.

318. Canada. Indian and Northern Affairs Canada; Committee for Original Peoples' Entitlement. *The Western Arctic claim: a guide to the Inuvialuit final agreement*. Ottawa: Indian and Northern Affairs Canada; 1984; 11, 11p.

319. Canada. Office of the Commissioner of Official Languages. *Annual report 1984, part iv: the minority challenge - extract*. [Ottawa]: The Commissioner; [1985]; 39, 39 p.

320. Canada. Parliament. House of Commons. Special Committee on Indian Self-Government. *Indian self-government in Canada*. [Ottawa]: Queen's Printer; [1983].

321. Canada. Prime Minister. *Statement by the Prime Minister of Canada to the Conference of First Ministers on Aboriginal Constitutional Matters*; March 8-9, 1984; Ottawa. [Ottawa]: Office of the Prime Minister; 1984.

322. Canadian Arctic Resources Committee; Canada. Bureau des Revendications des Autochtones. *Revendications foncières des autochtones: aperçu de la politique: dossier*. [Ottawa]: Bureau des Revendications des Autochtones; 1983; 21 p.

323. Canadian Bar Association of Ontario (Continuing Legal Education). *Canadian Bar Association Conference on Current Issues in Aboriginal and Treaty Rights*; May 25, 1984; University of Ottawa. Ottawa: Canadian Bar Association; July 1984.

324. Careless, Anthony. The struggle for jurisdiction: regionalism versus rationalism. *Publius*; 1984 Winter; 14(1): 61-77.

325. Carey, Miriam R.G. *The new ideology of aboriginal rights* [M.A. Thesis]. Calgary: University of Calgary; 1982; 148 p.

326. Carey-Belanger, Elaine. Regional development and collective intervention. In: Gagnon, Alain G., ed. *Quebec state and society*. Toronto: Methuen; 1984: 244-261; ix, 438 p.

327. Castonquay, Charles. La position des minorités francophones en 1976. *L'Action nationale*; 1980; 69(10): 825-829.

328. Centrale de l'enseignement du Québec. *La question nationale, le débat constitutionnel et nous: enjeux et perspectives*. [Sainte-Foy]: La Centrale; 1981; 32 p. (Les Dossiers CEQ).

329. Centre de formation populaire. *Au-dela du Parti québécois: lutte nationale et classes populaires*. Montréal: Nouvelle Optique, tirage de; 1982; 244 p. (Collection matériaux).

330. Chamberland, Paul. *Un parti pris anthropologique*. [Montréal]: Parti Pris; c1983; 325 p [3] p. (Collection Aspects; v. 43).

331. Chapeskie, Andrew. *This land is whose land? Aboriginal territories, aboriginal development and the Canadian state* [M.A. Thesis]. Ottawa, Ontario: Norman Paterson School of International Affairs, Carleton University; 1985; 125 p.

332. Chapman, R.J.K. *Regionalism, national development and governmental institutional arrangements: regions as moderating institutions.* Canberra: Centre for Research on Federal Financial Relations, Australian National University; 1982; v, 46 p. (Occasional paper; v. 24).

333. Chartier, Armand B. Franco-Americans and Quebec: linkages and potential in the Northeast. In: Hero, Alfred O. Jr.; Daneau, Marcel, eds. *Problems and opportunities in U.S.-Quebec relations.* Boulder, CO: Westview Press; 1984: 151-168; xv, 320 p. (Westview special studies in international relations).

334. Chouinard, Jean-Yves. Contraintes de la double légitimité. *L'Action nationale*; 1982 October; 72(2): 166-174.

335. Clarke, Harold D.; Kornberg, Allan, Stewart, Marianne C. Politically active minorities: political participation in Canadian democracy. In: Nevitte, Neill/Kornberg, Allan, eds. *Minorities and the Canadian state.* Oakville: Mosaic Press; 1985: 275-300; 324 p.

336. Clement, Wallace. More questions than answers ("Power shift west: myth or reality?"). *Canadian Journal of Sociology*; 1981 Spring; 6(2): 175-181.

337. Clement, Wallace. Regionalism as uneven development: class and region in Canada. In: Westfall, William, ed. *Perspectives on regions and regionalism in Canada.* Ottawa: Association for Canadian Studies; 1983; v: 68-80; 137 p.

338. Cleroux, Richard. Separatism in Quebec and Alberta. In: Pratt, Larry; Stevenson, Garth, eds. *Western separatism: myths, realities and dangers.* Edmonton: Hurtig Publishers; 1981: 105-118; 255 p.

339. Clift, Dominique. *Le déclin du nationalisme au Québec.* [Montréal]: Libre Expression; 1981; 195 p.

340. Clift, Dominique. *Quebec nationalism in crisis.* Kingston: McGill-Queen's University Press; c1982; viii, 155 p.

341. Coleman, William D. From Bill 22 to Bill 101: the politics of language under the Parti québécois. *Canadian Journal of Political Science*; 1981 September; 14(3): 459-486.

342. Coleman, William D. *The independence movement in Quebec 1945-1980.* Toronto: University of Toronto Press; c1984; xii, 274 p.

343. Coleman, William D. Social class and language policies in Quebec. In: Bourhis, Richard Y., ed. *Conflict and language planning in Quebec.* London: Multilingual Matters; 1984: 130-147; xvi, 304 p. (Multiligual Matters; v. 5).

344. Colvin, Eric. *Legal process and the resolution of Indian claims.* [Saskatoon]: University of Saskatchewan Native Law Centre; 1981; 29 p. (Studies of aboriginal rights).

345. Conseil de la vie française. Mémoire du Conseil de la vie française sur la révision de la constitution canadienne. *Vie française*; 1980 October-December; 34(10, 11, 12): 3-14.

346. Conway, J. F. *The West: the history of a region in Confederation.* Toronto: J. Lorimer; 1983; 261 p. (Canadian issues series).

347. Conway, J.F. *The place of the prairie West in the Canadian Confederation.* Edinburgh: Centre of Canadian Studies, Univ. of Edinburgh; 1982; 25 p.

348. Conway, J.F. *The recrudescence of western Canadian separatist sentiment: political and economic background.* London: Canadian High Commission; 1982; 30 p. (Canada house lecture series; v. 13).

349. Conway, J.F. Western alienation: a legacy of confederation. In: Fry, John, ed. *Contradictions in Canadian society.* Toronto: John Wiley; 1983.

350. Cook, Ramsay. The paradox of Quebec. In: Carty, R. Kenneth; Ward W. Peter, eds. *Entering the eighties.* Toronto: University of Toronto Press; 1980: 46-59; 160 p.

351. Coolican, Murray, Chmn. *Living treaties: lasting agreements. Report of the Task Force to Review Comprehensive Claims Policy.* Ottawa: Department of Indian Affairs and Northern Development; 1985; 132 p.

352. Coolican, Murray. *The northern agenda: a memorandum.* Northern Perspectives; 1984 November; 12(2): 2.

353. Cooper, Barry F. The West: a political minority. In: Nevitte, Neil; Kornberg, Allan, eds. *Minorities and the Canadian state.* Oakville: Mosaic Press; 1985: 203-220; 324 p.

354. Cooper, Barry F. Western political consciousness. In: Brooks, Steve, ed. *Political thought in Canada.* Toronto: Clark Irwin; 1984.

355. Cotterill, E.M.R. The territorial North. *Canadian Public Administration*; 1984 Summer; 27(2): 188-196.

356. Courtis, Kenneth S. *Fondements, forme et structure du sentiment d'appartenance nationale chez les jeunes Franco-québécois:* Laboratoire d'études politiques et administratives; 1983; 94 p.

357. Crean, Susan M.; Rioux, Marcel. *Two nations: an essay on the culture and politics of Canada and Quebec in a world of American pre-eminence.* Toronto: Lorimer; 1983; 167 p.

358. d'Anglejan, Alison. Language planning in Quebec: an historical overview and future trends. In: Bourhis, Richard Y., ed. *Conflict and language planning in*

Quebec. London: Multilingual Matters; 1984: 29-52; xvi, 304 p. (Multilingual Matters; v. 5).

359. Dacks, Gurston. Native claims: negotiating social contracts for the North. In Dacks, Gurston, ed. *A choice of futures: politics in the Canadian North*. Toronto: Methuen; 1981: 50-87.

360. Dagenais, André. *Dissolution de la Confédération canadienne: dialectique des "Nations-Etats", légitimité du Québec souverain: la non-validité du référendum du 20 mai 1980 : les confusions, contradictions et inversions de M. Pierre Elliott Trudeau, premier ministre du Contre-Canada*. Outremont: The Author; 1981; 127 p. (Liberer/Renverser; v. 1).

361. Dalon, Richard. An Alberta perspective on aboriginal peoples and the Constitution. In: Boldt, Menno; Long, J. Anthony, eds. *The quest for justice: aboriginal peoples and aboriginal rights*. Toronto: University of Toronto Press; 1985: 83-113; viii, 406 p.

362. De Brou, David. *French Canadian historians' interpretations of Confederation* [microfiche]: (M.A.) Université d'Ottawa; 1980 2 microfiches (126 fr.). Ottawa: National Library of Canada, 1981.

363. Decision-Canada (Association). *L'Illusion souverainiste: lecture critique du Livre blanc*. Montréal: Editions Héritage; c1980; 124 p. Note: Also published in English under the title "The impossible option: a post referendum comment".

364. Dempsey, Hugh A. *Western alienation in perspective*. Calgary: Glenbow Museum; 1981; 36 p.

365. Desbarats, Peter. *Canada lost, Canada found: the search for a new nation : a polemic*. Toronto: McClelland and Stewart; c1981; viii, 126 p.

366. Dick, Ronald S. Minorities and the Canadian visual media. In: Nevitte, Neil; Kornberg, Allan, eds. *Minorities and the Canadian state*. Oakville: Mosaic Press; 1985: 175-192; 324 p.

367. Diep, Bich Ngoc. Situation des minorités anglaise au Québec et francophone hors Québec. L'Action nationale; 1984 October; 74(2): 137-146.

368. Dion, Léon. *Le Québec et le Canada: les voies de l'avenir*. [Montréal]: Editions Québécor; [1980]; 236 p. (Collection politique).

369. Dobell, Peter C. Das Referendum in Quebec und die Zukunft Kanadas. *Europa Archive*; 1980 January; 35(9): 281-288.

370. Doering, Ronald, L. *Nunavut and land claims: options for a public land regime*. [Ottawa]: Nunavut Constitutional Forum; [1983]; i, 27 p. (Working paper).

371. Driben, Paul; Gummer, Burton. The native interface: an emerging role in government-native relations. *Native Studies Review*; 1985; 1(2): 33-47.

372. Driedger, Leo. Conformity vs pluralism: minority identities and inequalities. In: Nevitte, Neil; Kornberg, Allan, eds. *Minorities and the Canadian state*. Oakville: Mosaic Press; 1985: 157-174; 324 p.

373. Driedger, Leo. Multicultural regionalism: toward understanding the Canadian West. In: Rasporich, A.W., ed. *The making of modern West: western Canada since 1945*. Calgary: University of Calgary Press; 1984: 167-183.

374. Duhamel, Roger. M. Trudeau ou le triomphe de l'échec. *L'Action nationale*; 1984 May; 73(9): 827-836.

375. Dupras, Pierre; Dupras, Martin. *Oui ou non*. Saint-Lambert, Québec: Editions Héritage; c1980; 64 p.

376. Elkins, David J. The horizontal mosaic: immigrants and migrants in the provincial political cultures. In: Elkins, David J.; Simeon, Richard, eds. *Small worlds: provinces and parties in Canadian political life*. Toronto: Methuen; 1980: 106-130; xvi, 316 p.

377. Elkins, David J.; Simeon, Richard; Woolstencroft, Peter. *Small worlds: provinces and parties in Canadian political life*. Toronto: Methuen; 1980; 320 pp.

378. Elliot, Jean Leonard. Emerging ethnic nationalism in the Canadian Northwest Territories. *Canadian Review of Studies in Nationalism*; 1984 Fall; 11: 231-244.

379. Elton, David K. Contemporary western alienation: an option profile. In: Rasporich, A.W., ed. *The making of the modern West*. Calgary: University of Calgary Press; 1984: 47-54.

380. En Lutte (Organisation). *Ni fédéralisme renouvelé ni souveraineté-association*. [Montréal]: Organisation marxiste-léniniste du Canada en lutte; [1980?]; 76 p.

381. Engelen, E. *The challenges of Canada's regional diversity*. Toronto: Canada Studies Foundation; 1981; 5; 64 (70) p. (The Walter L. Gordon Lecture Series).

382. Engelmann, Frederick C. Reforming Canadian federalism. In: Pratt, Larry; Stevenson, Garth, eds. *Western separatism: myths, realities and dangers*. Edmonton: Hurtig Publishers; 1981: 229-242; 255 p.

383. Falconer, P. *Urban indian needs: federal policy responsibility in the context of the talks on aboriginal self-government*. Ottawa: Department of Indian Affairs and Northern Development; 1985; 50 p.

384. Fédération des groupes ethniques du Québec. *Les communautés ethniques face aux diverses options constitutionnelles*. Montréal: Fédération des groupes ethniques du Québec; 1980; 158 p.

385. Feldman, Elliot J.; Nevitte, Neil, eds. *The future of North America: Canada, the United States, and Quebec nationalism*. Lanham, MD: University Press of America; 1985; c1979. (Harvard studies in international affairs; v. 42).

386. Ferland, Marc; Vaillancourt, Yves. *Socialisme et indépendance au Québec: pistes pour le mouvement ouvrier et populaire*. Sainte-Foy [Québec]: Editions Socialisme et Indépendance, tirage de; 1981; 86 p.

387. Fitzmaurice, John. *Quebec and Canada: past, present, and future*. New York: St. Martin's Press; 1985; xxii, 343 p.

388. Flanagan, Thomas. The manufacture of minorities. In: Nevitte, Neil; Kornberg, Allan, eds. *Minorities and the Canadian state*. Oakville: Mosaic Press; 1985: 197-123; 324 p.

389. Flowers, Mary Kathryn. *Authority relations and legitimacy: a conflict analysis of Quebec nationalism* [microfiche]: (Ph.D.) New York University; 1980; 2 microfiches (188 fr.). Ann Arbor, Mich. University Microfilms International, 1980.

390. Foley, Edward C. Nova Scotia's case for coastal and offshore resources. *Ottawa Law Journal*; 1981; 13(2): 281-308.

391. Forster, Victor W. *Let Quebec go*. Norland, Ont.: V. Forster; c1983; 167 p.

392. Fortin, Pierre. *La souveraineté-association: est-ce économiquement viable?* [Chicoutimi]: G. Morin; c1980; 92 p.

393. Fortin, Pierre; Paquet, Gilles; Rabeau, Yves. Would Quebec be better in or out? In: Fox, Paul W., ed. *Politics: Canada*. Toronto: McGraw-Hill Ryerson; 1982: 209-218.

394. Fondation des Québécois pour le Oui. *Toute la question est là*. [Montréal]: La Fondation; [1980]; 48 p.

395. Fournier, Louis. *F.L.Q., the anatomy of an underground movement*. Toronto: NC Press; 1984; 373 p.

396. Fournier, Pierre. The future of Quebec nationalism. In: Banting, Keith; Simeon, Richard, eds. *And no one cheered*. Toronto: Methuen; 1983: 154-173; xii, 376 p.

397. Fournier, Pierre. The future of Quebec nationalism. *Journal of Commonwealth and Comparative Policy*; 1983; 21(1): 3-21.

398. Francoeur, Jacques. Pour un Québec différent dans un Canada pluraliste. *Vie Française*; 1981 October-December; 35: 10-12.

399. Gagnon, Alain G. The evolution of political forces in Quebec: the struggle for supremacy. In: *idem*, ed. *Quebec state and society*. Toronto: Methuen; 1984: 262-284; ix, 438 p.

400. Gagnon, Alain G., ed. *Quebec state and society*. Toronto: Methuen; 1984; ix, 438 p.

401. Gagnon, Alain G.; Montcalm, Mary Beth. Economic peripheralization and Quebec unrest. *Journal of Canadian Studies*; 1982 Summer; 17(2): 32-42.

402. Gagnon, Alain G.; Montcalm, Mary Beth. Economic peripheralization and Quebec unrest. In: Gagnon, Alain G., ed. *Quebec state and society*. Toronto: Methuen; 1984: 15-30; ix, 438 p.

403. Gagnon, Lysiane. *Chroniques politiques*. Montréal: Boréal Express; [1985]; 456 p. (Collection papiers collés).

404. Genest, Jean. Enfin, le livre blanc. *L'Action nationale*; 1980 January; 69(5): 341-349.

405. Genuist, Paul. *La faillite du Canada anglais*. Montreal: Quinze; c1980; 205 p.

406. Gibbins, Roger. American influence on western separatism. In: Pratt, Larry; Stevenson, Garth, eds. *Western separatism: myths, realities and dangers*. Edmonton: Hurtig Publishers; 1981: 193-208; 255 p.

407. Gibbins, Roger. Political change in the "new West". In: Rasporich, A.W., ed. *The making of the modern West*. Calgary: Univ. of Calgary Press; 1984: 37-46.

408. Gibbins, Roger. *Prairie politics and society: regionalism in decline*. Toronto: Butterworths; c1980; 228 p.

409. Gibbins, Roger. Regional politics in the wake of the Canada Act. In: Westfall, William, ed. *Perspectives on regions and regionalism in Canada*. Ottawa: Association for Canadian Studies; 1983; v: 131-137; 137 p.

410. Gibbins, Roger, ed. *Regionalism: territorial politics in Canada and the United States*. Toronto: Butterworths; 1982; 217 p.

411. Gibbins, Roger. The west - who governs? In: Josephy, Alvin M. Jr. *The revolt of the western colonies*; 1982; Sun Valley, Idaho: Institute of the American West; 1982: 65-72.

412. Gibbins, Roger; Ponting, J. Rick. An assessment of the probable impact of aboriginal self-government in Canada. In: Cairns, Alan; Williams, Cynthia, res. coords. *The politics of gender, ethnicity and language in Canada*. Toronto: University of Toronto Press; Royal Commission on the Economic Union and Development Prospects for Canada; 1986: 171-245; xvi, 247 p. (The collected research studies; v. 34).

413. Gibbins, Roger; Bakvis, Herman. *Regionalism: territorial politics in Canada and the United States*. Toronto: Butterworths; 1982; 217 pp.

414. Gibbins, Roger; Ponting J. Rick. The paradoxical nature of the Penner Report. *Canadian Public Policy*; 1984 June; 10(2): 221-224.

415. Gibson, Dale. Protection of minority rights under the Canadian Charter of Rights and Freedoms: can politicians and judges sing harmony? In: Nevitte, Neil; Kornberg, Allan, eds. *Minorities and the Canadian state*. Oakville: Mosaic Press; 1985: 31-51; 324 p.

416. Gibson, Dale. Stereotypes, statistics and slippery slopes: a reply to professors Flanagan and Knopff and other critics of human rights legislation. In: Nevitte, Neil; Kornberg, Allan, eds. *Minorities and the Canadian state.* Oakville: Mosaic Press; 1985: 125-138; 324 p.

417. Gingras, Francois-Pierre; Nevitte, Neil. The evolution of Quebec nationalism. In: Gagnon, Alain G., ed. *Quebec state and society.* Toronto: Methuen; 1984: 2-14; ix, 438 p.

418. Gingras, François-Pierre; Nevitte, Neil. La révolution en plan et le paradigme en cause. *Canadian Journal of Political Science;* 1983 December; 16(4): 691-716.

419. Godin, Gérald. La question du Manitoba. *L'Action nationale;* 1980; 69(7): 532-548.

420. Graham, K.A.; Brown, M.P.S.; McAllister, A.B.; Wojciechowski, M.J. *A climate for change:* alternatives for the central eastern Arctic. Kingston, Ontario: Institute of Local Government, Queen's University; 1984; xiv, 184 p.

421. Grencer, Gilles. Une analyse microéconomique des déterminants des transferts linguistiques des minorités hors - Québec en 1971. *L'Actualité économique;* 1984 June; 60(2): 149-163.

422. Griffin, Anne. *Quebec, the challenge of independence.* Rutherford [N.J.]: Fairleigh Dickinson University Press; c1984; 220 p.

423. Grube, John. La guerre de la centralisation. *L'Action nationale;* 1980; 69(8): 601-621.

424. Grube, John; Angers, Francois-Albert; Allen, Patrick. *Bâtisseur de pays: la pensée de Francois-Albert Angers.* Montreal: Editions de l'Action nationale; 1981; 256 p.

425. Guillaume, Pierre. Acadiens, droits linguistiques rapatriement de la constitution. *Etudes canadiennes;* 1982; 13: 153-156.

426. Hamilton, Richard; Pinard, Maurice. The Quebec independence movement. In: Williams, Colin H., ed. *National separatism.* Vancouver: University of British Columbia; 1982: 203-234; ix, 317 p.

427. Harrington, Denise. Who are the separatists? In: Pratt, Larry; Stevenson, Garth, eds. *Western separatism: myths, realities and dangers.* Edmonton: Hurtig Publishers; 1981: 23-44; 255 p.

428. Harvey, Fernand. La gestion régionale au Québec. *Journal of Canadian Studies;* 1980 Summer; 15(2): 74-87.

429. Harvey, Pierre. Le document du Parti libéral provincial. *L'Action nationale;* 1980 May; 69(9): 744-755.

430. Hawkes, David C. *Aboriginal self-government: what does it mean?* Kingston: Institute of Intergovernmental Relations; 1985; xiii, 99 p. (Aboriginal peoples and constitutional reform. Discussion paper).

431. Hawkes, David C. *Negotiating aboriginal self-government: developments surrounding the 1985 First Ministers' Conference.* Kingston, Ontario: Institute of Intergovernmental Relations, Queen's University; 1985; 48 p. (Background Paper; v. 7).

432. Hawkins, Freda. Multiculturalism in two countries: the Canadian and Australian experience. *Journal of Canadian Studies*; 1982 Spring; 17(1): 64-80.

433. Henderson, William B. *Canada's Indian reserves: the usufruct in our Constitution.* [Ottawa]: Department of Indian Affairs and Northern Development; 1980; ii, 45 p.

434. Holdsworth, Deryck. Dependence, diversity, and the Canadian identity. *Journal of Geography*; 1984 September-October; 83(5): 199-204.

435. Holloway, Kaye. *Le Canada, pourquoi l'impasse?* Montréal: Editions Nouvelle Optique; 1983.

436. In Struggle. *No to renewed federalism no to sovereignty - association.* Montréal: Marxist-Leninist Organization of Canada in struggle; 1980; 78 p.

437. In Struggle. *Quebec has the right to choose.* [Montreal]: Marxist-Leninist Organization of Canada in Struggle; [1980]; 72 p.

438. Institute of Intergovernmental Relations, Queen's University. *The question: the debate on the referendum question, Quebec National Assembly*, March 4-20, 1980. Kingston: Institute of Intergovernmental Relations, Queen's University; 1980; 93 p. (Documents of the debate; v. 1).

439. Institute of Intergovernmental Relations, Queen's University. *Response to Quebec: the other provinces and the Constitutional debate.* Kingston: Institute of Intergovernmental Relations, Queen's University; 1980. (Documents of the debate; v. 2).

440. Institute of Interogovernmental Relations, Queen's University. *La réponse au Québec: les autres provinces et le débat constitutionnel.* Kingston: Institute of Intergovernmental Relations, Queen's University; 1980; 74 p. (Documents du débat; v. 2).

441. Jacobs, Jane. *Canadian cities and sovereignty association.* Toronto: Canadian Broadcasting Corporation; 1980; 63 p.

442. Jacobs, Jane. *The question of separatism: Quebec and the struggle over sovereignty.* New York: Random House; 1980; 134 p.

443. Jaworsky, John. *A case study of the Canadian federal government's multiculturalism policy* [microfiche]: (M.A.) Carleton University; 1980; 2 microfiches (176 fr.). Ottawa: National Library of Canada, 1980.

444. Jobson, Keith and King, Richard, eds. *Aboriginal title, rights and the Canadian Constitution. Proceedings of a Symposium.* Victoria, B.C.: University of Victoria; December 1983.

445. Jull, Peter. Aboriginal peoples and political change in the North Atlantic area. *Journal of Canadian Studies*; 1981 Summer; 16(2): 41-52.

446. Jull, Peter. *Self-government for northern peoples: Canada and the circumpolar story; a report to the Government of the Northwest Territories, Aboriginal Rights and Constitutional Development Secretariat.* Yellowknife: Northwest Territories; 1985; i, 46 p.

447. Kakfwi, Stephen. *Constitutional rights: extinguishment or entrenchment.* Calgary: Arctic Institute of North America; 1984; 1 videorecording (50 min.); 1 in.

448. Kalin, Rudolf; Berry, J.W. Canadian ethnic attitudes in the conflict of national unity. *Journal of Canadian Studies*; 1982 Spring; 17(1): 103-110.

449. Kallen, Evelyn. Multiculturalism ideology, policy and reality. *Journal of Canadian Studies*; 1982 Spring; 17(1): 51-63.

450. Kirschenbaum, Stanislav J. Nationalisme et multiculturalisme au Canada: affinités et problèmes. *Etudes canadiennes*; 1981; 10: 139-148.

451. Knight, David B. Identity and territory: geographical perspectives on nationalism and regionalism. *Annals of the Association of American Geographers*; 1982; 72(4): 514-531.

452. Knight, David B. Regionalism and ethnicity. *Professional Geographer*; 1984; 36(4): 491.

453. Knopff, Rainer. Liberal democracy and the challenge of nationalism in Canadian politics. *Canadian Review of Studies in Nationalism*; 1982; 9(1): 23-42.

454. Knopff, Rainer. The statistical protection of minorities: affirmative action policy in Canada. In: Nevitte, Neil; Kornberg, Allan, eds. *Minorities and the Canadian state.* Oakville: Mosaic Press; 1985: 87-106; 324 p.

455. Knutson, Elmer. *Confederation or western independence?* [Edmonton]: E. Knutson; [1983]; 141 p.

456. Lallier, Adalbert. *La souveraineté-association: réalisme économique ou utopie.* Montréal: Cercle du Livre de France; 1980; 47 p.

457. Lambert, Ronald D. *The sociology of contemporary Quebec nationalism: an annotated bibliography and review.* New York: Garland Publishers; 1981; lxvi, 148 p.

458. Lamonde, Yvan. American cultural influence in Quebec: a one way mirror. In: Hero, Alfred O. Jr.; Daneau, Marcel, eds. *Problems and opportunities in U.S.-Quebec relations.* Boulder, CO: Westview Press; 1984: 106-126; xv, 320 p. (Westview special studies in international relations).

459. Lamontagne, Maurice. *The double deal: a response to the Parti Quebecois white paper and referendum question*. Montreal: Optimum Publishing Co; 1980; 100 p.

460. Lamontagne, Maurice. *La réponse au livre blanc du PQ: le référendum piège*. [Montréal]: Stanké; [1980]; 113 p.

461. Laponce, Jean. Nation-building as body-building: a comparative study of the personalization of city, province and state by anglophone and francophone Canadians. *Social Science Information*; 1984 December; 23(6): 977-991.

462. Lauren, Christer. *Canadian French and Finland Swedish: minority languages with outside standards, regionalisms, and adstrata*. Quebec: International Center for Research on Bilingualism; 1983; 28, xvi p.

463. Laurin-Frenette, Nicole. Divertimento pour deux états: *Canadian Journal of Political and Social Theory*; 1983 Fall; 7(3): 82-96.

464. Lautard, E. Hugh. Regional variation in Canada's cultural mosaic. In: Westfall, William, ed. *Perspectives on regions and regionalism in Canada*. Ottawa: Association for Canadian Studies; 1983; v: 59-67; 137 p.

465. Lavallée, Marc; Delisle, Carole. *Adieu la France, salut l'Amérique*. Montréal: Stanké; 1982; 156 p.

466. LeDuc, Lawrence; Murray, J. Alex. A resurgence of Canadian nationalism: attitudes and policy in the 1980's. In: Kornberg, Allan; Clarke, Harold D., eds. *Political support in Canada: the crisis years*. Durham, N.C.: Duke University Press; 1983: 270-292; xvi, 463 p. (Duke University centre for international studies publications).

467. LeDuc, Lawrence; Clarke, Harold D.; Jenson, Jane; Pammelt, Jon H. Sovereignty-association "Non"-Parti québécois "oui": trends in political support in Quebec. *American Review of Canadian Studies*; 1982 Fall; 12(3): 61-71.

468. Legendre, Camille. *French Canada in crisis: a new society in the making?* London: Minority Rights Group; 1980; 20 p.

469. Léonard, Jean-Francois. *L'impasse: enjeux et perspectives de l'après-référendum* [Montréal?]: Nouvelle Optique; 1980; 162 p.

470. Lescop, Renée. *Le pari québécois du Général de Gaulle*. Montréal: Boréal Express; 1981; 218 p.

471. Lévesque, René. On mérite mieux que ça (à propos du document Ryan). *L'Action nationale*; 1980 April; 59(8): 589-600.

472. Levesque, René. René Levesque talks about separatism - and other things. In: Fox, Paul W., ed. *Politics: Canada*. 5th ed. Toronto: McGraw-Hill Ryerson; 1982: 189-198; 693 p.

473. Levitt, Joseph. English Canadian nationalists and the Canadian character 1957-1974. *Canadian Review of Studies in Nationalism*; 1985 Fall; 12: 223-238.

474. Levitt, Joseph. *A vision beyond reach: a century of images of Canadian destiny*. Ottawa: Deneau; [1982]; iv, 237 p.

475. Li, Peter S.; Bolaria, B. Singh, eds. *Racial minorities in multicultural Canada*. [s.l.]: Garamond Press; 1983; 169 p.

476. Lithwick, N. H. Is federalism good for regionalism? *Journal of Canadian Studies*; 1980 Summer; 15(2): 62-73.

477. Little Bear, Leroy; Boldt, Menno; Long, J. Anthony, eds. *Pathways to self-determination: Canadian Indians and the Canadian state*. Toronto: University of Toronto Press; 1984; 197 p.

478. Little Bear, Leroy; Long, J. Anthony; Boldt, Menno. *Indian self-government: an emerging issue*. Lethbridge: University of Lethbridge; 1981; 24 p.

479. Long, J. Anthony; Little Bear, Leroy; Boldt, Menno. Federal Indian policy and Indian self-government in Canada: an analysis of a current proposal. *Canadian Public Policy*; 1982 Spring; 8(2): 189-199. Note: Language: English.

480. Louder, Dean R.; Waddell, Eric. *Du continent perdu à l'archipel retrouvé: le Québec et l'Amérique française*. Québec: Presses de l'Université Laval; 1983; cviii, 292 p. (Travaux du départment de géographie de l'Université Laval; v. 6).

481. Lupul, Manoly R. The political implementation of multiculturalism. *Journal of Canadian Studies*; 1982 Spring; 17(1): 93-102.

482. Lyon, Noel. *Aboriginal self-government: rights of citizenship and access to governmental services*. Kingston: Institute of Intergovernmental Relations; 1984; 70 (46) p. (Aboriginal peoples and constitutional reform. Background paper; v. 1).

483. Mackay, Jacques. *Le courage de se choisir: essai*. Montréal: L'Hexagone; 1983; 105 p.

484. MacKinnon, Frank. When "rights" are wrong: with examples from Atlantic Canada. In: Nevitte, Neil; Kornberg, Allan, eds. *Minorities and the Canadian state*. Oakville: Mosaic Press; 1985: 193-202; 324 p.

485. Magnet, Joseph Eliot. The future of official language minorities. *Les cahiers de droit*; 1986 March; (1): 189-202.

486. Mair, Nathan H. The Quebec protestant churches and the question of nationalism. *Social Compass*; 1984; 31(4): 379-390.

487. Mallet, Pascal. *Le Québec, pour quoi faire?* Paris: B. Grasset; 1980; 317 p.

488. Malloch, Lesley. *Dene government, past and future: a traditional Dene model of government and its implications for constitutional development in the Northwest Territories today*. Yellowknife: Western Constitutional Forum; 1984; 40 p.

489. Manitowabi, Mark. *The Indian Act and Indian self-government*. [Ottawa]: Dept. of Indian Affairs, Policy Coordination and Band Government Development Branch; 1980; 45 p.

490. Many Fingers, Wallace; Dacks, Gurston. Commentaries: aboriginal peoples and the Constitution. *Alberta Law Review*; 1981 Summer; 19(3): 428-434.

491. Marchak, Patricia. A contribution to the class and region debate. In: Westfall, William, ed. *Perspectives on regions and regionalism in Canada*. Ottawa: Association for Canadian Studies; 1983; v: 81-88; 137 p.

492. Marchak, Patricia. Limits on western growth ("Power shift west: myth or reality?"). *Canadian Journal of Sociology*; 1981 Spring; 6(2): 172-175.

493. Marchak, Patricia. The two dimensions of Canadian regionalism. *Journal of Canadian Studies*; 1980 Summer; 15(2): 88-97.

494. Marchant, C. Kenneth. *Analytic notes and structural layout: aboriginal self-government and the Constitution*. Ottawa: Corporate Policy Branch, Department of Indian Affairs and Northern Development; September 1982; 66 p. (Consultants report).

495. Mason, Michael D. Canadian and United States approaches to Indian sovereignty. *Osgoode Hall Law Journal*; 1983 September; 21(3): 422-474.

496. Matthews, Ralph. *The creation of regional dependency*. Toronto: University of Toronto Press; 1983; x, 246 p.

497. Matthews, Ralph. The significance and explanation of regional divisions in Canada: toward a Canadian sociology. *Journal of Canadian Studies*; 1980 Summer; 15(2): 43-61.

498. McConnell, W. H.; Milligan, S. M. The "Drury Report" on constitutional development in the Northwest Territories. *Musk-Ox*; 1981; 29: 10-24.

499. McCue, Harvey. The Constitutional Conference on aboriginal rights: where do we go from here? (editorial). *Journal of Canadian Studies*; 1983; 18(3): 3-4.

500. McInncs, Simon. The Inuit and the constitutional process: 1978-1981. In: Getty, Ian A.L.; Lussier, Antoine S., eds. *As long as the sun shines and the water flows*. Vancouver: University of British Columbia Press; 1983: 315-336.

501. McInnes, Simon. The Inuit and the constitutional process: 1978-81. *Journal of Canadian Studies*; 1981 Summer; 16(2): 53-68.

502. McInnes, Simon; Burnet, Peter. *Inuit and constitutional reform*. Ottawa: Inuit Committee on National Issues; 1981; 32 p.

503. McKinsey, Lauren. Watching the separatists. In: Pratt, Larry; Stevenson, Garth, eds. *Western separatism: myths, realities and dangers*. Edmonton: Hurtig Publishers; 1981: 209-228; 255 p.

504. McNeil, Kent. *Native claims in Rupert's Land and the North-West Territory: Canada's constitutional obligations.* Saskatoon: Native Law Centre, University of Saskatchewan; 1982; 37 p. (Studies in aboriginal rights).

505. McWhinney, Edward. The "language" problem in Quebec. *American Journal of Comparative Law;* 1981 Summer; 29: 413-427.

506. Melnyk, George. *Radical regionalism.* Edmonton: Newest; 1981; 114 p.

507. Milloy, John S. The early Indian acts: developmental strategy and constitutional change. In: Getty, Ian A.L.; Lussier, Antoine S., eds. *As long as the sun shines and water flows.* Vancouver: Univ. of British Columbia Press; 1983: 56-64.

508. Monière, Denis. Currents of nationalism in Quebec. In: Brooks, Stephen, ed. *Political thought in Canada.* Toronto: Irwin; 1980: 153-184; 277 p.

509. Monière, Denis. Motivations. *L'Action nationale;* 1985 April; 74(8): 779-786.

510. Montcalm, Mary Beth. *Class in ethnic nationalism Quebec nationalism in comparative perspective* [microfiche]: (Ph.D.) Carleton University; 1983 5 microfiches (414 fr.). Ottawa: National Library of Canada, 1984.

511. Montcalm, Mary Beth. Quebec nationalism in a comparative perspective. In: Gagnon, Alain G., ed. *Quebec state and society.* Toronto: Methuen; 1984: 45-58; ix, 438 p.

512. Moore, Kermot A. *The will to survive: native people and the Constitution.* Quebec: Hyperborea; 1984; 106 p.

513. Morchain, Janet Kerr; Wade, Mason. *Search for a nation: Canada's crisis in French-English relations 1759-1980.* Markham: Fitzhenry & Whiteside; 1984.

514. Morgan, Edward M. Self-government and the Constitution: a comparative look at native Canadians and American indians. *American Indian Law Review;* 1984; 12(1): 39-56.

515. Morisset, Jean. The aboriginal nationhood, the northern challenge and the construction of Canadian unity. *Queen's Quarterly;* 1981 Summer; 88(2): 237-249.

516. Morisset, Jean. *L'identité usurpée.* Montréal: Nouvelle Optique; 1985.

517. Morris, Raymond N. Canada as a family: Ontario responses to the Quebec independence movement. *Canadian Review of Sociology and Anthropology;* 1984 May; 21(2): 181-201.

518. Morse, Bradford W. *Aboriginal self-government in Australia and Canada.* Kingston, Ontario: Institute of Intergovernmental Relations, Queen's University; 1984; 130 p. (Background paper; v. 4).

519. Morton, F.L. Group rights individual rights in the Charter: the special cases of natives and quebecois. In: Nevitte, Neil; Kornberg, Allan, eds. *Minorities and the Canadian state.* Oakville: Mosaic Press; 1985: 71-85; 324 p.

520. Moss, J. E. Native proposals for constitutional reform. *Journal of Canadian Studies*; 1980-81 Winter; 15(4): 85-92.

521. Moulary, Josiane; Villemaire, Carmen. *Référendum québécois: bibliographie.* Montréal: Editions Bergeron; 1983; 276 p.

522. Nakatsura, Shaun. A constitutional right of Indian self-government. *University of Toronto Faculty of Law Review*; 1985; 23(2): 72-85.

523. Native Council of Canada. Métis and Non-Status Indian Constitutional Review Commission. *Native people and the Constitution of Canada - the report of the Métis and Non-status Indian Constitutional Review Commission*, by H. Daniels. [Ottawa]: Native Council of Canada; 1981; 99 p.

524. Nevitte, Neil; Gibbins, Roger. Minorities as an attitudinal phenomenon: a comparative analysis of youth elites. In: Nevitte, Neil; Kornberg, Allan, eds. *Minorities and the Canadian state*. Oakville: Mosaic Press; 1985: 257-273; 324 p.

525. *Nevitte, Neil; Kornberg, Allan, eds. Minorities and the Canadian state*. Oakville: Mosaic Press; 1985; 324 p.

526. Norrie, Kenneth; Percy, Michael. The economics of a separate west. In: Pratt, Larry; Stevenson, Garth, eds. *Western separatism: myths, realities and dangers.* Edmonton: Hurtig Publishers; 1981: 173-192; 255 p.

527. Northwest Territories. *Response to the report of the Task Force to Review Comprehensive Claims Policy: "Living treaties lasting agreements".* Yellowknife: Government of the Northwest Territories; May 27, 1986; 14 p.

528. Northwest Territories. Aboriginal Rights and Constitutional Development Secretariat. *Self-Government for the northern peoples: Canada and the circumpolar story. A report to the Government of the N.W.T.*, by Peter Jull. Yellowknife: Government of the Northwest Territories; 1985; 46 p.

529. O'Grady, William D. *The Quebec problem: an inquiry into the ethics of sovereignty and secession.* Ottawa: Borealis Press; 1981; c1980; 53 p.

530. O'Neill, Louis. Demain l'indépendance si nous le voulons. *L'Action nationale*; 1982 February; 71(6): 663-675.

531. Odjig, Alfred. *Aboriginal rights in Canada.* Ottawa: National Library of Canada; 1985; 17 (19) p.

532. Ontario. Provincial Secretariat for Resources Development, Native Affairs. *Aboriginal self-government: a discussion paper in preparation for the 1984 First Ministers Conference on Aboriginal and Treaty Rights.* Toronto: Provincial Secretariat for Resources Development, Native Affairs; 1984; 89 p.

533. Opekokew, Delia. *The first nations: Indian government and the Canadian Confederation.* Saskatoon: Federation of Saskatchewan Indians; 1980; viii, 92 p.

534. Orban, Edmond. Quebec alienation and the trend toward centralization. In: Gagnon, Alain G., ed. *Quebec state and society*. Toronto: Methuen; 1984: 31-44; ix, 438 p.

535. Ornstein, Michael D.; Stevenson, H. Michael. Elite and public opinion before the Quebec referendum: a commentary on the state in Canada: *Canadian Journal of Political Science*; 1981 December; 14(4): 745-774.

536. Ornstein, Michael D.; Stevenson, H. Michael; Williams, A. Paul. Region, class and political culture in Canada. *Canadian Journal of Political Science*; 1980 June; 13(2): 227-272.

537. Orridge, Andrew W. Separatist and autonomist nationalisms: the structure of regional loyalties in the modern state. In: Williams, Colin H., ed. *National separatism*. Vancouver: University of British Columbia; 1982: 43-74; ix, 317 p.

538. Owram, Doug. Reluctant hinterland. In: Pratt, Larry; Stevenson, Garth, eds. *Western separatism: myths, realities and dangers*. Edmonton: Hurtig Publishers; 1981: 45-64; 255 p.

539. Paquette, Gilbert. La souveraineté pour aller plus loin. *L'Action nationale*; 1985 April; 74(8): 787-791.

540. Parti Nationaliste. *La logique du Québec: projet de manifeste électoral*. Montréal: Parti nationaliste; [1983]; 18 p.

541. Parti québécois. The program of the Parti Québécois. In: Fox, Paul W., ed. *Politics: Canada*. 5th ed. Toronto: McGraw-Hill Ryerson; 1982: 197-202; 693 p.

542. Parti québécois. *Permanence nationale. Le parti québécois*. Montréal: Permanence nationale; [1983]; 32 p.

543. Pelletier, Gérard. *Les années d'impatience, 1950-1960*. [Montréal]: Stanké; 1983; 320 p.

544. Pelletier, Réjean. *Partis politiques et société québécoise 1960-1970*. Montréal: Laboratoire d'études politiques et administratives; Université Laval; 197 p. (Série 3: Notes et travaux de recherche; v. 5); ISBN: 292047059.

545. Percy, Michael. Assessing the economic evidence ("Power shift west: myth or reality?"). *Canadian Journal of Sociology*; 1980 Spring; 6(2): 169-172.

546. Polèse, Mario. Economic integration, national policies and the rationality of regional separatism. *Canadian Journal of Regional Science*; 1981 Spring; 4(1): 1-20.

547. Ponting, J. Rick; Gibbins, Roger. The reactions of English Canadians and French quebecois to native Indian protest: Canadian Review of Sociology and Anthropology; May 1981; 18(2): 222-238.

548. Ponting, J. Rick; Gibbins, Roger; Siggner, Andrew J. *Out of irrelevance: a socio-political introduction to Indian affairs in Canada*. Toronto: Butterworths; 1980; xvii, 360 p.

549. Pratt, Larry. Staples and the provincial state ("Power shift west: myth or reality?"). *Canadian Journal of Sociology*; 1981 Spring; 6(2): 181-183.

550. Pratt, Larry; Stevenson, Garth, eds. *Western separatism: myths, realities and dangers*. Edmonton: Hurtig Publishers; 1981; 255 p.

551. Puxley, Peter. The psychological appeals of separatism. In: Pratt, Larry; Stevenson, Garth, eds. *Western separatism: myths, realities and dangers*. Edmonton: Hurtig Publishers; 1981: 135-154; 255 p.

552. *Québec, un pays incertain: réflexions sur le Québec post-référendaire*, par Robert Boily. Montréal: Québec/Amérique; 1980; 312 p.

553. Québec. Assemblée nationale. *Oui: la tête et le coeur: le débat sur la question*. [Montréal]: Stanké; 1980; 86 (58) p.

554. Ralph Hedlin Associates. *Western Canada in Confederation: a short re-examination of some historic relationships and a record of how fair the system has been to the western region of Canada*. Toronto: Ralph Hedlin Associates; 1980; 26 leaves.

555. Ray, D.I. Western separatism: counter-elite of the marginalized. In: Reasons, Chuck, ed. *Stampede city: power and politics in the West*. Toronto: Between the Lines; 1984.

556. Reeves, William; Frideres, J.S. The resolution of complaints based on race and origin: the Canadian Human Rights Commission. In: Nevitte, Neil; Kornberg, Allan, eds. *Minorities and the Canadian state*. Oakville: Mosaic Press; 1985: 139-153; 324 p.

557. Reilly, Wayne G.; Preston, Richard A. *Encounter with Canada: essays in the social sciences: a publication in honor of Richard A. Preston*. [Durham, N.C.]: Duke University, Center for International Studies; 1980; vi, 120 p. (Occasional papers series).

558. Rhéaume, Gilles. L'affaire Riel. *L'Action nationale*; 1986 March; 75(7): 622-647.

559. Richards, John. The democratic potential of federalism. In: Westfall, William, ed. *Perspectives on regions and regionalism in Canada*. Ottawa: Association for Canadian Studies; 1983: 116-130; 137 p.

560. Richards, John. Populism and the West. In: Pratt, Larry; Stevenson, Garth, eds. *Western separatism: myths, realities and dangers*. Edmonton: Hurtig Publishers; 1981: 65-84; 255 p.

561. Richmond, Anthony H. *After the referenda: the future of ethnic nationalism in Britain and Canada: report of a joint international seminar; 5-9 November,*

1981. The University College of North Wales, Bangor. Downsview: York University, Institute for Behavioural Research; [1982]; 481 p.

562. Richmond, Anthony H., ed. *After the referenda: the future of ethnic nationalism in Britain and Canada.* Downsview: York University, Institute for Behavioural Research; [1981]; 481 p.

563. Rieber, Jesse A. *The United States federal government--Indian relationship: trusteeship and local government.* Ottawa: Indian and Northern Affairs Canada; 1984; iii, 128 p.

564. Rioux, Marcel; Crean, Susan. Overcoming dependency: a plea for two nations: *Canadian Journal of Political and Social Theory*; 1983; 7(3): 50-67.

565. Rioux, Marcel; Crean, Susan M. *Deux pays pour vivre: un plaidoyer.* Laval: Editions Coopératives A. Saint-Martin; 1980; 117 p.

566. Roberts, Stanley C. Sense and sensibility in the West. *Language and Society*; 1981 Winter; 4: 3-6.

567. Robillard, Jean-D. Au pays de Riel (2e partie). *L'Action nationale*; 1985 September; 75(1): 65-81.

568. Robillard, Jean-D. Au pays de Riel (3e partie). *L'Action nationale*; 1985 November; 75(3): 243-254.

569. Robillard, Jean-D. Nos cousins Franco-Ontariens. *L'Action nationale*; 1985 May; 74(9): 885-900.

570. Robillard, Jean-D. Politique d'assimilation et d'anglicisation. *L'Action nationale*; 1982 April; 71(8): 837-850.

571. Robinson, Eric; Bird Quinney, Henry. *The infested blanket: Canada's Constitution and the genocide of Indian nations.* Winnipeg: Queenston House Publishing; 1985; xxiv, 168 p.

572. Romanow, Roy J. Aboriginal rights in the constitutional process. In: Boldt, Menno; Long, J. Anthony, eds. *The quest for justice: aboriginal peoples and aboriginal rights.* Toronto: University of Toronto Press; 1985: 73-82; viii, 406 p.

573. Roy, Jean-Marce. Nationalisme et régionalisme dans la crise canadienne: essai d'interprétation geógraphique. *Cahiers de géographie du Québec*; 1980 April; 24(61): 109-122.

574. Roy, Raoul. *Le Canada réel.* [Montréal]: [R. Roy]; 1980; 30 p.

575. Roy, Raoul. *Lettre à René Lévesque.* Montréal: Editions du Franc-Canada; [1980]; 48 p. (Les Cahiers de la décolonisation du Franc-Canada; v. 10).

576. Roy, Raoul; Angers, Francois-Albert. *Peuple sans nom: oui a notre nom de canadiens non au sobriquet de québécois on est canadien ou bien on ne l'est pas.* [Montréal]: Franc-Canada; 1981; 116 p.

577. Rubinoff, Lionel. Multiculturalism and the metaphysics of pluralism. *Journal of Canadian Studies*; 1982 Spring; 17(1): 122-130.

578. Rudnicki, Walter. *The third option: a native role in Confederation*. Ottawa: Policy Development Group; April 4, 1980; 15 p.

579. Rudnicki, Walter. *List of current initiatives underway which impinge upon the general area of Indian self-government*. Ottawa: Department of Indian Affairs and Northern Development, Program Planning and Policy Coordination; November 1983; 227 p.

580. Rush, Gary. State, class and capital: demystifying the westward shift of power. *Canadian Review of Sociology and Anthropology*; 1983 August; 20(3): 255-289.

581. Rutan, Gerard F. Western Canada: the winds of alienation. *American Review of Canadian Studies*; 1982 Spring; 12(1): 74-97.

582. Rutan, Gerard F. Western Canada: alienation, separatism, and economic growth. *Journal of Contemporary Business*; 1981; 10(4): 43-57.

583. Sanders, Douglas. Aboriginal peoples and the Constitution. *Alberta Law Review*; 1981 Summer; 19(3): 410-427.

584. Sanders, Douglas. Prior claims: an aboriginal people in the Constitution of Canada. In: Beck, Stanley M.; Bernier, Ivan, eds. *Canada and the new Constituion: the unfinished agenda*. Montreal: Institute for Research on Public Policy; 1983; 1: 225-279; xii, 399 p.

585. Schuetz, C. F. The Acadians of Canada: the difficulties of a minority within a minority. *Europa Ethnica*; 1982; 39(2): 63-65.

586. Schwartz, Bryan. *Preliminary report of the Parliamentary Committee on Indian Self-Government: synopsis and comments*; October 4, 1983; 23 p.

587. Schwartz, Bryan. *First principles: constitutional reform with respect to the aboriginal peoples of Canada 1982-1984*. Kingston: Institute of Intergovernmental Relations; 1984; 292 p. (Background paper; v. 6).

588. Scott, Graham. *More than survival: viewpoints toward a theology of nation*. Don Mills: Canec; 1980; 125 p.

589. Seagram Company. *The Canadian journey, rivers of memory, river of dreams*. [Montreal]: [Seagram Company]; [1980]; 34 p.

590. Shaw, William F.; Albert, Lionel. *Partition: the price of Quebec's independence: a realistic look at the possibility of Quebec separating from Canada and becoming an independent state*. Montreal: Thornhill Publishers; 1980; 205 p.

591. Sherrill, Peter T. Separatism and Quebec. *Current History*; 1980; 79(460): 134-137.

592. Short, David E. Restrictions on access to English language schools in Quebec: an international human rights analysis. *Canada-United States Law Journal*; 1985; 10: 1-38.

593. Silver, A.I. *The French-Canadian idea of Confederation, 1864-1900*. Toronto: University of Toronto Press; 1982; ix, 257 p.

594. Sinclair-Faulkner, Tom. God's "Flower of Hope:" the religious matrix of Quebec's independantisme. In: Westfall, William [and others], eds. *Religion/culture: comparative Canadian studies*. Ottawa: Association for Canadian Studies; 1985; vii: 376-390; 410 p.

595. Sitwell, O.F.G.; Seifried, N.R.M. *The regional structure of the Canadian economy*. Toronto: Methuen; 1984; xv, 192 p.

596. Slattery, Brian. The hidden constitution: aboriginal rights in Canada. In: Boldt, Menno; Long J. Anthony, eds. *The quest for justice: aboriginal peoples and aboriginal rights*. Toronto: University of Toronto Press; 1985: 114-138; viii, 406 p.

597. Smith, Allan. National images and national maintenance: the ascendancy of the ethnic idea in North America. *Canadian Journal of Political Science*; 1981 June; 14(2): 227-258.

598. Smith, Carl F. *French-English relations in Canada*. Scarborough: Prentice-Hall; 1980; 141 p.

599. Smith, Joel; Kornberg, Allan. The Quebec referendum: national or provincial event. In: Kornberg, Allan; Clarke, Harold D., eds. *Political support in Canada: the crisis years*. Durham, N.C.: Duke University Press; 1983: 353-379; xvi, 463 p. (Duke University Centre for International Studies publications).

600. Smith, Joel; Kornberg, Allan; Rushing, Beth. The changing political situation of women in Canada. In: Nevitte, Neil; Kornberg, Allan, eds. *Minorities and the Canadian state*. Oakville: Mosaic Press; 1985: 221-238; 324 p.

601. Soderlund, Walter C.; Wagenberg, Ronald H.; Briggs, E. Donald; Nelson, Ralph C. Regional and linguistic agenda-setting in Canada: a study of newspaper coverage of issues affecting political integration in 1976. *Canadian Journal of Political Science*; 1980 June; 13(2): 347-356.

602. Soldatos, P. Le Canada après le référendum au Québec. *Etudes canadiennes*; 1982; 12: 103-118.

603. Spicer, Keith. *Cher péquiste... et néanmoins ami: propos pré-référendaires, dans un esprit post-référendaire*. [Montréal]: La Presse; [1980]; 183 p. (Collection temps présent).

604. Stevenson, Garth. Canadian regionalism in continental perspective. *Journal of Canadian Studies*; 1980 Summer; 15(2): 16-28.

605. Stevenson, Garth. Western alienation in Australia and Canada. In: Pratt, Larry; Stevenson, Garth, eds. *Western separatism: myths, realities and dangers*. Edmonton: Hurtig Publishers; 1981: 119-134; 255 p.

606. Stienstra, Deborah. *Provincial power at a premium: aboriginal rights, Alberta and the Constitution*. Edmonton: [s.n.]; 1984; 16 p.

607. Swainson, Donald Regionalism and the social scientists. *Acadiensis*; 1980; 10(1): 143-153.

608. Swindon, Hubert. Le référendum: une autre décennie d'instabilité politique. *L'Action nationale*; 1980 December; 60(4): 271-291.

609. Symons, T.H.B. Cultural diversity, Canadian identity and Canadian federalism. In: Mathews, Russell, ed. *Public policies in two federal countries: Canada and Australia*. Canberra: Centre for Research on Federal Financial Relations, Australian National University; 1982; 225-236.

610. Taylor, Charles. Nationalism and independence: an economic problem. In: Fox, Paul W., ed. *Politics: Canada*. 5th ed. Toronto: McGraw-Hill Ryerson; 1982: 169-179; 693 p.

611. Taylor, Donald M.; Sigal, Ronald J. Defining "Quebecois": the role of ethnic heritage, language, and political orientation. *Journal of Canadian Studies*; 1982; 14(2): 59-70.

612. Tennant, Paul. Indian self-government: progress or stalemate? *Canadian Public Policy*; 1984 June; 10(2): 211-215.

613. Thériault, Léon. La question du pouvoir en Acadie. *Etudes canadiennes*; 1982; 13: 119-142.

614. Tremblay, Marc-Adélard. L'identité des Québécois francophones: perspectives théoriques et tendances. *Transactions of the Royal Society of Canada*; 1984; 22: 3-18.

615. Tupper, Allan. Mr. Trudeau and the West. In: Pratt, Larry/Stevenson, Garth, eds. *Western separatism: myths, realities and dangers*. Edmonton: Hurtig Publishers; 1981: 85-104; 255 p.

616. Union bolchévique du Canada. *Oui, démasquons le PQ: position de l'Union bBolchévique sur le référendum* [Montréal]: L'Union; 1980; 36 p.

617. Union of New Brunswick Indians. *Views on the Canadian Constitution as it affects Indians of New Brunswick*. Fredericton: Union of New Brunswick Indians; 1981; 1v. Note: 36 cm.

618. Union of Nova Scotia Indians; Canada. Parliament. Special Joint Committee on the Constitution of Canada (1980-1981). *Statement of Union of Nova Scotia Indians, January 6, 1981 to the Joint Constitutional Committee of Senate and House of Commons of the Federal Parliament*. s.l.: [Ottawa]; 1981; 13 p.

619. Vadeboncoeur, Pierre. *To be or not to be: that is the question*. Montreal: Hexagone; [1980]; 169 p.

620. Valaskakis, Kimon. *Le Québec et son destin international: les enjeux géopolitiques*. [Montréal]: Quinze; [1980]; 149 p.

621. Valaskakis, Kimon. *Le référendum et les défis du futur.* Montréal: Parti libéral du Québec; 1980; 38 p. (Textes référendaires; v. 11).

622. Vallières, Pierre. *The impossible Quebec*. Montreal: Black Rose Books; 1980.

623. Waddell, Eric. State language and society: the vicissitudes of French in Quebec and Canada. In: Cairns, Alan; Williams, Cynthia, res. coords. *The politics of gender, ethnicity and language in Canada*. Toronto: University of Toronto Press; Royal Commission on the Economic Union and Development Prospects for Canada; 1986: 67-110; xvi, 247 p. (The collected research studies; v. 34).

624. Wah-Shee, James J. *Report to the Legislative Assembly of the N.W.T., by the Minister for Aboriginal Rights and Constitutional Development, the honourable James J. Wah-Shee*. Yellowknife: Government of N.W.T.; 1981; 6, 2 p.

625. Wardhaugh, Ronald. *Language and nationhood: the Canadian experience*. Vancouver: New Star Books; 1983; 269 p.

626. Weaver, Sally. Federal difficulties with aboriginal rights demands. In: Boldt, Menno; Long, J. Anthony, eds. *The quest for justice: aboriginal peoples and aboriginal rights*. Toronto: University of Toronto Press; 1985: 139-147; vii, 406 p.

627. Weaver, Sally M. A comment on the Penner report. *Canadian Public Policy*; 1984 June; 10(2): 215-221.

628. Weaver, Sally M. Federal policy-making for Métis and non-status Indians in the context of native policy. *Canadian Ethnic Studies*; 1985; 17(2): 80-102.

629. Westfall, William, ed. *Perspectives on regions and regionalism in Canada*. Ottawa: Association for Canadian Studies; 1983; 137 p.

630. Westfall, William. The regional patterns in Canada and Canadian culture. In: *idem.*, ed. *Perspectives on regions and regionalism in Canada*. Ottawa: Association for Canadian Studies; 1983: 2-15; 137 p.

631. Whalley, John; Trela, Irene. *Regional aspects of Confederation. Toronto: University of Toronto Press; Royal Commission on the Economic Union and Development Prospects for Canada; 1986: xvii, 269 p. (The collected research studies; v. 68)*.

632. Williams, Colin H. The desire of nations: Québécois ethnic separatism in comparative perspective. *Cahiers de geógraphie du Québec*; 1980 April; 24(61): 47-68.

633. Williams, Colin H., ed. *National separatism*. Vancouver: University of British Columbia; 1982; ix, 317 p.

634. Wonders, William C. Canadian regions and regionalisms: national enrichment or national disintegration? In: Westfall, William, ed. *Perspectives on regions and regionalism in Canada*. Ottawa: Association for Canadian Studies; 1983: 16-53; 137 p.

635. Woodcock, George. *Confederation betrayed*. Madeira Park, B.C.: Harbour Pub.; 1981; 198 p.

636. Zlotkin, Norman K. *Unfinished business: aboriginal peoples and the 1983 constitutional conference*. Kingston: Institute of Intergovernmental Relations, Queen's University; 1983; 91 p. (Discussion paper; v. 15).

3 Courts and Constitutions

637. Abel, Albert S. *Towards a constitutional charter for Canada.* Toronto: University of Toronto Press; c1980; 105 p. (Canadian University Paperbooks; v. 260).

638. Ackerman, Bruce A.; Charney, Robert E. Canada at the constitutional crossroads. *University of Toronto Law Journal*; 1984 Spring; 34(2): 117-135.

639. Adam, G.S. *The constitutional status of the press in Canada.* Montreal: McGill University, Graduate Communications Program; 1981; 12 p. (Working papers in communications).

640. Albert, Alan Dale. Constitutional law: patriation of Canadian Constitution - Canada Act, 1982, ch. 11, incorporating the Constitution Act, 1982; Reference re Amendment of the Constitution of Canada, 125 D.L.R.3d 1 (1981). *Harvard International Law Journal*; 1983 Winter; 23(2): 395-404.

641. Alberta. *Canada's Constitution: a proud moment for Alberta.* [Edmonton]: Government of Alberta; 1982.

642. Alberta. *Constitutional issues for the people of Alberta.* [Edmonton]: [Government of Alberta]; [1981]; 1 sheet.

643. Alberta. *Documents relating to the patriation of the British North America Act.* Edmonton: Government of Alberta; 1980; 27 p.

644. Alberta. *Submission by the Government of Alberta to the Select Committee on Foreign Affairs, House of Commons, Parliament of the United Kingdom, November 26, 1980.* [Edmonton]: Government of Alberta; 1980; (13) p.

645. Albinski, Henry S. Contemporary Canadian politics. *Current History*; 1984 May; 83(493): 296-210; 231-233.

646. Allen, J. Garfield. Canada's constitutional time-bomb (pt.1.): The divisive effects of Trudeau's approach. The Round Table; 1981; (281): 15-25.

647. Allen, J. Garfield. The flaw in Canadian federalism. *The Round Table*; 1980; 278: 172-176.

648. Anonymous. Comparison of the role of the Supreme Court in Canada and the United States: a one day conference, October 20, 1979, Case Western Reserve University, Cleveland, Ohio. *Canada-United States Law Journal*; 1980 Summer; (3): 1-102.

649. Anonymous. *Indians and the Canadian Constitution: Alberta chiefs seek support in England.* Standoff: Indian News Media; 1981; 16 p.

650. Apps, Eric. Minority language education rights. *University of Toronto Faculty of Law Review*; 1985 Fall; 43(2): 45.

651. Arbess, Daniel J. Limitations on legislative override under the Canadian Charter of Rights and Freedoms: a matter of balancing values. *Osgoode Hall Law Journal*; 1983 July; 21(1): 113-141.

652. Arès, Richard. L'impasse constitutionelle. *L'Action nationale*; 1981 January; 70(5): 361-363.

653. Arsenault, Pierre. *L'enchâssement des droits de la minorité canadienne-française dans la constitution du Canada.* [Moncton]: [n.b.]; Ecole de droit; c[1982?]; 3; 54 p.

654. Asplund, C. T. Mr. Trudeau's constitution: going in style. *Queen's Quarterly*; 1980 Winter; 87(4): 584-587.

655. Assemblée Constitutionnelle du Nunavut. *Bâtir le Nunavut; un document de travail accompagné de propositions en vue d'une constitution de l'Arctique.* Yellowknife: L'Assemblée; 1983; 54, (46) p.

656. Assemblée des évêques du Québec. *Observations des évêques du Québec sur la question constitutionnelle.* Montréal: L'Assemblée; [19] 81 p.

657. Association canadienne-française de l'Ontario. *Le droit de veto constitutionnel du Québec: un droit au service des Franco-Ontariens.* Ottawa: L'Association; [1982]; vii, iv, 131 [6] p.

658. Association of Metis and Non-Status Indians of Saskatchewan. *Position paper on native rights and constitutional patriation.* s.l.; 1980.

659. Baines, B. *Women, human rights, and the Constitution.* Rev. ed. [Ottawa]: Advisory Council on the Status of Women; 1980.

660. Bak, J. M.; Garabak, A. The ideology of a millennial Constitution in Hungary. *East European Quarterly*; 1981; 15(3): 307-326.

661. Bale, G. Reciprocal tax immunity in a federation - Section 125 of the Constitution Act, 1867 and the proposed federal tax on exported natural gas. *Canadian Bar Review*; 1983 September; 61(3): 652-681.

662. Bale, Gordon. Law, politics and the Manitoba school question: Supreme Court and Privy Council. *Canadian Bar Review*; 1985 September; 63(3): 461-518.

663. Ballem, John Bishop. Oil and gas under the Constitution. *Canadian Bar Review*; 1983 September; 61(3): 547-558.

664. Bankes, Nigel D.; Hunt, Constance D.; Saunders, J. Owen. Energy and natural resources: the Canadian constitutional framework. In: Krasnick, Mark, res. coord. *Case studies in the division of powers.* Toronto: University of Toronto Press; Royal Commission on the Economic Union and Development Prospects for Canada; 1986: 53-138; xvii, 269 p. (The collected research studies; v. 62).

665. Banks, Margaret A. The Canada Act 1982 - some facts and comments. *University of Western Ontario Law Review*; 1983; (1): 155-161.

666. Banting, Keith G.; Simeon, Richard. Introduction: the politics of constitutional change. In: *idem*, eds. *Redesigning the state: the politics of constitutional change in industrial nations*. Toronto: University of Toronto Press; 1985: 1-29; xii, 257 p.

667. Banting, Keith G.; Simeon, Richard, eds. *Redesigning the state: the politics of constitutional change in industrial nations*. Toronto: University of Toronto Press; 1985; xii, 257 p.

668. Banting, Keith; Simeon, Richard, eds. *And no one cheered: federalism, democracy and the Constitution Act*. Toronto: Methuen; 1983; xii, 376 p.

669. Banting, Keith; Simeon, Richard. Federalism, democracy and the future. In: *idem.*, eds. *And no one cheered*. Toronto: Methuen; 1983: 348-359; xii, 376 p.

670. Barry, Leo D. Law, policy and statutory interpretation under a constitutionally entrenched Canadian Charter of Rights and Freedoms. *Canadian Bar Review*; 1982 June; 60(2): 237-264.

671. Barsh, Russel Lawrence; Henderson, James Youngblood. Aboriginal rights, treaty rights, and human rights: indian tribes and "constitutional renewal". *Journal of Canadian Studies*; 1982 Summer; 17(2): 55-81.

672. Bastarache, Michael. Dualism and equality in the new Constitution. *University of New Brunswick Law Journal*; 1981; 30: 27-41.

673. Bayefsky, Anne F.; Eberts, Mary ed. *Equality rights and the Canadian Charter of Rights and Freedoms*: Carswell; 1985; xliv, 661 p.

674. Beaudoin, Gérald A. *La partage des pouvoirs*. 3rd ed. Ottawa: Editions de l'-Université d'Ottawa; 1983; xx, 634 p.

675. Beaudoin, Gérald-A. Les droits démocratiques (Canadian Charter of Rights and Freedoms). *Canadian Bar Review*; 1983 March; 61(1): 151-176.

676. Beaudoin, Gérald-A. *Le partage des pouvoirs*. Ottawa: Editions de l'-Université d'Ottawa; 1980; xix, 432 p. (Collection des travaux de la Faculté de droit de l'Université d'Ottawa).

677. Beaudoin, Gérald-A. *Le partage des pouvoirs*. 2nd ed. Ottawa: Editions de l'-Université d'Ottawa; 1982; xix, 527 p. (Monographies juridiques; Collection des travaux de la Faculté de droit de l'Université d'Ottawa; v. 16).

678. Beaudoin, Gérald-A. Le rapatriement: la fin du commencement? *University of Ottawa Quarterly*; 1982; 52(3): 287-301.

679. Beaupré, R. Michael. Vers l'interprétation d'une constitution bilingue. *Les Cahiers de droit*; 1984 December; 25(4): 939-958.

680. Beck, Stanley M.; Bernier, Ivan, eds. *Canada and the new Constitution: the unfinished agenda*. Montreal: Institute for Research on Public Policy; 1983; 2 v.; v.1: xii, 399 p.; v.2: 289 p.

681. Beckton, Clare. Freedom of expression - access to the courts. *Canadian Bar Review*; 1983 March; (1): 101-123.

682. Becton, Clare; MacKay, A Wayne, res. coords. *The courts and the Charter*. Toronto: University of Toronto Press; Royal Commission on the Economic Union and Development Prospects for Canada; 1985: xv, 279 p. (The collected research studies; v. 58).

683. Bélanger, Gérard. The division of powers in a federal system: a review of the economic literature, with applications to Canada. In: Simeon, Richard, res. coord. *Division of powers and public policy*. Toronto: University of Toronto Press; Royal Commission on the Economic Union and Development Prospects for Canada: 1-28; xiv, 206 p. (The collected research studies; v. 61).

684. Belobaba, Edward P.; Gertner, Eric, eds. *The new Constitution and the Charter of Rights: fundamental issues and strategies*. Toronto: Butterworth; c1983; xxi, 357 p.

685. Bender, Paul. The Canadian Charter of Rights and Freedoms and the United States Bill of Rights: a comparison. *McGill Law Journal*; 1983 September; 28(4): 811-866.

686. Bender, Paul A. Justifications for limiting constitutionally guaranteed rights and freedoms: some remarks about the proper role of Section One of the Canadian Charter. (Special Issue: The Charter: Initial Experience, Emerging Issues and Future Action). *Manitoba Law Journal*; 1983 Autumn; 13(4): 668-681.

687. Bennett, William R. *Submission of premier William R. Bennett on behalf of British Columbia to The Special Joint Committee on the Constitution of Canada, Ottawa, January 9, 1981*. Victoria: Government of British Columbia; 1981; 17 p.

688. Berger, Thomas R. The Charter and Canadian identity. *University of Western Ontario Law Review*; 1985 June; 23(1): 1-20.

689. Berger, Thomas R. The regime of tolerance. *Law Society Gazette*; 1981 March; 15(1): 51-63.

690. Bergeron, Gérard. Quebec in isolation. In: Banting, Keith; Simeon, Richard, eds. *And no one cheered*. Toronto: Methuen; 1983: 58-73; xii, 376 p.

691. Bernier, Ivan. Les affaires extérieures: la perspective juridique. In: Beck, Stanley M.; Bernier, Ivan, eds. *Canada and the new Constitution: the unfinished agenda*. Montreal: Institute for Research on Public Policy; 1983; 2: 187-218; 287 p.

692. Bernier, Ivan. La réforme de la Cour suprême: introduction. *Les Cahiers de droit*; 1985 March; 26(1): 187-188.

693. Bernier, Ivan; Lajoie, Andrée, res. coords. *The Supreme Court of Canada as an instrument of political change.* Toronto: University of Toronto Press, Royal Commission on the Economic Union and Development Prospects for Canada; 1986; xv, 211 p. (The collected research studies; v. 47).

694. Berube, A. Constitutional future of Canada and the territorial paradox. *Canadian Geographer*; 1981; 25(1): 1-3.

695. Binavince, Emilio S. The impact of the mobility rights: the Canadian economic union - a boom or a bust? *Ottawa Law Review*; 1982 Spring; 14(2): 340-365.

696. Blache, Pierre. La Cour suprême et le rapatriement de la constitution: l'impact des perceptions différentes de la question. *Les Cahiers de droit*; 1981 December; 22(3-4): 649-666.

697. Black, Edwin R. Trudeau's constitutional coup d'état. *Queen's Quarterly*; 1980 Winter; 87(4): 577-583.

698. Blair, D.G. The Charter and the judges: a view from the bench. *Manitoba Law Journal*; 1983 Autumn; 13(4): 445-454.

699. Blair, D.G. Do too many rights make a wrong? *Law Society Gazette*; 1983 June; 17(2): 156-165.

700. Blakeney, Allan E. Powers over the economy: securing the Canadian economic union in the Constitution - the Saskatchewan position [Regina]: Saskatchewan. Premier; 1980.

701. Blakeney, Allan E. *The patriation and amendment of the Constitution of Canada: brief presented to The Special Joint Committee on the Constitution by honourable Allan Blakeney, premier, Saskatchewan.* Regina: Government of Saskatchewan; 1980; 42 p.

702. Blanchard, René. Ni l'histoire, ni l'évolution politique redonnent ouverture au scénario de Pierre Trudeau. *L'Action nationale*; 1982 May-June; 71(9-10): 901-907.

703. Blanchard, René. Le projet constitutionnel, réforme ou contre-réforme? *L'Action nationale*; 1981 March; 70(7): 592-597.

704. Bliss, Michael. *Confederation: a new nationality.* Toronto: Grolier; c1981; 96 p. (Focus on Canadian history series).

705. Block, W. Government intervention. *Vital speeches*; Aug. 1, 1981; 47: 622-628.

706. Blom, Joost. Conflict of laws and constitutional law - extraterritorial provincial legislation The Queen v. Thomas Equipment Ltd. *University of British Columbia Law Review*; 1982 Summer; (2): 357-372.

707. Boadway, Robin; Norrie, Kenneth H. Constitutional reform Canadian-style: an economic perspective. *Canadian Public Policy*; 1980 Summer; 6(3): 492-505.

708. Bordeleau, A.G. *Pierre Elliott Trudeau's imprint on the Charter of Rights and Freedoms* (thesis) [Guelph]: University of Guelph. Dept. of Political Studies; 1984. (University of Guelph thesis).

709. Bossuyt, Marc. Droits linguistiques: une perspective européenne. *Manitoba Law Journal*; 1983 Fall; 13(4): 663-667.

710. Bouthillier, Guy. La genèse de l'article 23 de la constitution de Trudeau. *L'Action nationale*; 1982 February; 71(6): 651-662.

711. Brandt, G. J. Judicial mediation of political disputes: the patriation reference. *University of Western Ontario Law Review*; 1982 May; 20(1): 101-128.

712. Brandt, G. J. The Quebec veto reference: a constitutional postscript. *University of Western Ontario Law Review*; 1983; 21(1): 163-171.

713. Brazier, Rodney; Robilliard, St. John. Constitutional conventions: the Canada Supreme Court's views reviewed. *Public Law*; 1982 Spring: 28-34.

714. Breton, Albert. An analysis of constitutional change, Canada, 1980-82. *Public Choice*; 1984; 44(1): 251-72.

715. Brillinger, Don. Charter of Rights: the Canadian Charter in practice. *New Zealand Law Journal*; 1985 July: 231-233.

716. British Columbia. *Land and Constitution Acts*. Victoria: Queen's Printer for British Columbia; c1983; 1 sheet.

717. British Columbia. *Submission of the Government of British Columbia to the Foreign Affairs Committee House of Commons, London, England*. Victoria: Government of British Columbia; 1980; 110 p.

718. British Columbia. Ministry of Intergovernmental Relations. *Submission of the Government of British Columbia to the Foreign Affairs Committee, House of Commons, London, England*. [Victoria]: British Columbia, Ministry of Intergovernmental Relations; 1981; 47 p.

719. British Columbia. Premier. *British Columbia's constitutional proposals presented to the First Ministers' Conference on the Constitution October, 1978* [Victoria]: Government of British Columbia; 1980.

720. British Columbia. Premier; Canada. Parliament. Special Joint Committee on the Constitution of Canada (1980-1981). *Submission of Premier William R. Bennett on behalf of British Columbia to the Special Joint Committee on the Constitution of Canada, Ottawa, January 9, 1981*. [Victoria]: [Government of British Columbia]; [1981]; 17 p.

721. Brossard, Jacques; deMontigny, Yves. L'immigration ententes politiques et droit constitutionnel. *Revue juridique Thémis*; 1985; 19: 306-323.

722. Burg, Steven L. Republican and provincial constitution making in Yugoslav politics. *Publius*; 1982 Winter'; 12(1): 131-154.

723. Bushnell, S. I. The control of natural resources through the trade and commerce power and proprietary rights. *Canadian Public Policy*; 1980 Spring; 6(2): 313-324.

724. Cahow, Clark R. Comparative insights into constitutional history: Canada, the critical years. *Law and Contemporary Problems*; 1982 Autumn; 45(4): 33-52.

725. Cahow, Clark R. Comparative insights into constitutional history: Canada, the critical years. In: Davenport, Paul; Leach, Richard H, eds. *Reshaping Confederation: the 1982 reform of the Canadian Constitution.* Durham, N.C.: Duke University Press; 1984: 33-52; 329 p. (Duke University Centre for International Studies Publications).

726. Cairns, Alan C. The Canadian constitutional experiment. *Dalhousie Law Journal*; 1984 November; 9(1): 87-114.

727. Cairns, Alan C. Constitution-making, government self interest, and the problem of legitimacy. In: Kornberg, Allan; Clarke, Harold D, eds. *Political support in Canada: the crisis years.* Durham, N.C.: Duke University Press; 1983: 380-448; xvi, 463 p. (Duke University Centre for International Studies Publications).

728. Cairns, Alan C. The politics of constitutional conservatism. In: Banting, Keith; Simeon, Richard, eds. *And no one cheered.* Toronto: Methuen; 1983: 28-58; xii, 376 p.

729. Cairns, Alan C. Commentaries: an overview of the Trudeau constitutional proposals. *Alberta Law Review*; 1981 Summer; 19(3): 401-407.

730. Cairns, Alan C. The politics of constitutional renewal in Canada. In: Banting, Keith G.; Simeon, Richard, eds. *Redesigning the state: the politics of constitutional change in industrial nations.* Toronto: University of Toronto Press; 1985: 95-145; xii, 257 p.

731. Cairns, Alan C.; Williams, Cynthia, res. coords. *Constitutionalism, citizenship and society in Canada.* Toronto: University of Toronto Press; Royal Commission on the Economic Union and Development Prospects for Canada; 1985; xiv, 231 p. (The collected research studies; v. 33).

732. Cairns, Robert D. The Constitution as regulation: the case of natural resources. *Canadian Public Policy*; 1981 Winter; 7(1): 66-74.

733. Cairns, Robert D.; Chandler, Marsha A.; Moull, William D. The resource amendment (Section 92A) and the political economy of Canadian federalism. *Osgoode Hall Law Journal*; 1985 Summer; 23(2): 253-274.

734. Cameron, David M.; Dupré, J. Stephan. The financial framework of income distribution and social services. In: Beck, Stanley M.; Bernier, Ivan, eds. *Canada and the new Constitution: the unfinished agenda.* Montreal: Institute for Research on Public Policy; 1983; 1: 333-399; xii, 399 p.

735. Canada. *Accord constitutionnel: projet canadien de rapatriement de la constitution.* Ottawa: Government of Canada; 1981; 7 p.

736. Canada. *The Canadian Constitution 1980: explanation of a proposed resolution respecting the Constitution of Canada.* [Ottawa]: Canada; [1980]; 19, 20 p.

737. Canada. *The Canadian Constitution 1980: highlights of a proposed resolution respecting the Constitution of Canada.* [Ottawa]: [Government of Canada]; 1980; 4, 4 p.

738. Canada. *The Charter of Rights and Freedoms: a guide for Canadians.* Ottawa: Publications Canada; 1982; 76, 80 p.

739. Canada. *The Constitution Act, 1982.* Ottawa: Queen's Printer for Canada; c1982; 23 p.

740. Canada. *The Constitution Act, 1982.* Ottawa: Government of Canada; 1982; 23, 23 p.

741. Canada. *The Constitution and you - 1: what is the Constitution?* [folder]. [Ottawa]: Supply and Services Canada; 1980.

742. Canada. *The Constitution and you - 2: what good is a constitution to the average citizen?* [folder]. Ottawa: Supply and Services Canada; 1980.

743. Canada. *The Constitution and you - 3: why our Constitution must be renewed* [folder]. Ottawa: Supply and Services Canada; 1980.

744. Canada. *The Constitution and you - 4: why do we want to bring the Constitution home?* [folder]. Ottawa: Supply and Services Canada; 1980.

745. Canada. *The Constitution and you - 5: how to bring the Constitution home* [folder]. Ottawa: Supply and Services Canada; 1980.

746. Canada. *The Constitution and you - 7: what categories of rights and freedoms should be protected?* [folder]. [Ottawa]: Government of Canada; 1980.

747. Canada. *Constitutions of Canada: federal and provincial.* Dobbs Ferry, N.Y.: Oceana Publications; 1978-1983; 4 v.

748. Canada. *Powers over the economy : options submitted for consideration by the Government of Canada to safeguard the Canadian Economic Union in the Constitution.* Ottawa: Government of Canada; 1980; 2, 4, 3 p.

749. Canada. *Securing the Canadian economic union in the Constitution.* Ottawa: Government of Canada; 1980; viii, 50, 53, viii p. (Discussion paper).

750. Canada. *Text of the resolution respecting the Constitution of Canada adopted by the House of Commons on December 2, 1981.* [Ottawa]: [Government of Canada]; [1981]; 24 p.

751. Canada. *The Constitution and you - 6: a Charter of Rights and Freedoms in the Constitution - why do we need it?* [folder]. Ottawa: Supply and Services Canada; 1980.

752. Canada. Canadian Unity Information Office. *Canadian Constitution - proposed resolution respecting the Constitution of Canada, 1980*. [Ottawa]: Canadian Unity Information Office; 1980.

753. Canada. Canadian Unity Information Office. *The Canadian Constitution, 1981: a resolution adopted by the Parliament of Canada, December 1981. Constitution Act, 1982*. Ottawa: Canadian Unity Information Office; [1984]; 28 p.

754. Canada. Canadian Unity Information Office. *Constitutional reform 1980*. [Ottawa]: Canadian Unity Information Office; 1980.

755. Canada. Canadian Unity Information Office. *Notes on Canadian federalism (Constitution)* [Ottawa]: Canadian Unity Information Office; 1984.

756. Canada. Department of Indian Affairs and Northern Development. 1983 *Constitutional record on aboriginal rights* [Ottawa]: DIAND; 1983.

757. Canada. Department of Indian Affairs and Northern Development. *Constitutional development in Canada's North* [Ottawa]: DIAND; 1982.

758. Canada. Department of Indian Affairs and Northern Development. *Division of Northwest Territories; constitutional development in Canada's North* [Ottawa]: DIAND; 1982.

759. Canada. Department of Justice. *Constitutional reform - notes for a speech by the Honourable Jean Chretien, Minister of Justice, House of Commons*; October 6, 1980. [Ottawa]: Department of Justice; 1980.

760. Canada. Department of Justice. *Statement by the Honourable Jean Chretien, Minister of Justice to the Special Joint Committee on the Constitution*, January 12, 1981. [Ottawa]: Department of Justice; 1981.

761. Canada. Department of Justice. *Amending our Constitution - the rights of the aboriginal peoples.* [Ottawa]: Department of Justice; 1984.

762. Canada. Department of Justice. *Consolidation of proposed constitutional resolutions tabled by the Minister of Justice...April 24, 1981; Text of proposed constitutional resolution filed by the Deputy General...with the Supreme Court.* [Ottawa]: Department of Justice; 1981.

763. Canada. Department of Justice. *Consolidation of proposed regulation and amendments to the Constitution of Canada, January 1981.* [Ottawa]: Department of Justice; 1980.

764. Canada. Department of Justice. *A consolidation of the Constitution Acts, 1867-1982.* Ottawa: Department of Justice; c1983; 83, 83 p.

765. Canada. Department of Justice. *Correspondence between the Prime Minister of Canada and the Premiers regarding a constitutional amendment on the powers of the Senate.* [Ottawa]: Department of Justice; 1985.

766. Canada. Department of Justice. *Equality issues in federal law : a discussion paper*. Ottawa: Department of Justice; c1985; 65, 79 p.

767. Canada. Department of Justice. *Manual of commentaries on the Charter of Rights and Freedoms*. [Ottawa]: Department of Justice; 1982.

768. Canada. Department of Justice. *Notes for a speech by the Honourable Jean Chretien, Minister of Justice, House of Commons - constitutional reform*. [Ottawa]: Department of Justice; 1980.

769. Canada. Department of Justice. *Report to Cabinet on constitutional discussions, summer 1980, and the outlook for the First Ministers Conference and beyond*. [Ottawa]: Department of Justice; 1980.

770. Canada. Department of Justice. *The role of the United Kingdom in the amendment of the Canadian Constitution: background paper*. [Ottawa]: Government of Canada; 1981; 54, 62 p.

771. Canada. Department of Justice. *Text of proposed constitutional resolution filed by the Deputy Attorney General of Canada with the Supreme Court of Canada on April 24, 1981*. [Ottawa]: Department of Justice; 1981.

772. Canada. Department of the Solicitor General. *Canadian Federal-Provincial Task Force on Justice for Victims of Crime Report - highlights*. [Ottawa]: Department of the Solicitor General; 1983.

773. Canada. Federal-Provincial Relations Office. *Highlights of the Constitutional Amendment Bill 1978*. [Ottawa]: Federal-Provincial Relations Office; 1984.

774. Canada. Ministère de la Justice. *Le rôle du Royaume-Uni dans la modification de la constitution canadienne: texte documentaire*. Ottawa: Government of Canada; 1981; 62, 54 p.

775. Canada. Ministry of Justice and Attorney General. *Government response to representations for change to the proposed resolution respecting the Constitution of Canada*. [Ottawa]: The Ministry; 1981.

776. Canada. Parliament. *Canada Gazette, part 3 - resolution respecting the Constitution of Canada...Canada Act, 1982 - Constitution Act, 1982 - proclamation respecting the Constitution Act, 1982*. [Ottawa]: Supply and Services Canada; 1982.

777. Canada. Parliament. *Canadian Constitution 1980 - proposed resolution respecting the Constitution of Canada*. [Ottawa]: Government of Canada; 1980.

778. Canada. Parliament. *Canadian Constitution, 1981 - highlights of the resolution adopted by the Parliament of Canada, December 1981*. [Ottawa]: Supply and Services Canada; 1981.

779. Canada. Parliament. *Canadian Constitution, 1981: text of the resolution ... adopted by the House of Commons on Dec. 2, 1981, and by the Senate on Dec. 8, 1981*. [Ottawa]: Supply and Services Canada; 1981.

780. Canada. Parliament. *Canadian Constitution: proposed resolution for joint address to Her Majesty the Queen respecting the Constitution of Canada.* [Ottawa]: Government of Canada; 1980.

781. Canada. Parliament. *Canadian Constitution: proposed resolution respecting the Constitution of Canada tabled in the Senate and the House of Commons 1980.* [Ottawa]: Supply and Services Canada; 1980.

782. Canada. Parliament. *La loi constitutionnelle de 1982.* Ottawa: Supply and Services Canada; 1982; 23, 23 p.

783. Canada. Parliament. *Resolution respecting the Constitution of Canada adopted by the Parliament of Canada in December, 1981.; Canada Act, 1982.; Constitution Act, 1982.* [Ottawa]: Supply and Services Canada; 1982.

784. Canada. Parliament. House of Commons. *Constitution and you.* [Ottawa]: Supply and Services Canada; 1982.

785. Canada. Parliament. Library. Research Branch. *Impact of the Charter of Rights and Freedoms on the criminal justice system* (rev.1982), by P. Rosen. [Ottawa]: Library of Parliament; 1982.

786. Canada. Parliament. Library. Research Branch. *Some comments on the Charter of Rights and Freedoms,* by D. Cheifetz and P. Rosen. [Ottawa]: Library of Parliament; 1982.

787. Canada. Parliament. Senate. Standing Committee on Legal and Constitutional Affairs. *Report on certain aspects of the Canadian Constitution,* by H. Carl Goldenberg. [Ottawa]: The Committee; 1980; 44, 45 p.

788. Canada. Parliament. Special Joint Committee on the Consitution of Canada; Canadian Human Rights Foundation. *Brief to the Special Joint Committee of the Senate and the House of Commons on the Constitution of Canada - Canadian Human Rights Foundation.* [Ottawa]: The Committee; 1980.

789. Canada. Parliament. Special Joint Committee on the Constitution of Canada. *Background material prepared for the Canada West Foundation presented to the Special Joint Committee of the Senate and of the House of Commons on the Constitution of Canada November 25, 1980.* [Ottawa]: The Committee; 1980.

790. Canada. Parliament. Special Joint Committee on the Constitution of Canada. *Brief presented to the Special Joint Committee on the Constitution - Saskatchewan. Patriation and amendment of the Constitution of Canada - brief presented to the Special Joint Committee on the Constitution,* by Honourable Allan Blakeney, Premier. [Ottawa]: The Committee; 1980.

791. Canada. Parliament. Special Joint Committee on the Constitution of Canada. *Brief to the Special Joint Committee of the Senate and the House of Commons on the Constitution of Canada - Union of British Columbia Municipalities.* [Ottawa]: The Committee; 1980.

792. Canada. Parliament. Special Joint Committee on the Constitution of Canada. *Minutes of proceedings and evidence of the Special Joint Committee of the Senate and the House of Commons on the Constitution of Canada - 3rd session, 32nd parliament,1980-81*. [Ottawa]: The Committee; 1980.

793. Canada. Parliament. Special Joint Committee on the Constitution of Canada. *Presentation by the Government of the Northwest Territories to the Joint Committee of the House of Commons and the Senate on the Constitution of Canada by the Honourable George Braden*. [Ottawa]: The Committee; 1980.

794. Canada. Parliament. Special Joint Committee on the Constitution of Canada. *Submission of Premier William R. Bennett on behalf of British Columbia to the Special Joint Committee on the Constitution of Canada, Ottawa, January 9, 1981*. [Ottawa]: The Committee; 1981; 17 p.

795. Canada. Parliament. Special Joint Committee on the Constitution of Canada. *Submission to the Special Joint Parliamentary Committee of the Senate and the House of Commons on the Constitution...presented by the Honourable J. Angus Maclean on behalf of the Government of Prince Edward Island*. [Ottawa]: The Committee; 1980.

796. Canada. Parliament. Special Joint Committee on the Constitution of Canada; Federation of Canadian Municipalities. *Brief to the Special Joint Committee of the Senate and the House of Commons on the Constitution of Canada*. [Ottawa]: The Committee; 1980.

797. Canada. Prime Minister. *Prime Minister's address to the House of Commons in the constitutional debate; March 23, 1981*. [Ottawa]: Office of the Prime Minister; 1981.

798. Canada. Prime Minister. *Charter of Rights and Freedoms: guide for Canadians*. [Ottawa]: Supply and Services Canada; 1982.

799. Canada. Prime Minister. *Letter sent to all Premiers on April 19, 1975 on the patriation of the Constitution*. [Ottawa]: Office of the Prime Minister; 1981.

800. Canada. Prime Minister. *The Prime Minister's address to the House of Commons in the Constitutional debate - edited version*. Ottawa: Office of the Prime Minister; 1981; 25 p.

801. Canada. Prime Minister. *Proposed resolution for a joint address to Her Majesty the Queen respecting the Constitution of Canada*. [Ottawa]: Office of the Prime Minister; 1980; 20 leaves.

802. Canada. Prime Minister. *Proposed resolution to authorize His Excellency the Governor General to issue a proclamation respecting amendments to the Constitution of Canada*. [Ottawa]: Office of the Prime Minister; 1983.

803. Canada. Prime Minister. *Text of a letter to the Premier of Quebec in response to Mr. Levesque's letter of November 25, 1981 (on the Constitution)*. Ottawa: Office of The Prime Minister; 1981.

804. Canada. Secretary of State. *Canadian Bill of Rights - an act for the recognition and protection of human rights and fundamental freedoms (passed by the Parliament of Canada and assented to 10th August, 1960)*. [Ottawa]: Secretary of State; 1985.

805. Canada. Secretary of State. *Constitution, 1982.; Patriation of the the Constitution of Canada 1982, a pictorial record*. [Ottawa]: Secretary of State; 1983.

806. Canada. Special Representative for Constitutional Development in the Northwest Territories. *Constitutional development in the Northwest Territories: report of the special representative*. [Ottawa]: Supply and Services Canada; 1980; 194 p.

807. Canada. Supreme Court. *Appeals by the provinces of Canada to the Attorney General of Canada - questions concerning the amendments to the Constitution of Canada*. [Ottawa]: Supreme Court; 1981.

808. Canada. Supreme Court. *Canadian Charter of Rights and Freedoms and its interpretation by the courts - an address by the Honourable Brian Dickson, P.C. Supreme Court of Canada to the Princeton Alumni Association*. [Ottawa]: Supreme Court; 1985.

809. Canada. Supreme Court. *Constitutional decisions, September 28, 1981*. [Ottawa]: Canada. Supreme Court; [1981]; 130 p.

810. Canada. Supreme Court. *The Supreme Court decisions on the Canadian Constitution*. Toronto: Lorimer; 1981; xxi, 141 p.

811. Canada. Supreme Court. *Supreme Court of Canada - the Constitution and early beginning of the court*. [Ottawa]: Supreme Court; 1980.

812. Canada. Supreme Court; Manitoba. Department of the Attorney General; Newfoundland. Department of Justice; Quebec. Department of Justice. *Reference re amendment of the Constitution of Canada, 1982*. [Ottawa]: [Supreme Court of Canada]; [1981]; [11] p.

813. Canadian Association of Statutory Human Rights Agencies Conference (1982). *Documents* (1982 CASHRA Conference); May 31-June 2, 1982; Montebello, Que. [Ottawa]: Canadian Intergovernmental Conference Secretariat; 1982; various pagings.

814. Canadian Bar Association. *The native peoples of Canada and the Canadian Constitution*. Calgary: Canadian Bar Association; [1980]; 28 leaves.

815. Canadian Charter of Rights and Freedoms (actual text). *Canadian Bar Review*; 1983 March; 61(1): 4-18.

816. Canadian Federal-Provincial Task Force on Justice for Victims of Crime. *Canadian Federal-Provincial Task Force on justice for victims of crime*: report, by Don Sinclair. [Ottawa]: The Task Force; c1983; viii, 202 p.

817. Canadian Human Rights Commission. *Presentation by the Canadian Human Rights Commission to the Special Joint Committee on the Constitution of Canada, November, 1980 - the Canadian Charter of Rights and Freedoms*. [Ottawa]: Canadian Human Rights Commission; 1980.

818. Canadian Intergovernmental Conference Secretariat. *Constitutional Accord: Canadian patriation plan*. Ottawa: [Canadian Intergovernmental Conference Secretariat]; 1981; 1 portfolio (6 pieces).

819. Canadian Law Information Council. *Constitutional language rights of official-language minorities in Canada : a study of the legislation of the provinces and territories respecting education rights of official-language minorities and compliance with section 23 of the Canadian Charter of Rights and Freedoms*, by Pierre Foucher. Ottawa: Canadian Law Information Council; 1985; viii, 460 p.

820. Canadian Study of Parliament Group. *Seminar on the constitutional resolution and legislative authority in Canada; January 9, 1981*; Ottawa. [Ottawa]: Canadian Study of Parliament Group; 1981.

821. Careless, Anthony; Stevenson, Donald W. Canada: constitutional reform as a policy making instrument. *Publius*; 1982 Summer; 12(3): 85-98.

822. Carignan, Pierre. De la notion de droit collectif et de son application en matière scolaire au Québec. (La Charte canadienne des droits et libertés: concepts et impacts). *Revue juridique Thémis*; 1984; 18: 1-103.

823. Carmichael, D.J.C. The constitutional debate: reflections upon right and legitimacy in Canada. *Chitty's Law Journal*; 1981 September; 29: 217-227.

824. Carson, Bruce. Parliament and the Charter. *Canadian Parliamentary Review*; Winter 84/85; 7: 8-11.

825. Catholic Church. Assemblée des évêques du Québec. *Remarks from the Catholic bishops of Quebec on the constitutional question*. Montreal: L'Assemblée; [19] 81, 2 leaves.

826. Chambre de commerce du Canada. *Mémoire sur la réforme constitutionnelle*. [Montréal]: La Chambre; 1980; 6 p.

827. Cheffins, Ronald I. The Constitution Act, 1982 and the amending formula: political and legal implications. *Supreme Court Law Review*; 1982; 4: 43-54.

828. Chevrette, François. *Recueil de droit constitutionnel*. [Montréal]: Librairie de l'Université de Montréal; [1980?]; 183 p.

829. Chevrette, François. Les ressources naturelles dans une perspective de changement constitutionnel: le cas du Québec. In: Beck, Stanley M.; Bernier, Ivan, eds. *Canada and the new Constitution: the new agenda*. Montreal: Institute for Research on Public Policy; 1983; 2: 89-112; 289 p.

830. Chevrette, François; Marx, Herbert. *Droit constitutionnel: notes et jurisprudence*. Montréal: Presses de l'Université de Montréal; 1982; xv, 1728 p.

831. Chouinard, Jean-Yves. Les droits collectifs inséparables des droits individuels. *L'Action nationale*; 1981 November; 71(3): 371-384.

832. Chrétien, Jean. *Notes for a speech by the honourable Jean Chretien, P.C., M.P., Minister of Justice and Minister of State for Social Development to the Canadian Bar Association, Montreal, August 25, 1980*. Ottawa: Government of Canada; 1980; 14 p.

833. Christian, Timothy J. The limitation of liberty: a consideration of Section 1 of the Charter of Rights and Freedoms. *University of British Columbia Law Review*; 1982; 16: 105-140.

834. Christian, Timothy J. Section 7 of the Charter of Rights and Freedoms: constraints on state action. *Alberta Law Review*; 1984 Spring; 22(2): 222-246.

835. Clarke, J.; Wise, S.F., eds. *Aspects of the constitutional debate: 1981*. Ottawa: Carleton University; 1982; vii, 271 p. (Occasional papers; v. 1).

836. Claydon, John. International human rights law and the interpretation of the Canadian Charter of Rights and Freedoms. *Supreme Court Law Review*; 1982; 4: 287-302.

837. Close, D. Politics and constitutional reform in Canada: a study in political opposition. *Publius*; 1985 Winter; 15(1): 161-176.

838. Coffin, Marie-Claire L. *An agenda-setting study of the coverage of the 1981 constitutional debate: a comparison between English Toronto newspapers and French Montreal newspapers* [microfiche]: (M.A.) University of Windsor; 1983; 2 microfiches (120 fr.). Ottawa: National Library of Canada, 1985.

839. Cohen, Maxwell; Bayefsky, Anne F. The Canadian Charter of Rights and Freedoms and public international law. *Canadian Bar Review*; 1983 March; 61(1): 265-313.

840. Colvin, Eric. Constitutional jurisprudence in the Supreme Court of Canada. *Supreme Court Law Review*; 1982; 4: 3-22.

841. Communist Party of Canada. *Way out of the constitutional crisis*. [s.l.]: Communist Party of Canada; 1982.

842. Conklin, Francis. The Canadian Constitution as viewed from certain historical perspectives to the south. *Canadian-American Law Journal*; 1983 Fall; 2(1): 37-41.

843. Conklin, William E. Interpreting and applying the limitations clause: an analysis of Section 1. *Supreme Court Law Review*; 1982; 4: 75-87.

844. Le Conseil de la langue française. Des garanties constitutionnelles pour le français. *L'Action nationale*; 1985 June; 74(10): 1047-1051.

845. Conseil pour l'unité canadienne. *Perspectives du conseil pour l'unité canadienne sur la réforme constitutionnelle*. Montréal: Le Conseil; 1980; 22 p.

846. Constitution Act, 1982 (transcript). *University of British Columbia Law Review*; 1982; 16: 227-236.

847. Constitutional Alliance of the Northwest Territories. *Chronological notes on the Western Constitutional Forum of the Constitutional Alliance of the Northwest Territories.* Yellowknife: Constitutional Alliance of the Northwest Territories; 1984; 24 p.

848. Continuing Committee of Ministers on the Constitution. *The Canadian economic union: for discussion purposes only - Saskatchewan; July 22-24, 1980*; Vancouver. [s.l.]: The Committee; 1980.

849. Continuing Committee of Ministers on the Constitution. *Charter of Rights and Freedoms tabled by the delegation of the Government of Canada: background notes; July 8-11, 1980*; Montreal. [Ottawa]: The Committee; 1980.

850. Continuing Committee of Ministers on the Constitution. *Charter of Rights and Freedoms: statement by the Hon. Jean Chretien; July 8-11, 1980*; Montreal. [s.l.]: The Committee; 1980.

851. Continuing Committee of Ministers on the Constitution. *The Charter of Rights: Quebec's position*; July 14-18, 1980; Toronto. [s.l.]: The Committee; 1980.

852. Continuing Committee of Ministers on the Constitution. *Comments of Quebec on federal positions regarding powers over the economy*; July 22-24, 1980; Vancouver. [s.l.]: The Committee; 1980.

853. Continuing Committee of Ministers on the Constitution. *Communications: statement by the Hon. Jean Chretien; July 8-11, 1980*; Montreal. [s.l.]: The Committee; 1980.

854. Continuing Committee of Ministers on the Constitution. *Communications: notes for a statement by Quebec*; July 8-11, 1980; Montreal. [s.l.]: The Committee; 1980.

855. Continuing Committee of Ministers on the Constitution. *Documents* (Continuing Committee Of Ministers on the Constitution, 1980); July 8-11, 1980; Montreal. [s.l.]: The Committee; 1980.

856. Continuing Committee of Ministers on the Constitution. *Documents* (Continuing Committee of Ministers on the Constitution, 1980); July 14-18, 1980; Toronto. [s.l.]: The Committee; 1980.

857. Continuing Committee of Ministers on the Constitution. *Documents* (Continuing Committee of Ministers on the Constitution, 1980); July 22-25, 1980; Vancouver. [s.l.]: The Committee; 1980.

858. Continuing Committee of Ministers on the Constitution. *Economic union in the Canadian federation: a positive approach: statement by the Hon. Roy Romanow ... Saskatchewan*; July 22-24, 1980; Vancouver. [s.l.]: The Committee; 1980.

859. Continuing Committee of Ministers on the Constitution. *Entrenching a Charter of Rights: background notes tabled by the delegation of the Government of Canada*; July 8-11, 1980; Montreal. [s.l.]: The Committee; 1980.

860. Continuing Committee of Ministers on the Constitution. *Fisheries: statement by the Hon. Jean Chretien*; July 8-11, 1980; Montreal. [s.l.]: The Committee; 1980.

861. Continuing Committee of Ministers on the Constitution. *Fishing: notes for a statement by Quebec*; July 8-11, 1980; Montreal. [s.l.]: The Committee; 1980.

862. Continuing Committee of Ministers on the Constitution. *Natural resources: notes for a statement by Quebec*; July 8-11, 1980; Montreal. [s.l.]: Committee of Ministers; 1980.

863. Continuing Committee of Ministers on the Constitution. *Offshore resources: statement by the Hon. Jean Chretien*; July 8-11, 1980; Montreal. [s.l.]: Committee of Ministers; 1980.

864. Continuing Committee of Ministers on the Constitution. *Offshore resources: notes for a statement by Quebec*; July 8-11, 1980; Montreal. [s.l.]: The Committee; 1980.

865. Continuing Committee of Ministers on the Constitution. *Patriation of the Constitution: statement by the Hon. Jean Chretien; July 8-11, 1980*; Montreal. [s.l.]: Committee of Ministers; 1980.

866. Continuing Committee of Ministers on the Constitution. *Patriation and the amending formula: Quebec's position*; July 14-18, 1980; Toronto. [s.l.]: The Committee; 1980.

867. Continuing Committee of Ministers on the Constitution. *Powers over the economy: securing the Canadian economic union in the Constitution - discussion paper submitted by the Government of Canada*; July 8-11, 1980; Montreal. [s.l.]: The Committee; 1980.

868. Continuing Committee of Ministers on the Constitution. *Powers over the economy: statement by the Hon. Jean Chretien*; July 8-11, 1980; Montreal. [s.l.]: The Committee; 1980.

869. Continuing Committee of Ministers on the Constitution. *Powers affecting the economy: notes for a speech by Quebec*; July 8-11, 1980; Montreal. [s.l.]: The Committee; 1980.

870. Continuing Committee of Ministers on the Constitution. *Rights and freedoms within the Canadian federation: discussion draft*; July 8-11, 1980; Montreal. [s.l.]: The Committee; 1980.

871. Continuing Committee of Ministers on the Constitution. *The Senate: notes for a statement by Quebec*; July 8-11, 1980; Montreal. [s.l.]: The Committee; 1980.

872. Continuing Committee of Ministers on the Constitution. *Senate: statement by the Hon. Jean Chretien*; July 8-11, 1980; Montreal. [s.l.]: The Committee; 1980.

873. Continuing Committee of Ministers on the Constitution. *Sharing and/or equalization and regional disparities: statement by the Hon. Jean Chretien*; July 8-11, 1980; Montreal. [s.l.]: The Committee; 1980.

874. Continuing Committee of Ministers on the Constitution. *Statement of principles: statement by the Hon. Jean Chretien*; July 8-11, 1980; Montreal. [s.l.]: The Committee; 1980.

875. Continuing Committee of Ministers on the Constitution. *The Supreme Court of Canada; notes for a statement by Quebec*; July 8-11, 1980; Montreal. [s.l.]: The Committee; 1980.

876. Continuing Committee of Ministers on the Constitution. *Supreme Court: statement by the Hon. Jean Chretien*; July 8-11, 1980; Montreal. [s.l.]: The Committee; 1980.

877. Continuing Committee of Ministers on the Constitution. *Meeting of the Continuing Committee of Ministers on the Constitution: statements, by Jean Chrétien*. Ottawa: Canadian Intergovernmental Conference Secretariat; 1980; 8 pts.

878. Continuing Meeting of Ministers on the Constitution. *Equalization and regional disparities: notes for a statement by Quebec*; July 8-11, 1980; Montreal. [s.l.]: The Committee; 1980.

879. Cooper, Jordan, D. The influence of U.S. jurisprudence on the interpretation of the Canadian Charter of Rights and Freedoms: an initial survey. *Boston College International and Comparative Law Review*; 1986 Winter; (1): 73-105.

880. Corry, James Alexander. Renewal of the Constitution. *Law Society Gazette*; 1980; 14(4): 309-316.

881. Côté, Pierre-André. La préséance de la Charte canadienne des droits et libertés. (La Charte canadienne des droits et libertés: concepts et impacts). *Revue juridique Thémis*; 1984; 18: 105-130.

882. Council for Canadian Unity. *C.C.U. and the Constitution - the position of the Council for Canadian Unity concerning the proposed resolution on the Constitution* [folding sheet]. [Montreal]: Council for Canadian Unity; 1980.

883. Council for Canadian Unity. *Views on the Council for Canadian Unity on constitutional reform*. Montreal: The Council; 1980; 21 p.

884. Courchene, Thomas J. The political economy of Canadian constitution-making: the Canadian economic union issue. *Public Choice*; 1984; 44(1): 201-249.

885. Courchene, Thomas J. *Economic management and the division of powers*. Toronto: University of Toronto Press; Royal Commission on the Economic Union and Development Prospects for Canada; 1986; xvii, 256 p. (The collected research studies; v. 67).

886. Covell, Maureen. Possibly necessary but not necessarily possible: revision of the Constitution in Belgium. In: Banting, Keith G.; Simeon, Richard, eds.

Redesigning the state: the politics of constitutional change in industrial nations.
Toronto: University of Toronto Press; 1985: 71-94; xii, 257 p.

887. Crisp, L. F. *Australian national government.* 5th ed. Melbourne: Longman Cheshire; 1983; xii, 523 p.

888. Cuming, Ronald C. C., res. coord. *Harmonization of business law in Canada.* Toronto: University of Toronto Press; Royal Commission on the Economic Union and Development Prospects for Canada; 1986; xx, 245 p. (The collected research studies; v. 56).

889. Cuming, Ronald C. C. Harmonization of law in Canada. In: Cuming, Ronald C. C., res. coord. *Perspectives on the harmonization of law in Canada.* Toronto: University of Toronto Press; Royal Commission on the Economic Union and Development Prospects for Canada; 1985: 1-58; xviii, 178 p. (The collected studies; v. 55).

890. Cuming, Ronald C. C., res. coord. *Perspectives on the harmonization of law in Canada.* Toronto: University of Toronto Press; Royal Commission on the Economic Union and Development Prospects for Canada; 1985; xviii, 178 p. (The collected research studies; v. 55).

891. d'Onorio, Joel-Benoit. Le conflit constitutionnel canado-québécois. *Rev. int. de droit comparé*; 1984; 36(1): 111-143.

892. Dacks, Gurston. *Liberal-democratic society and government in Canada: constitutional development in the western Northwest Territories.* Yellowknife: Western Constitutional Forum; 1983; iv, 27 p.

893. Dalfen, Charles M.; Dunbar, Laurence J. E. Transportation and communications: the Constitution and the Canadian economic union. In: Krasnick, Mark, res. coord. *Case studies in the division of powers.* Toronto: University of Toronto Press; Royal Commission on the Economic Union and Development Prospects for Canada; 1986: 139-202; xvii, 269 p. (The collected research studies; v. 62).

894. Davenport, Paul. The Constitution and the sharing of wealth in Canada. In: Davenport, Paul; Leach, Richard H., eds. *Reshaping Confederation: the 1982 reform of the Canadian Constitution.* Durham, N.C.: Duke University Press; 1984: 109-148; 329 p. (Duke University Centre for International Studies Publications).

895. Davenport, Paul. Reshaping confederation: the 1982 reform of the Canadian Constitution. *Law and Contemporary Problems*; 1982 Autumn; 45(4): 1-10.

896. Davenport, Paul; Leach, Richard H., eds. Canadian Constitution (symposium). *Law and Contemporary Problems*; 1982 Autumn; 45: 1-302.

897. Davenport, Paul; Leach, Richard H., eds. *Reshaping Confederation: the 1982 reform of the Canadian Constitution.* Durham, N.C.: Duke University Press; 1984; 329 p. (Duke University Centre for International Studies publications).

898. Davis, William G. *Statement in the legislature by the Hon. William G. Davis, Premier of Ontario on constitutional negotiations, Tuesday, June 10, 1980*; June 10, 1980; [s.l.]. Toronto: Ontario. Office of the Premier; 1980.

899. Davis, William G. *Statement by the Hon. William G. Davis, Premier of Ontario, re position on Constitutional patriation and amendment, Wednesday, Oct. 1, 1980*; October 1, 1980; [Toronto]. Toronto: Ontario. Office of the Premier; 1980.

900. Davis, William G. *Statement by the Hon. William G. Davis, Premier of Ontario, on the Constitution, Friday, Oct. 3, 1980*; October 3, 1980; [Toronto]. Toronto: Ontario. Office of the Premier; 1980.

901. Davis, William G. *Statement by the Hon. William G. Davis, Premier of Ontario, on the Constitution in the legislature, Monday, Oct. 6, 1980; October 6, 1980*; [Toronto]. Toronto: Ontario. Office of the Premier; 1980.

902. Davis, William G. *Statement by the Hon. William G. Davis, Premier of Ontario to the legislature on constitutional reform; November 6, 1980*; Toronto. Toronto: Ontario. Office of the Premier; 1980.

903. Davis, William G. *Statement by the Hon. William G. Davis, Premier of Ontario, re: Constitution; April 9, 1981; Toronto*. Toronto: Ontario. Office of the Premier; 1981.

904. Davis, William G. *Statement by the Hon. William G. Davis, premier of Ontario, re: Constitution; April 16, 1981; Toronto*. Toronto: Ontario. Office of the Premier; 1981.

905. Dawson, D. Commonwealth perogatives. In: Saunders, Cheryl [and others]. *Current constitutional problems in Australia*. Canberra: Centre for Research on Federal Financial Relations, Australian National University; 1982; 62-67 p.

906. Days, Drew S. III. Civil rights in Canada: an American perspective (Symposium: the Canadian Constitution). *American Journal of Comparative Law*; 1984 Spring; 32(2): 307-338.

907. de Grandpré, Louis-Philippe. Faut-il réformer la Cour suprême du Canada? Les Cahiers de droit; 1985 March; 26(1): 189-193.

908. de Mestral, A. L. C. Treaty-power, and more on rules and obiter dicta. *Canadian Bar Review*; 1983 December; (4): 856-865.

909. Dellinger, Walter. The amending process in Canada and the United States: a comparative perspective. *Law and Contemporary Problems*; 1982 Fall; 45(4): 283-302.

910. Dellinger, Walter. The amending process in Canada and the United States: a comparative perspective. In: Davenport, Paul; Leach, Richard H., eds. *Reshaping Confederation: the 1982 reform of the Canadian Constitution*. Durham, N.C.: Duke University Press; 1984: 283-302; 329 p. (Duke University centre for international relations publications); ISBN: 082230578X.

911. Delperee, Francis. Cour suprême, Cour d'arbitrage ou Cour constitutionnelle? *Les Cahiers de droit*; 1985 March; 26(1): 205-216.

912. deMontigny, Yves. La Charte des droits et libertés, la prérogative royale et les "questions politiques". *Revue du barreau du Québec*; 1984 January-February; 44(1): 156-172.

913. deMontigny, Yves. Preuve d'une convention constitutionnelle devant les tribunaux - Modification de l'Acte de l'Amérique du Nord - Rôle du Québec. *Revue du barreau du Québec*; 1983 November-December; 43(5): 1133-1150.

914. Dickinson, I. S. Patriation of the Canadian Constitution: a background note. *Journal of the Law Society of Scotland*; 1981 December; 26(12): 485-488.

915. Dickinson, I.S. Severing the legislative link - some reflections on the Canada Act 1982. *New Law Journal*; 1982 August; (6065): 777-780.

916. Dobell, Peter C. Constitutional and political confrontation in Canada. *World Today*; 1981; 37(6): 223-234.

917. Doerr, Audrey D.; Carrier, Micheline. *Women and the Constitution in Canada*. Ottawa: Canadian Advisory Council on the Status of Women; 1981; x, 223 p.

918. Doody, Michael R. Freedom of the press, the Canadian Charter of Rights and Freedoms, and a new category of qualified privilege. *Canadian Bar Review*; 1983 March; 61(1).

919. Dorion, Henri. La constitution canadienne et les partages géographiques. *Cahiers de géographie du Québec*; 1980 April; 24(61): 69-80.

920. Douglas, Colin. Conflicting claims to oil and natural gas resources off the eastern coast of Canada. *Alberta Law Review* (Canadian Petroleum Law Supplement); 1980 Winter; 18(1): 54-69.

921. Driedger, Elmer A. The Canadian Charter of Rights and Freedoms. *Ottawa Law Review*; 1982 Spring; 14(2): 366-378.

922. Driedger, Elmer A. The spending power. *Queen's Law Journal*; 1981 Fall; 7(1): 124-134.

923. Drury, C.M. *Constitutional development in the Northwest Territories report of the Special Representative*. Ottawa: Supply and Services Canada; 1980; 194 p.

924. Duhamel, Roger. L'accident et la nécessité. *L'Action nationale*; 1981 December; 71(4): 467-485.

925. Duplé, Nicole. L'article 7 de la Charte canadienne des droits et libertés et les principes de justice fondamentale. *Les Cahiers de droit*; 1984 March; 25(1): 99-124.

926. Duplé, Nicole. La Cour suprême et le rapatriement de la constitution: la victoire du compromis sur la rigueur. *Les Cahiers de droit*; 1981 December; 22(3-4): 619-648.

927. Duplé, Nicole. La réforme constitutionnelle et l'article 96 de l'Acte de l'Amérique du Nord britannique 1867. In: Beck, Stanley M.; Bernier, Ivan, eds. *Canada and the new Constitution: the unfinished agenda.* Montreal: Institute for Research on Public Policy; 1983: 129-159; xii, 399 p.

928. Eberts, Mary. The use of litigation under the Canadian Charter of Rights and Freedoms as a strategy for achieving change. In: Nevitte, Neil; Kornberg, Allan, eds. *Minorities and the Canadian state.* Oakville: Mosaic Press; 1985: 53-69; 324 p.

929. Eberts, Mary. *Women and constitutional renewal.* [Ottawa]: Canadian Advisory Council on the Status of Women; 1980.

930. Edinger, Elizabeth. Constitutional law: the doctrines of colorability and extra-territoriality. *Canadian Bar Review*; 1985; 63(1): 203-221.

931. Edinger, Elizabeth. Territorial limitations of provincial powers. *Ottawa Law Review*; 1982 Winter; 14(1): 57-99.

932. Elazar, Daniel J. The principles and traditions underlying American state constitutions. *Publius*; 1982 Winter; 12(1): 11-26.

933. Elazar, Daniel J. Constitution-making: the pre-eminently political act. In: Banting, Keith G.; Simeon, Richard, eds. *Redesigning the state: the politics of constitutional change in industrial nations.* Toronto: University of Toronto Press; 1985: 232-248; xii, 257 p.

934. Elliot, Robin. Interpreting the Charter - use of the earlier versions as an aid. *University of British Columbia Law Review*; 1982; 16: 11-57.

935. Else-Mitchell, R. Australian processes for constitutional amendment. In: Mathews, Russell, ed. *Public policies in two federal countries: Canada and Australia.* Canberra: Centre for Research on Federal Financial Relations, Australian National University; 1982; 83-87 p.

936. Emery, Georges. Réflexions sur le sens et la portée au Québec des articles 25, 35, et 37 de la Loi constitutionnelle de 1982. *Les Cahiers de droit*; 1984 March; 25(1).

937. Fairley, H. Scott. Canadian federalism, fisheries and the Constitution: external constraints on internal ordering. *Ottawa Law Review*; 12; 2(257-318).

938. Fairley, H. Scott. Constitutional aspects of external trade policy. In: Krasnick, Mark, res. coord. *Case studies in the division of powers.* Toronto: University of Toronto Press; Royal Commission on the Economic Union and Development Prospects for Canada; 1986: 1-51; xvii, 269 p. (The collected research studies; v. 62).

939. Fairley, H. Scott. Developments in constitutional law: the 1983-84 term. *Supreme Court Law Review*; 1985; 7: 63-129.

940. Fairley, H. Scott. Enforcing the Charter: some thoughts on an appropriate and just standard for judicial review. *Supreme Court Law Review*; 1982; 4: 217-254.

941. Fashler, Robert; Thompson, Andrew. Constitutional change and the forest industry. In: Beck, Stanley M.; Bernier, Ivan, eds. *Canada and the new Constituion: the unfinished agenda*. Montreal: Institute for Research on Public Policy; 1983; 2: 55-87; 289 p.

942. Federal-Provincial Task Force on Justice for Victims of Crime. report, by D. Sinclair. [Ottawa]: The Task Force; 1981.

943. Federal-Provincial Task Force on the Uniform Rules of Evidence. *Report of the Federal-Provincial Task Force on the Uniform Rules of Evidence*. Toronto: Carswell; 1982; xxxiv, 615 p.

944. Federation of Canadian Municipalities. Resource Task Force on Constitutional Reform. *Municipal government in a new Canadian federal system: second report*. Ottawa: Federation of Canadian Municipalities; 1982; 31 p.

945. Federation of Canadian Municipalities. Resource Task Force on Constitutional Reform. *Municipal government in a new Canadian federal system: report of the Resource Task Force on Constitutional Reform*, by Edward McWhinney. [Ottawa]: Federation of Canadian Municipalities; 1980.

946. Flavelle, L. *Equality rights provisions of the Canadian Charter of Rights and Freedoms*. [Toronto]: Ontario Legislative Library; 1985. (Ontario legislative library current issue paper; v. 35).

947. La Forest, G. V. *The allocation of taxing power under the Canadian Constitution*. 2nd ed. Toronto: Canadian Tax Foundation; 1981; viii, 219 p. (Canadian tax papers).

948. La Forest, Gerard V. The Canadian Charter of Rights and Freedoms: an overview. *Canadian Bar Review*; 1983; 61: 19-29.

949. Forsey, Eugene A. The courts and the conventions of the Constitution. *University of New Brunswick Law Journal*; 1984; 33: 11-42.

950. Forsey, Eugene A. The Constitution bill. *Queen's Quarterly*; 1980 Winter; 87(4): 566-569.

951. Foucher, Pierre. *Constitutional language rights of official-language minorities in Canada*. [Ottawa]: Canadian Law Information Council; 1985.

952. Friedenberg, E. Z. Canada's new Constitution: the struggle for human rights. *Nation*; 1982; 234(11): 335-338.

953. Friedland, Martin L. Criminal justice and the Charter. (Special Issue: The Charter: Initial Experience, Emerging Issues and Future Action). *Manitoba Law Journal*; 1983 Fall; 13(4): 549-572.

954. Gaffney, R.E.; Gould, G.P.; Semple, A.J. *Broken promises: the aboriginal constitutional conferences.* Fredericton: New Brunswick Association of Metis and Non-Status Indians; 1984; 115 p.

955. Gagnon, Jacques. Les constitutions américaines et l'expérience canadienne. *L'Action nationale*; 1984 October; 74(2): 107-110.

956. Gagnon, Jean Denis. Les effets de la Charte canadienne des droits et libertés sur le droit du travail (La Charte canadienne des droits et libertés: concepts et impacts). *Revue juridique Thémis*; 1984; 18: 131-181.

957. Gall, Gerald L. Some miscellaneous aspects of Section 15 of the Canadian Charter of Rights and Freedoms. *Alberta Law Review*; 1986 Spring; 24(3): 462-476.

958. Garant, Patrice. L'article 7 de la Charte - toujours énigmatique après 18 mois de jurisprudence. (Special Issue: The Charter; Initial Experience, Emerging Issues and Future Actin). *Manitoba Law Journal*; 1983 Fall; 13(4): 477-487.

959. Garant, Patrice. L'article 96 de la Loi constitutionnelle de 1867. *Les Cahiers de droit*; 1985 March; 26(1): 217-222.

960. Garrow, D. Bruce. *The constitutionality of the Carriage by Air Act in Canada: Marier v. Air Canada* [microfiche]: (L.L.M.) McGill University; 1981; 2 microfiches (174 fr.). Ottawa: National Library of Canada, 1983.

961. Gault, Ian Townsend. Jurisdiction over the petroleum resources of the Canadian continental shelf: the emerging picture. *Alberta Law Review*; 1985 Winter; 23(1): 75-100.

962. Gautron, Alain. French-English discrepancies in the Canadian Charter of Rights and Freedoms. *Manitoba Law Journal*; 1982 Spring; 12(2): 220-231.

963. Gibbins, Roger. Constitutional politics and the West. In: Banting, Keith; Simeon, Richard, eds. *And no one cheered.* Toronto: Methuen; 1983: 119-132; xii, 376 p.

964. Gibson, Dale. The Charter of Rights and the private sector. *Manitoba Law Journal*; 1982 Spring; 12(2): 213-219.

965. Gibson, Dale. Constitutional arrangements for environmental protection and enhancement under a new Canadian Constitution. In: Beck, Stanley M.; Bernier, Ivan, eds. *Canada and the new Constitution: the unfinished agenda.* Montreal: Institute for Research on Public Policy; 1983; 2: 113-153; 289 p.

966. Gibson, Dale. The constitutional position of local government in Canada. *Manitoba Law Journal*; 1980 Spring; 11(1): 1-19.

967. Gibson, Dale. Determining disrepute: opinion polls and the Canadian Charter of Rights and Freedoms. *Canadian Bar Review*; 1983 March; 61(1): 377-390.

968. Gibson, Dale. Distinguishing the governors from the governed: the meaning of "government" under Section 32(1) of the Charter. (Special Issue: The Charter: Initial Experience, Emerging Issues and Future Action). *Manitoba Law Journal*; 1983 Autumn; 13(4): 505-522.

969. Gibson, Dale. Protection of minority rights under the Canadian Charter of Rights and Freedoms: can politicians and judges sing harmony? *Hamline Law Review*; 1985 May; 8(2): 343-371.

970. Gibson, Dale. Reasonable limits under the Canadian Charter of Rights and Freedoms. *Manitoba Law Journal*; 1985 Spring; 15(1): 27-52.

971. Gilbert, Christopher David. *Judicial interpretation of the Australian and Canadian constitutions, 1867-1982* [microfiche]: (D.Jur.), York University; 1983; 8 microfiches (708 fr.). Ottawa: National Library of Canada, 1984.

972. Giroux, Jean-Baptiste. La "confédération" engloutie parmi les convulsions de reptiles. *L'Action nationale*; 1982 January; 71(5): 539-548.

973. Giroux, Jean-Baptiste. Le projet Trudeau. *L'Action nationale*; 1981 February; 70(6): 495-510.

974. Giroux, Jean-Baptiste. Québec partenaire majeur ou province minorisée? *L'Action nationale*; 1984 June; 73(10): 972-936.

975. Giroux, Jean-Baptiste. La réforme constitutionnelle: 1 - le partage des pouvoirs. *L'Action nationale*; 1981 January; 70(5): 395-407.

976. Gold, Alan D. The legal rights provisions - a new vision or déjà vu? *Supreme Court Law Review*; 1982; 4: 107-130.

977. Gold, Marc. A principled approach to equality rights: a preliminary inquiry. *Supreme Court Law Review*; 1982; 4: 131-161.

978. Gold, Marc E.; Dussault, René. *Materials on current issues of Canadian federalism, 1983*. Toronto: Osgoode Hall Law School of York University; 1983; 1; various pagings.

979. Graham, K.A.; McAllister, A.B. *The Inuit land claims, constitutional development, and local government reform in the Northwest Territories: an overview*. Kingston: Institute of Local Government, Centre for Resource Studies, Eastern Arctic Study, Queen's University; 1981; 150 p.

980. Gray, M.F. Relation of industrial powers to current constitutional problems. In: Saunders, Cheryl [and others]. *Current constitutional problems in Australia*. Canberra: Centre for Research on Federal Financial Relations, Australian National University; 1982; 56-61 p.

981. Great Britain. Parliament. House of Commons. *Canada Bill: to give effect to a request by the Senate and House of Commons Canada*.; Canada bill: proposals to legislate the Constitution Act 1982 and terminate the power of the United Kingdom to legislate for Canada. [London]: Queen's Printer; 1981.

982. Great Britain. Parliament. House of Commons. Foreign Affairs Committee. *First report from the Foreign Affairs Committee, session 1980-81: British North American Acts, the role of parliament: together with appendices thereto, part of the proceedings of the committee relating to the report, and the minutes of evidence taken before the committee on 12 November in the last session, and on 3 and 10 December, with appendices.* London: H.M.S.O.; 1981; 2.

983. Green, L.C. Aboriginal peoples, international law and the Canadian Charter of Rights and Freedoms. *Canadian Bar Review*; 1983 March; 61(1): 339-353.

984. Green, L.C. The Canadian Charter of Rights and international law. *Canadian Yearbook of International Law*; 1982; 3(23).

985. Green, L.C. Commentaries: The entrenchment of a Bill of Rights. *Alberta Law Review*; 1981 Summer; 19(3): 384-387.

986. Grey, Julius H. Federal "consumer protection law" in the field of publicity. Revue du Barreau de Québec; 1981 November-December; 41(5): 1001-1015.

987. Grubel, Herbert G. Reflections on a Canadian bill of economic rights. *Canadian Public Policy*; 1982 Winter; 8(1): 57-68.

988. Gunther, Richard. Constitutional change in contemporary Spain. In: Baning Keith G.; Simeon, Richard, eds. *Redesigning the state: the politics of constitutional change in industrial nations.* Toronto: University of Toronto Press; 1985: 42-70; xii, 257 p.

989. Hadfield, Brigid. Westering home: the patriation of the Canadian Constitution. *Northern Ireland Legal Quarterly*; 1982 Autumn; 33(3): 265-276.

990. Hahn, Randolph. Canada's Charter of Rights and Freedoms. *Public Law*; 1984 Winter: 530-538.

991. Harrison, Rowland J. Natural resources and the Constitution: some recent developments and their implications for the future regulation of the resource industries. *Alberta Law Review*; 1980 Winter; 18(1): 1-25.

992. Harvey, Julien. Les interventions fédérales et leurs conséquences. *L'Action nationale*; 1985 January; 74(5): 519-522.

993. Hatfield, Richard. *Brief to the Special Joint Committee of the Senate and the House of Commons on the Constitution of Canada.* [St. John]: New Brunswick. Office of the Premier; 1980.

994. Helliwell, John F. Energy and the Canadian federation: some economic aspect of optional constitutions. In: Beck, Stanley M.; Bernier, Ivan, eds. *Canada and the new Constitution: the unfinished agenda.* Montreal: Institute for Research on Public Policy; 1983; 2: 1-17; 289 p.

995. Henderson, Gordon F.; Binavince, Emiliv S. Doing business in Canada and the judicial review of wrongful government statutory and regulatory action. *Canada-United States Law Journal*; 1984; 7: 1-60.

996. Henderson, William B. Canada's Indian reserves: the usufruct in our Constitution. *Ottawa Law Review*; 1980 Winter; 12(1): 167-194.

997. Herriges, Guy M. *A manual on the Charter of Rights and Freedoms*. Saskatoon: Saskatchewan Human Rights Commission; Saskatchewan Association on Human Rights; 1983; 65, (18) p.

998. Hodge, William C. Patriation of the Canadian Constitution: comparative federalism in a new context. *Washington Law Review*; 1985 June; 60(3): 585-632.

999. Hogg, Peter W. Canada's new Charter of Rights. *American Journal of Comparative Law*; 1984 Spring; 32(2): 283-305.

1000. Hogg, Peter W. Comment on James C. MacPherson's paper on economic regulation and the British North America Act. *Canadian Business Law Journal*; 1981 April; 5(2): 220-224.

1001. Hogg, Peter W. Commentaries: amendment and patriation [Canadian Constitution]. *Alberta Law Review*; 1981 Summer; 19(3): 369-374.

1002. Hogg, Peter W. Constitutional law - amendment of the British North America act - role of the provinces. *Canadian Bar Review*; 1982 June; 60(2): 307-334.

1003. Hogg, Peter W. Constitutional law - federal power to amend the Constitution of Canada - reform of the Senate. *Canadian Bar Review*; 1980 September; 61(3): 631-645.

1004. Hogg, Peter W. Constitutional reform. *Canadian Bar Review*; 1980; 58(2): 481-482.

1005. Hogg, Peter W. Constitutional reform in Canada. *Yale Studies in World Public Order*; 1980 Spring; (2): 285-296.

1006. Hogg, Peter W. Federalism and the jurisdiction of Canadian courts. *University of New Brunswick Law Journal*; 1981; 30: 9-25.

1007. Hogg, Peter W. The new Canadian Constitution: introduction. *American Journal of Comparative Law*; 1984 Spring; 32(2): 221-239.

1008. Hogg, Peter W. Patriation of the Canadian Constitution: has it been achieved? *Queen's Law Journal*; 1983 Fall-Spring; 8(2): 123-130.

1009. Hogg, Peter W. Supremacy of the Canadian Charter of Rights and Freedoms. *Canadian Bar Review*; 1983 March; 61(1): 69-80.

1010. Hogg, Peter W. The theory and practice of constitutional reform. *Alberta Law Review*; 1981 Summer; 19(3): 335-351.

1011. Hogg, Peter W. Administration of justice: an introduction. In: Beck, Stanley M.; Bernier, Ivan, eds. *Canada and the new Constitution: the unfinished agenda*. Montreal: Institute for Research on Public Policy; 1983; 1: 91-127.

1012. Hogg, Peter W. *Cases on Constitutional law*. rev. Nov. 1982 ed. Toronto: Osgoode Hall Law School, York University; 1982; iii, 679 p.

1013. Hogg, Peter W. *Constitutional law of Canada*. 2nd ed. Toronto: Carswell; 1985; lxxv, 988 p.

1014. Hogg, Peter W. *Constitutional law of Canada; Canada Act 1982 annotated* (combined ed.). [Toronto]: [Carswell]; [1982]; xlii, 548, xiv, 155 p.

1015. Horth, Camille. *Le droit constitutionnel et la sécurité nationale au Canada* [microfiche]: (L.L.M.) Université Laval; 1982; 2 microfiches (126 Fr.). Ottawa: Bibliothèque nationale du Canada, 1984.

1016. Hosek, Chaviva. Women and the Constitutional process. In: Banting, Keith; Simeon, Richard, eds. *And no one cheered*. Toronto: Methuen; 1983: 280-300; xii, 376 p.

1017. Hovius, Berend. The legacy of the Supreme Court of Canada's approach to the Canadian Bill of Rights: prospects for the Charter. *McGill Law Journal*; 1982 December; 28(1): 31-58.

1018. Hovius, Berend; Martin, Robert. The Canadian Charter of Rights and Freedoms in the Supreme Court of Canada. *Canadian Bar Review*; March 1983; 61(1): 354-376.

1019. Howard, C.; Saunders, C.A. Constitutional amendment and constitutional reform in Australia. In: Mathews, Russell, ed. *Public policies in two federal countries: Canada and Australia*. Canberra: Centre for Research on Federal Financial Relations, Australian National University; 1982; 69-82 p.

1020. Hudon, Raymond. Quebec, the economy and the Constitution. In: Banting, Keith; Simeon, Richard, eds. *And no one cheered*. Toronto: Methuen; 1983: 133-153; xii, 376 p.

1021. Hughes, Patricia. Indian lands reserved for the Indians: off-limits to the provinces? *Osgoode Hall Law Journal*; 1983 July; 21(1): 82-112.

1022. Huppe, Luc. *Le pouvoir accessoire en droit constitutionnel canadien*. Canadian Bar Review; 1985 December; 63(4): 744-763.

1023. Hurley, John. Aboriginal rights, the Constitution and the Marshall court. *Revue juridique Thémis*; 1983 Summer; 17(3): 403-443.

1024. Hutton, Brian. In re: Resolution to amend the Constitution. *Canadian-American Law Journal*; 1983 Fall; 1: 88-99.

1025. Inions, Noella J. Newfoundland offshore claims. *Alberta Law Review*; 19; 3(461-482).

1026. Inuit Tapirisat of Canada. *Creation of the Nunavut Territorial Government*. Ottawa: Inuit Tapirisat of Canada; 1982; 58 p.

1027. Jackman, Martha. Interprovincial mobility rights under the Charter. *University of Toronto Faculty of Law Review*; 1985 Fall; 43(2): 16-44.

1028. Janisch, H. Beyond jurisdiction: judicial review and the Charter of Rights. *Revue du Barreau du Québec*; 1983 March-April; 43(2): 401-407.

1029. Jennings, R.C. The imperial connection: residual constitutional links. In: Saunders, Cheryl [and others]. *Current constitutional problems in Australia*. Canberra: Centre for Research on Federal Financial Relations, Australian National University; 1982; 68-75 p.

1030. Jinadu, L. Adele. The constitutional situation of the Nigerian states. *Publius*; 1982 Winter; 12(1): 155-186.

1031. Jull, Peter. *A necessary victory: a perspective on the Aboriginal Rights Coalition and the restoration of constitutional aboriginal rights in Canada, November, 1981*. [Charlottetown]: [P. Jull]; 1981; 35 leaves.

1032. Kay, Richard S. Constitution-making in Canada. *Worldview*; 1981; 24(5): 21-23.

1033. Kay, Richard S. Courts as Constitution-makers in Canada and the United States. *Supreme Court Law Review*; 1982; 4: 23-41.

1034. Kay, Richard S. The creation of constitutions in Canada and the United States. *Canada-United States Law Journal*; 1984; 7(7): 111-163.

1035. Kellas, James D. The politics of constitution-making: the experience of the United Kingdom. In: Banting, Keith G.; Simeon, Richard, eds. *Redesigning the state: the politics of constitutional change in industrial nations*. Toronto: University of Toronto Press; 1985: 146-159; xii, 257 p.

1036. Kerr, Robert W. Constitution Act, 1980: is it constitutional? *University of New Brunswick Law Journal*; 1981; 30: 73-90.

1037. Kerr, Robert W. The future of language rights under Canada's constitutional options. In: Beck, Stanley M.; Bernier, Ivan, eds. *Canada and the new Constitution: the unfinished agenda*. Montreal: Institute for Research on Public Policy; 1983; 1: 307-331; xii, 399 p.

1038. Kershaw, Sir Anthony. The Canadian Constitution and the Foreign Affairs Committee of the U.K. House of Commons, 1980 and 1981. *Parliamentarian*; 1981 July; 62(3): 173-182.

1039. Kilgour, D. Marc. Distributing the power to amend Canada's Constitution: reply. *Canadian Journal of Political Science*; 1985 June; 18(2): 389-396.

1040. Kilgour, D. Marc. A formal analysis of the amending formula of Canada's Constitution Act, 1982. *Canadian Journal of Political Science*; 1983 December; 16(4): 771-777.

1041. Kilgour, D. Marc; Levesque, Terrence J. The Canadian constitutional amending formula: bargaining in the past and the future. *Public Choice*; 1984; 44(3): 457-80.

1042. Kilgour, D. Marc; Levesque, Terrence J. The choice of a permanent amending formula for Canada's Constitution. *Canadian Public Policy*; 1984 September; 10(3): 359-361.

1043. Kilgour, D. Marc; Levesque, Terrence J. *The Canadian constitutional amending formula: bargaining in the past and the future*. Waterloo: School of Business and Economics, Wilfred Laurier University; 1983; 41 p. (Research paper series).

1044. Knopff, Rainer. Federalism, the charter and the court: the origins of judicial review in Canada - comment. *Canadian Journal of Political Science*; 1983 September; 16(3): 585-591.

1045. Knopff, Rainer. Legal theory and the "patriation" debate. *Queen's Law Journal*; 1981 Fall; 7(1): 41-65.

1046. Knopff, Rainer. Nationalism, liberalism, and federalism: elements of Canada's constitutional crisis. *Dalhousie Review*; 1979-1980 Winter; 59: 651-658.

1047. Knopff, Rainer; Morton, F. L. Nation-building and the Canadian Charter of Rights and Freedoms. In: Cairns, Alan; Williams, Cynthia, res. coord's. *Constitutionalism, citizenship and society in Canada*. Toronto: University of Toronto Press; Royal Commission on the Economic Union and Development Prospects for Canada; 1985: 133-182 p; xiv, 231 p. (The collected research studies; v. 33).

1048. Knopff, Rainer; Morton, F.L. Judicial statesmanship and the Canadian Charter of Rights and Freedoms. In: McKercher, William R., ed. *The U.S. Bill of Rights and the Canadian Charter of Rights and Freedoms*. Toronto: Ontario Economic Council; 1983: 184-200; 270 p. (Special research report/Ontario Economic Council).

1049. Kome, Penney. *The taking of twenty-eight: women challenge the Constitution*. Toronto: Women's Press; 1983; 125 p.

1050. Kornberg, Allan; Archer, Keith. A note on Quebec attitudes toward constitutional options. *Law and Contemporary Problems*; 1982 Autumn; 45(4): 71-85.

1051. Kornberg, Allan; Archer, Keith. A note on Quebec attitudes toward constitutional options. In: Davenport, Paul; Leach, Richard H., eds. *Reshaping Confederation: the 1982 reform of the Canadian Constitution*. Durham, N.C.: Duke University Press; 1984: 71-87; 329 p. (Duke University Centre for International Studies Publications).

1052. Krasnick, Mark, res. coord. *Case studies in the division of powers*. Toronto: University of Toronto Press; Royal Commission on the Economic Union and Development Prospects for Canada; 1986; xvii, 269 p. (The collected research studies; v. 62).

1053. Kushner, Howard. Election polls, freedom of speech and the Constitution. *Ottawa Law Review*; 1983 Summer; 15(3): 515-552.

1054. Kushner, Howard L. Dominion Stores and Labatt Breweries: signals of a return to the theory of provincial rights. *Osgoode Hall Law Journal*; 1981 March; 19(1): 118-139.

1055. Kyer, Clifford Ian. Has history a role to play in constitutional adjudication: some preliminary considerations. *Law Society Gazette*; 1981; 15(2): 135-157.

1056. Laberge, Henri. Les objets de négociations fédérales-provinciales dans la révision constitutionnelle. *L'Action nationale*; 1981 January; 70(5): 383-394.

1057. Laberge, Henri. Pour une approche constitutionnelle renouvelée. *L'Action nationale*; 1980; 70(3): 211-222.

1058. Laberge, Henri. Une nouvelle constitution québécoise. *L'Action nationale*; 1980 December; 60(4): 318-327.

1059. Lajoie, Andrée; Mulazzi, Pierrette; Gamache, Michèle. Political ideas in Quebec and the evolution of Canadian constitutional law, 1945 to 1985. In: Bernier, Ivan; Lajoie, Andrée, res. coords. *The Supreme Court of Canada as an instrument of political change*. Toronto: University of Toronto Press; Royal Commission on the Economic Union and Development Prospects for Canada; 1986: 1-103; xv, 211 p. (The collected research studies; v. 47).

1060. Lange, Donald J. Constitutional jurisprudence, politics, and minority language rights. *Manitoba Law Journal*; 1980 Winter-Spring; 11(1): 33-57.

1061. Langford, J. Stuart. *The law of your land: a practical guide to the new Canadian Constitution*. Toronto: CBC Enterprises; 1982; 112 p.

1062. LaSelva, Samuel V. Federalism and unanimity: the Supreme Court and constitutional amendment. *Canadian Journal of Political Science*; 1983 December; 16(4): 757-770.

1063. LaSelva, Samuel V. Only in Canada: reflections on the Charter's notwithstanding clause. *Dalhousie Review*; 1983 Autumn; 63(3): 383-398.

1064. Laskin, John B. The Canadian Constitution. *Public Law*; 1982 Winter: 549-553.

1065. Laskin, John B. Mobility rights under the Charter. *Supreme Court Law Review*; 1982; 4: 89-106.

1066. Laskin, John B. The Canadian constitutional proposals. *Public Law*; 1981 Autumn: 340-354.

1067. Latouche, Daniel. Les calculs stratégiques derrière le "Canada Bill". In: Davenport, Paul; Leach, Richard H., eds. *Reshaping Confederation: the 1982 reform of the Canadian Constitution*. Durham, N.C.: Duke University Press; 1984: 165-176; 329 p. (Duke University centre for international relations publications).

1068. Latouche, Daniel. Les calculs stratégiques derrière le "Canada Bill." (Reshaping Confederation: the 1982 Reform of the Canadian Constitution). *Law and Contemporary Problems*; 1982 Autumn; 45(4): 165-176.

1069. Latouche, Daniel. *Canada and Quebec, past and future: an essay*. Toronto: University of Toronto Press; Royal Commission on the Economic Union and Development Prospects for Canada; 1986; Xviii, 157 p. (The collected research studies; v. 70). Note: Also published in French under the title *Canada et le Québec: un essai rétrospectif et prospectif*.

1070. Latouche, Daniel. The constitutional misfire of 1982. In: Banting, Keith; Simeon, Richard, eds. *And no one cheered*. Toronto: Methuen; 1983: 96-118; xii, 376 p.

1071. Law Reform Commission of Canada. *The legal status of the federal administration*. Ottawa: The Commission; 1985; 106 (111) p. (Working paper; v. 40).

1072. Leach, Richard H. Implications for federalism of the reformed Constitution of Canada. *Law and Contemporary Problems*; 1982 Autumn; 45(4): 149-164.

1073. Leach, Richard H. Implications for federalism of the reformed Constitution of Canada. In: Davenport, Paul; Leach, Richard H., eds. *Reshaping Confederation: the 1982 reform of the Canadian Constitution*. Durham, N.C.: Duke University Press; 1984: 149-164; 329 p. (Duke University centre for international relations publications).

1074. Leavy, James. *Mise à jour 1967-1982 de la Cour suprême et la constitution [de]* Jacques Brossard. [Montréal]: Presses de l'Université de Montréal; 1983; 92 p.

1075. Leavy, James; Brossard, Jacques. *Mise à jour 1967-1982 de la Cour suprême et la constitution*. [Montréal]: Presses de l'Université de Montréal; 1983; 92 p.

1076. Lederman, W. R. Canada's current constitutional crisis. *Parliamentarian*; 1981 July; 62(3): 192-198.

1077. Lederman, W. R. The Canadian Charter of Rights and Freedoms: one year later. *Transactions of the Royal Society of Canada*; 1983; 21: 81-91.

1078. Lederman, W. R. Canadian constitutional amending procedures: 1867-1982. *American Journal of Comparative Law*; 1984 Spring; 32(2): 339-359.

1079. Lederman, W. R. Constitutional procedure and the reform of the Supreme Court of Canada. *Les Cahiers de droit*; 1985 March; 26(1): 195-204.

1080. Lederman, W. R. Mr. Justice Rand and Canada's federal Constitution. *University of Western Ontario Law Review*; 1980 Winter; 18(1): 31-49.

1081. Lederman, W. R. The power of the judges and the new Canadian Charter of Rights and Freedoms. *University of British Columbia Law Review*; 1982; 16: 1-10.

1082. Lederman, William R. The Supreme Court of Canada and basic constitutional amendment. In: Banting, Keith; Simeon, Richard, eds. *And no one cheered.* Toronto: Methuen; 1983: 176-188; xii, 376 p.

1083. Lederman, William R.; McConnell, W. H. *Continuing Canadian constitutional dilemmas: essays on the constitutional history, public law and federal system of Canada.* Toronto: Butterworths; 1981; xiii, 442 p.

1084. Lehmbruch, Gerhard. Constitution-making in young and aging federal systems. In: Banting, Keith G.; Simeon, Richard, eds. *Redesigning the state: the politics of constitutional change in industrial countries.* Toronto: University of Toronto Press; 1985: 30-41; xii, 257 p.

1085. Leigh, L.H. Canada's constitutional time bomb (pt.2): The end of an unwanted imperial obligations. *Round Table*; 1981; 281: 26-32.

1086. Levesque, Terrence J.; Moore, James W. Citizen and provincial power under alternative amending formulae: an extension of Kilgour's analysis. *Canadian Journal of Political Science*; 1984 March; 17(1): 157-166.

1087. Levy, J. C. The invocation of remedies under the Charter of Rights and Freedoms: some procedural considerations. *Manitoba Law Journal*; 1983 Fall; 13(4): 523-545.

1088. Lieberman, Michael. Foreword (North America: law, politics and economics; Canadian federalism). *Law and Contemporary Problems*; 1981 Summer; 44(3): 163-167.

1089. Lluelles, Didier; Trudel, Pierre. L'application de la Charte canadienne des droits et libertés aux rapports de droit privé (La Charte canadienne des droits et libertés: concepts et impacts). *Revue juridique Thémis*; 1984; 18: 219-252.

1090. Low, D. Martin. The Canadian Charter of Rights and Freedoms and the role of the courts: an initial survey. *University of British Columbia Law Review*; 1984 Winter; (1): 69-94.

1091. Lucas, Alastair R.; McDougall, Ian. Petroleum and natural gas and constitutional change. In: Beck, Stanley M.; Bernier, Ivan, eds. *Canada and the new Constitution: the unfinished agenda.* Montreal: Institute for Research on Public Policy; 1983; 2: 19-54; 289 p.

1092. Lucas, Alistair R. Constitutional law - federal fisheries power - provincial resource management and property and civil rights powers. *University of British Columbia Law Review*; 1982 Winter; (1): 145-154.

1093. Lucas, Alistair R. Natural resources and the new Constitution. *Newsletter of Canadian Institute of Resources Law*; 1982 September; 2: 1-2.

1094. Lutz, Donald S. The purposes of American state constitutions. *Publius*; 1982 Winter; 12(1): 27-44.

1095. Lyon, J.N. Constitutional theory and the Martland-Richie dissent. *Queen's Law Journal*; 1981 Fall; 7(1): 135-143.

1096. Lyon, Noel. The teleological mandate of the fundamental freedoms guarantee: what to do with vague but meaningful generalities. *Supreme Court Law Review*; 1982; 4: 57-73.

1097. Lysyk, K. Developments in constitutional law: the 1980-81 term. *Supreme Court Law Review*; 1982; 3: 65-113.

1098. Macdonald, R. A. Postscript and prelude - the jurisprudence of the Charter: eight theses. *Supreme Court Law Review*; 1982; 4: 321-350.

1099. Macdonald, R. A. The proposed section 96B: an ill-conceived reform destined to failure. *Les Cahiers de droit*; March 1985; 26(1): 251-282.

1100. Macdonald, R. A. Absence of juridiction: a perspective. *Revue du Barreau du Québec*; 1983; March-April(43): 2; CODEN: 307-351.

1101. MacGuigan, Mark. *Possible amendment of section 96 - an address by the Honourable Mark MacGuigan, Minister of Justice and Attorney General of Canada, to the Canadian Bar Association*; February 28, 1984; Whitehorse. [Ottawa]: Department of Justice; 1984.

1102. MacGuigan, Mark. The Charter - emerging issues and future action. *Manitoba Law Journal*; 1983 Fall; 13(4): 683-694.

1103. MacGuigan, Mark. *Comments on the report of the UK Select Committee on Foreign Affairs on the BNA Acts, notes for a speech by the Secretary of State for External Affairs, Dr. Mark MacGuigan, to the Edmonton Chamber of Commerce Constitutional Conference, February 6, 1981*. Ottawa: Canada Dept. of External Affairs; 1981; 8 p.

1104. MacGuigan, Mark. *The Constitution of Canada: a suggested amendment relating to provincial administrative tribunals: a discussion paper*. [Ottawa]: Department of Justice; 1983; 13 (14) p.

1105. MacKay, A. Wayne. Fairness after the Charter: a rose by any other name? (Administrative law and the Charter). *Queen's Law Journal*; 1985 Spring; 10(2): 263-335.

1106. MacKay, A. Wayne. Judicial process in the Supreme Court of Canada: the patriation reference and its implications for the Charter of Rights. *Osgoode Hall Law Journal*; 1983 July; 21(1): 55-81.

1107. MacKay, A. Wayne; Bauman, Richard W. The Supreme Court of Canada: reform implications for an emerging national institution. In: Becton, Clare; MacKay, A. Wayne, res. coords. *The courts and the Charter*. Toronto: University of Toronto Press; Royal Commission on the Economic Union and Development Prospects for Canada; 1985: 37-131; xv, 279 p. (The collected research studies; v. 58).

1108. MacKinnon, Frank. Half the constitutional story is still to be told. *Canadian Public Administration*; 1983 Spring; 26(1): 113-120.

1109. Maclean, J. Angus. *Notes for premier J. Angus Maclean's press conference of Tuesday, 29 September 1981, on the Supreme Court of Canada's decision on the constitutional reference; September 29, 1981.* [Charlottetown]: Prince Edward Island. Office of the Premier; 1981.

1110. MacLean, J. Angus. *A submission to the Special Joint Parliamentary Committee of the Senate and the House of Commons on the Constitution concerning the proposed resolution for a joint address to Her Majesty the Queen respecting the Constitution of Canada.* Charlottetown: Prince Edward Island. Legislative Assembly; 1980; 24, 61 p.

1111. MacPherson, James C. Developments in constitutional law: the 1978-79 term. *Supreme Court Law Review*; 1980; 1: 77-135.

1112. MacPherson, James C. Developments in constitutional law: the 1979-80 term. *Supreme Court Law Review*; 1981; 2: 49-123.

1113. MacPherson, James C. Economic regulation and the British North America Act: Labatt Breweries and other constitutional imbroglios. *Canadian Business Law Journal*; 1981 April; 5(2): 172-219.

1114. MacPherson, James C. The potential implications of constitutional reform for the Supreme Court of Canada. In: Beck, Stanley M.; Bernier, Ivan, eds. *Canada and the new Constitution: the unfinished agenda.* Montreal: Institute for Research on Public Policy; 1983: 161-223; xii, 399 p.

1115. Maffini, G.; Wood, S. *Issues and economic implications of constitutional change in Nova Scotia: an analytical framework.* [Halifax]: Dalhousie University. Institute of Public Affairs; 1980.

1116. Magnet, Joseph Eliot. The Charter's official languages provisions: the implications of entrenched bilingualism. *Supreme Court Law Review*; 1982; 4: 163-193.

1117. Magnet, Joseph Eliot. *Constitutional law of Canada: cases, notes and materials.* Toronto: Carswell; 1984; xxii, 309 p. (Carswell student editions).

1118. Magnet, Joseph Eliot. *Constitutional law of Canada: cases, notes, and materials.* Toronto: Carswell; 1983; xxii, 1229 p.

1119. Magnet, Joseph Eliot. *Constitutional law of Canada: cases, notes, and materials.* 2nd ed. Toronto: Carswell; 1985.

1120. Magnet, Joseph Eliot. Minority-language educational rights. *Supreme Court Law Review*; 1982; 4: 195-216.

1121. Mallory, J. *Charter of Rights and Freedoms and Canadian democracy.* [Saskatoon]: University of Saskatchewan; 1984.

1122. Mallory, J. R. The politics of constitutional change. *Law and Contemporary Problems*; 1982 Autumn; 45(4): 53-69.

1123. Mallory, J. R. The politics of constitutional change. In: Davenport, Paul; Leach, Richard H., eds. *Reshaping Confederation: the 1982 reform of the Canadian Constitution*. Durham, N.C.: Duke University Press; 1984: 53-70; 329 p. (Duke University Centre for International Studies publications).

1124. Malone, S. Marc. *Guaranteed representation of aboriginal peoples in institutions of public government: constitutional development in the western Northwest Territories*. Yellowknife: Legislative Assembly; 1983; v, 134 p.

1125. Malone, S. Marc. *Nunavut: the division of power*. Yellowknife, N.W.T.: Nunavut Constitutional Forum; March, 1983; 125 p. (Working Paper No. 1).

1126. Manitoba. *Constitutional issues for the people of Manitoba*. [Winnipeg]: Province of Manitoba; [1981]; 1 sheet.

1127. Manitoba. Court of Appeal. *Manitoba constitutional reference: re an act for expediting the decision of constitutional and other provincial questions, C.C.S.M., C. C180 and re a reference pursuant thereto by the Lieutenant Governor in council*. [Winnipeg]: Manitoba Court of Appeal; 1981.

1128. Manitoba. Department of the Attorney -General. *Constitutionally speaking - published by the Department of the Attorney-General to inform Manitobans about proposed constitutional amendments*. [Winnipeg]: Dept. of the Attorney-General; 1983.

1129. Manitoba. Office of the Premier. *Constitutional issues for the people of Manitoba* [folder]. [Manitoba]: Office of the Premier; 1981.

1130. Mann, F. The Constitution after the Supreme Court decision: the next phase of the debate. *Business Quarterly*; 1981 Autumn; 46(3): 74-81.

1131. Mann, F. The Ottawa accord and the resolution of the Canadian Parliament: now who has our Constitution? *Business Quarterly*; 1982; 47(1): 47-53.

1132. Manning, Morris. *Rights, freedoms and the courts: a practical analysis of the Constitution Act, 1982*. Toronto: Emond-Montgomery; 1983; lxiv, 760 p.

1133. Maps, Thomas W. Law reform in Canada: the impact of the provincial law reform agencies on uniformity. *Dalhousie Law Journal*; 1983 April; 7(2): 257-276.

1134. Marshall, Geoffrey. Beyond the B.N.A. Act: amendment and patriation. *Alberta Law Review*; 1981 Summer; 19(3): 363-368.

1135. Marshall, Geoffrey. Canada's Constitution (editorial). *Public Law*; 1981 Spring: 7-11.

1136. Marshall, Geoffrey. The law and the Canadian Constitution. *Public Law*; 1981 Winter: 433-435.

1137. Marshall, Geoffrey. The United Kingdom Parliament and the British North America Acts. *Alberta Law Review*; 1981 Summer; 19(3): 352-362.

1138. Martin, Maedythe J.; McGraw, Donna. *Canadian constitutional reform: a checklist and index to the papers presented at federal-provincial conferences, 1976-1979*. Toronto: Legislative Library, Research and Information Services; 1980; iii, 34 p.

1139. Marvin Shaffer & Associates Ltd. *Impact of division on distribution of NWT non-renewable resource wealth.* Yellowknife: Western Constitutional Forum; 1984; 147 p.

1140. Mascotto, Jacques; Soucy, Pierre Yves. The Quebec workers' movement and the constitutional crisis of the Canadian state: a survey of some practical and theoretical issues. *Journal of Area Studies*; 1982; 5: 30-34.

1141. McConnell, W. H. Constitutional law (annual survey of Canadian law). *Ottawa Law Review*; 1982 Summer; 14(3): 502-616.

1142. McConnell, W. H. Cutting the Gordian knot: the amending process in Canada. *Law and Contemporary Problems*; 1981 Summer; 44(3): 195-230.

1143. McConnell, W. H. A western view of constitution-building. *Queen's Quarterly*; 1980 Winter; 87(4): 570-576.

1144. McDonald, David C. *Legal rights in the Canadian Charter of Rights and Freedoms: a manual of issues and sources.* Toronto: Carswell; 1982; xxv, 275 p.

1145. McDonald, Susan A. The problem of treaty-making and treaty implementation in Canada. *Alberta Law Review*; 1981 Spring; 19(2): 293-302.

1146. McEvoy, J. Atlantic Canada: the constitutional offshore regime. *Dalhousie Law Journal*; 1984; 8(2): 284-343.

1147. McEvoy, J. The Charter as a bilingual instrument. *Canadian Bar Review*; 1986 March; (1): 155-171.

1148. McKercher, William R., ed. *The U.S. Bill of Rights and the Canadian Charter of Rights and Freedoms.* Toronto: Ontario Economic Council; 1983; 270 p. (Special research report/Ontario Economic Council).

1149. McKercher, William R. The United States Bill of Rights: implications for Canada. In: McKercher, William R., ed. *The U.S. Bill of Rights and the Canadian Charter of Rights and Freedoms*. Toronto: Ontario Economic Council; 1983: 7-26; 270 p. (Special research report/Ontario Economic Council).

1150. McLellan, A. Anne; Elman, Bruce P. To whom does the Charter apply? Some recent cases on section 32. *Alberta Law Review*; 1986 Winter; 24(2): 361-375.

1151. McLellan, A. Anne; Elman, Bruce, P. The enforcement of the Canadian Charter of Rights and Freedoms: an analysis of section 24. *Alberta Law Review*; 1983 Spring; 21(2): 205-250.

1152. McMurtry, R. Roy. The Canadian Charter of Rights and Freedoms: an Ontario view. In: McKercher, William R., ed. *The U.S. Bill of Rights and the Canadian Charter of Rights and Freedoms*. Toronto: Ontario Economic Council; 1983: 151-157; 270 p. (Special research report/Ontario Economic Council).

1153. McMurtry, R. Roy. The search for a constitutional accord - a personal memoir. *Queen's Law Journal*; 1983 Fall-Spring; (1-2): 28-73.

1154. McNeil, Kent. The constitutional rights of the aboriginal peoples of Canada. *Supreme Court Law Review*; 1982; 4: 255-265.

1155. McWhinney, Edward. *Canada and the Constitution 1979-1982: patriation and the Charter of Rights*. Toronto: University of Toronto Press; 1982; xii, 227 p.

1156. McWhinney, Edward. The Canadian Charter of Rights and Freedoms: the lessons of comparative jurisprudence. *Canadian Bar Review*; 1983 March; 61(1): 55-68.

1157. McWhinney, Edward. Constitutional patriation as prologue: phase two constitution-making and reform of federal institutions. *Les Cahiers de droit*; 1984 March; 25(1): 165-171.

1158. McWhinney, Edward. The constitutional patriation project, 1980-82. *American Journal of Comparative Law*; 1984 Spring; 32(2): 241-267.

1159. McWhinney, Edward. International law and the "patriation" of the Canadian Constitution. *Canadian Yearbook of International Law*; 1983: 294-301.

1160. Meekison, J. Peter. The amending formula. *Queen's Law Journal*; 1983 Fall-Spring; 8(1-2): 99-122.

1161. Meekison, J. Peter; Romanow, Roy J.; Moull, William D. *Origins and meaning of section 92a: the 1982 constitutional amendment on resources*. Montreal: Institute for Research on Public Policy; 1984.

1162. Millar, Perry S.; Baar, Carl. *Judicial administration in Canada*. Montreal: McGill-Queen's University Press; 1981; xxiii, 452 p. (Canadian public administration series).

1163. Milne, David. *The new Canadian Constitution*. Toronto: J. Lorimer; 1982; 240 p. (Canadian issues).

1164. Mintz, Eric. Banzhaf's power index and Canada's constitutional amending formula: a comment on Kilgour's analysis. *Canadian Journal of Political Science*; 1985; 18(2): 385-387.

1165. Mintz, Eric. Changing Canada's constitutional amending formula: a comment. *Canadian Public Policy*; 1985 September; 11(3): 623-624.

1166. Monahan, Patrick J. The Supreme Court and the economy. In: Bernier, Ivan; Lajoie, Andrée, res. coords. *The Supreme Court of Canada as an instrument of political change*. Toronto: University of Toronto Press; Royal Commission on the

Economic Union and Development Prospects for Canada; 1986: 105-178; xv, 211 p. (The collected research studies; v. 47).

1167. Monet, Jacques. *"Maintaining a Constitution worthy of such a country:" reflections on values in Canadian society.* Regina: Campion College; 1983; 18 p.

1168. Monière, Denis. Le Québec fait-il encore partie du Canada? *L'Action nationale*; 1983; 72(6): 487-508.

1169. Morel, André. La clause limitative de l'article 1 de la Charte canadienne des droits et libertés: une assurance contre le gouvernement des juges. *Canadian Bar Review*; 1983 March; 61(1): 81-100.

1170. Morin, Claude. Le 5 novembre 1981. *L'Action nationale*; 1983 January; 72(5): 425-444.

1171. Morin, Claude. L'expérience canadienne et québécoise de révision constitutionnelle: leçons et perspectives. *Les Cahiers de droit*; 1985 March; 26(1): 29-55.

1172. Morin, Rosaire. Le gouvernement fédéral occupe le territoire québécois. *L'Action nationale*; 1981 October; 71(2): 139-148.

1173. Morin, Rosaire. Notre opposition au fédéral. *L'Action nationale*; 1981 February; 70(6): 483-494.

1174. Morris, Sharon R. The Constitution and family law in Canada: prospects and proposals. *Canadian Community Law Journal*; 1981; 5: 106-129.

1175. Morton, F. L.; Pal, Leslie A. The impact of the Charter of Rights on public administration: a case study of sex discrimination in the Unemployment Insurance Act. *Canadian Public Administration*; 1985 Summer; 28(2): 221-243.

1176. Moull, William D. Business law implications of the Canadian Charter of Rights and Freedoms. *Canadian Business Law Journal*; 1984 February; 8(4): 449-484.

1177. Moull, William D. Intergovernmental immunity from taxation: the unresolved issues. *Canadian Tax Journal*; 1984 January-February; 32(1): 54-63.

1178. Moull, William D. Natural resources: provincial proprietary rights, the Supreme Court of Canada, and the resource amendment to the Constitution. *Alberta Law Review*; 1983 Summer; 21(3): 472-487.

1179. Moull, William D. Section 92A of the Constitution Act, 1867. *Canadian Bar Review*; 1983 December; 61(4): 715-734.

1180. Moull, William D. Newfoundland resources: the Supreme Court strikes again. *Supreme Court Law Review*; 1985: 419-440.

1181. Muldoon, Francis C. Law reform in Canada: diversity or uniformity? *Manitoba Law Journal*; 1983 Summer; (3): 257-269.

1182. Mullan, David J. Developments in administrative law: the 1982-83 term. *Supreme Court Law Review*; 1984; 6: 1-48.

1183. Mullan, David J. The uncertain constitutional position of Canada's administrative appeal tribunals. *Ottawa Law Review*; 1982 Spring; 14(2): 239-269.

1184. Munro, John. *Speaking notes for the Honourable John C. Munro, Minister of Indian Affairs and Northern Development, for the constitutional resolution debate, February 20, 1981*. Ottawa: Indian and Northern Affairs Canada; 1981; 19 p.

1185. Nathanson, David, C. *The Canadian Charter of Rights and Freedoms and the Income Tax Act (transcript)*. Canadian Tax Foundation (Conference Report); 1983; Ann: 636-688.

1186. National Association of Women and the Law; Canada. Parliament. Special Joint Committee on the Constitution of Canada (1980-1981). *Women's human right to equality, a promise unfulfilled: submitted to the Special Joint Committee on the Constitution*. Ottawa: The Association; 1980; ii, 18 p.

1187. Neary, Peter. The Supreme Court of Canada and "the Bowater's law", 1950. *Dalhousie Law Journal*; 1984 January; 8(1): 201-215.

1188. Neilson, William A. W. Interjurisdictional harmonization of consumer protection laws and administration in Canada. In: Cuming, Ronald C. C., res. coord. *Perspectives on the harmonization of law in Canada*. Toronto: University of Toronto Press; Royal Commission on the Economic Union and Development Prospects for Canada; 1985: 59-116; xviii, 178 p. (The collected research studies; v. 55).

1189. Nesgos, Peter, D. Aeronautics law and the Canadian Constitution. *Annals of Air and Space Law*; 1981; 6: 89-113.

1190. New Brunswick. Advisory Council on the Status of Women. *Bringing all of New Brunswick laws into conformity with section 15 of the Canadian Charter of Rights and Freedoms*. Moncton: Advisory Council on the Status of Women; 1985; 12, 4 p.

1191. Newfoundland. Court of Appeal. *Newfoundland constitutional reference: re a reference by the Lieutenant-Governor in council concerning the effect and validity of the amendments to the Constitution of Canada sought in the proposed resolution*. [St John's]: Newfoundland Court of Appeal; 1981.

1192. Newfoundland. Department of Intergovernmental Affairs. *Towards the twenty-first century - together: the position of the Government of Newfoundland regarding constitutional change*. [St John's]: Intergovernmental Affairs; 1980.

1193. Newfoundland. Office of the Premier. *Brief to the Select Committee on Foreign Affairs, House of Commons - subject: the legal and constitutional responsibilities of the Parliament of the United Kingdom with respect to the proposed Constitution Act, 1980*. [St. John's]: Office of the Premier; 1980.

1194. Northwest Territories. *The Constitutional debate: a northern perspective.* Paper presented to the Alternatives Conference of the Canada West Foundation; November 27-29, 1980; Banff, Alberta.

1195. Northwest Territories. Aboriginal Rights and Constitutional Development. *Building Nunavut: a working document with a proposal for an Arctic constitution: Nunavut Constitutional Forum.* [Yellowknife]: Government of the Northwest Territories; 1983.

1196. Northwest Territories. Aboriginal Rights and Constitutional Development Secretariat. *A proposal for addressing the issue of aboriginal rights and freedoms as they relate to the February 1983 Conference of First Ministers on the Canadian Constitution;* 1983. Yellowknife: The Secretariat; 1983; 4 p.

1197. Northwest Territories. Aboriginal Rights and Constitutional Development Secretariat. *Our land our future: discussion paper on political and constitutional development in the Northwest Territories.* Yellowknife: Government of the N.W.T.; 1981; 16 (16) p.

1198. Northwest Territories. Executive Committee. *Aboriginal rights and constitutional development in the Northwest Territories.* Yellowknife: Government of the Northwest Territories; 1980; 5 (4) p.

1199. Northwest Territories. Legislative Assembly. *Minutes of the second Western Arctic Constitutional Conference; September 14-16, 1982;* Yellowknife. Yellowknife: Government of the Northwest Territories; [1982]; 281 p.

1200. Northwest Territories. Legislative Assembly. *Position of the Legislative Assembly on constitutional development in the Northwest Territories.* Yellowknife: Government of the Northwest Territories; [1980]; 59 p.

1201. Northwest Territories. Legislative Assembly. Special Committee on Constitutional Development. *Working paper for the second Western Arctic Constitutional Conference, September 14-16, 1982.* Yellowknife: Northwest Territories Legislative Assembly; September 1, 1982; 39 p.

1202. Northwest Territories. Legislative Assembly. Special Committee on Constitutional Development. *Constitutional development and the protection of aboriginal rights.* [Yellowknife]: Government of the Northwest Territories; 1983.

1203. Northwest Territories. Legislative Assembly. Special Committee on Constitutional Development. *Constitutional development in the western Northwest Territories: protection of aboriginal rights.* [Yellowknife]: Government of the Northwest Territories; 1980.

1204. Northwest Territories. Legislative Assembly. Special Committee on Constitutional Development. *Constitutional development in the western Northwest Territories: liberal - democratic government: principles and practice; Liberal - democratic society and government in Canada.* [Yellowknife]: Government of the Northwest Territories; 1980.

1205. Northwest Territories. Legislative Assembly. Special Committee on Constitutional Development. *Residency requirements - part 1: residence requirements limiting voting rights to permanent residents - part 2: a statistical analysis of residency and mobility patterns in the Northwest Territories - residency requirements*. [Yellowknife]: Government of the Northwest Territories; 1983.

1206. Northwest Territories. Legislative Assembly. Special Committee on Constitutional Developments. *Constitutional development in the western Northwest Territories: regional government; Regional government in the western Northwest Territories: a discussion paper*, by W. Bean and K.A. Graham. [Yellowknife]: Government of the Northwest Territories; 1980.

1207. Northwest Territories. Legislative Council. Special Committee on Constitutional Development. *Discussion paper on the Denendeh government proposal; Working paper for the second Western Arctic Constitutional Conference*; September 14-16, 1982. [Yellowknife]: Government of the Northwest Territories; 1982.

1208. Northwest Territories; Constitutional Alliance of the Northwest Territories. *The constitutional alliance of the N.W.T. and the Nunavut and western constitutional forums: report to the Legislative Assembly*. Yellowknife: Constitutional Alliance of the Northwest Territories; 1983; 3, 9 p.

1209. Nouailhat, Yves-Henri. Les provinces atlantiques dans le débat sur le rapatriement de la constitution. Etudes Canadiennes; 1982; 13: 143-149.

1210. Nova Scotia. House of Assembly. Select Committee on Constitutional Matters. *The report of the Nova Scotia House of Assembly Select Committee on Constitutional Matters*, by Arthur R. Donahoe. [Halifax]: The Committee; 1981; 2 v.

1211. Nova Scotia. House of Assembly. Select Committee on Constitutional Matters; Alberta. Legislative Assembly. Special Select Committee on constitutional matters. *Verbatim transcript of a meeting of the Nova Scotia House of Assembly Select Committee on constitutional matters and the Alberta Special Select committee on Constitutional Matters: 9:30 a.m., Friday January 23, 1981*; January 23, 1981; Halifax. Halifax: The Committee; 1981; 60 p.

1212. Nunavut Constitutional Forum. *Building Nunavut: a working document with a proposal for an Arctic constitution*. [Ottawa]: The Forum; 1983; 46, 54 p.

1213. Nunavut Constitutional Forum. *Building Nunavut: today and tomorrow. 2nd ed. Ottawa, Ontario*: Nunavut Constitutional Forum; March 1985; 56 p.

1214. Nurgitz, Nathan; Segal, Hugh. *No small measure: the Progressive Conservatives and the Constitution*. Ottawa: Deneau Publishers; [1983]; ix, 136 p.

1215. O'Reilly, James O. La Loi constitutionnelle de 1982, droit des autochtones. Les Cahiers de droit; 1984 March; 25(1): 125-144.

1216. Olling, R. D.; Westmacott, M. W. Canada and the constitutional question 1970-1980: themes and variations. *Business Quarterly*; 1980 Autumn; 45(2): 41-48.

1217. Olling, R. D.; Westmacott, M. W, eds. *The Confederation debate: the Constitution in crisis.* Dubuque, Iowa: Kendall/Hunt Pub. Co; 1980; xviii, 217 p.

1218. Ontario. *Statement by the Hon. T.L. Wells following the Supreme Court decision on the Constitution, Sept. 28, 1981.* [Toronto]: Ontario; 1981.

1219. Ontario. Legislative Assembly. Select Committee on Constitutional Reform. *Committee hearings of the Select Committee on Constitutional Reform.* [Toronto]: The Committee; 1980.

1220. Ontario. Legislative Assembly. Select Committee on Constitutional Reform. *Report of the Select Committee on Constitutional Reform.* [Toronto]: [Legislative Assembly]; [1980]; v, 74 p.

1221. Ontario. Legislative Assembly. Select Committee on Constitutional Reform. *Summary of recommendations and positions on select aspects of Canadian constitutional reform,* by L. Grayson. [Toronto]: Government of Ontario; 1980.

1222. Ontario. Ministry of Intergovernmental Affairs. *Canada's new Constitution - some personal reminiscences, impressions and feelings,* by Thomas L. Wells. [Toronto]: Ministry of Intergovernmental Affairs; 1983.

1223. Ontario. Ministry of Intergovernmental Affairs. *The Constitution Act, 1982: potential impact of the provisions regarding the aboriginal peoples, and the options for Ontario.* Toronto: Ministry of Intergovernmental Affairs; January, 1983; 123 p.

1224. Ontario. Ministry of Intergovernmental Affairs. *For change in the interests of Canada: Ontario's constitutional position.* Toronto: Ontario Ministry of Intergovernmental Affairs; 1980; 6 p.

1225. Ontario. Ministry of Intergovernmental Affairs. *Partners in a strengthened Canada.* [Toronto]: Ministry of Intergovernmental Affairs; 1980.

1226. Ontario. Ministry of Intergovernmental Affairs. *Statement by the Honourable Thomas L. Wells, Minister of Intergovernmental Affairs, opening the debate on Confederation in the Ontario legislature, May 5, 1980.* [Toronto]: Ministry of Intergovernmental Affairs; 1980.

1227. Ontario. Ministry of Intergovernmental Affairs. *Statement by the Honourable Thomas L. Wells, Minister of Intergovernmental Affairs on the report of the Constitutional Committee of the Quebec Liberal Party "a new Canadian federation", Tuesday, January 29, 1980.* [Toronto]: Ministry of Intergovernmental Affairs; 1980.

1228. Ontario. Ministry of Labour. *Canadian Charter of Rights and Freedoms: a selected bibliography.* Toronto: Ministry of Labour; 1985.

1229. Ontario. Ministry of the Attorney General. *Statement by the Honourable Roy McMurtry following the Supreme Court decision on the Constitution,* September 28, 1981; Ottawa. [Toronto]: Ministry of the Attorney General; 1981.

1230. Ontario. Ministry of the Attorney General. *Sources for the interpretation of equality rights under the Charter: a background paper*. Rev ed. Toronto: Ministry of the Attorney General; 1985; xvi, 463 p.

1231. Orban, Edmond. *Mécanismes pour une nouvelle constitution*. Ottawa: Editions de l'Université d'Ottawa; 1981; x, 146 p.

1232. Orban, Edmond. *Mécanismes pour une nouvelle constitution*. Ottawa: Editions de L'Université d'Ottawa; 1981; x 146 p.

1233. Ouellette, Yves. La Charte canadienne et les tribunaux administratifs. (La Charte canadienne des droits et libertés: concepts et impacts). *Revue juridique Thémis*; 1984; 18: 295-328.

1234. Parti libéral du Québec. Commission constitutionnelle. *Une nouvelle fédération canadienne*. Montréal: Parti libéral du Québec; 1980; 145 p.

1235. Parti liberal du Québec. Commission constitutionelle. *A new Canadian federation, by the Constitutional Committee of the Quebec Liberal Party*. Montreal: Quebec Liberal Party; 1980; 141 p. Note: Includes: 28 cm. Language: English.

1236. Paul, Victor, C.A, ed. *Le dossier de la crise constitutionnelle, 1981: O' Canada vs. je me souviens*. Victoriaville: Publications Vic; [1981]; 132 p.

1237. Peiris, G. L. Legal protection of human rights: the contemporary Canadian experience. *Legal Studies*; 1985 November; 5(3): 261-295.

1238. Pelletier, Benoit B. Les pouvoirs de légiférer en matière de langue après la "Loi constitutionnelle de 1982". *Les Cahiers de droit*; 1984 March; 25(1): 227-297.

1239. Pelot, Bernard J. *The buckskin curtain: a discussion paper on aboriginal rights in the Constitution*. Ottawa: s.n.; 1985; 22 p.

1240. Penton, M. James. Collective versus individual rights: the Canadian tradition and the Charter of Rights and Freedoms. In: McKercher, William R., ed. *The U.S. Bill of Rights and the Canadian Charter of Rights and Freedoms*. Toronto: Ontario Economic Council; 1983: 174-183; 270 p. (Special research report / Ontario Economic Council).

1241. Pépin, Gilles. L'indépendance judiciaire et l'indépendance des tribunaux au sens des articles 11 et 23 des Chartes canadienne et québécoise. *Revue du barreau du Québec*; 1984 November-December; 44(5): 901-924.

1242. Pépin, Gilles. L'irrecevabilité du projet de modification de l'article 96 de la Loi constitutionnelle de 1867. *Les Cahiers de droit*; 1985 March; 26(1): 239-249.

1243. Pépin, Gilles. The problem of section 96 of the Constitution Act, 1867. In: Becton, Clare; MacKay, A. Wayne, res. coords. *The courts and the Charter*. Toronto: University of Toronto Press; Royal Commission on the Economic Union and Development Prospects for Canada; 1985: 223-227; xv, 279 p. (The collected research studies; v. 58).

1244. Pestieau, Caroline. External economic relations and constitutional change. In: Beck, Stanley M.; Bernier, Ivan, eds. *Canada and the new Constitution: the unfinished agenda.* Montreal: Institute for Research on Public Policy; 1983; 2: 219-248; 289 p.

1245. Petter, Andrew. Constitutional law: rearranging the administration of criminal justice. *Canadian Bar Review*; 1985; 63(1): 162-178.

1246. Petter, Andrew. Maitre chez who? The Quebec veto reference. *Supreme Court Law Review*; 1984; 6: 387-399.

1247. Philip, Christian. Le Québec et le "repatriement" de la constitution canadienne. Revue de droit public; 1982; 98(6): 1567-1600.

1248. Phillips, O. Hood. The Canada Act 1982. *International and Comparative Law Quarterly*; 1982 October; 31(4): 845-848.

1249. Phillips, O. Hood. Constitutional conventions in the Supreme Court of Canada. *Law Quarterly Review*; 1982 April; 98: 194-197.

1250. Posluns, Michael. *Constitutional development and the protection of aboriginal rights.* Yellowknife: Western Constitutional Forum and the Legislative Assembly Special Committee on Constitutional Development; 1983; viii, 113 p.

1251. Press, Charles. Assessing the policy and operational implications of state constitutional change. *Publius*; 1982 Winter; 12(1): 99-112.

1252. Prince Edward Island. *A submission to the Special Joint Parliamentary Committee of the Senate and the House of Commons on the Constitution concerning the proposed resolution of a joint address to Her Majesty the Queen respecting the Constitution of Canada, presented by Honourable J. Angus Maclean on behalf of the Government of Prince Edward Island.* [Charlottetown]: Government of Prince Edward Island; 1980; 24 p.

1253. Prince Edward Island. Legislative Assembly. *Representation of the Government of Prince Edward Island to the Foreign Affairs Committee of the House of Commons of the United Kingdom regarding the British North America Act.* [Charlottetown]: Government of Prince Edward Island; 1980.

1254. Pye, A. Kenneth. The rights of persons accused of crime under the Canadian Constitution: a comparative perspective *Law and Contemporary Problems*; 1982 Autumn; 45(4): 221-248.

1255. Pye, A. Kenneth. The rights of persons accused of crime under the Canadian Constitution: a comparative perspective. In: Davenport, Paul; Leach, Richard H., eds. *Reshaping Confederation: the 1982 reform of the Canadian Constitution.* Durham, N.C.: Duke University Press; 1984: 221-248; 329 p. (Duke University Center for International Relations publications).

1256. Québec. *Draft agreement on the Constitution: proposals by the Government of Quebec.* Quebec: Gouvernement du Québec; 1985; 35 p.

1257. Québec. *Projet d'accord constitutionnel: propositions du gouvernement du Québec*. Québec: Assemblée nationale; 1985; 39 p.

1258. Quebec Liberal Party. *Choose Quebec and Canada*. [Montreal]: Quebec Liberal Party; [1980?]; v.

1259. Quebec Liberal Party. Policy Commission. *Mastering our future, working paper*. Montreal: Quebec Liberal Party; 1985; various pagings.

1260. Québec. Assemblée nationale. Commission permanente de la présidence du conseil, de la constitution et des affaires intergouvernementales. *Dossier sur les discussions constitutionnelles: extraits*. [Québec]: Gouvernement du Québec, Ministère des Affaires intergouvernementales; 1980; 52 leaves.

1261. Québec. Cour d'appel. *Renvoi à la Cour d'appel relatif à un projet de résolution portant addresse commune à sa majesté la reine concernant la constitution du Canada*. [Québec]: Québec. Cour d'appel; 1981.

1262. Québec. Ministère des affaires intergouvernementales. *Constitution express*. [Québec]: Gouvernement du Québec; [1980-1981]; 14 folders.

1263. Québec. Ministère des Communications. *Minute Ottawa. Constitution*. [Québec]: Ministère des Communications; 1981.

1264. Radkowski-Harmstone, Teresa. Communist constitutions and constitutional change. In: Banting, Keith G.; Simeon, Richard, eds. *Redesigning the state: the politics of constitutional change in industrial nations*. Toronto: University of Toronto Press; 1985: 203-231; xii, 257 p.

1265. Regan, Gerald A. *Notes for an address by the Honourable Gerald A. Regan, P.C., Q.C., M.P. Minister of Labour on the constitutional resolution - House of Commons; March 2, 1981*; Ottawa. [Ottawa]: Department of Labour; 1981.

1266. Rémillard, Gil. Commentaries: The entrenchment of a Bill of Rights. *Alberta Law Review*; 1981 Summer; 19(3): 387-390.

1267. Rémillard, Gil. The Constitution Act, 1982: an unfinished compromise. *American Journal of Comparative Law*; 1984 pring; 32(2): 269-281.

1268. Rémillard, Gil. Historique du rapatriement. *Les Cahiers de droit*; 1984 March; 25(1): 15-97.

1269. Rémillard, Gil. Legality, legitimacy and the Supreme Court. In: Banting, Keith; Simeon, Richard, eds. *And no one cheered*. Toronto: Methuen; 1983: 189-209; xii, 376 p.

1270. Rémillard, Gil; Bérubé, Guylaine. Le contrôle de la constitutionnalité des lois au lendemain de la Loi constitutionnelle de 1982. *Revue du barreau du Québec*; 1982 Sept-Oct; 42(4): 565-596.

1271. Rémillard, Gil. The Trudeau resolution and constitutional reform in Canada. In: Mathews, Russell, ed. *Public policies in two federal countries: Canada and*

Australia. Canberra: Centre for Research on Federal Financial Relations, Australian National University; 1982; 59-64.

1272. Review Committee on Newfoundland Legislation. *Provincial legislation and the Canadian Charter of Rights and Freedoms*. St. John's: The Committee; 1985; vi, 44 p.

1273. Richards, J. G; Smith, G. J. Applying the Charter. *Advocates' Quarterly*; 1983 July; (2): 129-158.

1274. Rights and constitutional change in Canada: a roundtable discussion. In: McKercher, William R., ed. *The U.S. Bill of Rights and the Canadian Charter of Rights and Freedoms*. Toronto: Ontario Economic Council; 1983: 139-150; 270 p. (Special research report/Ontario Economic Council).

1275. Robertson, Gordon. The position of the government of Canada on constitutional reform 1980-81. In: Mathews, Russell, ed. *Public policies in two federal countries: Canada and Australia*. Canberra: Centre for Research on Federal Financial Relations, Australian National University; 1982; 65-68 p.

1276. Robinette, J. J. The future of our Constitution. *University of British Columbia Law Review*; 1984 Summer; 18(2): 335-349.

1277. Rokas, Teresa Andrea. *Canadian political economy and constitutional review: a case study of Ontario and British Columbia* [microfiche]: (M.A.) McMaster University; 1980 3 microfiches (202 fr.). Ottawa: National Library of Canada; Canadian theses on microfiche, 1982.

1278. Roman, Andrew. The Charter of Rights: renewing the social contract. *Queen's Law Journal*; 1983 Fall-Spring; 8(1-2): 188-203.

1279. Roman, Andrew. The possible impact of the Canadian Charter of Rights and Freedoms on administrative law. *Les Cahiers de droit*; 1985 June; 26(2): 339-359.

1280. Romanow, Roy. "Reworking the miracle:" the Constitutional Accord 1981. *Queen's Law Journal*; 1983 Fall-Spring; 8(1-2): 74-98.

1281. Romanow, Roy J.; Whyte, John; Leeson, Howard. *Canada - notwithstanding: the making of the Constitution, 1976-1982*. Toronto: Carswell/Methuen; 1984; xxi, 286 p.

1282. Ross, Rupert. Transfer of the residuary power to the provinces. *University of Toronto Faculty of Law Review*; 1981 Spring; 39(1): 30-42.

1283. Russell, Peter H. Constitutional reform of the judicial branch: symbolic vs. operational considerations. *Canadian Journal of Political Science*; 1984 June; 17(2): 227-252.

1284. Russell, Peter H. The effect of a Charter of Rights on the policy-making role of Canadian courts. *Canadian Public Administration*; 1982 Spring; 25(1): 1-33.

1285. Russell, Peter H. The first three years in Charterland. *Canadian Public Administration*; 1985 Fall; 28(3): 367-396.

1286. Russell, Peter H. The political purposes of the Canadian Charter of Rights and Freedoms. *Canadian Bar Review*; 1983 March; 61(1): 30-54.

1287. Russell, Peter H. Bold statescraft, questionable jurisprudence. In: Banting, Keith; Simeon, Richard, eds. *And no one cheered*. Toronto: Methuen; 1983: 210-238; xii, 376 p.

1288. Russell, Peter H. *The Court and the Constitution: comments on the Supreme Court reference on constitutional amendment*. Kingston: Institute of Intergovernmental Relations, Queen's University; 1982; viii, 81 p.

1289. Russell, Peter H. *Leading constitutional decisions: cases on the British North America Act*. 3rd ed. Ottawa: Carleton University Press; 1982; vii, 578 p.

1290. Russell, Peter H. The Supreme Court's interpretation of the Constitution. In: Fox, Paul W., ed. *Politics: Canada*. Toronto: McGraw-Hill Ryerson: 592-620; 693 p.

1291. Sabetti, Filippo. The historical context of constitutional change in Canada. *Law and Contemporary Problems*; 1982 Autumn; 45(4): 11-32.

1292. Sabetti, Filippo. The historical context of constitutional change in Canada. In: Davenport, Paul; Leach, Richard H., eds. *Reshaping Confederation: the 1982 reform of the Canadian Constitution*. Durham, N.C.: Duke University Press; 1984: 11-32; 329 p. (Duke University Centre for International Studies publications).

1293. Sabetti, Filippo. The making of Italy as an experiment in constitutional choice. *Publius*; 1982 Summer; 12(3): 65-84.

1294. Sanders, Douglas. The indian lobby. In: Banting, Keith; Simeon, Richard, eds. *And no one cheered*. Toronto: Methuen; 1983: 301-332; xii, 376 p.

1295. Sanders, Douglas. Prior claims: an aboriginal people in the Constitution of Canada. In: Beck, Stanley M.; Bernier, Ivan, eds. *Canada and the new Constitution*: the unfinished agenda. Montreal: Institute for Research on Public Policy; 1983: 225-279.

1296. Sanders, Douglas. The rights of the aboriginal peoples of Canada. *Canadian Bar Review*; 1983 March; 61(1): 314-338.

1297. Saskatchewan. *An act to amend the Constitutional Questions Act: chapter 31, 1983-84*. [Regina]: [Queen's Printer]; [1984]; 2 p.

1298. Saskatchewan. *The patriation and amendment of the Constitution of Canada : brief, presented to the Special Joint Committee on the Constitution by Allan Blakeney*. [Regina]: Government of Saskatchewan; [1980]; 42 p.

1299. Saskatchewan. Advisory Council on the Status of Women. *Position paper on the constitutional proposal to transfer family law to the provincial jurisdiction.* [Saskatoon]: The Council; 1980; 21 leaves.

1300. Saskatchewan. Department of Intergovernmental Affairs. *Canada's Constitution - the Saskatchewan position - March 13, 1981.* [Regina]: Department of Intergovernmental Affairs; 1981.

1301. Saskatchewan. Department of Justice. *Compliance of Saskatchewan laws with Canadian Charter of Rights and Freedoms: discussion paper.* Regina: Department of Justice; 1984; iii, 28 p.

1302. Saskatchewan. Legislative Assembly. *Bringing home Canada's Constitution - Saskatchewan's position.* [Regina]: Legislative Assembly; 1981.

1303. Saskatchewan; Continuing Committee of Ministers on the Constitution. *Powers over the economy: securing the Canadian economic union in the Constitution: discussion paper.* Regina: Government of Saskatchewan; 1980; 9 leaves.

1304. Saunders, Cheryl. Parliamentary appropriation. In: Saunders, Cheryl [and others]. *Current constitutional problems in Australia.* Canberra: Centre for Research on Federal Financial Relations, Australian National University; 1982; 1-36 p.

1305. Saunders, Cheryl [and others]. *Current constitutional problems in Australia.* Canberra: Centre for Research on Federal Financial Relations, Australian National University; 1982; viii, 75 p.

1306. Schechter, Stephen L. Amending the United States Constitution: a new generation on trial. In: Banting, Keith G.; Simeon, Richard, eds. *Redesigning the state: the politics of constitutional change in industrial nations.* Toronto: University of Toronto Press; 1985: 160-202; xii, 257 p.

1307. Schmeiser, Douglas A. Entrenchment revisited: the effect of the Canadian Charter of Rights and Freedoms. In: McKercher, William R., eds. *The U.S. Bill of Rights and the Canadian Charter of Rights and Freedoms.* Toronto: Ontario Economic Council; 1983: 158-173; 270 p. (Special research report/Ontario Economic Council).

1308. Schmeiser, Douglas A.; Young, Katherine J. Mobility rights in Canada. *Manitoba Law Journal*; 1983 Fall; 13(4): 615-649.

1309. Schmeiser, Douglas A. The entrenchment of a bill of rights. *Alberta Law Review*; 1981 Summer; 19(3): 375-383.

1310. Schwartz, Bryan; Whyte, John D. The patriation references and the idea of Canada. *Queen's Law Journal*; 1983 Fall-Spring; 8(1-2): 158-187.

1311. Scott, Anthony. Divided jurisdiction over natural-resource revenues. *Transactions of the Royal Society of Canada*; 1980; 18: 203-222.

1312. Scott, Stephen A. The Canadian constitutional amendment process. *Law and Contemporary Problems*; 1982 Autumn; 45(4): 249-281.

1313. Scott, Stephen A. Entrenchment by executive action: a partial solution to "legislative override". *Supreme Court Law Review*; 1982; 4: 303-320.

1314. Scott, Stephen A. Law and convention in the patriation of the Canadian Constitution. *Parliamentarian*; 1981 July; 62(3): 183-191.

1315. Scott, Stephen A. Pussycat, pussycat, or patriation and the new constitutional amendment processes. *University of Western Ontario Law Review*; 1982 December; 20(2): 247-306.

1316. Scott, Stephen A. The Canadian constitutional amendment process. In: Davenport, Paul; Leach, Richard H., eds. *Reshaping Confederation: the 1982 reform of the Canadian Constitution*. Durham, N.C.: Duke University Press; 1984: 249-282; 329 p. (Duke University Centre for International Studies Publications); ISBN: 0-8223-0578-X. Note: Includes: index.

1317. Scott, Stephen A. The Canadian constitutional amendment process: mechanisms and prospects. In: Becton, Clare; MacKay, A. Wayne, res. coord. *Recurring issues in Canadian federalism*. Toronto: University of Toronto Press; Royal Commission on the Economic Union and Development Prospects for Canada; 1986: 77-112; xv, 187 p. (The collected research studies; v. 57).

1318. Scott, Stephen A. Canadian federal courts and the constitutional limits of their jurisdiction. *McGill Law Journal*; 1982; 27(2): 137-195.

1319. Sedler, Robert A. Constitutional protection of individual rights in Canada: the impact of the new Canadian Charter of Rights and Freedoms. *Notre Dame Law Review*; 1984; 59(5): 1191-1242.

1320. Semkow, Brian. Energy and the new Constitution. *Alberta Law Review*; 1982 Winter; 23(1): 101-134.

1321. Sharman, Campbell. The strange case of a provincial constitution: the British Columbia Constitution Act. *Canadian Journal of Political Science*; 1984 March; 17(1): 87-108.

1322. Sharpe, Robert J. *Interprovincial product liability litigation: jurisdiction, enforcement and choice of law*. [Ottawa]: Consumer and Corporate Affairs Canada; 1981; 236 p.

1323. Sheppard, Robert; Valpy, Michael. *The national deal: the fight for a Canadian Constitution*. Toronto: Fleet Books; 1982; viii, 360 p.

1324. Simeon, Richard. Constitutional development and reform. In: Whittington, Michael S.; Williams, Glen, eds. *Canadian politics in the 1980's*. Toronto: Methuen; 1981: 243-259; xiv, 336 p.

1325. Simeon, Richard, res. coord. *Division of powers and public policy*. Toronto: University of Toronto Press; Royal Commission on the Economic Union and

Development Prospects for Canada; 1985; xiv, 206 p. (The collected research studies; v. 61).

1326. Simeon, Richard. *Le guide du citoyen sur la question constitutionnelle.* Montréal: Héritage; 1981; 47 p.

1327. Simeon, Richard. An overview of the Trudeau constitutional proposals. *Alberta Law Review*; 1981 Summer; 19(3): 391-400.

1328. Slattery, Brian. The constitutional guarantee of aboriginal and treaty rights. *Queen's Law Journal*; 1983 Fall-Spring; 8(1-2): 232-273.

1329. Slattery, Brian. The hidden Constitution: aboriginal rights in Canada. *American Journal of Comparative Law*; 1984 Spring; 32(2): 361-391.

1330. Slattery, Brian. The independence of Canada. *Supreme Court Law Review*; 1983; 5: 369-404.

1331. Smiley, Donald V. The Canadian Charter of Rights and Freedoms with special emphasis on Quebec-Canada relations. In: McKercher, William R., ed. *The U.S. Bill of Rights and the Canadian Charter of Rights and Freedoms.* Toronto: Ontario Economic Council; 1983: 218-225; 270 p. (Special research report/Ontario Economic Council).

1332. Smiley, Donald V. *The Canadian Charter of Rights and Freedoms,* 1981. Toronto: Ontario Economic Council; 1981; iii, 71 p. (Discussion paper series / Ontario economic council).

1333. Smiley, Donald V. The challenge of Canadian ambivalence. *Queen's Quarterly*; 1981 Spring; 88(1): 1-12.

1334. Smiley, Donald V. A dangerous deed: the Constitution Act, 1982. In: Banting, Keith; Simeon, Richard, eds. *And on one cheered.* Toronto: Methuen; 1983: 74-95; xii, 376 p.

1335. Smith, Garry J. *Charter of Rights and administrative law, 1983-1984: the Law Society of Upper Canada bar admission course materials.* [Toronto]: Carswell; 1983; xxix, 184 p.

1336. Smith, Jennifer. Federalism, the Charter and the court: the origins of judicial review in Canada. *Canadian Journal of Political Science*; 1983 March; 16(3): 115-134.

1337. Smith, Jennifer. Federalism, the Charter and the court: the origins of judicial-review in Canada - reply. *Canadian Journal of Political Science*; 1983 September; 16(3): 597-599.

1338. Smith, Jennifer. Origins of the Canadian amendment dilemma. *Dalhousie Review*; 1981; 61(2): 291-306.

1339. Smith, Jennifer Irene. *A treatment of political institutions in the Confederation debate* [microfiche]: (Ph.D.) Dalhousie University; 1981 4 microfiches (331 fr.). Ottawa: National Library of Canada, 1982.

1340. Smith, Lynn. Charter equality rights: some general issues and specific applications in British Columbia to elections, juries and illegitimacy. *University of British Columbia Law Review*; 1984 Summer; 18(2): 351-406.

1341. Smith, Peter J. *The ideological genesis of Canadian Confederation.* (Ph.D.) Carleton University; 1984 5 microfiches (465 fr.). Ottawa: National Library of Canada, 1985.

1342. Snell, James G. Relations between the Maritimes and the Supreme Court of Canada: the patterns of the early years (transcript). *Dalhousie Law Journal*; 1984 June; 8(3): 143-163.

1343. Snell, James G. The West and the Supreme Court of Canada: the process of institutional accommodation of regional attitudes and needs. *Manitoba Law Journal*; 1984; 14(3): 287-304.

1344. Snell, James G.; Vaughan, Frederick. *The Supreme Court of Canada: history of the institution.* Toronto: The Osgoode Society, University of Toronto Press; 1985; xv, 319 p.

1345. Soberman, D. A. Canada's institutional "deficit". *Queen's Law Journal*; 1983 Fall-Spring; 8(1-2): 204-210.

1346. Sproule-Jones, Marc. On the analysis of constitutional change in Canada - comments. *Public Choice*; 1984; 44(1): 279-283.

1347. Sproule-Jones, Mark. The enduring colony? Political-institutions and political science in Canada. *Publius*; 1984 Winter; 14(1): 93-108.

1348. Stairs, Denis. Foreign policy. In: Beck, Stanley M.; Bernier, Ivan, eds. *Canada and the new Constitution*: the unfinished agenda. Montreal: Institute for Research on Public Policy; 1983; 2: 155-186; 289 p.

1349. Stanfield, Robert L. Constitutional reform: Canadian issues. In: Mathews, Russell, ed. *Public policies in two federal countries: Canada and Australia.* Canberra: Centre for Research on Federal Financial Relations, Australian National University; 1982; 53-58 p.

1350. Stein, Michael B. Canadian constitutional reform, 1927-1982 - a comparative case analysis over time. *Publius*; 1984 Winter; 14(1): 121-139.

1351. Stephen, N. Constitutional change in Canada: lessons and analogies from across the Pacific. *Australian Journal of Public Administration*; 1983; 42(1): 173-186.

1352. Stephen, Ninian. *Constitutional change in Canada: lessons and analogies from across the Pacific.* [North Ryde, N.S.W.]: Australian and New Zealand Association for Canadian Studies; 1984; 15 p. (Monograph series).

1353. Stevenson, Garth. Commentaries: an overview of the Trudeau constitutional proposals. *Alberta Law Review*; 1981 Summer; 19(3): 407-409.

1354. Stevenson, Garth. The division of powers. In: Simeon, Richard, res. coord. *Division of powers and public policy*. Toronto: University of Toronto Press; Royal Commission on the Economic Union and Development Prospects for Canada; 1985: 71-124; xiv, 206 p. (The collected research studies; v. 61).

1355. Stone, Dennis; Walpole, F. Kim. The Canadian Constitution Act and the Constitution of the United States: a comparative analysis. *Canadian-American Law Journal*; 1983 Fall; 2(1): 1-36.

1356. Strayer, Barry. The implications of the Canadian Charter of Rights and Freedoms. In: McKercher, William R., ed. *The U.S. Bill of Rights and the Canadian Charter of Rights and Freedoms*. Toronto: Ontario Economic Council; 1983: 226-234; 270 p. (Special research report/Ontario Economic Council).

1357. Strayer, Barry L. *The Canadian Constitution and the Courts: the function and scope of judicial review*. 2nd ed. Toronto: Butterworths; c1983; xxxiv, 310 p.

1358. Sturm, Albert L. The development of American state constitutions. *Publius*; 1982 Winter; 12(1): 57-98.

1359. Swan, John. The Canadian Constitution, federalism and the conflict of laws. *Canadian Bar Review*; 1985 June; 63(2): 271-321.

1360. Swinton, Katherine. Bora Laskin and federalism. *University of Toronto Law Journal*; 1985; 35: 353-391.

1361. Tarnopolsky, W. S. Human rights and constitutional options for Canada. In: Beck, Stanley M.; Bernier, Ivan, eds. *Canada and the new Constitution: the unfinished agenda*. Montreal: Institute for Research on Public Policy; 1983; 1: 281-305; xii, 399 p.

1362. Tarnopolsky, Walter S. A comparison between the Canadian Charter of Rights and Freedoms and the International Covenant on Civil and Political Rights. *Queen's Law Journal*; 1983 Fall-Spring; 8(1-2): 211-231.

1363. Tarnopolsky, Walter S. The equality rights in the Canadian Charter of Rights and Freedoms. *Canadian Bar Review*; 1983 March; 61(1): 242-264.

1364. Tarnopolsky, Walter S. The historical and constitutional context of the proposed Canadian Charter of Rights and Freedoms. *Law and Contemporary Problems*; 1981 Summer; 44(3): 169-193.

1365. Tarnopolsky, Walter S. The new Canadian Charter of Rights and Freedoms as compared and contrasted with the American Bill of Rights. *Human Rights Quarterly*; 1983 August; (3): 227-274.

1366. Tarnopolsky, Walter S. The Constitution and human rights. In: Banting, Keith; Simeon, Richard, eds. *And no one cheered*. Toronto: Methuen; 1983: 261-279; xii, 376 p.

1367. Tarnopolsky, Walter S. Human rights protection by statute - the Canadian experience. *Law Society Journal*; 1986 June; (5): 34-35.

1368. Tarnopolsky, Walter S. *Religious freedom: freedom of religion in Canada: the legal and constitutional basis*. Limited ed. Vancouver: Bible Holiness Movement; 1985; 27 p.

1369. Tarnopolsky, Walter S. Some perspectives on the Canadian Charter of Rights and Freedoms. In: McKercher, William R., ed. *The U.S. Bill of Rights and the Canadian Charter of Rights and Freedoms*. Toronto: Ontario Economic Council; 1983: 203-217; 270 p. (Special research report/Ontario Economic Council).

1370. Tarnopolsky, Walter S.; Beaudoin, Gerald A. *The Canadian Charter of Rights and Freedoms: commentary*. Toronto: Carswell; 1982; liii, 590 p.

1371. Tetley, William. Language and education rights in Quebec and Canada (a legislative history and personal political diary). In: Davenport, Paul; Leach, Richard H., eds. *Reshaping Confederation: the 1982 reform of the Canadian Constitution*. Durham, N.C.: Duke University Press; 1984: 177-220; 329 p. (Duke University Centre for International Studies publications).

1372. Theauvette, Carole. *La domiciliation de la constitution canadienne: l'affrontement de deux conceptions du fédéralisme* [microfiche]: (M.A.) Université d'Ottawa; 1983 3 microfiches (229 IM.). Ottawa: Bibliothèque nationale du Canada, 1985.

1373. Tremblay, André. *Précis de droit constitutionnel*. Montréal: Editions Thémis; 1982; ix, 341 p.

1374. Tremblay, Guy. La Cour suprême et l'amendement constitutionnel. *Les Cahiers de droit*; 1980 June; (1): 31-41.

1375. Tremblay, Guy. La procédure de modification de la constitution du Canada et ses puzzles. *Revue du barreau du Québec*; 1983 Nov-Dec; 43(5): 1151-1159.

1376. Tremblay, Guy. The Supreme Court of Canada: final arbiter of political disputes. In: Bernier, Ivan; Lajoie, Andrée, res. coords. *The Supreme Court of Canada as an instrument of political change*. Toronto: University of Toronto Press; Royal Commission on the Economic Union and Development Prospects for Canada; 1986: 179-209; xv, 211 p. (The collected research studies; v. 47).

1377. Tschaeni, Hanspeter. Constitutional change in Swiss cantons: an assessment of a recent phenomenon. *Publius*; 1982 Winter; 12(1): 113-130.

1378. Turp, Daniel. Le recours au droit international aux fins de l'interprétation de la Charte canadienne des droits et libertés: un bilan jurisprudentiel. (La Charte canadienne des droits et libertés: concepts et impacts). *Revue juridique Thémis*; 1984; (18): 353-411.

1379. Vipond Robert C. Constitutional politics and the legacy of the provincial rights movement in Canada. *Canadian Journal of Political Science*; 1985 June; 18(2): 266-294.

1380. Vipond, Robert C. *Federalism and the problem of sovereignty: constitutional politics and the rise of the provincial rights movement in Canada* [microfiche]: (Ph.D.) Harvard University; 1983 4 microfiches (359 fr.). Michigan: University Microfilms International, 1984.

1381. Wah-Shee, James J. *Statement to western N.W.T. constitutional conference*; January 19-22, 1982; Yellowknife. Yellowknife: s.n.; 1982; 8 p.

1382. Walsh, Sandra A. *The Constitution of Canada and its amendment: a selected bibliography*. Monticello, ILL.: Vance Bibliographies; 1981; 7 p. (Public administration series).

1383. Watson, William G. The economics of constitution-making. *Law and Contemporary Problems*; 1982 Autumn; 45(4): 87-108.

1384. Watson, William G. The economics of Constitution making. In: Davenport, Paul; Leach, Richard H., eds. *Reshaping Confederation: the 1982 reform of the Canadian Constitution*. Durham, N.C.: Duke University Press; 1984: 88-108; 329 p. (Duke University Centre for International Studies publications).

1385. Weiler, Paul C. Of judges and rights or should Canada have a constitutional Bill of Rights. *Dalhousie Review*; 1980-81; 60(2): 205-237.

1386. Welling, Bruce; McLaren, Richard. The Charter of Rights and the "fundamental wrong". *Business Quarterly*; 1981 Spring; 46(1): 5-9.

1387. Wells, Thomas L. *Statement by the Honourable Thomas L. Wells, Minister of Intergovernmental affairs on the report of the Constitutional Committee of the Quebec Liberal Party "a new Canadian federation", Tuesday, January 29, 1980*; Toronto: Ontario. Ministry of Intergovernmental Affairs; 1980.

1388. West, Edwin G.; Winer, Stanley L. The individual, political tension, and Canada's quest for a new Constitution. *Canadian Public Policy*; 1980 Winter; 6(1): 3-15.

1389. Westin, Alan F. The United States Bill of Rights and the Canadian Charter: a socio-political analysis. In: McKercher, William R., ed. *The U.S. Bill of Rights and the Canadian Charter of Rights and Freedoms. Toronto: Ontario Economic Council; 1983: 27-50 p; 270 p. (Special research report/Ontario Economic Council)*.

1390. Whitaker, Reginald. Democracy and the Canadian constitution. In: Banting, Keith; Simeon, Richard, eds. *And no one cheered*. Toronto: Methuen; 1983: 240-260; xii, 376 p.

1391. Whittington, Michael S., res. coord. *The North*. Toronto: University of Toronto Press; Royal Commission on the Economic Union and Development Prospects for Canada; 1985; xvii, 183 p. (The collected research studies; v. 72).

1392. Whittington, Michael S. Political and constitutional development in the N.W.T. and Yukon: the issues and the interests. In: *idem.*, coord. *The North*. Toronto: University of Toronto Press; Royal Commission on the Economic Union and Development Prospects for Canada; 1985: 53-108; xvii, 183 p. (The collected research studies; v. 72).

1393. Whyte, John D. Developments in constitutional law: the 1982-83 term. *Supreme Court Law Review*; 1984; 5: 49-94.

1394. Whyte, John D. Fundamental justice: the scope and application of Section 7 of the Charter. *Manitoba Law Journal*; 1983 Fall; 13(4): 455-475.

1395. Whyte, John D. *The Constitution and natural resource revenues*. Kingston: Institute of Intergoverenmental Relations, Queen's University; 1982; iii, 50 p.

1396. Whyte, John D. Constitutional aspects of economic development policy. In: Simeon, Richard, res. coord. *Division of powers and public policy*. Toronto: University of Toronto Press; Royal Commission on the Economic Union and Development Prospects for Canada; 1985: 29-70; xiv, 206 p. (The collected research studies; v. 61).

1397. Williford, Mary Elizabeth. Canadian constitutional law - Supreme Court of Canada holds consent of Quebec not necessary for amendment to Canadian constitution. *Texas International Law Journal*; 1984 Winter; 19(1): 233-246.

1398. Woehrling, José. La Cour suprême et les conventions constitutionnelles: les renvois relatifs au "rapatriement" de la constitution canadienne. *Revue de droit Université de Sherbrooke*; 1984 Spring; (2): 391-440.

1399. Woodcock, George. Confederation as a world example. In: Banting, Keith; Simeon, Richard, eds. *And no one cheered*. Toronto: Methuen; 1983: 333-346; xii, 376 p.

1400. Woods, Gerald; Sim, Heather. *Highlights of federal initiatives in criminal justice, 1966-1980*. Ottawa: Ministry of the Solicitor General of Canada; 1981; vii, 78 p.

1401. Woodward, Michael; George, Bruce. The Canadian Indian lobby of Westminster 1979-1982. *Journal of Canadian Studies*; 1983 Fall; 18(3): 119-143.

1402. Yurko, William J. *Parliament and patriation: the triumph of unilateralism: a personal perspective*. [s.l.]: [W.J. Yurko]; [1984]; 413 p.

1403. Ziegel, Jacob S. Harmonization of provincial laws, with particular reference to commercial, consumer and corporate law. In: Cuming, Ronald C. C., res. coord. *Harmonization of business law in Canada*. Toronto: University of Toronto Press;

Royal Commission on the Economic Union and Development Prospects for Canada; 1986: 1-75; xx, 245 p. (The collected research studies; v. 56).

1404. Zylstra, B.F. *Liberalism or liberty, an assessment of Canada's new Constitution.* [Toronto?]: Christian Labour Association of Canada; 1983; [8] p.

4 Intergovernmental Relations

1405. Abizadeh, Sohrab; Hudson, Richard. Trends in the federal-provincial tax collection agreements: the case of Alberta. *Canadian Tax Journal*; 1983 July-August; 31(4): 653-664.

1406. Advisory Commission on Intergovernmental Relations. *Awakening the slumbering giant: intergovernmental relations and federal grant law.* Washington D.C.: ACIR; 1980; vi, 101 p. (Information report; v. M-122).

1407. Advisory Commission on Intergovernmental Relations. *The federal role in the federal system: the dynamics of growth. Hearings on the federal role.* Washington D.C.: ACIR; 1980; v, 90 p. (Commission report; A-87).

1408. Advisory Commission on Intergovernmental Relations. *Significant features of fiscal federalism 1979-80 edition.* Washington D.C.: ACIR; 1980; xii, 189 p. (Advisory Commission on Intergovernmental Relations report; M-123).

1409. Advisory Commission on Intergovernmental Relations. *Significant features of fiscal federalism 1980-81 edition.* [Washington, D.C.]: ACIR; 1981. (Advisory Commission on Intergovernmental Relations report; M-132).

1410. Advisory Commission on Intergovernmental Relations. *Significant features of fiscal federalism 1981-82 edition.* Washington D.C.: ACIR; 1983; xii, 146 p. (Advisory Commission on Intergovernmental Relations report; M-135).

1411. Advisory Commission on Intergovernmental Relations. *Significant features of fiscal federalism 1982-83 edition.* [Washington, D.C.]: ACIR; 1981. (Advisory Commission on Intergovernmental Relations report; M-137).

1412. Advisory Commission on Intergovernmental Relations. *Significant features of fiscal federalism 1984 edition.* Washington D.C.: ACIR; 1985; xv, 236 p.

1413. Advisory Commission on Intergovernmental Relations. *State administrators' opinions on administrative change, federal aid, federal relationships.* Washington D.C.: ACIR; 1980; vii, 64 p. (Information report; M-120).

1414. Advisory Commission on Intergovernmental Relations. *State-local relations bodies: state ACIRs and other approaches.* Washington D.C.: ACIR; 1981; vii, 67 p. (Information report; v. M-124).

1415. Advisory Council for Inter-government Relations. *Australian housing policy and intergovernmental relations.* Hobart, Tasmania: ACIR; 1984; v, 156 p. (Discussion papers; 14).

1416. Advisory Council for Inter-government Relations. *The Australian Loan Council and intergovernmental relations.* Canberra: Australian Government Publishing Service; 1982; ix,145 p. (Relationships Reference; v. 5).

1417. Advisory Council for Inter-government Relations. *Eighth annual report for the year ending 31 August 1984.* Hobart, Tasmania: A.B. Caudell; 1985; viii, 38 p.

1418. Advisory Council for Inter-government Relations. *Fifth annual report year ending 31 August 1981.* Canberra: Australian Government Publishing Service; 1982; viii, 69 p.

1419. Advisory Council for Inter-government Relations. *Fourth annual report year ending 31 August 1980.* Canberra: Australian Government Publishing Service; 1981; viii, 48 p.

1420. Advisory Council for Inter-government Relations. *Implications of constitutional recognition for Australian local government.* Hobart, Tasmania: Tasmanian Government Printer; 1985. (Relationships Reference; 8).

1421. Advisory Council for Inter-government Relations. *Intergovernmental aspects of major resource projects and their infrastructure.* Hobart, Tasmania: ACIR; 1984: xiv, 186 p. (Discussion papers; 15).

1422. Advisory Council for Inter-government Relations. *Local government systems of Australia.* Canberra: Australian Government Publishing Service; 1981; xi, 830 p. (Relationships Reference; Information Papers; 7).

1423. Advisory Council for Inter-government Relations. *Resource development and inter-government relations.* Hobart, Tasmania: A.B. Caudell; [1985]; vii, 70 p. (Relationships Reference; 9).

1424. Advisory Council for Inter-government Relations. *Revenue sharing for local government.* Hobart, Tasmania: ACIR; 1985; ii, 31 p. (Information papers; 11).

1425. Advisory Council for Inter-government Relations. *Seventh annual report for the year ending 31 August 1983.* Canberra: Australian Government Publishing Service; 1984; ix, 103 p.

1426. Advisory Council for Inter-government Relations. *Sixth annual report for the year ending 31 August 1982.* Canberra: Australian Government Publishing Service; 1983; ix, 97 p.

1427. Alberta. *Alberta in Canada: strength in diversity : a Government of Alberta discussion paper.* [Edmonton]: [Government of Alberta]; [1983]; 76 p.

1428. Alberta. Alberta Federal and Intergovernmental Affairs. *Eighth annual report to March 31, 1981.* [Edmonton]: FIGA; [1982]; vii, 79 p.

1429. Alberta. Alberta Federal and Intergovernmental Affairs. *Eleventh annual report, to March 31, 1984.* [Edmonton]: FIGA; [1985]; 52 p.

1430. Alberta. Alberta Federal and Intergovernmental Affairs. *Inventory of Federal-provincial programs in Alberta, March 31, 1981*. Rev. ed. [Edmonton]: [FIGA]; 1981; vi, 502 p.

1431. Alberta. Alberta Federal and Intergovernmental Affairs. *Ninth annual report to March 31, 1982*. [Edmonton]: FIGA; [1982].

1432. Alberta. Alberta Federal and Intergovernmental Affairs. *Seventh annual report to March 31, 1980*. [Edmonton]: FIGA; [1981]; 53 p.

1433. Alberta. Alberta Federal and Intergovernmental Affairs. *Tenth annual report to March 31, 1983*. [Edmonton]: FIGA; [1984]; 43 p.

1434. Alberta. Premier. *Premier Lougheed's press conference; Friday July 25, 1980, Ottawa*. Edmonton: Government of Alberta; 1980; 13 leaves.

1435. Anderson, D.L. Market power and the Saskatchewan potash industry. *Canadian Public Policy*; 1985; 11: 321-328.

1436. Annual conference of New England Governors and eastern Canadian Premiers (10th, 1982). *Documents* (10th Annual Conference of New England Governors and eastern Canadian Premiers, 1982); June 20-22, 1982; Rockport, Maine. [Ottawa]: Canadian Intergovernmental Conference Secretariat; 1982; various pagings.

1437. Annual Conference of New England Governors and eastern Canadian Premiers (11th, 1983). *Documents* (11th Annual Conference of New England Governors and eastern Canadian Premiers, 1983); June 19-21, 1983; Charlottetown. [Ottawa]: Canadian Intergovernmental Conference Secretariat; 1983; various pagings.

1438. Annual Conference of New England Governors and eastern Canadian Premiers (12th, 1984). *Documents* (12th Annual Conference of New England Governors and eastern Canadian Premiers, 1984); June 17-19, 1984; Newport, R.I. [Ottawa]: Canadian Intergovernmental Conference Secretariat; 1984.

1439. Annual conference of New England Governors and eastern Canadian Premiers (13th, 1985). *Documents* (13th Annual Conference of New England Governors and eastern Canadian Premiers, 1985); June 16-18, 1985; St. Andrews, N.B. [Ottawa]: Canadian Intergovernmental Affairs Secretariat; 1985; 2 v.; various pagings.

1440. Annual Interprovincial Conference of Ministers Responsible for Northern Development, 1981. *Alberta: housing design, construction and delivery, 1981*; Goose Bay. [Ottawa]: Canadian Intergovernmental Conference Secretariat; 1981; various pagings.

1441. Annual Interprovincial Conference of Ministers with Responsibility for Northern Development, 1981. Northern preference policies in contracting and business development in northern Saskatchewan; 1981; Goose Bay. [Ottawa]: Canadian Intergovernmental Conference Secretariat; 1981.

1442. Annual Interprovincial Conference of Ministers with Responsibility for Northern Development, 1981. *Northern development and the environmental assessment procedure in Saskatchewan*; 1981; Goose Bay. [Ottawa]: Canadian Intergovernmental Conference Secretariat; 1981.

1443. Annual Interprovincial Conference of Ministers with Responsibility for Northern Development, 1981. *Northern development and the environment: the planning and assessment process in British Columbia*; 1981; Goose Bay. [Ottawa]: Canadian Intergovernmental Conference Secretariat; 1981.

1444. Annual Interprovincial Conference of Ministers with Responsibility for *Northern Development, 1981. Northern development and the environment: summary, Quebec; 1981*; Goose Bay. [Ottawa]: Canadian Intergovernmental Conference Secretariat; 1981.

1445. Annual Interprovincial Conference of Ministers with Responsibility for Northern Development, 1981. *Northern development and the environment: Ontario; 1981*; Goose Bay. [Ottawa]: Canadian Intergovernmental Conference Secretariat; 1981.

1446. Annual Interprovincial Conference of Ministers with Responsibility for Northern Development, 1981. *Northern development and the environment: basic document, Quebec; 1981*; Goose Bay. [Ottawa]: Canadian Intergovernmental Conference Secretariat; 1981.

1447. Annual Interprovincial Conference of Ministers with Responsibility for Northern Development, 1981. *Provincial update, Alberta: transition from traditional to wage economy; 1981*; Goose Bay. [Ottawa]: Canadian Intergovernmental Conference Secretariat; 1981.

1448. Annual Interprovincial Conference of Ministers with Responsibility for Northern Development, 1981. *Saskatchewan: status report and update*; 1981; Goose Bay. [Ottawa]: Canadian Intergovernmental Conference Secretariat; 1981.

1449. Annual Premiers' Conference (22nd, 1981). *Notes for remarks by the Premier of Quebec Hon. René Levesque - the state of federal-provincial relations - at the 22nd Annual Premiers' Conference*; Aug. 1981; Victoria. [Ottawa]: Canadian Intergovernmental Conference Secretariat; 1981.

1450. Annual Premiers' Conference (23rd, 1982). *Communiqué: federal-provincial relations - 23rd Annual Premiers' Conference*; Aug. 1982; Halifax. [Ottawa]: Canadian Intergovernmental Conference Secretariat; 1982.

1451. Appel, David. *Interprovincial product liability litigation: jurisdiction, enforcement and choice of law in Quebec private international law.* [Ottawa]: Policy Research, Analysis and Liaison Directorate, Consumer and Corporate Affairs Canada; c1982; 35 p.

1452. Armstrong, C. *Politics of federalism: Ontario's relations with the federal government, 1867-1942*. Toronto: Ontario. Ministry of Culture and Recreation; 1981.

1453. Armstrong, Christopher. *The politics of federalism: Ontario's relations with the federal government, 1867-1942*. Toronto: University of Toronto Press; 1981; xiv, 279 p.

1454. Auld, D. A. L. Financing Confederation: stabilization and harmonization. *Canadian Public Policy*; 1982 Summer; 8(3): 307-10.

1455. Auld, D. A. L.; Eden, L. B. Federal provincial financial equalization and the Canadian Constitution. *Environment and Planning C: Government & Policy*; 1983; 1(4): 475-487.

1456. Auld, D.A.L. *Optimal fiscal balance and provincial-local finance*. Canberra: Centre for Research on Federal Financial Relations, Australian National University; 1981; vi, 34 p. (Occasional paper; v. 17).

1457. Auld, D.A.L. The scope for short-run fiscal stabilization policy within Confederation. In: Bird, Richard M., ed. *Fiscal dimensions of Canadian federalism*. Toronto: Canadian Tax Foundation; c1980: 91-109; v, 151 p. (Financing Canadian federation; v. 4).

1458. Auld, D.A.L. Tax harmonization and its importance in the Canadian federation. In: Bird, Richard M., ed. *Fiscal dimensions of Canadian federalism*. Toronto: Canadian Tax Foundation; 1980: 118-142; v, 151 p. (Financing Canadian federation; v. 4).

1459. Auld, D.A.L.; Eden, L.B. *Provincial-municipal fiscal equalization and revenue sharing* [Guelph]: University of Guelph. Dept. of Economics; 1983. (University of Guelph dept. of economics discussion paper; 1983-01).

1460. Ballentine, J. Gregory; Thirsk, Wayne R. The effects of revenue sharing on the distribution of disposable incomes. *Canadian Public Policy*; 1980 Winter; 6(1): 30-40.

1461. Balthazar, Louis. Quebec's policies toward the United States. In: Hero, Alfred O. Jr.; Daneau, Marcel, eds. *Problems and opportunities in U.S.-Quebec relations*. Boulder, CO: Westview Press; 1984: 220-248; xv, 320 p. (Westview special studies in international relations).

1462. Banker, Stephen. How America sees Quebec. In: Hero, Alfred O. Jr.; Daneau, Marcel, eds. *Problems and opportunities in U.S.-Quebec relations*. Boulder, CO: Westview Press; 1984: 169-184; xv, 320 p. (Westview special studies in international relations).

1463. Banting, Keith G. Federalism and income security: themes and variations. In: Courchene, Thomas J.; Conklin, David W.; Cook, Gail C.A., eds. *Ottawa and the provinces: the distribution of money and power*. Toronto: Ontario Economic

Council; 1985; 1: 253-276; xii, 341 p. (Special research report/Ontario Economic Council).

1464. Barfield, Claude E. *Rethinking federalism : block grants and federal, state, and local responsibilities.* Washington: American Enterprise Institute for Public Policy Research; c1981; ix, 99 p. (AEI studies; v. 349).

1465. Beer, Samuel H. *Federalism, making the system work.* Washington, D.C.: Center for National Policy; 1982; 60 p. (Alternatives for the 1980's; 6).

1466. Bélanger, Gérard. Dans un système fédéral le gouvernement central doit-il essayer d'imposer l'harmonisation fiscale? *L'Actualité économique*; 1982 December; 58(4): 493-513.

1467. Bennett, R. J. *Intergovernmental financial relations in Austria.* Canberra: Centre for Research on Federal Financial Relations, Australian National University; 1985; xi, 97 p. (Research monograph; v. 39).

1468. Bercuson, David Jay. *Canada and the burden of unity.* Toronto: Gage; c1980; 191 p.

1469. Bergeron, Gérard. Lecture du Livre blanc et du Livre beige selon une perspective 'super-fédéraliste'. *Canadian Public Policy*; 1980 Summer; 6(3): 506-520.

1470. Bergeron, Gérard. *Syndrome québécois et mal canadien:* Québec; Presses de l'Université Laval; c1981; xi, 297 p.

1471. Beriault, Yves. *Municipal government in a new Canadian federal system: report of the Resource Task Force on Constitutional Reform, Federation of Canadian Municipalities, Ottawa.* Ottawa: [Federation of Canadian Municipalities]; 1980; iv, 155 p.

1472. Bertrand, Guy. L'axe Québec - Etats-Unis. *L'Action nationale*; 1984 April; 73(8): 691-708.

1473. Bhajan, Grewal; Mathews, Russell. *Federalism, locational surplus, and the redistributive role of subnational governments.* Canberra: Centre for Research on Federal Financial Relations, Australian National University; 1983; 31 p. (Reprint Series; 53).

1474. Bird, Richard. Fiscal finance in comparative perspective. In: Courchene, Thomas J.; Conklin, David W.; Cook, Gail C.A., eds. *Ottawa and the provinces: the distribution of money and power.* Toronto: Ontario Economic Council; 1985; 1: 137-178; xii, 341 p. (Special research report).

1475. Bird, Richard M. *Fiscal dimensions of Canadian federalism.* Toronto: Canadian Tax Foundation; c1980; 4; v, 151 p. (Financing Canadian federation; v.4).

1476. Bissonnette, Lise. Orthodoxie fédéraliste et relations régionales transfrontières: une menace illusoire. *Etudes internationales*; 1981 December; 12(4): 635-656.

1477. Blackburn, V.C. Urban policy aspects of grants to local government. In: Mathews, Russell, ed. *Urban federalism: urban studies in a federal context.* Canberra: Centre for Research on Federal Financial Relations, Australian National University; 1981; 142-169.

1478. Boadway, Robin. *Intergovernmental transfers in Canada.* Toronto: Canadian Tax Foundation; 1980; ix, 93 p. (Financing Canadian federation; v. 2).

1479. Boadway, Robin; Flatters, Frank. Efficiency and equalization payments in a federal system of government: a synthesis and extension of recent results. *Canadian Journal of Economics*; 1982 November; 15(4): 613-633.

1480. Boadway, Robin; Flatters, Frank. *Equalization in a federal state: an economic analysis.* Ottawa: Economic Council of Canada; 1982; vii, 65 p.

1481. Boadway, Robin; Flatters, Frank. Financing Confederation: rejoinder. *Canadian Public Policy*; 1982 Autumn; 8(4): 621-623.

1482. Boadway, Robin; Flatters, Frank. *The role of equalization payments in a federal system of government: a synthesis and extension of recent results.* Kingston: Institute for Economic Research, Queen's University; c1981; 46 p. (Discussion paper).

1483. Boadway, Robin; Mintz, Jack. Issues in public finance: reflections on a conference held at Queen's University. *Canadian Tax Journal*; 1982 July-August; 30(4): 537-561.

1484. Boadway, Robin; Flatters, Frank: Leblanc, A. Revenue sharing and the equalization of natural resource revenues. *Canadian Public Policy*; 1983 June; 9(2): 174-180.

1485. Bourassa, Robert. *L'union monétaire et l'union politique sont indissociables.* Montréal: Parti libéral du Québec; 1980; 30 p. (Textes référendaires; v. 10).

1486. Bradford, David F.; Oates, Wallace E. Towards a predictive theory of intergovernmental grants. In: Grewal, Bhajan S. [and others], ed. *The economics of federalism.* Canberra: Australian National University; 1980: 321-333; xiii, 432 p.

1487. Break, George F. Fiscal federalism in the United States: the first 200 years, evolution and outlook. In: Advisory Council on Intergovernmental Relations. *The future of federalism in the 1980's.* Washigton D.C.: ACIR; 1981: 39-66; vii, 135 p. (Advisory Council on Intergovernmental Relations report; v. M-126).

1488. Brennan, H. Geoffrey. Criteria for state and local taxes. In: Grewal, Bhajan S. [and others], ed. *The economics of federalism.* Canberra: Australian National University; 1980: 341-350; xiii, 432 p.

1489. Breton, Albert. A theory of government grants. In: Grewal. Bhajan S. [and others], ed. *The economics of federalism.* Canberra: Australian National University; 1980: 9-24; xiii, 432 p.

1490. British Columbia. Ministry of Agriculture and Food. *Report on the evaluation of ARDSA (Agriculture and Rural Development Subsidiary Agreement)*. Victoria: British Columbia, Ministry of Agriculture and Food; 1982; xvi, 143 p.

1491. British Columbia. Ministry of Intergovernmental Relations. *Annual report April 1, 1982 to March 31, 1983*. Victoria: The Ministry; [1984]; 14 p.

1492. British Columbia. Ministry of Intergovernmental Relations. *Annual report April 1, 1983 to March 31, 1984*. Victoria: The Ministry; [1985]; 16 p.

1493. British Columbia. Ministry of Intergovernmental Relations. *Annual Report April 1, 1984 to March 31, 1985*. Victoria: Ministry of Intergovernmental Relations; 1985; 35 p.

1494. British Columbia. Ministry of Intergovernmental Relations. *First annual report November 23, 1979 to March 31, 1981*. [Victoria]: [The Ministry]; [1982]; 32 p.

1495. British Columbia. Ministry of Intergovernmental Relations. *Second annual report April 1, 1981 to March 31, 1982*. [Victoria]: [The Ministry]; [1983]; 24 p.

1496. British Columbia; *Canada. Department of Regional Economic Expansion. Canada-British Columbia subsidiary agreement on intensive forest management*. [Victoria]: Province of British Columbia, Ministry of Forests; [1980]; 34 p.

1497. Brown, Douglas. *Intergovernmental relations in Canada: the year in review 1979*. Kingston: Institute of Intergovernmental Relations, Queen's University; c1980; 129 p.

1498. Brown, Malcolm C. *Established program financing: evolution or regression in Canadian fiscal federalism?* Canberra: Centre for Research on Federal Financial Relations, Australian National University; 1984; viii, 108 p. (Research monograph; v. 38).

1499. Brown, Malcolm C. The implications of Established Program Finance for national health insurance. *Canadian Public Policy*; 1980 Summer; 6(3): 521-532.

1500. Brown, Malcolm C. Provincial government saving and the equity rationale of Canada's equalization program. *Canadian Taxation*; 1981 Fall; 3(3): 155-161.

1501. Buchanan, James M. Federalism and fiscal equity. In: Grewal, Bhajan S. [and others], ed. *The economics of federalism*. Canberra: Australian National University; 1980: 183-200; xiii, 432 p.

1502. Buchanan, James M.; Wagner, Richard E. An efficiency basis for federal fiscal equalization. In: Grewal, Bhajan S. [and others], ed. *The economics of federalism*. Canberra: Australian National University; 1980: 235-253; xiii, 432 p.

1503. Buchanan, Jim; Buchanan, Diana. *Revenue sharing: the literature of the new federalism*. Monticello, Ill.: Vance Bibliographies; 1980; 47 p. (Public administration series; v. P-504).

1504. Calgary. Corporate Resource Department. *Financing urban growth: a brief to the provincial government by the Council of the City of Calgary.* Calgary: Corporate Resource Dept.; 1983; 56 p.

1505. Cameron, David M. Financing Confederation: equity and efficiency. *Canadian Public Policy*; 1982 Summer; 8(3): 299-303.

1506. Cameron, David M. Provincial responsibilities for municipal government. *Canadian Public Administration*; 1980 Summer; 23(2): 222-235.

1507. Cameron, Kenneth D. Summary of discussions (Municipal government in the intergovernmental maze). *Canadian Public Administration*; 1980 Summer; 23(2): 195-206.

1508. Canada. *Federal-provincial Fiscal Arrangements and Federal Post-secondary Education and Health Contributions Act, 1977: B1976-77, C.10 amended by 1980-81-82-82, CC. 46, 48, 94, 121; 1984, CC. 6, 13, 31.* [Ottawa]: Supply and Services Canada; c1984; 45 p.

1509. Canada Advisory Council on the Status of Women. *Equality and equalization: brief by the Canadian Advisory Council on the Status of Women to the Parliamentary Task Force on Federal-provincial Arrangements; June 29, 1981.* [s.l.]: The Task Force; 1981.

1510. Canada. Ministry of State for *Economic and Regional Development. Economic and regional development agreements - backgrounder.* [Ottawa]: The Ministry; 1984.

1511. Canada. Parliament. House of Commons. Standing Committee on Finance, Trade and Economic Affairs. *Summary statement on federal-provincial relations: by the Canadian Labour Congress to the Finance, Trade and Economic Affairs Committee of the House of Commons.* Ottawa: The Committee; 1982; 10 p.

1512. Canada. Canadian Forestry Service; New Brunswick. Department of Natural Resources. *Canada/New Brunswick forest renewal agreement.* Rev ed. [Ottawa]: Government of Canada; [1985]; 28 (28) p.

1513. Canada. Department of Agriculture [loose leaf]. *Notes for an address to the opening of the 37th Federal-Provincial Agriculture Ministers' Meeting*; 1981; Lethbridge. [s.l.]: Dept. of Agriculture; 1981.

1514. Canada. Department of Finance. *Notes on the fiscal equalization program by the Hon. Allan J. MacEachen, ... at the Federal-Provincial Meeting of Ministers of Finance and Provincial Treasurers, Dec. 14-15, 1981*; Toronto. [s.l.]: Dept. of Finance; 1981.

1515. Canada. Department of Finance. *Description of fiscal equalization program* [Ottawa]: Department of Finance; 1983.

1516. Canada. Department of Finance. *Fiscal federalism in the eighties - position of the Government of Canada preparatory to a federal-provincial meeting of*

Finance Ministers and Treasurers, Lord Nelson Hotel, Halifax, Nova-Scotia, November 23-24, 1981 [pamphlet: 11-49 p]. Ottawa: Department of Finance; 1981.

1517. Canada. Department of Finance; Canada. Parliament. House of Commons. Special Committee on the Federal-Provincial Fiscal Arrangements. *Federal-provincial fiscal arrangements in the eighties: a submission to the Parliamentary Task Force on the Federal-Provincial Fiscal Arrangements*, by Allan J. Mac-Eachen. Ottawa: Department of Finance; 1981; 89 p.

1518. Canada. Department of Fisheries and Oceans; New Brunswick. Department of Fisheries. *Canada-New Brunswick Subsidiary Agreement on Fisheries Development under the Economic and Regional Development Agreement*. [Ottawa]: Department of Fisheries and Oceans; 1984; 15, 16 p.

1519. Canada. Department of Regional Economic Expansion. *Canada-New-foundland Rural Development Subsidiary Agreement regional development programs* [Ottawa]: DREE; 1983.

1520. Canada. Department of Regional Economic Expansion. *Canada/Nova Scotia Economic and Regional Development Agreement - course of action: 1984-85* [Ottawa]: DREE; 1984.

1521. Canada. Department of Regional Economic Expansion. *Summaries of Federal-Provincial General Development Agreements and currently active Subsidiary Agreements - April 1, 1980; Free development agreements April 1, 1980* [Ottawa]: Department of Regional Economic Expansion; 1980.

1522. Canada. Department of Regional Economic Expansion. *Summaries of Federal-Provincial General Development Agreements and currently active Subsidiary Agreements*. [Ottawa]: DREE; 1980; vi, 177 p.

1523. Canada. Department of Regional Economic Expansion. *Summaries of Federal-Provincial General Development Agreements and currently active Subsidiary Agreements*. [Ottawa]: [DREE]; [1981]; vii, 217 p.

1524. Canada. Department of Regional Industrial Expansion; Alberta. Alberta Tourism and Small Business. *Canada-Alberta Subsidiary Agreement on Northern Development*. [Ottawa]: Department of Regional Industrial Expansion; Alberta Tourism and Small Business, Northern Branch; 1985; [33, 36] p.

1525. Canada. Department of Regional Industrial Expansion; Alberta. Alberta Tourism and Small Business. *Canada-Alberta Subsidiary Agreement on Northern Development between the Government of Canada, presented by the Minister of Regional Industrial Expansion and the Government of the Province of Alberta, represented by the Minister of Tourism and Small Business*. Ottawa: Department of Regional Industrial Expansion; 1985; 33 (36) p.

1526. Canada. Department of Regional Industrial Expansion; Alberta. Department of Federal and Intergovernmental Affairs. *Canada/Alberta Economic and Regional Development Agreement - course of action 1985/86* [Ottawa]: DRIE; 1985.

1527. Canada. Federal-Provincial Relations Office. *A descriptive inventory of federal-provincial programs and activities in operation during fiscal years 1980-81 and 1981-1982.* [Ottawa]: Federal-Provincial Relations Office; 1982; iv, 272 p.

1528. Canada. Federal-Provincial Relations Office. *A descriptive inventory of federal-provincial programs and activities in operation during fiscal year 1982-1983.* [Ottawa]: Federal-Provincial Relations Office; 1983; iii, 295 p.

1529. Canada. Federal-Provincial Relations Office. *A descriptive inventory of federal-provincial programs and activities in operation during fiscal year 1983-1984.* [Ottawa]: Federal-Provincial Relations Office; 1984; iii, 307 p.

1530. Canada. Federal-Provincial Relations Office. *A descriptive inventory of federal-provincial programs and activities in operation during the fiscal year 1984-1985.* [Ottawa]: Federal-Provincial Relations Office; 1985; iii, 308 p.

1531. Canada. Groupe de travail parlementaire sur les accords fiscaux entre le gouvernement fédéral et les provinces. Fédéralisme fiscal au Canada [s.l.]: Groupe de travail parlementaire sur les accords fiscaux entre le gouvernement fédéral et les provinces; 1981.

1532. Canada. House of Commons. Special Committee on the Federal-Provincial Fiscal Arrangements. *Fiscal federalism in Canada (equalization payments, transfers)* Ottawa: Special Committee on the Federal-Provincial Fiscal Arrangements; 1981.

1533. Canada. Minister Responsible for the Status of Women. *Federal-provincial-territorial report on wife battering to the Meeting of Ministers Responsible for the Status of Women*; 1984; Niagara-on-the-Lake. [Ottawa]: [Supply and Services Canada]; c1984; 460 p.

1534. Canada. Ministry of State for Economic and Regional Development. *Canada-Prince Edward Island Economic and Regional Development Agreement - course of action: 1984-85.* [Ottawa]: The Ministry; 1984.

1535. Canada. Ministry of State for Economic and Regional Development. *Canada/New Brunswick Economic and Regional Development Agreement.* [Ottawa]: The Ministry; 1984.

1536. Canada. Ministry of State for Economic and Regional Development. *Canada/Saskatchewan Economic and Regional Development Agreement.* [Ottawa]: The Ministry; 1984.

1537. Canada. National Emergency Planning Establishment. *Release - Conference of Federal and Provincial Ministers, and representatives of Territorial Governments Responsible for Emergency Planning.* [Ottawa]: National Emergency Planning Establishment; 1981.

1538. Canada. Parliament. *An Act to amend the Federal-Provincial Fiscal Arrangements and Established Programs Financing Act, 1977 and to Provide for Payments to Certain Provinces.* Ottawa: Supply and Services Canada; 1982; 15 p.

1539. Canada. Parliament. House of Commons. Special Committee on Federal-Provincial Fiscal Arrangements. *Brief - submitted by the National Indian Brotherhood to the Task Force on Federal-Provincial Fiscal Arrangements.* [Ottawa]: The Committee; 1981.

1540. Canada. Parliament. House of Commons. Special Committee on Federal-Provincial Fiscal Arrangements. *Submission to the Parliamentary Task Force on Federal-Provincial Fiscal Arrangements - Canadian Association for Adult Education.* [Ottawa]: The Task Force; 1981.

1541. Canada. Parliament. House of Commons. Special Committee on Federal-Provincial Fiscal Arrangements. *Submission to the Parliamentary Task Force on Federal-Provincial Fiscal Arrangements - National Council of Welfare.* [Ottawa]: The Task Force; 1981.

1542. Canada. Parliament. House of Commons. Special Committee on Federal-Provincial Fiscal Arrangements. *Submission to the Parliamentary Task Force on Federal-Provincial Arrangements - Canadian Council on Social Development.* [Ottawa]: The Task Force; 1981; 18 [6] p.

1543. Canada. Parliament. House of Commons. Special Committee on Federal-Provincial Fiscal Arrangements. *Submission to the Parliamentary Task Force on Federal-Provincial Fiscal Arrangements by the Canadian Union of Public Employees.* [Ottawa]: The Task Force; 1981.

1544. Canada. Parliament. House of Commons. Special Committee on Federal-Provincial Fiscal Arrangements; Canadian Association of University Teachers. *Funding of Canadian universities: a brief submitted to the Parliamentary Task Force on Federal-Provincial Fiscal Arrangements by the Canadian Association of University Teachers.* [Ottawa]: The Special Committee; 1981.

1545. Canada. Parliament. House of Commons. Special Committee on Federal-Provincial Fiscal Arrangements; Ontario Welfare Council; Committee of Social Planning Councils. *Joint submission to the Parliamentary Task Force on Federal-Provincial Fiscal Arrangements by Ontario Welfare Council - Committee of Social Planning Councils - PROACT.* [Ottawa]: The Committee; 1981.

1546. Canada. Parliament. House of Commons. Special Committee on the Federal-Provincial Fiscal Arrangements. *Federal-provincial fiscal arrangements in the eighties : a submission to the Parliamentary Task Force on the Federal-Provincial Fiscal Arrangements*, by Allan J. MacEachen. Ottawa: Department of Finance; 1981; 89 p.

1547. Canada. Parliament. House of Commons. Special Committee on the Federal-Provincial Fiscal Arrangements. *Fiscal federalism in Canada: report of the Parliamentary Task Force on Federal-Provincial Fiscal Arrangements*, by H. Breau. Ottawa: The Task Force; 1981; xix, 214 p.

1548. Canada. Parliament. House of Commons. Special Committee on the Féderal-Provincial Fiscal Arrangements. *Minutes of proceedings and evidence of the Special Committee on the Federal-Provincial Fiscal Arrangements*, by H. Breau. [Ottawa]: The Committee; 1981.

1549. Canada. Parliament. House of Commons. Special Committee on the Federal-Provincial Fiscal Arrangements. *Submission to the Parliamentary Task Force on Federal-Provincial Fiscal Arrangements presented on behalf of the Government of Manitoba by A. Brian Ransom.* Winnipeg: The Task Force; 1981; 28 [26] p.

1550. Canada. Parliament. House of Commons. Task Force on Federal-Provincial Fiscal Arrangements. *Submission to the Parliamentary Task Force on Federal-Provincial Fiscal Arrangements - Canadian Council on Social Development.* [Ottawa]: The Task Force; 1981.

1551. Canada. Prime Minister. *Text of The Prime Minister's telex to the Provincial Premiers concerning a Federal-Provincial Conference on the Economy.* [Ottawa]: Office of The Prime Minister; 1981.

1552. Canada. Public Works Canada. *The need for and the feasibility of an appeals process in regard to municipal grants-in-lieu of taxes: a report prepared for the Minister of Public Works Canada by I.C. Pollack, R. Gaulin, G. Simpson.* [Ottawa]: Supply and Services Canada; 1983; [324] p. in various pagings.

1553. Canada.; Alberta.; Saskatchewan.; British Columbia. *The Western Accord: an agreement between the governments of Canada, Alberta, Saskatchewan and British Columbia on oil and gas pricing and taxation.* Ottawa: Canada; [1985]; 5 p.

1554. Canada; Alberta. *Canada-Alberta cooperation on native (Indian-Metis) development: memorandum of understanding.* Ottawa: Government of Canada; Government of Alberta; 1985; 9 p.

1555. Canada; Manitoba. *Canada-Manitoba Subsidiary Agreement on Churchill.* [Ottawa]: Government of Canada; [1984]; 26 p.

1556. Canada; Manitoba. *Canada-Manitoba Subsidiary Agreement on Communications and Cultural Enterprises.* [Ottawa]: Government of Canada; [1984]; 22 p.

1557. Canada; Manitoba. *Canada-Manitoba Subsidiary Agreement on Transportation Development.* [Ottawa]: Government of Canada; [1984]; 21 p.

1558. Canada; Manitoba. *Canada-Manitoba Subsidiary Agreement on Urban Bus Industrial Development.* [Ottawa]: Government of Canada; [1984]; 23, (6) p.

1559. Canada; Manitoba. *Canada/Manitoba Northern Development Agreement 1982-87: progress report 1982/83.* [Ottawa]: Government of Canada; 1983; v, 44 p.

1560. Canada; Manitoba. *Canada/Manitoba Northern Development Agreement 1982-87: progress report 1983-84*. [Ottawa]: Government of Canada; 1984; vi, 79 p.

1561. Canada; Manitoba. *Canada/Manitoba Northern Development Agreement: 1982-87: progress report 1984-85*. [Ottawa]: Government of Canada; 1985; vi, 83 p.

1562. Canada; Ontario. *Forest Resource Development Agreement*. [Ottawa]: Government of Canada; [1985]; 34 (35) p.

1563. Canada; Prince Edward Island. *Canada-Prince Edward Island Agreement on Alternative Energy Development*. [Ottawa]: Government of Canada; [1984]; 11, (4) p.

1564. Canada; Prince Edward Island. *Canada-Prince Edward Island Agreement on Transportation Development*. [Ottawa]: Government of Canada; [1984]; 15, (7) p.

1565. Canada; Prince Edward Island. *Canada-Prince Edward Island Economic and Regional Development Agreement*. [Ottawa]: Government of Canada; [1984]; 8 p.

1566. Canada; Prince Edward Island. *Canada-Prince Edward Island Forest Resource Development Agreement*. [Ottawa]: Government of Canada; [1984]; 3 p.

1567. Canada; Prince Edward Island. *Canada-Prince Edward Island Subsidiary Agreement for Planning*. [Ottawa]: Government of Canada; [1984]; 9, (3) p.

1568. Canada; Prince Edward Island. *Canada-Prince Edward Island Subsidiary Agreement on Fisheries Development*. [Ottawa]: Government of Canada; [1984]; 12, (10) p.

1569. Canada; Prince Edward Island. *Canada-Prince Edward Island Subsidiary Agreement on Agri-food Development 1984-1989*. [Ottawa]: Government of Canada; [1984]; 13, 13 p. Note: Agriculture subsidiary agreement backgrounder (3 p.) laid in.

1570. Canadian Intergovernmental Conference Secretariat. *Federal-Provincial First Ministers' Conferences, 1906-1985*. Ottawa: Canadian Intergovernmental Conference Secretariat; 1986; iv, 86 p. [iv, 91 p.].

1571. Canadian Labour Congress. *Proposals for the reform of federal-provincial financial relations*. [Ottawa]: [Canadian Labour Congress]; 1982; 12 p.

1572. Canadian Study of Parliament Group. *Seminar on First Minister's Conferences, held in the Province House, federal-provincial; May 30th, 1981*; Halifax. [Ottawa]: Canadian Study of Parliament Group; 1981.

1573. Carey, William D. Intergovernmental relations: guides to development. In: Wright, Deil S.; White, Harvey L., eds. *Federalism and intergovernmental relations*. Washington: American Society for Public Administration; 1984: 238-244; 33 p.

1574. Carroll, John E. Environmental issues. In: Hero, Alfred O. Jr.; Daneau, Marcel, eds. *Problems and opportunities in U.S.-Quebec relations*. Boulder, CO: Westview Press; 1984: 80-105; xv, 320 p. (Westview special studies in international relations).

1575. Carter, George E. *New directions in financing Canadian federalism*. Canberra: Centre for Research on Federal Financial Relations, Australian National University; 1980; vii, 29 p. (Occasional paper; no. 13).

1576. Centrale de l'Enseignement du Québec. *Ce qui nous interesse, c'est la conquête de la plus grande autonomie possible du peuple québécois face à tous les pouvoirs qui l'oppriment*: mémoire déposé par la CEQ à la commission parlementaire de la présidence du conseil et de la constitution, 21 Janvier 1981. [Sainte-Foy]: Centrale de l'Enseignement du Quebec; 1981; 41 p.

1577. Chaput-Rolland, Solange. La réforme des relations fédérales-provinciales: introduction. *Les Cahiers de droit*; 1985 March; 26(1): 9-13.

1578. Chenoweth, Don. Political parties, provinces and Canadian foreign policy: Trudeau and beyond. *American Review of Canadian Studies*; 1985 Summer; 15(2): 188-204.

1579. Clark, Gordon L. A theory of local autonomy. *Annals of the Association of American Geographers*; 1984; 74: 195-206.

1580. Cleland, Mike. The General Development Agreement and provincial economic development. In: Jamieson, Barbara, ed. *Governing Nova Scotia: policies, priorities, and the 1984-85 budget*. Halifax: School of Public Administration, Dalhousie University; 1984: 163-177; x, 226 p.

1581. Conference of Ministers of Finance and Provincial Treasurers (5th, 1968). *Documents* (Conference of Ministers of Finance and Provincial Treasurers, 5th); November 4-5, 1968; Ottawa: Canadian Intergovernmental Conference Secretariat; 1968; Various pagings.

1582. Conference of New England Governors and eastern Canadian Premiers (1982). *Conference on energy in the 80's* (Conference of New England Governors and eastern Canadian Premiers); April 10-11, 1982; Quebec. [Ottawa]: Canadian Intergovernmental Conference Secretariat; 1986; various pagings.

1583. Conference of Provincial Ministers of Mines (41st, 1984). *Documents* (Forty-first Conference of Provincial Ministers of Mines, 1984); August 8, 1984; Yellowknife. [Ottawa]: Canadian Intergovernmental Conference Secretariat; 1984; various pagings.

1584. Conference of the Council of Ministers Responsible for Transportation and Highway Safety. *Communiqué - transborder-trucking*. [Ottawa]: Canadian Intergovernmental Conference Secretariat; 1982.

1585. Conference of the Council of Provincial and Territorial Attorneys General and Ministers of Justice (1985). *Documents* (Conference of the Council of Provincial and Territorial Attorneys General, 1985); September 19-20, 1985; Regina. [Ottawa]e: Canadian Intergovernmental Conference Secretariat; 1985; various pagings.

1586. Conference of the Provincial Council of Attorneys General and Ministers of Justice (1981). *Documents* (Conference of the Provincial Council of Attorneys General and Ministers of Justice, 1981); October 1-2, 1981; St. John's. [Ottawa]: Canadian Intergovernmental Conference Secretariat; 1981; various pagings.

1587. Conference of the Provincial Council of Attorneys General and Ministers of Justice (1983). *Documents* (Conference of the Provincial Council of Attorneys General and Ministers of Justice, 1983); May 26-27, 1983; Charlottetown. [Ottawa]: Canadian Intergovernmental Conference Secretariat; 1983; various pagings.

1588. Conklin, David W.; Cook, Gail C. A.; Courchene, Thomas J. *Ottawa and the provinces: the distribution of money and power.* Toronto: Ontario Economic Council; 1985.

1589. Council of Maritime Premiers. *Intergovernmental cooperation among the governments of New Brunswick, Nova Scotia and Prince Edward Island.* [Halifax]: Council of Maritime Premiers; 1984.

1590. Council of Ministers Responsible for Transportation and Highway Safety. *Documents* (Council of Ministers Responsible for Transportation and Highway Safety); December 5, 1983; Hull. [Ottawa]: Canadian Intergovernmental Conference Secretariat; 1983; various pagings.

1591. Council of Ministers Responsible for Transportation and Highway Safety. *Notes for remarks by the Hon. Lloyd Axworthy to the 20th conference of the Council of Ministers Responsible for Transportation and Highway Safety; Dec. 3, 1983*; Hull. [Ottawa]: Canadian Intergovernmental Conference Secretariat; 1983.

1592. Courchene, Thomas J. Canada's new equalization program: description and evaluation. *Canadian Public Policy*; 1983 December; 9(4): 458-475.

1593. Courchene, Thomas J. Energy and equalization. In: Ontario Economic Council. *Energy policies for the 1980's: an economic analysis.* Toronto: Ontario Economic Council; 1980; 1: 103-143; 176 p. (Special research report/Ontario Economic Council).

1594. Courchene, Thomas J. Equalization payments in the 1990's. In: Courchene, Thomas J.; Conklin, David W.; Cook, Gail C.A., eds. *Ottawa and the provinces: the distribution of money and power.* Toronto: Ontario Economic Council; 1985; 2: 73-104; 343 p. (Special research report/Ontario Economic Council).

1595. Courchene, Thomas J. *Equalization payments: past, present and future.* Toronto: Ontario Economic Council; 1984; xiii, 433 p. (Federal-provincial relations series).

1596. Courchene, Thomas J. *The evolution of equalization payments: the BNA Act to the Constitution Act, 1982.* Kingston: Institute for Economic Research, Queen's University; 1983; 67 p. (Discussion paper).

1597. Courchene, Thomas J. The fiscal arrangements: focus on 1987. In: Courchene, Thomas J.; Conklin, David W.; Cook, Gail C.A., eds. *Ottawa and the provinces: the distribution of money and power.* Toronto: Ontario Economic Council; 1985; 1: 3-21; xii, 341 p. (Special research report/Ontario Economic Council).

1598. Courchene, Thomas J.; Copplestone, Glen H. Alternative equalization programs: two-tier systems. In: Bird, Richard M., ed. *Fiscal dimensions of Canadian federalism.* Toronto: Canadian Tax Foundation; 1980: 9-45; v, 151 p. (Financing Canadian Federation; v. 4).

1599. Courchene, Thomas J.; Melvin, James R. Energy revenues: consequences for the rest of Canada. *Canadian Public Policy* (supplement); 1980 February; 6: 192-204.

1600. Courchene, Thomas J.; Wildasin, D. *Note on the analytics of the new equalization formula.* Kingston: Queen's University. Institute for Economic Research; 1983. (Queen's University Institute for Economic Research discussion paper; no. 531).

1601. Courchene, Thomas J.; Conklin, D. W.; Cook, Gail A, eds. *Ottawa and the provinces : the distribution of money and power.* Toronto: Ontario Economic Council; c1985; 2 v. (v.1:xii, 341 p.; v.2: 343 p.). (Federal-provincial relations series; Special research report / Ontario Economic Council).

1602. Creighton, Donald G. *British North America at Confederation: a study, prepared for the Royal Commission on Dominion-Provincial Relations.* [Ottawa]: [Supply and Services Canada]; [1981]. Note: Originally published in 1939.

1603. Cullen, A.S.; Jarvis, W.D. *Preview: the 1982 federal-provincial fiscal arrangements negotiations.* Ottawa: Informetrica; 1981; iv, 77 leaves [46] p.

1604. Cumming, Peter. Equitable fiscal federalism: the problems in respect of resources revenue sharing. In: Krasnick, Mark, res. coord. *Fiscal federalism.* Toronto: University of Toronto Press; Royal Commission on the Economic Union and Development Prospects for Canada; 1986: 49-95; xvi, 211 p. (The collected research studies; v. 65).

1605. Cumming, Peter. Federal-provincial fiscal arrangements and the search for fiscal equity through reformulation of the equalization program. In: Courchene, Thomas J.; Conklin, David W.; Cook, Gail C.A., eds. *Ottawa and the provinces: the distribution of money and power.* Toronto: Ontario Economic Council; 1985; 1: 96-136; xii, 341 p. (Special research report/Ontario Economic Council).

1606. Datla, Abbijit. *State-municipal fiscal relations: a comparative study of Australia and India.* Canberra: Centre for Research on Federal Financial Relations, Australian National University; 1982; x, 70 p. (Research monograph; no. 37).

1607. Davenport, Paul. *The Constitution and the sharing of wealth in Canada.* Law and Contemporary Problems; 1982 Autumn; 45(4): 109-147.

1608. Davis, William G. *Perspectives on institutions of Canadian federalism* (25th Annual Premiers' Conference); 1984; Charlottetown. Toronto: Ontario Premier; 1984; 11 p.

1609. Dean, James M. The appropriate fiscal transfer to the Northwest Territories: a structure. *Canadian Public Policy*; 1981 Summer; 7(3): 408-417.

1610. Dean, James M. The interaction of federal and territorial income tax rates: the case of the Northwest Territories. *Canadian Journal of Regional Science*; 1981 Autumn; 4(2): 243-259.

1611. deBellefeuille, Pierre. Les relations fédérales-provinciales. *L'Action nationale*; 1985 March; 74(7): 685-688.

1612. Denton, Frank T.; Spencer, Byron G. Prospective changes in population and their implications for government expenditures. In: Courchene, Thomas J.; Conklin, David W.; Cook, Gail C.A., eds. *Ottawa and the provinces: the distribution of money and power.* Toronto: Ontario Economic Council; 1985; 1: 44-95; xii, 341 p. (Special research report/Ontario Economic Council).

1613. Deutsch, Antal. The rationale for equalization payments. *Canadian Taxation*; 1981 Spring; 3(1): 34-37.

1614. Deutsch, Antal. Three fiscal irritants in Confederation. *Canadian Public Policy*; 1981 Spring; 7(2): 343-347.

1615. Divay, Gérard. Le développement d'initiative locale. Canadian Public Administration; 1980 Summer; 23(2): 236-251.

1616. Dobell, A. R. Financing Confederation: politics and process. *Canadian Public Policy*; 1982 Summer; 8(3): 303-07.

1617. Dobell, Rodney. The consultation process: prospects for 1987 and beyond. In: Courchene, Thomas J.; Conklin, David W.; Cook, Gail C.A., eds. *Ottawa and the provinces: the distribution of money and power.* Toronto: Ontario Economic Council; 1985; 2: 144-161; 343 p. (Special research report/Ontario Economic Council).

1618. Dolan, Michael B.; Tomlin, Brian W.; VonRiekhoff, Harald. Integration and autonomy in Canada-United States relations, 1963-1972. *Canadian Journal of Political Science*; 1982 June; 15(2): 331-363.

1619. Dowd, Kevin; Sayeed, Adil. Federal-provincial fiscal relations: some background. In: Courchene, Thomas J.; Conklin, David W.; Cook, Gail C.A., eds. *Ottawa and the provinces: the distribution of money and power.* Toronto: Ontario Economic Council; 1985; 2: 253-275; 343 p. (Special research report/Ontario Economic Council).

1620. Duchacek, Ivo D. The international dimension of subnational self-government. *Publius*; 1984 Fall; 14(4): 5-31.

1621. Duhamel, Roger. De Paris à Varsovie sans oublier Ottawa. L'Action nationale; 1982 February; 71(6): 639-649.

1622. Dunn, Sheilagh M. *The year in review, 1981: intergovernmental relations in Canada*. Kingston: Institute of Intergovernmental Relations, Queen's University; c1982; x, 228 p.

1623. Dunn, Sheilagh M. *The year in review, 1982: intergovernmental relations in Canada*. Kingston: Institute of Intergovernmental Relations, Queen's University; c1982; v, 189 p.

1624. Dupré, J. Stefan. Intergovernmental relations and the metropolitan area. In: Feldman, Lionel D., ed. *Politics and government in urban Canada*. 4th ed. Toronto: Methuen; 1981: 151-161; xii, 451 p.

1625. Dupré, J. Stephan. Reflections on the fiscal and economic aspects of government by conference. *Canadian Public Administration*; 1980 Spring; 23(1): 54-59.

1626. Economic Council of Canada. *Financing Confederation: today and tomorrow*. [Ottawa]: Economic Council of Canada; 1982; viii, 182 p.

1627. Economic Council of Canada. *Financing Confederation today and tomorrow: summary and conclusions*. [Ottawa]: [Economic Council of Canada]; 1982; (vii), 58 p.

1628. Elazar, Daniel J. Fiscal questions and political answers in intergovernmental finance. In: Wright, Deil S.; White, Harvey L., eds. *Federalism and intergovernmental relations*. Washington: The American Society for Public Administration; c1984: 158-170. (PAR Classics).

1629. Emerson, David, L. The tightrope of fiscal federalism. *Canadian Business Review*; 1981 Winter; 8(4): 37-45.

1630. Federal-Provincial Conference of Communications Ministers. *Report* (Federal-Provincial Conference of Ministers of Communications, 1981); September 1981; Winnipeg. [Ottawa]: Canadian Intergovernmental Conference Secretariat; 1981.

1631. Federal-Provincial Conference of Deputy Ministers Responsible for Criminal Justice. *Documents* (Federal-Provincial Conference of Ministers Responsible for Criminal Justice, 1981); June 22-23, 1981; Mont Sainte-Anne. [Ottawa]: Canadian Intergovernmental Conference Secretariat; various pagings.

1632. Federal-Provincial Conference of First Ministers on Aboriginal Constitutional Matters. *Opening remarks for presentation by Dr. David Ahenakew, national chief, Assembly of First Nations* (First Ministers' Conference on Aboriginal Constitutional Matters, 1983); March 15, 1983; Ottawa. [Ottawa]: Canadian Intergovernmental Conference Secretariat; 1983.

1633. Federal-Provincial Conference of First Ministers Conference on Aboriginal Constitutional Matters. *Proposals for amendments and additions to the Constitution Act, 1982 presented by: Dr. David Ahenakew, national chief, on behalf of the Assembly of First Nations* (First Ministers' Conference of Aboriginal Constitutional Matters, 1983); March 1983; Ottawa. [Ottawa]: Canadian Intergovernmental Conference Secretariat; 1983.

1634. Federal-Provincial Conference of First Ministers on Aboriginal Constitutional Matters. *Documents* (Federal-provincial Conference of First Ministers on Aboriginal Constitutional Matters, 1983); March 15-16, 1983; Ottawa. [Ottawa]: Canadian Intergovernmental Conference Secretariat; 1983; 3 v; various pagings.

1635. Federal-Provincial Conference of First Ministers on Aboriginal Constitutional Matters. *Framework agreement concerning charter of aboriginal rights - Province of Manitoba;* March 1983; Ottawa. [Ottawa]: Canadian Intergovernmental Conference Secretariat; 1983.

1636. Federal-Provincial Conference of First Ministers on Aboriginal Constitutional Matters. *Notes for an opening statement by the Honourable Howard R. Pawley, premier of Manitoba* (First Ministers' Conference on Aboriginal Constitutional Matters, 1983); March 1983; Ottawa. [Ottawa]: Canadian Intergovernmental Conference Secretariat; 1983.

1637. Federal-Provincial Conference of First Ministers on Aboriginal Constitutional Matters. *Notes for a statement on aboriginal rights by the Honourable James M. Lee, P.C., Premier of Prince Edward Island* (First Ministers' Conference on Aboriginal Constitutional Matters, 1983); March 1983; Ottawa. [Ottawa]: Canadian Intergovernmental Conference Secretariat; 1983.

1638. Federal-Provincial Conference of First Ministers on Aboriginal Constitutional Matters. *Opening statement, Native Council of Canada* (Federal-Provincial Conference of First Ministers on Aboriginal Constitutional Matters, 1983); March 1983; Ottawa. [Ottawa]: Canadian Intergovernmental Conference Secretariat; 1983.

1639. Federal-Provincial Conference of First Ministers on Aboriginal Constitutional Matters. *Opening statement by the Honourable Edmund L. Morris, M.L.A. Minister Responsible for Native Affairs, Nova Scotia* (First Ministers' Conference on Aborioginal Constitutional Matters, 1983); March 1983; Ottawa. [Ottawa]: Canadian Intergovernmental Conference Secretariat; 1983.

1640. Federal-Provincial Conference of First Ministers on Aboriginal Constitutional Matters. *Opening statement by Quebec Premier Rene Levesque* (First Ministers' Conference on Aboriginal Constitutional Matters, 1983); March 1983; Ottawa. [Ottawa]: Canadian Intergovernmental Conference Secretariat; 1983.

1641. Federal-Provincial Conference of First Ministers on Aboriginal Constitutional Matters. *Opening remarks by the Hon. Grant Devine, Saskatchewan* (First

Ministers' Conference on Aboriginal Constitutional Matters, 1983); March 1983; Ottawa. [Ottawa]: Canadian Intergovernmental Conference Secretariat; 1983.

1642. Federal-Provincial Conference of First Ministers on Aboriginal Constitutional Matters. *Opening statement by the Prime Minister of Canada, the Rt. Honourable Pierre Elliott Trudeau* (First Ministers' Conference on Aboriginal Constitutional Matters, 1983); March 15, 1983; Ottawa. [Ottawa]: Canadian Intergovernmental Conference Secretariat; 1983.

1643. Federal-Provincial Conference of First Ministers on Aboriginal Constitutional Matters. *Opening statement by the Honourable William G. Davis, Premier of Ontario* (First Ministers' Conference on Aboriginal Constitutional Matters, 1983); March 15, 1983; Ottawa. [Ottawa]: Canadian Intergovernmental Conference Secrtariat; 1983.

1644. Federal-Provincial Conference of First Ministers on Aboriginal Constitutional Matters. *Quebec's answers to proposals by the aboriginal peoples, Quebec* (First Ministers' Conference on Aboriginal Constitutional Matters, 1983); March 1983; Ottawa. [Ottawa]: Canadian Intergovernmental Conference Secretariat; 1983.

1645. Federal-Provincial Conference of First Ministers on Aboriginal Constitutional Matters. *Statement of principles - Province of Manitoba* (First Ministers'- Conference on Aboriginal Constitutional Issues, 1983); March 1983; Ottawa. [Ottawa]: Canadian Intergovernmental Conference Secretariat; 1983.

1646. Federal-Provincial Conference of First Ministers on Aboriginal Constitutional Matters. *Verbatim transcript - unverified and unoffical* (Federal-Provincial Conference of First Ministers on Aboriginal Constitutional Matters, 1983); March 15-16, 1983; Ottawa. [Ottawa]: Canadian Intergovernmental Conference Secretariat; 1983.

1647. Federal-Provincial Conference of First Ministers on Aboriginal Constitutional Matters. *Draft amendment to section 35(4) - Native Council of Canada* (First Ministers' Conference on Aboriginal Constitutional Matters, 1984); March 8-9, 1984; Ottawa. [Ottawa]: Canadian Intergovernmental Conference Secretariat; 1984.

1648. Federal-Provincial Conference of First Ministers on Aboriginal Constitutional Matters. *Equality rights - federal government* (First Ministers' Conference on Aboriginal Constitutional Matters); March 8-9, 1984; Ottawa. [Ottawa]: Canadian Intergovernmental Conference Secretariat; 1984.

1649. Federal-Provincial Conference of First Ministers on Aboriginal Constitutional Matters. *Equality rights - alternate wording for section 35 Nova Scotia proposal* (First Ministers' Conference on Aboriginal Constitutional Matters, 1984); March 8-9, 1984; Ottawa. [Ottawa]: Canadian Intergovernmental Conference Secretariat; 1984.

1650. Federal-Provincial Conference of First Ministers on Aboriginal Constitutional Matters. *Métis National Council draft constitutional accords on Métis self-identification and enumeration* (First Ministers' Conference on Aboriginal Constitutional Matters, 1984); March 8-9, 1984; Ottawa. [Ottawa]: Canadian Intergovernmental Conference Secretariat; 1984.

1651. Federal-Provincial Conference of First Ministers on Aboriginal Constitutional Matters. *Native women of Quebec: declaration by Mrs. Bibiane Courtois* (First Ministers' Conference on Aboriginal Constitutional Matters, 1984); March 8-9, 1984; Ottawa. [Ottawa]: Canadian Intergovernmental Conference Secretariat; 1984.

1652. Federal-Provincial Conference of First Ministers on Aboriginal Constitutional Matters. *Opening statement - the Hon. C.W. Pearson, Yukon* (First Ministers' Conference on Aboriginal Constitutional Matters, 1984); March 8-9, 1984; Ottawa. [Ottawa]: Canadian Intergovernmental Conference Secretariat; 1984.

1653. Federal-Provincial Conference of First Ministers on Aboriginal Constitutional Matters. *Opening statement of Premier Richard Hatfield* (First Ministers Conference on Aboriginal Constitutional Matters, 1984); March 8-9, 1984; Ottawa. [Ottawa]: Canadian Intergovernmental Conference Secretariat; 1984.

1654. Federal-Provincial Conference of First Ministers on Aboriginal Constitutional Matters. *Opening statement of Premier Peter Lougheed* (First Ministers Conference on Aboriginal Constitutional Matters, 1984); March 8-9, 1984; Ottawa. [Ottawa]: Canadian Intergovernmental Conference Secretariat; 1984.

1655. Federal-Provincial Conference of First Ministers on Aboriginal Constitutional Matters. *Opening statement by the Prime Minister of Canada the Right Honourable Pierre Elliot Trudeau* (First Ministers Conference on Aboriginal Constitutional Matters, 1984); March 8, 1984; Ottawa. [Ottawa]: Canadian Intergovernmental Conference Secretariat; 1984.

1656. Federal-Provincial Conference of First Ministers on Aboriginal Constitutional Matters. *Opening statement by the Honourable William G. Davis, Premier of Ontario* (First Ministers'Conference on Aboriginal Constitutional Matters, 1984); March 8-9, 1984; Ottawa. [Ottawa]: Canadian Intergovernmental Conference Secretariat; 1984.

1657. Federal-Provincial Conference of First Ministers on Aboriginal Constitutional Matters. *Opening statement by the Honourable A. Brian Peckford, Premier of Newfoundland* (First Ministers' Conference on Aboriginal Constitutional Matters, 1984); March 8-9, 1984; Ottawa. [Ottawa]: Canadian Intergovernmental Conference Secretariat; 1984.

1658. Federal-Provincial Conference of First Ministers on Aboriginal Constitutional Matters. *Opening statement by the Hon. William R. Bennett, Premier of British Columbia* (First Ministers' Conference on Aboriginal Constitutional Matters,

1984); March 8-9, 1984; Ottawa. [Ottawa]: Canadian Intergovernmental Conference Secretariat; 1984.

1659. Federal-Provincial Conference of First Ministers on Aboriginal Constitutional Matters. *Opening statement by the Hon. Rene Levesque* (First Ministers Conference on Aboriginal Constitutional Matters, 1984); March 8-9, 1984; Ottawa. [Ottawa]: Canadian Intergovernmental Conference Secretariat; 1984.

1660. Federal-Provincial Conference of First Ministers on Aboriginal Constitutional Matters. *Opening statement by Louis Bruyere, president, Harry W. Daniels, vice president, Native Council of Canada* (First Ministers' Conference on Aboriginal Constitutional Matters, 1984); March 8-9, 1984; Ottawa. [Ottawa]: Canadian Intergovernmental Conference Secretariat; 1984.

1661. Federal-Provincial Conference of First Ministers on Aboriginal Constitutional Matters. *Opening remarks - I.C.N.I* (Inuit Committee on National Issues) (First Ministers' Conference on Aboriginal Constitutional Matters, 1984); March 8-9, 1984; Ottawa. [Ottawa]: Canadian Intergovernmental Conference Secretariat; 1984.

1662. Federal-Provincial Conference of First Ministers on Aboriginal Constitutional Matters. *Opening remarks for presentation by Dr. David Ahenakew, national chief, Assembly of First Nations* (First Ministers' Conference on Aboriginal Constitutional Matters, 1984); March 8-9, 1984; Ottawa. [Ottawa]: Canadian Intergovernmental Conference Secretariat; 1984.

1663. Federal-Provincial Conference of First Ministers on Aboriginal Constitutional Matters. *Opening remarks by the Hon. Grant Devine - Saskatchewan* (First Ministers' Conference on Aboriginal Constitutional Matters, 1984); March 8-9, 1984; Ottawa. [Ottawa]: Canadian Intergovernmental Conference Secretariat; 1984.

1664. Federal-Provincial Conference of First Ministers on Aboriginal Constitutional Matters. *Opening remarks - Metis National Council* (First Ministers' Conference on Aboriginal Constitutional Matters, 1984); March 8-9, 1984; Ottawa. [Ottawa]: Canadian Intergovernmental Conference Secretariat; 1984.

1665. Federal-Provincial Conference of First Ministers on Aboriginal Constitutional Matters. *Proposal of the Government of Canada for the review of social, cultural and economic programs and services to the regional peoples of Canada tabled by the Prime Minister of Canada* (First Ministers' Conference on Aboriginal Constitutional Matters, 1984); March 8-9, 1984; Ottawa. [Ottawa]: Canadian Intergovernmental Conference Secretariat; 1984.

1666. Federal-Provincial Conference of First Ministers on Aboriginal Constitutional Matters. *Proposed 1984 Constitutional Accord on the rights of the aboriginal peoples of Canada* (tabled by the Prime Minister of Canada) (First Ministers' Conference on Aboriginal Constitutional Matters, 1984); March 8-9, 1984; Ottawa. [Ottawa]: Canadian Intergovernmental Conference Secretariat; 1984.

1667. Federal-Provincial Conference of First Ministers on Aboriginal Constitutional Matters. *Proposed 1984 constitutional accord on the rights of the aboriginal peoples of Canada - Assembly of First Nations, Inuit Committee on National Issues, Native Council of Canada* (First Ministers' Conference on Aboriginal Constitutional Matters, 1984); March 8-9, 1984; Ottawa. [Ottawa]: Canadian Intergovernmental Conference Secretariat; 1984.

1668. Federal-Provincial Conference of First Ministers on Aboriginal Constitutional Matters. *Documents* (Federal-Provincial Conference of First Ministers on Aboriginal Constitutional Matters, 1984); March 8-9, 1984; Ottawa. [Ottawa]: Canadian Intergovernmental Conference Secretariat; 1984.

1669. Federal-Provincial Conference of First Ministers on Aboriginal Constitutional Matters. *Verbatim transcript - unrevised and unofficial* (First Ministers' Conference on Aboriginal Constitutional Matters, 1985); April 2-3, 1985; Ottawa. [Ottawa]: Canadian Intergovernmental Conference Secretariat; 1985.

1670. Federal-Provincial Conference of First Ministers on Aboriginal Constitutional Matters (1983). *Agenda item: Charter of Rights of First Nations - sub item: equality.* Federal-Provincial Conference of First Ministers on Aboriginal Constitutional Matters (1983); 1983; Ottawa. [Ottawa]: Canadian Intergovernmental Conference Secretariat; 1983.

1671. Federal-Provincial Conference of First Ministers on Aboriginal Constitutional Matters (1983). *Conférence des premiers ministres sur les questions constitutionnelles intéressant les Autochtones, 1983: déclaration de Max Gros-Louis, grand chef des Hurons*; 1983; Ottawa. [Ottawa]: Canadian Intergovernmental Conference Secretariat; 1983.

1672. Federal-Provincial Conference of First Ministers on Aboriginal Constitutional Matters (1983). *Constitutional position of the Blood tribe* (Federal-Provincial Conference of First Ministers on Aboriginal Constitutional Matters, 1983); 1983; Ottawa. [Ottawa]: Canadian Intergovernmental Conference Secretariat; 1983. (Federal-provincial conference of first ministers on aboriginal constitutional matters 1983 document 800; v. 17-035).

1673. Federal-Provincial Conference of First Ministers on Aboriginal Constitutional Matters (1983). *Manitoba Metis rights position paper* (Federal-Provincial Conference of First Ministers on Aboriginal Constitutional Matters ,1983); 1983; Ottawa. [Ottawa]: Canadian Intergovernmental Conference Secretariat; 1983. (Federal-provincial conference of first ministers on aboriginal constitutional matters 1983 document 800).

1674. Federal-Provincial Conference of First Ministers on Aboriginal Constitutional Matters (1983). *Opening remarks ... by Dr. David Ahenakew, national chief, Assembly of First Nations* (Federal-Provincial Conference of First Ministers on Aboriginal Constitutional Matters, 1983); 1983; Ottawa. [Ottawa]: Canadian Intergovernmental Conference Secretariat; 1983.

1675. Federal-Provincial Conference of First Ministers on Aboriginal Constitutional Matters (1983). *Presentation of the Indian nations of Hobbema to the S.37(1) conference on aboriginal and treaty rights* (Federal-Provincial Conference of First Ministers on Aboriginal Constitutional Matters, 1983); 1983; Ottawa. [Ottawa]: Canadian Intergovernmental Conference Secretariat; 1983.

1676. Federal-Provincial Conference of First Ministers on Aboriginal Constitutional Matters (1983). *Proposals for amendments and additions to the Constitution Act, 1982, by D. Ahenakew* (Federal-Provincial Conference of First Ministers on Aboriginal Constitutional Matters, 1983); 1983; Ottawa. [Ottawa]: Canadian Intergovernmental Conference Secretariat; 1983.

1677. Federal-Provincial Conference of First Ministers on Aboriginal Constitutional Matters (1983). *Statement by Sandra Lovelace on behalf of the Indian women of New Brunswick* (Federal-Provincial Conference of First Ministers on Aboriginal Constitutional Matters, 1983); 1983; Ottawa. [Ottawa]: Canadian Intergovernmental Conference Secretariat; 1983.

1678. Federal-Provincial Conference of First Ministers on Aboriginal Constitutional Matters (1984). *Documents* (Federal-Provincial Conference of First Ministers on Aboriginal Constitutional Matters, 1984); March 8-9, 1984; Ottawa. [Ottawa]: Canadian Intergovernmental Conference Secretariat; various pagings.

1679. Federal-Provincial Conference of First Ministers on Aboriginal Constitutional Matters (1984). *Verbatim transcript - unverified and unofficial* (Federal-Provincial Conference of First Ministers on Aboriginal Constitutional Matters, 1984); March 8-9, 1984; Ottawa. [Ottawa]: Canadian Intergovernmental Conference Secretariat; 1984.

1680. Federal-Provincial Conference of First Ministers on Aboriginal Constitutional Matters (1985). *Documents* (Federal-Provincial Conference of First Ministers on Aboriginal Constitutional Matters, 1985); April 2-3, 1985; Ottawa. [Ottawa]: Canadian Intergovernmental Conference Secretariat; 1985.

1681. Federal-Provincial Conference of First Ministers on the Constitution. *Documents* (Federal-provincial Conference of First Ministers on the Constitution, 1980); Sept. 8-13, 1980; Ottawa. [Ottawa]: Canadian Intergovernmental Conference Secretariat; 1980; various pagings.

1682. Federal-Provincial Conference of First Ministers on the Constitution. *Verbatim transcript - unverified and unofficial* (Federal-Provincial Conference of First Ministers on the Constitution, 1980); Sept. 8-13, 1980; Ottawa. [Ottawa]: Canadian Intergovernmental Conference Secretariat; 1980; 2 v.

1683. Federal-Provincial Conference of First Ministers on the Constitution. *Documents* (Federal-Provincial Conference of First Ministers on the Constitution, 1981); Nov. 2-5, 1981; Ottawa. [Ottawa]: Canadian Intergovernmental Conference Secretariat; 1981; various pagings.

1684. Federal-Provincial Conference of First Ministers on the Constitution. *Verbatim transcript - unverified and unofficial* (Federal-Provincial Conference of First Ministers on the Constitution, 1981); Nov. 2-5, 1981; Ottawa. [Ottawa]: Canadian Intergovernmental Conference Secretariat; 1981.

1685. Federal-Provincial Conference of First Ministers on the Constitution (1980). *Revised discussion draft of September 3, 1980, the Canadian Charter of Rights and Freedoms* (Federal-Provincial Conference of First Ministers on the Constitution, 1980); 1980; Ottawa. Ottawa: Canadian Intergovernmental Conference Secretariat; 1980; 9 p.

1686. Federal-Provincial Conference of First Ministers on the Economy. *Brief review of free expenditures in Newfoundland and proposals currently pending - the Honourable A. Brian Peckford* (Federal-Provincial Conference of First Ministers on the Economy, 1982); February 2-4, 1982; Ottawa. [Ottawa]: Canadian Intergovernmental Conference Secretariat; 1982.

1687. Federal-Provincial Conference of First Ministers on the Economy. *Comments by Premier John M. Buchanan, Nova Scotia* (Federal-Provincial Conference of First Ministers on the Economy, 1982); February 2-4, 1982; Ottawa. [Ottawa]: Canadian Intergovernmental Conference Secretariat; 1982.

1688. Federal-Provincial Conference of First Ministers on the Economy. *Development of the economy* (Federal-Provincial Conference of First Ministers on the Economy, 1982); February 2-4, 1982; Ottawa. [Ottawa]: Canadian Intergovernmental Conference Secretariat; 1982.

1689. Federal-Provincial Conference of First Ministers on the Economy. *Documents* (Federal-Provincial Conference of First Ministers on the Economy, 1982); February 2-4, 1982; Ottawa. [Ottawa]: Canadian Intergovernmental Conference Secretariat; 1982; various pagings.

1690. Federal-Provincial Conference of First Ministers on the Economy. *Documents* (Federal-Provincial Conference of First Ministers on the Economy); February 2-4, 1982; Ottawa. [Ottawa]: Canadian Intergovernmental Conference Secretariat; 1982.

1691. Federal-Provincial Conference of First Ministers on the Economy. *Equalization proposal "a viable option," Saskatchewan* (Federal-Provincial Conference of First Ministers on the Economy, 1982); February 2-4, 1982; Ottawa. [Ottawa]: Canadian Intergovernmental Conference Secretariat; 1982.

1692. Federal-Provincial Conference of First Ministers on the Economy. *Gouvernement du Québec: research and development* (Federal-Provincial Conference of First Ministers on the Economy, 1982; Ottawa; February 2-4, 1982. [Ottawa]: Canadian Intergovernmental Conference Secrtariat; 1982.

1693. Federal-Provincial Conference of First Ministers on the Economy. *Gouvernement du Québec: summary of Quebec's position* (Federal-Provincial Conference of First Ministers on the Economy, 1982); February 2-4, 1982; Ottawa. [Ottawa]: Canadian Intergovernmental Conference Secretariat; 1982.

1694. Federal-Provincial Conference of First Ministers on the Economy. *Gouvernement du Québec: regional development* (Federal-Provincial Conference of First Ministers on the Economy, 1982); February 2-4, 1982; Ottawa. [Ottawa]: Canadian Intergovernmental Conference Secretariat; 1982.

1695. Federal-Provincial Conference of First Ministers on the Economy. *Gouvernement du Québec: management of the economy* (Federal-Provincial Conference of First Ministers on the Economy, 1982); February 2-4, 1982; Ottawa. [Ottawa]: Canadian Intergovernmental Conference Secretariat; 1982.

1696. Federal-Provincial Conference of First Ministers on the Economy. *Gouvernement du Québec: human resources* (Federal-Provincial Conference of First Ministers on the Economy, 1982); February 2-4, 1982; Ottawa. [Ottawa]: Canadian Intergovernmental Conference Secretariat; 1982.

1697. Federal-Provincial Conference of First Ministers on the Economy. *Gouvernement du Québec: fiscal arrangements* (Federal-Provincial conference of First Ministers on the Economy, 1982); February 2-4, 1982; Ottawa. [Ottawa]: Canadian Intergovernmental Conference Secretariat; 1982.

1698. Federal-Provincial Conference of First Ministers on the Economy. *Gouvernement du Québec: economic development* (Federal-Provincial Conference of First Ministers on the Economy, 1982); February 2-4, 1982; Ottawa. [Ottawa]: Canadian Intergovernmental Conference Secretariat; 1982.

1699. Federal-Provincial Conference of First Ministers on the Economy [loose leaf]. *Highlights: British Columbia position on transportation and Canadian economic development* (Federal-Provincial Conference of First Ministers on the Economy, 1982); February 1982; Ottawa. [s.l.]: The Conference; 1982.

1700. Federal-Provincial Conference of First Ministers on the Economy. *Joint provincial statement on fiscal arrangements* (Federal-Provincial Conference of First Ministers on the Economy, 1982); February 2-4, 1982; Ottawa. [Ottawa]: Canadian Intergovernmental Conference Secretariat; 1982.

1701. Federal-Provincial Conference of First Ministers on the Economy. *Notes for a closing statement by the Honourable William R. Bennett, Premier of British Columbia* (Federal-Provincial Conference of First Ministers on the Economy, 1982); February 1982; Ottawa. [Ottawa]: Canadian Intergovernmental Conference Secretariat; 1982.

1702. Federal-Provincial Conference of First Ministers on the Economy. *Notes for opening remarks by Premier Lougheed, Alberta* (Federal-Provincial Conference of First Ministers on the Economy, 1982); February 2-4, 1982; Ottawa. [Ottawa]: Canadian Intergovernmental Conference Secretariat; 1982.

1703. Federal-Provincial Conference of First Ministers on the Economy. *Notes for an opening statement by the Right Honourable P.E. Trudeau, Prime Minister of Canada* (Federal-Provincial Conference of First Minsiters on the Economy, 1982); February 2-4, 1982; Ottawa. [Ottawa]: Canadian Intergovernmental Conference Secretariat; 1982.

1704. Federal-Provincial Conference of First Ministers on the Economy. *Notes for an opening statement by the Honourable Howard Pawley, Premier of Manitoba* (Federal-Provincial Conference of Ministers on the Economy, 1982); February 2-4, 1982; Ottawa. [Ottawa]: Canadian Intergovernmental Conference Secretariat; 1982.

1705. Federal-Provincial Conference of First Ministers on the Economy. *Notes for an opening statement by Premier Allan Blakeney of Saskatchewan* (Federal-Provincial Conference of First Minsiters on the Economy, 1982); February 2-4, 1982; Ottawa. [Ottawa]: Canadian Intergovernmental Conference Secretariat; 1982.

1706. Federal-Provincial Conference of First Ministers on the Economy. *Notes for a statement by the Hon. William R. Bennett, Premier of British Columbia* (Federal-Provincial Conference of First Ministers on the Economy, 1982); February 2-4, 1982; Ottawa. [Ottawa]: Canadian Intergovernmental Conference Secretariat; 1982.

1707. Federal-Provincial Conference of First Ministers on the Economy. *Notes on transportation and Canadian economic development - the Honourable William R. Bennett, Premier of British Columbia* (Federal-Provincial Conference of First Ministers on the Economy, 1982); February 2-4, 1982; Ottawa. [Ottawa]: Canadian Inergovernmental Conference Secretariat; 1982.

1708. Federal-Provincial Conference of First Ministers on the Economy. *Opening statement by the Honourable William G. Davis, Premier of Ontario* (Federal-Provincial Conference of First Ministers on the Economy, 1982); February 2-4, 1982; Ottawa. [Ottawa]: Canadian Intergovernmental Conference Secretariat; 1982.

1709. Federal-Provincial Conference of First Ministers on the Economy. *Opening statement by the Honourable James M. Lee, Premier of Prince Edward Island* (Federal-Provincial Conference of First Ministers on the Economy, 1982); February 2-4, 1982; Ottawa. [Ottawa]: Canadian Intergovernmental Conference Secretariat; 1982.

1710. Federal-Provincial Conference of First Ministers on the Economy. *Opening statement by the Honourable A. Brian Peckford, Premier of Newfoundland* (Federal-Provincial Conference of First Ministers on the Economy, 1982); February 2-4, 1982; Ottawa. [Ottawa]: Canadian Intergovernmental Conference Secretariat; 1982.

1711. Federal-Provincial Conference of First Ministers on the Economy. *Opening remarks by Mr. Rene Levesque, Prime Minister of Quebec* (Federal-provincial Conference of First Ministers on the Economy, 1982); February 2-4, 1982; Ottawa. [Ottawa]: Canadian Intergovernmental Conference Secretariat; 1982.

1712. Federal-Provincial Conference of First Ministers on the Economy. *Prime Minister's statement for revised federal proposal on EPF* (Federal-Provincial Conference of First Ministers on the Economy, 1982); February 2-4, 1982; Ottawa. [Ottawa]: Canadian Intergovernmental Conference Secretariat; 1982.

1713. Federal-Provincial Conference of First Ministers on the Economy. *Public investment in Canada - a background paper, Saskatchewan* (Federal-Provincial Conference of First Ministers on the Economy, 1982); February 2-4, 1982; Ottawa. [Ottawa]: Canadian Intergovernmental Conference Secretariat; 1982.

1714. Federal-Provincial Conference of First Ministers on the Economy. *Quebec proposal* (Federal-Provincial Conference of First Ministers on the Economy, 1982); February 2-4, 1982; Ottawa. [Ottawa]: Canadian Intergovernmental Conference Secretariat; 1982.

1715. Federal-Provincial Conference of First Ministers on the Economy. *Regional development - background papers;* 1982; Ottawa. [Ottawa]: Canadian Intergovernmental Conference Secretariat; 1982.

1716. Federal-Provincial Conference of First Ministers on the Economy. *The relative size of the provincial government sector 1977/1978-1981/1982*, British Columbia; February 2-4, 1982; Ottawa. [Ottawa]: Canadian Intergovernmental Conference Secretariat; 1982.

1717. Federal-Provincial Conference of First Ministers on the Economy. *The road out of recession - highlights of Saskatchewan's alternative economic policy for Canadians;* February 2-4, 1982; Ottawa. [Ottawa]: Canadian Intergovernmental Conference Secretariat; 1982.

1718. Federal-Provincial Conference of First Ministers on the Economy. *Text of opening remarks by Premier Hatfield (in language spoken), New Brunswick* (Federal-Provincial Conference of First Ministers on the Economy, 1982); February 2-4, 1982; Ottawa. [Ottawa]: Canadian Intergovernmental Conference Secretariat; 1982.

1719. Federal-Provincial Conference of First Ministers on the Economy. *Transcript of the Prime Minister's closing statement at the final session of the First Ministers' Conference on the Economy* (1982); February 2-4, 1982; Ottawa. [Ottawa]: Canadian Intergovernmental Conference Secretariat; 1982.

1720. Federal-Provincial Conference of First Ministers on the Economy (1982). *Verbatim report* (Federal-Provincial Conference of First Ministers on the Economy, 1982); February 4, 1982; Ottawa. [Ottawa]: Canadian Intergovernmental Conference Secretariat; 1982; 107 p.

1721. Federal-Provincial Conference of First Ministers on the Economy (1985). *Documents* (Federal-Provincial Conference of First Ministers on the Economy,

1985); February 14-15, 1985; Regina. [Ottawa]: Canadian Intergovernmental Conference Secretariat; 1985; various pagings.

1722. Federal-Provincial Conference of First Ministers on the Economy (1985) [boxed set]. *Documents* (Federal-Provincial Conference of First Ministers on the Economy, 1985); November 28-29, 1985; Halifax. [Ottawa]: Canadian Intergovernmental Conference Secretariat; 1985; various pagings.

1723. Federal-Provincial Conference of First Ministers on the Economy (1985). *Manitoba position paper on : the state of federal-provincial relations* (Federal-Provincial Conference of First Ministers on the Economy, 1985); 1985; Halifax. [Winnipeg]: Manitoba; 1985; various pagings.

1724. Federal-Provincial Conference of First Ministers on the Economy (1985). *A plan to encourage equity investment by individual Canadians : a proposal by the Government of British Columbia* (Federal-Provincial Conference of First Ministers on the Economy, 1985); 1985; Regina. Victoria: Province of British Columbia; 1985; 2 p.

1725. Federal-Provincial Conference of First Ministers on the Economy (1985). *Verbatim transcript* (Federal-Provincial Conference of First Ministers on the Economy, 1985); February 14-15, 1985; Regina. [Ottawa]: Canadian Intergovernmental Conference Secretariat; 1985; 401 p.

1726. Federal-Provincial Conference of Mines Ministers (1985). *Documents* (Federal-Provincial Conference of Mines Ministers, 1985); May 27, 1985; Ottawa. [Ottawa]: Canadian Intergovernmental Conference Secretariat; 1985; various pagings.

1727. Federal-Provincial Conference of Mines Ministers (1985). *Documents* (Federal-Provincial Conference of Mines Ministers, 1985); September 17, 1985; Charlottetown. [Ottawa]: Canadian Intergovernmental Conference Secretariat; 1985; various pagings.

1728. Federal-Provincial Conference of Ministers and Deputy Ministers of Agriculture. *Documents* (Federal-Provincial Conference of Ministers and Deputy Ministers of Agriculture, 1982); July 13-14, 1982; Halifax. [Ottawa]: Canadian Intergovernmental Conference Secretariat; 1982; various pagings.

1729. Federal-Provincial Conference of Ministers and Deputy Ministers of Agriculture. *Opening remarks by the Hon. Eugene F. Whelan, Minister of Agriculture* (Federal-Provincial Conference of Ministers and Deputy Ministers of Agriculture, 1983); July 19-20, 1983; Brudenell, P.E.I. [Ottawa]: Canadian Intergovernmental Conference Secretariat; 1983.

1730. Federal-Provincial Conference of Ministers and Deputy Ministers of Agriculture (1984). *Documents* (Federal-Provincial Conference of Ministers and Deputy Ministers of Agriculture, 1984); July 24, 1984; Winnipeg. [Ottawa]: Canadian Intergovernmental Conference Secretariat; 1984; various pagings.

1731. Federal-Provincial Conference of Ministers and Deputy Ministers of Agriculture on Farm Credit (1984). *Documents* (Federal-Provincial Conference of Ministers and Deputy Ministers of Agriculture on Farm Credit, 1984); Nov. 8-9, 1984; Toronto. [Ottawa]: Canadian Intergovernmental Conference Secretariat; 1984.

1732. Federal-Provincial Conference of Ministers and Deputy Ministers of Agriculture on Farm Credit (1985). *Documents* (Federal-Provincial Conference of Ministers and Deputy Ministers of Agriculture on Farm Credit, 1985); July 23-24, 1985; St. John's. [Ottawa]: Canadian Intergovernmental Conference Secretariat; 1985; various pagings.

1733. Federal-Provincial Conference of Ministers and Deputy Ministers of Public Works, Supply and Government Services (1982). *Documents* (Federal-Provincial Conference of Ministers and Deputy Ministers of Public Works, Supply and Government Services, 1982); August 24-28, 1982; Halifax. [Ottawa]: Canadian Intergovernmental Conference Secertariat; various pagings.

1734. Federal-Provincial Conference of Ministers and Deputy Ministers of the Departments of Public Works and Supply and Services. *Report* (Federal-Provincial Conference of Ministers and Deputy Ministers of the Departments of Public Works and Supply and Services). [Ottawa]: Canadian Intergovernmental Conference Secretariat; 1981.

1735. Federal-Provincial Conference of Ministers of Agriculture (1981). *Documents* (Federal-Provincial Conference of Ministers of Agriculture, 1981); July 13, 1981; Lethbridge. [Ottawa]: Canadian Intergovernmental Conference Secretariat; various pagings.

1736. Federal-Provincial Conference of Ministers of Agriculture (1983). *Documents* (Federal-Provincial Conference of Ministers of Agriculture, 1983); July 18, 1983; Brudenell, P.E.I. [Ottawa]: Canadian Intergovernmental Conference Secretariat; 1983; various pagings.

1737. Federal-Provincial Conference of Ministers of Communications. *Documents* (Federal-Provincial Conference of Ministers of Communications, 1981); September 9-10, 1981; Winnipeg. [Ottawa]: Canadian Intergovernmental Conference Secretariat; 1981; various pagings.

1738. Federal-Provincial Conference of Ministers of Communications. *Backgrounder: federal-provincial co-operation in communications programs: a synopsis, rev. April 1982;* [s.l.]. [Ottawa]: Canadian Intergovernmental Conference Secretariat; 1982.

1739. Federal-Provincial Conference of Ministers of Communications (1982). *Documents* (Federal-Provincial Conference of Ministers of Communications, 1982); May 21, 1982; Calgary. [Ottawa]: Canadian Intergovernmental Conference Secretariat; 1982; various pagings.

1740. Federal-Provincial Conference of Ministers of Communications (1985). *Documents* (Federal-Provincial Conference of Ministers of Communications, 1985); September 9-10, 1985; Winnipeg. [Ottawa]: Canadian Intergovernmental Conference Secretariat; 1981; various pagings.

1741. Federal-Provincial Conference of Ministers of Consumer Affairs (1981). *Documents* (Federal-Provincial Conference of Ministers of Consumer Affairs, 1981); September 3-4, 1981; Quebec. [Ottawa]: Canadian Intergovernmental Conference Secretariat; 1981; various pagings.

1742. Federal-Provincial Conference of Ministers of Culture and Historical Resources. *Documents* (Federal-Provincial Conference of Ministers of Culture and Historical Resources, 1980); Sept. 19, 1980; Toronto. [Ottawa]: Canadian Intergovernmental Conference Secretariat; 1980; various pagings.

1743. Federal-Provincial Conference of Ministers of Culture and Historical Resources. *Report* (Federal-Provincial Conference of Ministers of Culture and Historical Resources). [Ottawa]: Canadian Intergovernmental Conference Secretariat; 1980.

1744. Federal-Provincial Conference of Ministers of Housing. *Documents* (Federal-Provincial Conference of Ministers of Housing, 1981); June 1-2, 1981; Ottawa. [Ottawa]: Canadian Intergovernmental Conference Secretariat; 1981; various pagings.

1745. Federal-Provincial Conference of Ministers of Housing (1984). *Documents* (Federal-Provincial Conference of Ministers of Housing, 1984); December 7, 1984; Ottawa. [Ottawa]: Canadian Intergovernmental Conference Secretariat; 1984.

1746. Federal-Provincial Conference of Ministers of Science and Technology (1985). *Documents* (Federal-Provincial Conference of Ministers of Science and Technology, 1985); February 5, 1985; Calgary. [Ottawa]: Canadian Intergovernmental Conference Secretariat; 1985; various pagings.

1747. Federal-Provincial Conference of Ministers of the Departments of Public Works and Supply and Services (1981). *Documents* (Federal-Provincial Conference of Ministers of the Departments of Public Works and Supply and Services, 1981); September 9-11, 1981; St. John's. [Ottawa]: Canadian Intergovernmental Conference Secretariat; 1981; various pagings.

1748. Federal-Provincial Conference of Ministers of Tourism. *Documents* (Federal-Provincial-Territorial Conference of Ministers of Tourism, 1983); September 8, 1983; Whitehorse. [Ottawa]: Canadian Intergovernmental Conference Secretariat; 1983; various pagings.

1749. Federal-Provincial Conference of Ministers of Wildlife. *Documents* (Federal-Provincial Conference of Ministers of Wildlife, 1981); May 25-26, 1981;

Edmonton. [Ottawa]: Canadian Intergovernmental Conference Secretariat; 1981; various pagings.

1750. Federal-Provincial Conference of Ministers of Wildlife (1981). *News release* (Federal-Provincial Conference of Ministers of Wildlife, 1981); 1981; Edmonton. [Ottawa]: Canadian Intergovernmental Conference Secretariat; 1981.

1751. Federal-Provincial Conference of Ministers on Aboriginal Constitutional Matters. *Documents* (Federal-Provincial Conference of Ministers on Aboriginal Constitutional Matters, 1985); June 5-6, 1985; Ottawa. [Ottawa]: Canadian Intergovernmental Conference Secretariat; 1985.

1752. Federal-Provincial Conference of Ministers Responsible for Corrections, Criminal Justice, Law Enforcement, and of Attorneys General (Criminal Justice). *Documents* (Federal-Provincial Conference of Ministers Responsible for Corrections, Criminal Justice, Law Enforcement, and of Attorneys - General (criminal justice), 1981); December 7-9, 1981; Ottawa. [Ottawa]: Canadian Intergovernmental Conference Secretariat; 1981; various pagings.

1753. Federal-Provincial Conference of Ministers Responsible for Criminal Justice and Juvenile Justice (1984). *Documents* (Federal-Provincial Conference of Ministers Responsible for Criminal Justice and Juvenile Justice, 1984); November 22-23, 1984; St. John's. [Ottawa]: Canadian Intergovernmental Conference Secretariat; 1984.

1754. Federal-Provincial Conference of Ministers Responsible for Culture and Historical Resources. *Documents* (Federal-Provincial Conference of Ministers Responsible for Culture and Historical Resources, 3rd, 1982); May 4, 1982; Regina. [Ottawa]: Canadian Intergovernmental Conference Secretariat; 1982; various pagings.

1755. Federal-Provincial Conference of Ministers Responsible for Economic and Regional Development (1985). *Documents* (Federal-Provincial Conference of Ministers Responsible for Economic and Regional Development, 1985); March 24-25, 1985; Quebec City. [Ottawa]: Canadian Intergovernmental Conference Secretariat; 1985; various pagings.

1756. Federal-Provincial Conference of Ministers Responsible for Economic Regional Development (1985). *Documents* (Federal-Provincial Conference of Ministers Responsible for Economic Regional Development, 1985); 1985-1986: Canadian Intergovernmental Conference Secretariat; various pagings.

1757. Federal-Provincial Conference of Ministers Responsible for International Trade. *Documents* (Federal-Provincial Conference of Ministers Responsible for International Trade, 1982); June 21, 1982; Ottawa. [Ottawa]: Canadian Intergovernmental Conference Secretariat; 1982; various pagings.

1758. Federal-Provincial Conference of Ministers Responsible for International Trade (1982). *Documents* (Federal-Provincial Conference of Ministers Responsible for International Trade, 1982); September 14, 1982; Ottawa. [Ottawa]: Canadian Intergovernmental Conference Secretariat; 1982; various pagings.

1759. Federal-Provincial Conference of Ministers Responsible for International Trade (1985). *Documents* (Federal-Provincial Conference of Ministers Responsible for International Trade, 1985); May 28, 1985; Vancouver. [Ottawa]: Canadian Intergovernmental Conference Secretariat; 1985; various pagings.

1760. Federal-Provincial Conference of Ministers Responsible for Sport and Recreation. *Documents* (Federal-Provincial Conference of Ministers Responsible for Sport and Recreation, 1981); October 22, 1981; Vancouver. [Ottawa]: Canadian Intergovernmental Conference Secretariat; 1981; various pagings.

1761. Federal-Provincial Conference of Ministers Responsible for Sport and Recreation. *Documents* (Federal-Provincial Conference of Ministers Responsible for Sport and Recreation, 1984); Sept. 26, 1984; Grand Falls. [Ottawa]: Canadian Intergovernmental Conference Secretariat; 1984.

1762. Federal-Provincial Conference of Ministers Responsible for Sport and Recreation (1985). *Documents* (Federal-Provincial Conference of Ministers Responsible for Sport and Recreation, 1985); September 11, 1985; Calgary. [Ottawa]: Canadian Intergovernmental Conference Secretariat; 1985; various pagings.

1763. Federal-Provincial Conference of Ministers Responsible for Sport, Fitness and Recreation (1980). *Documents* (Federal-Provincial Conference of Ministers Responsible for Sport, Fitness and Recreation, 1980); 1980; Toronto. [Ottawa]: The Conference; [1980]; 1; various pagings.

1764. Federal-Provincial Conference of Ministers Responsible for Transportation and Highway Safety. *Documents* (Federal-Provincial Conference of Ministers Responsible for Transportation and Highway Safety (special session); May 31, 1984; Ottawa. [Ottawa]: Canadian Intergovernmental Conference Secretariat; 1984.

1765. Federal-Provincial Conference of Ministers with Manpower Responsibilities (1982). *Documents* (Federal-Provincial Conference of Ministers with Manpower Responsibilities, 1982); January 11, 1982; Vancouver. [Ottawa]: Canadian Intergovernmental Conference Secretariat; 1982; various pagings.

1766. Federal-Provincial Conference of the First Ministers on the Economy. *Alternative equalization formula - proposal of the province of Saskatchewan;* 1982; Ottawa. [s.l.]: The Conference; 1982.

1767. Federal-Provincial Conferences of Attorneys General, Ministers Responsible for Criminal Justice and Ministers Responsible for Corrections (1983). *Documents* (Federal-Provincial Conferences of Attorneys General, Ministers Responsible for Criminal Justice and Ministers Responsible for Corrections, 1983); July 11-12, 1983; Ottawa. [Ottawa]: Canadian Intergovernmental Conference Secretariat; 1983; various pagings.

1768. Federal-Provincial Conferences of Attorneys General, Ministers Responsible for Criminal Justice and Ministers Responsible for Corrections. *Final report of the Federal-Provincial Committee on Enforcement of Maintenance and Custody Orders in Canada* (Federal-Provincial Conferences of Attorneys General, Ministers Responsible for Corrections, 1983); July 11-12, 1983; Ottawa. [Ottawa]: Canadian Intergovernmental Conference Secretariat; 1983.

1769. Federal-Provincial Conferences of Ministers of Agriculture (1982). *Documents* (Federal-Provincial Conferences of Ministers of Agriculture, 1982); 1982; Halifax, Regina. [Ottawa]: Canadian Intergovernmental Conference Secretariat; 1982; various pagings.

1770. Federal-provincial discussions raise some key issues. *Au Courant;* 1981; 2(2): 5-7.

1771. Federal-Provincial First Ministers' Conference on the Economy. *Canada and the world: competing for international markets* (Federal-Provincial Conference of First Ministers on the Economy, 1985); Feb. 14-15, 1985; Regina. [Ottawa]: Canadian Intergovernmental Conference Secretariat; 1985.

1772. Federal-Provincial Meeting of Finance Ministers and Provincial Treasurers. *Provincial report on the revised equalization program proposed in the November 12, 1982 federal budget* (Federal-Provincial Meeting of Finance Ministers and Provincial Treasurers, 1981); December 14-15, 1981; Toronto. [Ottawa]: Canadian Intergovernmental Conference Secretariat; 1981.

1773. Federal-Provincial Meeting of Finance Ministers and Provincial Treasurers (1981). *Provincial report on the Established Programs Financing arrangement* (Federal-Provincial Meeting of Finance Ministers and Provincial Treasurers, 1981); 1981; Toronto. [Toronto]: [Ministry of Treasury and Economics]; [1982?]; 14 p.

1774. Federal-Provincial Meeting of Finance Ministers and Provincial Treasurers (1981). *Provincial report on the revised equalization program proposed in the November 12, 1981 federal budget* (Federal-Provincial Meeting of Finance Ministers and Provincial Treasurers, 1981); 1981; Toronto. [Toronto]: Ministry of Treasury and Economics; 1982; 14 p.

1775. Federal-Provincial Meeting of Ministers of Mines (1983). *Documents* (Federal-Provincial Meeting of Ministers of Mines, 1983); September 20, 1983; Regina. [Ottawa]: Canadian Intergovernmental Conference Secretariat; various pagings.

1776. Federal-Provincial Meeting of Ministers on Aboriginal Constitutional Matters. *Comments made by the Honourable Mark MacQuigan* (Federal-Provincial Meeting of Ministers on Aboriginal Constitutional Matters, 1983); Jan. 31 - Feb. 1, 1983; Ottawa. [Ottawa]: Canadian Intergovernmental Conference Secretariat; 1983.

1777. Federal-Provincial Meeting of Ministers on Aboriginal Constitutional Matters. Declaration of the first nations (Federal-Provincial Meeting of Ministers on Aboriginal Consitutional Matters, 1983); Jan. 31 - Feb. 1, 1983; Ottawa. [Ottawa]: Canadian Intergovernmental Conference Secretariat; 1983.

1778. Federal-Provincial Meeting of Ministers on Aboriginal Constitutional Matters. *Notes for address to Constitutional Ministers Conference on aboriginal rights - Hon. G. Braden, Minister of Justice and Public Services, Government of Northwest Territories;* January 31 - February 1, 1983; Ottawa. [Ottawa]: Canadian Intergovernmental Conference Secretariat; 1983.

1779. Federal-Provincial Meeting of Ministers on Aboriginal Constitutional Matters. *Statement by the Hon. Thomas L. Wells, Minister of Intergovernmental Affairs, Province of Ontario to the Meeting of Ministers and Aboriginal Leaders on Aboriginal Rights and the Constitution;* January 31, 1983; Ottawa. [Ottawa]: Canadian Intergovernmental Conference Secretariat; 1983.

1780. Federal-Provincial Meeting of Ministers on Aboriginal Constitutional Matters. *Documents* (Federal-Provincial Meeting of Ministers on Aboriginal Constitutional Matters, 1983); Nov. 2-3, 1983; Ottawa. [Ottawa]: Canadian Intergovernmental Conference Secretariat; 1983.

1781. Federal-Provincial Meeting of Ministers on Aboriginal Constitutional Matters. *Documents* (Federal-Provincial Meeting of Ministers on Aboriginal Constitutional Matters, 1984); Dec. 17-18, 1984. [Ottawa]: Canadian Intergovernmental Conference Secretariat; 1984.

1782. Federal-Provincial Meeting of Ministers on Aboriginal Constitutional Matters. *Documents* (Federal-Provincial Meeting of Ministers on Aboriginal Constitutional Matters, 1984); Jan. 25-26, 1984. [Ottawa]: Canadian Intergovernmental Conference Secretariat; 1984.

1783. Federal-Provincial Meeting of Ministers on Aboriginal Constitutional Matters. *Documents* (Federal-Provincial Meeting of Ministers on Aboriginal Constitutional Matters, 1984); February 13-14, 1984. [Ottawa]: Canadian Intergovernmental Conference Secretariat; 1984.

1784. Federal-Provincial Meeting of Ministers on Aboriginal Constitutional Matters. *Documents* (Federal-Provincial Meeting of Ministers on Aboriginal Constitutional Matters, 1985); March 11-12, 1985. [Ottawa]: Canadian Intergovernmental Conference Secretariat; 1985.

1785. Federal-Provincial Meeting of Ministers on Aboriginal Constitutional Matters. *Documents* (Federal-Provincial Conference of First Ministers on Aboriginal Constitutional Matters, 1985); April 2-3, 1985; Ottawa. [Ottawa]: Canadian Intergovernmental Conference Secretariat; 1985.

1786. Federal-Provincial Meeting of Ministers on Aboriginal Constitutional Matters (1983). *Documents* (Federal-Provincial Meeting of Ministers on Aboriginal

Constitutional Matters, 1983); 1983; Ottawa. [Ottawa]: Canadian Intergovernmental Conference Secretariat; 1983; various pagings.

1787. Federal-Provincial Meeting of Ministers on Aboriginal Constitutional Matters (1985). *Accord respecting matters affecting the aboriginal peoples of Canada, 1985* (Federal-Provincial Meeting of Ministers on Aboriginal Constitutional Matters, 1985); March 11-12, 1985; Toronto. [Ottawa]: Canadian Intergovernmental Conference Secretariat; 1985.

1788. Federal-Provincial Meeting of Ministers Responsible for International Trade (1985). *Documents* (Federal-Provincial Meeting of Ministers Responsible for International Trade, 1985); October 10, 1985; Halifax. [Ottawa]: Canadian Intergovernmental Conference Secretariat; 1985; various pagings.

1789. Federal-Provincial Meeting of the Continuing Committee of Ministers on the Constitution. *Documents* (Federal-Provincial Meeting of the Continuing Committee of Ministers on the Constitution, 1980); July 22-24, 1980; Ottawa. [Ottawa]: Canadian Intergovernmental Conference Secretariat; 1980.

1790. Federal-Provincial Meeting on Aboriginal Constitutional Matters (1984). *Documents* (Federal-Provincial Meeting on Aboriginal Constitutional Matters, 1984); January 25-26, 1984; Yellowknife. [Ottawa]: Canadian Intergovernmental Conference Secretariat; 1984; various pagings.

1791. Federal-Provincial Trade Ministers Conference. *Documents* (Federal-Provincial Trade Ministers Conference); June 21, 1982; Ottawa. [Ottawa]: Canadian Intergovernmetnal Conference Secretariat; 1982.

1792. Federal-Provincial-Territorial Conference of Ministers of Consumer and Corporate Affairs (1985). *Documents* (Federal-Provincial-Territorial Conference of Ministers of Consumer and Corporate Affairs, 1985); September 10-11, 1985; Hecla Island, Man. [Ottawa]: Canadian Intergovernmental Conference Secretariat; various pagings.

1793. Federal-Provincial-Territorial Conference of Ministers of Housing. *Documents* (Federal-Provincial-Territorial Conference of Ministers of Housing, 1985); July 4, 1985. [Ottawa]: Canadian Intergovernmental Conference Secretariat; 1985.

1794. Federal-Provincial-Territorial Conference of Ministers of Housing (1985). *Documents* (Federal-Provincial-Territorial Conference of Ministers of Housing, 1985); July 4, 1985; Calgary. [Ottawa]: Canadian Intergovernmental Conference Secretariat; 1985; various pagings.

1795. Federal-Provincial-Territorial Conference of Ministers of Tourism. *Documents* (Federal-Provincial-Territorial Conference of Ministers of Tourism, 1984); Nov. 29, 1984; Moncton. [Ottawa]: Canadian Intergovernmental Conference Secretariat; 1984.

1796. Federal-Provincial-Territorial Conference of Ministers Responsible for Social Services. *Documents* (Federal-Provincial-Territorial Conference of Ministers

Responsible for Social Services, 1985); 1985; Ottawa. [Ottawa]: Canadian Intergovernmental Conference Secretariat; 1985.

1797. Federal-Provincial-Territorial Conference of Ministers Responsible for Social Services (1985). *Documents* (Federal-Provincial-Territorial Conference of Ministers Responsible for Social Services, 1985); April 26, 1985; Ottawa. [Ottawa]: Canadian Intergovernmental Conference Secretariat; 1985.

1798. Federal-Provincial-Territorial Conference of Ministers Responsible for the Status of Women. *Closing statement, federal* (Federal-Provincial-Territorial Conference of Minsiters Responsible for the Status os Women, 1983); May 31 - June 1, 1983; Ottawa. [Ottawa]: Canadian Intergovernmental Conference Secretariat; 1983.

1799. Federal-Provincial-Territorial Conference of Ministers Responsible for the Status of Women. *Documents* (Annual Federal-Provincial-Territorial Conference of Ministers Responsible for the Status of Women, 3rd, 1984); May 29-30, 1984; Niagara-on-the-Lake. [Ottawa]: Canadian Intergovernmental Conference Secretariat; 1985; various pagings.

1800. Federal-Provincial-Territorial Conference of Ministers Responsible for the Status of Women. *Documents* (Annual Federal-Provincial-Territorial Conference of Ministers Responsible for the Status of Women, 4th, 1985); June 6-7, 1985; Winnipeg. [Ottawa]: Canadian Intergovernmental Conference Secretariat; 1985.

1801. Federal-Provincial-Territorial Conference of Ministers Responsible for the Status of Women (1982). *Documents* (Federal-Provincial-Territorial Conference of Ministers Responsible for the Status of Women, 1982); May 10-11, 1982; Ottawa. [Ottawa]: Canadian Intergovernmental Conference Secretariat; 1982; various pagings.

1802. Federal-Provincial-Territorial Conference of Ministers Responsible for the Status of Women (1983). *Documents* (Federal-Provincial-Territorial Conference of Ministers Responsible for the Status of Women, 1983); May 31- June 1, 1983; Ottawa. Ottawa: Canadian Intergovernmental Conference Secretariat; various pagings.

1803. Federal-Provincial-Territorial Meeting of Ministers and Deputy Ministers Responsible for Indian Affairs. *Documents* (Federal-Provincial-Territorial Meeting of Ministers and Deputy Ministers Responsible for Indian Affairs, 1982); May 3-4, 1982; Fredericton. [Ottawa]: Canadian Intergovernmental Conference Secretariat; 1982.

1804. Federal-Provincial-Territorial Meeting of Ministers Responsible for the Status of Women (1985). *Documents* (Federal-Provincial-Territorial Meeting of Ministers Responsible for the Status of Women, 1985); October 17, 1985; Ottawa. [Ottawa]: Canadian Intergovernmental Conference Secretariat; 1985; various pagings.

1805. Federal-Provincial-Territorial Ministerial Conference on Human Rights. Joint statement of the Federal-Provincial Territorial Ministerial Conference on Human Rights; Sept. 12-13, 1985. [Ottawa]: Canadian Intergovernmental Conference Secretariat; 1985.

1806. Federal-Provincial-Territorial Ministerial Conference on Human Rights (1983). *Documents* (Federal-Provincial-Territorial Ministerial Conference on Human Rights, 1983); September 8-9, 1983; Ottawa. [Ottawa]: Canadian Intergovernmental Conference Secretariat; 1983.

1807. Federation of Canadian Municipalities; Canada. Parliament. House of Commons. Special Committee on the Federal-Provincial Fiscal Arrangements. *Submission to the Parliamentary Task Force on Federal-Provincial Fiscal Arrangements.* [Ottawa]: Federation of Canadian Municipalities; 1981; 4 p.

1808. Feldman, Elliot J.; Milch, Jerome. Coordination or control? the life and death of the Ministry of State for Urban Affairs. In: *idem.*, ed. *Politics and government of urban Canada.* 4th ed. Toronto: Methuen; 1981: 246-264; xii, 451 p.

1809. Feldman, Lionel D. *Politics and government of urban Canada.* 4th ed. Toronto: Methuen; 1981; xii, 451 p.

1810. Feldman, Lionel D.; Graham, Katherine A. Intergovernmental relations and urban growth: a Canadian view. In: Feldman, Lionel D., ed. *Politics and government of urban Canada.* 4th ed. Toronto: Methuen; 1981: 202-218; xii, 451 p.

1811. First Ministers' Conference on Aboriginal Constitutional Matters. *Aboriginal peoples and political institutions; The experience and direction in Canada's Northwest Territories - First Ministers' Conference on Aboriginal Constitutional Matters*; March 8-9, 1984; Ottawa. [Ottawa]: Canadian Intergovernmental Conference Secretariat; 1984.

1812. First Ministers' Conference on Aboriginal Constitutional Matters. *Notes for the address of the Honourable Richard Nerysoo - Northwest Territories* (First Ministers Conference on Aboriginal Constitutional Matters); March 8-9, 1984; Ottawa. [Oattawa]: Canadian Intergovernmental Conference Secretariat; 1984.

1813. First Ministers' Conference on Aboriginal Constitutional Matters. *Notes for opening statement by John H. Buchanan, P.C., D.C., M.L.A., Premier of Nova Scotia* (First Ministers' Conference on Aboriginal Constitutional Matters, 1984); March 8-9, 1984; Ottawa. [Ottawa]: Canadian Intergovernmental Conference Secretariat; 1984.

1814. First Ministers' Conference on Aboriginal Constitutional Matters. *Notes for an opening statement by the Hon. Howard R. Pawley* (First Ministers' Conference on Aboriginal Constitutional Matters, 1984); March 8-9, 1984; Ottawa. [Ottawa]: Canadian Intergovernmental Conference Secretariat; 1984.

1815. First Ministers' Conference on Aboriginal Constitutional Matters. *Verbatim transcript, unrevised and unofficial* (First Ministers' Conference on Aboriginal

Constitutional Matters, 1985); April 2 and 3, 1985; Ottawa. [Ottawa]: Canadian Intergovernmental Conference Secretariat; 1985; iv, 294 p.

1816. Fletcher, Frederick J.; Wallace, Donald C. Federal-provincial relations and the making of public policy in Canada: a review of case studies. In: Simeon, Richard, res. coord. *Division of powers and public policy.* Toronto: University of Toronto Press; Royal Commission on the Economic Union and Development Prospects for Canada; 1985: 125-206; xiv, 206 p. (The collected research studies; v. 61).

1817. Foot, David K. The demographic future of fiscal federalism in Canada. *Canadian Public Policy;* 1984 December; 10(4): 406-414.

1818. Foot, David K. *The demographic future of fiscal federalism in Canada.* Toronto: Institute for Policy Analysis; 1984; 18 p. (Working Paper).

1819. Forget, C. *Finances publiques et le fédéralisme canadien* [booklet: 50-99 p.]. [s.l.]: Parti Libéral du Québec; 1980. (Parti libéral du Québec textes référendaires; v. 6).

1820. Forget, Claude E. The harmonization of social policy. In: Krasnick, Mark, res. coord. *Fiscal federalism.* Toronto: University of Toronto Press; Royal Commission on the Economic Union and Development Prospects for Canada; 1986: 970148; xvi, 211 p. (The collected research studies; v. 65).

1821. Forsey, Eugene A. *Notes on the Ryan proposals: "A new Canadian federation".* [s.l.]: [s.n.]; [1980]; 13 leaves ; 29 cm.

1822. Fox, Paul W., ed. *Politics: Canada.* 5th ed. Toronto: McGraw-Hill Ryerson; c1982; 693 p. (McGraw-Hill Ryerson series in Canadian politics).

1823. Funston, Bernard William. *The Northwest Territories in Canadian federalism* 1963-79: Scott Polar Research Institute; 1980; iv, 287 p.

1824. Gallegher, Stephen J. *Government autonomy, federal-provincial conflict and the regulation of oil* [microfiche]: (M.A.) McGill University; 1983; 2 microfiches (148 fr.). Ottawa: National Library of Canada, 1985.

1825. Ghent, Jocelyn. The participation of provincial governments in international science and technology. *American Review of Canadian Studies;* 1980 Spring; 10(1): 48-62.

1826. Giroux, Jean-Baptiste. Les Québécois doivent s'opposer au régime fédéral et non au parti politique de M. Trudeau. *L'Action nationale;* 1981 November; 71(3): 361-369.

1827. Gotlieb, Marc J. George Drew and the Dominion-Provincial Conference on Reconstruction of 1945-6. *Canadian Historical Review;* 1985; 66(1): 27-47.

1828. Graham, John F. Equalization and Canadian federalism. *Public Finance;* 1982; 37(2): 246-62.

1829. Groenewegen, Peter. Tax assignment and revenue sharing in Australia. In: McLure, Charles E. (Jr.), ed. *Tax assignment in federal countries*. Canberra: ANU Press; 1983: 293-327; xix, 370 p.

1830. Grube, John. M. François-Albert Angers et l'indépendance fiscale. *L'Action nationale*; 1980 June; 59(10): 796-821.

1831. Hartle, Douglas G. Some political realities in the world of stagflation. In: Courchene, Thomas J. [and others]. *Ottawa and the provinces: the distribution of money and power*. Toronto: Ontario Economic Council; 1985; 2: 217-234; 343 p. (Special research report/Ontario Economic Council).

1832. Head, J. G. Public goods and multilevel government. In: Grewal, Bhajan S. [and others], ed. *The economics of federalism*. Canberra: Australian National University; 1980: 383-405; xiii, 432 p.

1833. Helliwell, John F.; Scott, Anthony. *Canada in fiscal conflict: resources and the West - summary version*. [Vancouver]: Pemberton Securities; [1981]; 18 p.

1834. Herber, Bernard P. *Poor persons and poor governments: economic criteria for the distribution function and its performance in the American federation*. Canberra: Centre for Research on Federal Financial Relations, Australian National University; 1985. (Research monograph; v. 42).

1835. Hero, Alfred O., Jr.; Daneau, Marcel, eds. *Problems and opportunities in U.S.-Quebec relations*. Boulder, CO: Westview Press; 1984; xv, 320 p. (Westview special studies in international relations).

1836. L'Heureux, Jacques. Municipalities and the division of powers. In: Simeon, Richard, res. coord. *Intergovernmental relations*. Toronto: University of Toronto Press; Royal Commission on the Economic Union and Development Prospects for Canada; 1985: 179-214; xiv, 263 p. (The collected research studies; v. 63).

1837. Howard, C. *The federal fiscal imbalance*. Canberra: Centre for Research on Federal Financial Relations, Australian National University; 1984; 14 p. (Reprint Series; v. 61).

1838. Hum, Derek; Thomas, Paul. Less equal than others. *Policy Options*; 1985 May; 6(4): 14-16.

1839. Hunt, Wayne Austin. *The federal-provincial conference of first ministers, 1960-1976* [microfiche]: (Ph.D.) University of Toronto; 1982; 3 microfiches (289 fr.). Ottawa: National Library of Canada, 1983.

1840. Hunter, J.S.H. Intergovernmental fiscal adjustment in Australia: a review of recent developments in the light of experience in Canada and West Germany. *Finanzarchiv*; 1980; 38(3): 424-42.

1841. Intergovernmental Conference on Acid Rain (1985). *Documents* (Intergovernmental Conference on Acid Rain, 1985); April 10-12, 1985; Quebec. [Ottawa]: Canadian Intergovernmental Conference Secretariat; 1985; various pagings.

1842. Intergovernmental Conference on Local Government Information Development. *Documents* (Intergovernmental Conference on Local Government Information Development, 1980); May 21-22, 1980; Winnipeg. Ottawa: Statistics Canada, Public Finance Division; 1980; 238 p (in various pagings).

1843. Interprovincial Conference of Agriculture Ministers. *Documents* (Interprovincial Conference of Agriculture Ministers, 1981). [Ottawa]: Canadian Intergovernmental Conference Secretariat; 1981.

1844. Interprovincial Conference of Ministers and Deputy Ministers of Agriculture. *Documents* (Interprovincial Conference of Ministers and Deputy Ministers of Agriculture, 1982); July 12, 1982; Halifax. [Ottawa]: Canadian Intergovernmental Conference Secretariat; 1982.

1845. Interprovincial Conference of Ministers and Deputy Ministers of Agriculture. *Documents* (Interprovincial Conference of Ministers and Deputy Ministers of Agriculture, 1983); July 18, 1983; Brudenell, P.E.I. [Ottawa]: Canadian Intergovernmental Conference Secretariat; 1983.

1846. Interprovincial Conference of Ministers and Deputy Ministers of Agriculture. *Documents* (Interprovincial Conference of Ministers and Deputy Ministers of Agriculture, 1984); July 23 and 25, 1984; Winnipeg. [Ottawa]: Canadian Intergovernmental Conference Secretariat; 1984.

1847. Interprovincial Conference of Ministers and Deputy Ministers of Agriculture (1984). *Documents* (Interprovincial Conference of Ministers and Deputy Ministers of Agriculture, 1984); Winnipeg; 1984. [Ottawa]: The Conference; [1984]; 2 p.

1848. Interprovincial Conference of Ministers and Deputy Ministers of Agriculture (1985). *Documents* (Interprovincial Conference of Ministers and Deputy Ministers of Agriculture, 1985); July 22-24, 1985; St. John's. [Ottawa]: Canadian Intergovernmental Conference Secretariat; 1985; various pagings.

1849. Interprovincial Conference of Ministers of Agriculture. *Documents* (Interprovincial Conference of Ministers of Agriculture, 1982); Nov. 4, 1982; Regina. [Ottawa]: Canadian Intergovernmental Conference Secretariat; 1982.

1850. Interprovincial Conference of Ministers of Agriculture. *Documents* (Interprovincial Conference of Ministers of Agriculture, 1983); March 1, 1983; Toronto. [Ottawa]: Canadian Intergovernmental Conference Secretariat; 1983.

1851. Interprovincial Conference of Ministers of Communications. *Documents* (Interprovincial Conference of Ministers of Communications, 1981); Feb. 11-12, 1981; Quebec. [Ottawa]: Canadian Intergovernmental Conference Secretariat; 1981.

1852. Interprovincial Conference of Ministers of Culture and Historical Resources. *Documents* (Interprovincial Conference of Ministers of Culture and Historical Resources, 1980); Sept. 18, 1980; Toronto. [Ottawa]: Canadian Intergovernmental Conference Secretariat; 1980.

1853. Interprovincial Conference of Ministers of Health. *Documents* (Interprovincial Conference of Ministers of Health, 1980); Sept. 30 - Oct. 1, 1980; Winnipeg. [Ottawa]: Canadian Intergovernmental Conference Secretariat; 1980.

1854. Interprovincial Conference of Ministers of Health. *Documents* (Interprovincial Conference of Ministers of Health, 1981; Sept. 30 - Oct. 1, 1981; St. John's. [Ottawa]: Canadian Intergovernmental Conference Secretariat; 1981.

1855. Interprovincial Conference of Ministers of Housing. *Documents* (Interprovincial Conference of Ministers of Housing, 1984); July 4, 1984; St. John's. [Ottawa]: Canadian Intergovernmental Conference Secretariat; 1984.

1856. Interprovincial Conference of Ministers of Municipal Affairs. *Documents* (Interprovincial Conference of Ministers of Municipal Affairs, 1980); August 13-15, 1980; St. Andrews. [Ottawa]: Canadian Intergovernmental Conference Secretariat; 1980.

1857. Interprovincial Conference of Ministers of Municipal Affairs. *Documents* (Interprovincial Conference of Ministers of Municipal Affairs, 1982); August 17-20, 1982; Digby. [Ottawa]: Canadian Intergovernmental Conference Secretariat; 1982.

1858. Interprovincial Conference of Ministers of Municipal Affairs. *Documents* (Interprovincial Conference of Ministers of Municipal Affairs, 1983); August 9-12, 1983; Victoria. [Ottawa]: Canadian Intergovernmental Conference Secretariat; 1983.

1859. Interprovincial Conference of Ministers of Municipal Affairs. *Letter to the Prime Minister from the Premier of Quebec concerning availability of federal grants to municipalities* (Interprovincial Conference of Ministers of Municipal Affairs, 1983); August 9-12, 1983; Victoria. [Ottawa]: Canadian Intergovernmental Conference Secretariat; 1983.

1860. Interprovincial Conference of Ministers of Municipal Affairs (1985). *Communiqué* (Interprovincial Conference of Ministers of Municipal Affairs, 1985); August 13-16, 1985; Saskatoon. [Ottawa]: Canadian Intergovernmental Conference Secretariat; 1985.

1861. Interprovincial Conference of Ministers of Social Service. *Documents* (Interprovincial Conference of Ministers of Social Service, 1982); Nov. 24-25, 1982; St. John's. [Ottawa]: Canadian Intergovernmental Conference Secretariat; 1982.

1862. Interprovincial Conference of Ministers Responsible for Cultural Affairs and Historic Resources. *Documents* (Interprovincial Conference of Ministers Responsible for Cultural Affairs and Historic Resources, 1983); September 27, 1983; Grand Falls. [Ottawa]: Canadian Intergovernmental Conference Secretariat; 1983.

1863. Interprovincial Conference of Ministers Responsible for Culture and Historical Resources (4th), 1982. *Documents* (Interprovincial Conference of Ministers Responsible for Culture and Historical Resources, 4th); May 3, 1982; Regina. [Ottawa]: Canadian Intergovernmental Conference Secretariat; 1982.

1864. Interprovincial Conference of Ministers Responsible for Native People. *Communiqué* (Interprovincial Conference of Ministers Responsible for Native People, 1981); 1981; Montreal. [Ottawa]: Canadian Intergovernmental Conference Secretariat; 1981. (Interprovincial Conference of ministers Responsible for Native People 1981, document 860; 104-106).

1865. Interprovincial Conference of Ministers Responsible for Native People. *Communiqué* (Interprovincial Conference of Ministers Responsible for Native People, 1982). [Ottawa]: Canadian Intergovernmental Conference Secretariat; 1982.

1866. Interprovincial Conference of Ministers Responsible for Social Services. *Documents* (Interprovincial Conference of Ministers Responsible for Social Services, 1980); Sept. 11-12, 1980; Fredericton. [Ottawa]: Canadian Intergovernmemtal Conference Secretariat; 1980.

1867. Interprovincial Conference of Ministers Responsible for Social Services. *Documents* (Interprovincial Conference of Ministers Responsible for Social Services, 1981); Oct. 15-16, 1981; Quebec. [Ottawa]: Canadian Intergovernmental Conference Secretariat; 1981.

1868. Interprovincial Conference of Ministers Responsible for Sport and Recreation. *Documents* (Interprovincial Conference of Ministers Responsible for Sport and Recreation, 1981); October 21, 1981; Vancouver. [Ottawa]: Canadian Intergovernmental Conference Secretariat; 1981.

1869. Interprovincial Conference of Ministers Responsible for Sport and Recreation. *Documents* (Interprovincial Conference of Ministers Responsible for Sport and Recreation, 1982); Oct. 26-27, 1982; Saskatoon. [Ottawa]: Canadian Intergovernmental Conference Secretariat; 1982.

1870. Interprovincial Conference of Ministers Responsible for Sport and Recreation. *Documents* (Interprovincial Conference of Ministers Responsible for Sport and Recreation, 1983); 19-20 April 1983. [Ottawa]: Candian Intergovernmental Conference Secretariat; 1983.

1871. Interprovincial Conference of Ministers Responsible for Sport and Recreation. *Documents* (Interprovincial Conference of Ministers Responsible for Sport and Recreation, 1983); Oct. 18-19, 1983; Fredericton. [Ottawa]: Canadian Intergovernmental Conference Secretariat; 1983.

1872. Interprovincial Conference of Ministers Responsible for Sport and Recreation. *Leisure opportunities for disabled - Alberta* (Interprovincial Conference of

Ministers Responsible for Sport and Recreation, 1983); October 18-19, 1983; Fredericton. [Ottawa]: Canadian Intergovernmental Conference Secretariat; 1983.

1873. Interprovincial Conference of Ministers Responsible for Sport and Recreation. *Documents* (Interprovincial Conference of Ministers Responsible for Sport and Recreation, 1984); Sept. 24-25, 1984; Grand Falls. [Ottawa]: Canadian Intergovernmental Conference Secretariat; 1984.

1874. Interprovincial Conference of Ministers Responsible for Sport and Recreation (1980). *Documents* (Interprovincial Conference of Ministers Responsible for Sport and Recreation, 1980); 1980; Toronto. [Ottawa]: Canadian Intergovernmental Conference Secretariat; [1980].

1875. Interprovincial Conference of Ministers Responsible for Sport and Recreation (1981). *Proposed initiatives for the Interprovincial Sport and Recreation Council regarding leisure opportunities for disabled people* (Interprovincial Conference of Ministers Responsible for Sport and Recreation, 1981); 1981; Vancouver. [Ottawa]: Canadian Intergovernmental Conference Secretariat; 1981.

1876. Interprovincial Conference of Ministers with Responsibility for Northern Development. *Documents* (Interprovincial Conference of Ministers with Responsibility for Northern Development, 3rd, 1980); Sept. 10-11, 1980; Thompson, Man. [Ottawa]: Canadian Intergovernmental Conference Secretariat; 1981.

1877. Interprovincial Conference of Ministers with Responsibility for Northern Development. *Documents* (Interprovincial Conference of Ministers with Responsibility for Northern Development, 4th, 1981); September 15-17, 1981; Goose Bay. [Ottawa]: Canadian Intergovernmental Conferences Secretariat; 1981.

1878. Interprovincial Conference of Municipal Affairs. *Interprovincial Conference of Municipal Affairs Ministers - documents*; August 18-20, 1981; Winnipeg. [Ottawa]: Canadian Intergovernmental Conference Secretariat; 1981.

1879. Interprovincial Conference on Privacy. *Documents* (Interprovincial Conference on Privacy: initiatives for 1984 (symposium), 1984); May 23-24, 1984; Toronto. [Ottawa]: Canadian Intergovernmental Conference Secretariat; 1984.

1880. Interprovincial Housing Ministers' Conference. *Documents* (Interprovincial Housing Ministers' Conference, 1981); Feb. 26, 1981; St. John's. [Ottawa]: Canadian Intergovernmental Conference Secretariat; 1981.

1881. Interprovincial Meeting of Ministers Responsible for Pensions. *Documents of the Interprovincial Meeting of Ministers Responsible for Pensions, 1984*; June 5, 1984; Toronto. [Ottawa]: Canadian Intergovernmental Conference Secretariat; 1984.

1882. Interprovincial Meeting of Ministers Responsible for Pensions. *Documents* (Interprovincial Meeting of Ministers Responsible for Pensions, 1984); Dec. 3, 1984; Toronto. [Ottawa]: Canadian Intergovernmental Conference Secretariat; 1984.

1883. Interprovincial Meeting of Ministers Responsible for Pensions (1984). *Documents* (Interprovincial Meeting of Ministers Responsible for Pensions, 1984); December 3, 1984; Toronto. [Ottawa]: Canadian Intergovernmental Conference Secretariat; 1984.

1884. Jobin, Jacques; Dufour, Jean-Marie. Mesure et incidence des dépenses fiscales au Québec. L'Actualité économique; 1985 March; 61(1): 93-111.

1885. Johnson, A.W. Federal-provincial fiscal relations: an historical perspective. In: Courchene, Thomas J.; Conklin, David W.; Cook, Gail C.A., eds. *Ottawa and the provinces: the distribution of money and power.* Toronto: Ontario Economic Council; 1985; 2: 107-143; 343 p. (Special research report/Ontario Economic Council).

1886. Johnson, James A. *Federal sales tax reform in Canada: some parallels with Australia.* Canberra: Centre for Research on Federal Financial Relations, Australian National University; 20 p. (Reprint Series; v. 65).

1887. Jones, Kenneth Gary. *Response to regional disparity in the Maritime provinces, 1926-1942: a study in Canadian intergovernmental relations* [microfiche]: (M.A.) University of New Brunswick; 1980; 3 microfiches (211 fr.). Ottawa: National Library of Canada, 1981.

1888. Jones, P. F. M. Jurisdiction at sea. *Supreme Court Law Review*; 1982 Ann.: 445-451.

1889. Kerr, Robert. The scope of federal power in relation to consumer protection. *Ottawa Law Review*; 1980; 12(1): 119-144.

1890. Kettner, Bonni Raines. *Canadian federalism and the international activities of three provinces Alberta, Ontario and Quebec* [microfiche]: (M.A.) Simon Fraser University; 1980; 3 microfiches (207 fr.). Ottawa: National Library of Canada, 1980.

1891. Kitchen, Harry M.; McMillan, Melville L. Local government and Canadian federalism. In: Simeon, Richard, res. coord. *Intergovernmental relations.* Toronto: University of Toronto Press; Royal Commission on the Economic Union and Development Prospects for Canada; 1985: 215-261; xiv, 263 p. (The collected research studies; v. 63).

1892. Kitchen, Harry M.; McMillan, Melville L. *Local government and Canadian federalism: review and assessment.* Edmonton: Dept. of Economics, University of Alberta; 1984; various pagings.

1893. Krasnick, Mark, res. coord. *Fiscal federalism.* Toronto: University of Toronto Press; Royal Commission on the Economic Union and Development Prospects for Canada; 1986; xvi, 211 p. (The collected research studies; v. 65).

1894. Lapointe, Jean-Louis. La réforme de la fiscalité municipale au Québec. Canadian Public Administration; 1980 Summer; 23(2): 269-280.

1895. Lazar, Fred. Resource revenues and fiscal equalization: a proposal. *Canadian Taxation*; 1981 Fall; 3(3): 162-166.

1896. Leach, Richard H., ed. *Intergovernmental relations in the 1980's*. New York: Marcel Dekker; 1983; 99 p. (Annals of public administration; v. 4).

1897. Lemelin, Claude. A federal view of consultation. In: Courchene, Thomas J.; Conklin, David W.; Cook, Gail C.A, eds. *Ottawa and the provinces: the distribution of money and power*. Toronto: Ontario Economic Councilil; 1985; 2: 183-188; 343 p. (Special research report/Ontario Economic Council).

1898. Leslie, Peter M. National standards in public services. In: Courchene, Thomas J.; Conklin, David W.; Cook, Gail C.A., eds. *Ottawa and the provinces: the distribution of money and power*. Toronto: Ontario Economic Council; 1985; 2: 195-216; 343 p. (Special research report/Ontario Economic Council).

1899. Leslie, Peter M. *Politics, policy and federalism: defining the role of the Institute of Intergovernmental Relations*. Kingston: Institute of Intergovernmental Relations; Queen's University; c1984; vi, 26 p.

1900. Lower, Arthur. The Prime Minister and the Premiers. *Queen's Quarterly*; 1980 Winter; 87(4): 560-565.

1901. Macdonald, H. Ian. Federal-provincial fiscal issues in Canada. In: Mathews, Russell, ed. *Public policies in two federal countries: Canada and Australia*. Canberra: Centre for Research on Federal Financial Relations, Australian National University; 1982; 145-152 p.

1902. MacEachen, Allan J. *Fiscal arrangements in the eighties: proposals of the Government of Canada*. [Ottawa]: Dept. of Finance; 1981; 55 (59) p.

1903. MacLaren Plansearch Ltd. *The evaluation study report of the Canada-New Brunswick Subsidiary Agreement for Forestry Development*. [s.l.]: MacLaren Plansearch Lavalin; 1984; 2 v.

1904. Magnusson, Warren. The local state in Canada: theoretical perspectives. *Canadian Public Administration*; 1985 Winter; 28(4): 575-599.

1905. Mallory, J. R. Conflict management in the Canadian federal system (North America: law, politics and economics: Canadian federalism). *Law and Contemorary Problems*; 1981 Summer; 44(3): 231-246.

1906. Manitoba. Trade: *Manitoba position paper: for First Ministers' Conference*; November 28-29, 1985; Halifax. Winnipeg: Manitoba; 1985; 22 p.

1907. Manitoba. *Submission to the Parliamentary Task Force on Federal-Provincial Fiscal Arrangements*, by Brian Ransom. Winnipeg: [Government of Manitoba]; 1980; 40 p.

1908. Manitoba. *Submission to the Parliamentary Task Force on Federal-Provincial Fiscal Arrangements*, by Brian Ransom. Winnipeg: [Government of Manitoba]; 1981; [12] leaves.

1909. Manitoba. Department of Energy and Mines. *Canada-Manitoba Mineral Development Agreement, 1984/89. sector "A" geoscientific activities: progress report, 1984/85.* Winnipeg: Department of Energy & Mines; 1985; 82 p.

1910. Manitoba. Department of Finance. *Background information on equalization.* Winnipeg: Manitoba Finance; 1984; 136 p.

1911. Manitoba. Municipal Planning Branch. Northern Planning Section. *Canada-Manitoba Northlands Agreement 1981-82 progress report: northern planning program.* Winnipeg: Northern Planning; 1982; 16 p.

1912. Markusen, Ann R.; Saxenian, Annalee; Weiss, Marc A. Who benefits from intergovernmental transfers. *Publius*; 1981 Winter; 11(1): 5-36.

1913. Maskell, C.A. *Changing perceptions of the Australian Inter-State Commission.* Canberra: Centre for Research on Federal Financial Relations, Australian National University; vi, 43 p. (Occasional paper; 26).

1914. Mathews, Russell. *The Australian Loan Council: co-ordination of public debt policies in a federation.* Canberra: Centre for Research on Federal Financial Relations, Australian National University; 1984; 23 p. (Reprint series; v. 62.)

1915. Mathews, Russell. *Commonwealth - Northern Territory financial relations.* Canberra: Centre for Research on Federal Financial Relations, Australian National University; 1983; 40 p. (Reprint Series; v. 56).

1916. Mathews, Russell. *The Commonwealth - state financial contract.* Canberra: Centre for Research on Federal Financial Relations, Australian National University; 1982; 33 p. (Reprint Series; v. 46).

1917. Mathews, Russell. *Federal-state fiscal arrangements in Australia.* Canberra: Centre for Research on Federal Financial Relations, Australian National University; 1983; 35 p. (Reprint Series; v. 57).

1918. Mathews, Russell. *Federalism in retreat: the abandonment of tax sharing and fiscal equalization.* Canberra: Centre for Research on Federal Financial Relations, Australian National University; 26 p. (Reprint Series; v. 50).

1919. Mathews, Russell. *Fiscal equalization in education.* Canberra: Centre for Research on Federal Financial Relations, Australian National University; 1983; x, 180 p.

1920. Mathews, Russell. *Fiscal equalization through the local grant system.* Canberra: Centre for Research on Federal Financial Relations, Australian National University; 1981; 18 p. (Reprint Series; v. 43).

1921. Mathews, Russell. *Fiscal federalism - 1951 style - revisited.* Canberra: Centre for Research on Federal Financial Relations, Australian National University; 1982; 29 p. (Reprint Series; v. 45).

1922. Mathews, Russell. Intergovernmental financial arrangements and taxation. In: Mathews, Russell, ed. *Public policies in two federal countries: Canada and*

Australia. Canberra: Centre for Research on Federal Financial Relations, Australian National University; 1982; 153-182 p.

1923. Mathews, Russell. *Intergovernmental fiscal relations and regional growth in a federal context*. Canberra: Centre for Research on Federal Financial Relations, Australian National University; 1981; 28 p. (Reprint Series; v. 42).

1924. Mathews, Russell. Mechanisms for fiscal equalization. In: Grewal, Bhajan S. [and others], ed. *The economics of federalism*. Canberra: Australian National University; 1980: 255-284; xiii, 432 p.

1925. Mathews, Russell, ed. *Urban federalism: urban studies in a federal context*. Canberra: Centre for Research on Federal Financial Relations, Australian National University; 1981; xiii, 169 p.

1926. Mathews, Russell; Else-Mitchell, R. *Federal grants to states*. Canberra: Centre for Research on Federal Financial Relations, Australian National University; 1980; 20 p. (Reprint Series; v. 38).

1927. McFadden, M.; Wittenberg, R. *Regional development plans project no. 271024 under Canada-British Columbia Subsidiary Agreement on Agriculture and Rural Development - regional profile for Quesnel district office area*. [Victoria]: British Columbia. Ministry of Agriculture and Food; 1980.

1928. McLarty, R.A. *Current issues in Canadian fiscal federalism*. Canberra: Centre for Research on Federal Financial Relations, Australian National University; 1980; 21 p. (Reprint series; v. 36).

1929. McLarty, R.A. *Federal-provincial conditional transfers: from cost-sharing to block funding*. Canberra: Centre for Research on Federal Financial Relations, Australian National University; 1981; vi, 30 p. (Occasional paper; 15).

1930. McMillan, Melville L. *Rethinking fiscal equalization for local governments*. Canberra: Centre for Research on Federal Financial Relations, Australian National University; 1981; 29 p. (Reprint Series; v. 47).

1931. McMillan, Melville L.; Norton, Derek G. The distribution of unconditional transfers to Alberta municipalities: existing and alternative methods. *Canadian Tax Journal*; 1981 March-April; 29(2): 171-183.

1932. Meekison, J. Peter. First ministers' conferences in the Canadian federal system. In: Courchene, Thomas J.; Conklin, David W.; Cook, Gail C.A., eds. *Ottawa and the provinces: the distribution of money and power*. Toronto: Ontario Economic Council; 1985; 2: 162-182; 343 p. (Special research report/Ontario Economic Council).

1933. Meeting of Federal-Provincial Ministers on Grain Handling and Transportation (1980). *Documents* (Meeting of Federal-Provincial Ministers on Grain Handling and Transportation, 1980); June 3, 1980; Toronto. [Ottawa]: Canadian Intergovernmental Conference Secretariat; 1980; various pagings.

1934. Meeting of the Continuing Committee of Ministers on the Constitution (1980). *Documents* (Meeting of the Continuing Committee of Ministers on the Constitution, 1980); July 8-11, 1980; Montreal. [Ottawa]: Canadian Intergovernmental Conference Secretariat; 1980; various pagings.

1935. Meeting of the Continuing Committee of Ministers on the Constitution (1980). *Documents* (Meeting of the Continuing Committee of Ministers on the Constitution, 1980); July 14-18, 1980; Toronto. [Ottawa]: Canadian Intergovernmental Conference Secretariat; 1980; various pagings.

1936. Meeting of the Continuing Committee of Ministers on the Constitution (1980). *Documents* (Meeting of the Continuing Committee of Ministers on the Constitution, 1980); July 22-25, 980; Vancouver. [Ottawa[: Canadian Intergovernmental Conference Secretariat; 1980; various pagings.

1937. Meeting of the Council of Provincial Energy Ministers (1983). *Documents* (Meeting of the Council of Provincial Energy Ministers, 1983); September 19, 1983; Regina. [Ottawa]: Canadian Intergovernmental Conference Secretariat; 1983; various pagings.

1938. Meeting of the Interprovincial Sport and Recreation Council (1983). *Documents* (Meeting of the Interprovincial Sport and Recreation Council, 1983); April 19-20, 1983; Ottawa. [Ottawa]: Canadian Intergovernmental Conference Secretariat; 1981; various pagings.

1939. Meeting of the Interprovincial Sport and Recreation Council (1985). *Documents* (Meeting of the Interprovincial Sport and Recreation Council, 1985); September 12, 1985; Calgary. [Ottawa]: Canadian Intergovernmental Conference Secretariat; 1985; unpaged.

1940. Monière, Denis. *Pour la suite de l'histoire: essai sur la conjoncture politique au Québec.* Montréal: Québec-Amerique; 1982; 182 p.

1941. Monière, Denis. Le Québec doit être représenté à Ottawa par des députés souverainistes. *L'Action nationale*; 1982 January; 71(5): 555-567.

1942. Musgrave, Richard A. Approaches to a fiscal theory of political federalism. In: Bhajan, Grewal S. [and others], ed. *The economics of federalism.* Canberra: Australian National University; 1980: 209-233; xiii, 432 p.

1943. Nahwegahbow, David C. *Federal-provincial implications of various concepts of Indian self-government.* Ottawa: Corporate Policy Branch, Department of Indian Affairs and Northern Development; June 1983; 179 p. (Consultant's eport).

1944. National Conference on Social Welfare. Committee on Federalism and National Purpose. *To form a more perfect union: the report of the Committee on Federalism and National Purpose,* by Daniel J. Evans and Charles S. Robb, chairmen. Washington, D.C.: National Conference on Social Welfare; 1985; xi, 52 p.

Bibliography

1945. New Brunswick. Department of Finance. *Federal-provincial fiscal arrangements, 1982-1987*. [Fredericton]: New Brunswick. Department of Finance; 1982; 30 (30) p.

1946. Newfoundland. Newfoundland's position on extension of services, by N. Doyle. *Federal-Provincial Conference of Ministers of Communications* (1981); 1981; Winnipeg. [Ottawa]: Canadian Intergovernmental Conference Secretariat; 1981.

1947. Newfoundland. Department of Finance. *Provincial submission to the Parliamentary Task Force on Federal-Provincial Fiscal Arrangements*, by John F. Collins and Thomas V. Hickey. [St. John's]: Government of Newfoundland and Labrador; 1981; 13, 5, [2] leaves.

1948. Newfoundland. Office of the Premier. *Discussion paper on major bilateral issues: Canada - Newfoundland.* [St. John's]: Newfoundland. Office of the Premier; 1980.

1949. Norrie, Kenneth H.; Percy, Michael B.; Wilson, L. S. Financing confederation: principles and practices of equalization. *Canadian Public Policy*; 1982 Summer; 8(3): 290-93.

1950. Norrie, Kenneth H.; Percy, Michael B.; Wilson, L. S. Financing confederation: rejoinder. *Canadian Public Policy*; 1982 Autumn; 8(4): 623-625.

1951. Northwest Territories. Department of Information. *First Ministers' Conference on Aboriginal Rights and the Constitution*; March 15-16, 1983; Ottawa. Yellowknife: Northwest Territories Information; 1983; 28, (1) p.

1952. Northwest Territories. Economic Development Agreement Secretariat. *A guide to the economic development agreement in the Northwest Territories: building a better future*. [Yellowknife]: EDA Secretariat; [1983?]; 24 p.

1953. Northwest Territories. Energy, Mines and Resources Secretariat. *NWT - Canada resource management and revenue sharing agreement: a proposal for settlement, draft No.5*. Yellowknife: Energy, Mines and Resources Secretariat; 1983; 63 p.

1954. Nova Scotia. Department of Development. Federal-Provincial Development Agreements Branch. *Federal-provincial development agreements branch: a status report*. [Halifax]: Development Nova Scotia; 1981; 10 p.

1955. Nova Scotia. Intergovernmental Affairs. *A descriptive inventory of federal-provincial programs and activities in the province of Nova Scotia as of April 1981*. [Halifax]: Intergovernmental Affairs; 1981; 225 p.

1956. Olson, Mancur, Jr. The principle of 'fiscal equivalence': the division of responsibilities among different levels of government. In: Grewal, Bahajan S. [and others], ed. *The economics of federalism*. Canberra: Australian National University; 1980: 25-37; xiii, 432 p.

1957. Ontario Welfare Council. *Joint submission to the Parliamentary Task Force on Federal-Provincial Fiscal Arrangements.* Toronto: Ontario Welfare Council; 1981.

1958. Ontario. Intergovernmental Finance Policy Branch. *Ontario papers on federal-provincial fiscal arrangements: reprinted and summarized for the Meeting of Provincial Ministers of Finance, Victoria, B.C., June 25 and 26, 1982; 1981*; Victoria. Toronto: Ontario Ministry of Treasury and Economics, Intergovernmental Finance Policy Branch; [1982]; 75 p.

1959. Ontario. Intergovernmental Finance Policy Branch. *Fiscal federalism in Canada, the record to date, the challenge ahead: summary budget paper B.* Toronto: Intergovernmental Finance Policy Branch; 1982; 2 leaves.

1960. Ontario. Intergovernmental Finance Policy Branch. *Ontario papers on federal-provincial fiscal arrangements: reprinted and summarized for the Meeting of Provincial Ministers of Finance, Victoria, B.C., June 25 and 26, 1981.* Toronto: Ministry of Treasury and Economics; [1981?]; 20 p.

1961. Ontario. Ministry of Industry and Tourism. *Proposals for interprovincial economic co-operation and for the establishment of a Canadian domestic market development agency.* [Toronto]: Ontario Ministry of Industry and Tourism; 1981; 53 p.

1962. Ontario. Ministry of Intergovernmental Affairs. *Ministry of Intergovernmental Affairs Ontario.* [Toronto]: Ministry of Intergovernmental Affairs; 1983.

1963. Ontario. Ministry of Intergovernmental Affairs. *Ontario's perspective on Canadian federalism today - an address by the Hon. Thomas L. Wells, Minister of Intergovernmental Affairs, Province of Ontario to the Royal Commission Society, London, England, April 14, 81.* Toronto: The Ministry; 1981.

1964. Ontario. Ministry of Intergovernmental Affairs. *Remarks by the Hon. Thomas L. Wells, Minister of Intergovernmental Affairs, Government of Ontario to "consortium on North American affairs", Harvard University, Cambridge, Massachusetts, Tuesday, Feb. 3, 1981.* [Toronto]: Ministry of Intergovernmental Affairs; 1981.

1965. Ontario. Ministry of Intergovernmental Affairs. *Remarks by the Honourable Thomas L. Wells, Minister of Intergovernmental Affairs re: provincial transfer payments to municipalities for 1981, Thursday, Jan. 22, 1981.* [Toronto]: Ministry of Intergovernmental Affairs; 1981.

1966. Ontario. Ministry of Intergovernmental Affairs. *Statement by the Hon. T.L. Wells, Minister of Intergovernmental Affairs to the Glendon College symposium "Quebec - year of the referendum", Toronto, Ontario, Saturday, March 8, 1980.* [Toronto]: Ministry of Intergovernmental Affairs; 1980.

1967. Ontario. Ministry of Treasury and Economics. *Notes for a statement on federal-provincial fiscal arrangements by the Hon. Frank S. Miller, Treasurer of*

Ontario, *Federal-Provincial Conference of Finance Ministers; January 22, 1982*; Ottawa. Toronto: The Ministry; 1982.

1968. Ontario. Ministry of Treasury and Economics. Intergovernmental Finance Policy Branch. *Fiscal federalism in Canada: the record to date, the challenge ahead - summary of the Ontario budget paper b.* [Toronto]: Ministry of Treasury and Economics; 1981.

1969. Ontario. Office of the Premier. *A blueprint for economic recovery.* Federal-Provincial Conference of First Ministers on the Economy; February 2-4, 1982; Ottawa. [Toronto]: Office of the Premier; [1982]; 24, vi p.

1970. Ouellette, Yves. Le partage des compétences en matière de constitution des sociétés. *Revue juridique Thémis*; 1980-81; 15(1): 113-141.

1971. Pacific Rim Metropolitan Conference. *Pacific Rim Metropolitan Conference proceedings: April 5 to 10, 1981, Vancouver, British Columbia, Canada*; 1981; Vancouver. [Vancouver]: [s.n.]; [1982]; iv, 186 p.

1972. Peckford, A. Brian. *Annual Interprovincial Conference of Ministers with Responsibility for Northern Development, 1981: notes for a speech by the Hon. A. Brian Peckford*; 1981; Goose Bay. [Ottawa]: Canadian Intergovernmental Affairs Secretariat; 1981.

1973. Peckford, A. Brian. *The past in the present: a personal perspective on Newfoundland's future.* St. John's: H. Cuff Publications; 1983; 127 p.

1974. Pernthaler, Peter. *Federal fiscal relations in Austria.* Canberra: Centre for Research on Federal Financial Relations, Australian National University; ii, 51 p. (Occasional paper; v. 30).

1975. Perry, David B. Established programs financing. *Canadian Tax Journal*; 1981 March-April; 29(2): 246-249.

1976. Perry, David B. The federal-provincial fiscal arrangements for 1982-87. *Canadian Tax Journal*; 1983 January-February; 31(1): 30-47.

1977. Perry, David B. The growth of government transfer payments to individuals. *Canadian Tax Journal*; 1983 March-April; 31(2): 292-300.

1978. Perry, David B. An historical perspective on public finance in the provinces. *Canadian Tax Journal*; 1981 July-August; 29(4): 570-575.

1979. Pollack, I. C.; Simpson, G.; Gaulin, Robert. *The need for and the feasibility of an appeals process in regard to municipal grants-in-lieu of taxes: a report.* [Ottawa]: [Public Works Canada]; 1982; c1983; xv, 105 p.

1980. Powrie, T. L. Natural resource revenues and federal-provincial fiscal arrangements. *Canadian Tax Journal*; 1981 July-August; 29(4): 499-502.

1981. Premiers' Conference on the Patriation of the Canadian Constitution (April 16, 1981). *Premiers' Conference - Constitutional Accord*; April 16, 1981; Ottawa. [Ottawa]: Canadian Intergovernmental Conference Secretariat; 1981.

1982. Premiers' Conference on the Patriation of the Canadian Constitution (April 16, 1981). *Verbatim transcript* (Constitutional Accord patriation plan amending formula, 8 provinces); 1981; Ottawa. [Ottawa]: Canadian Intergovernmental Conference Secretariat; 1981.

1983. Prince Edward Island. *Province of Prince Edward Island: position statement.* Federal-Provincial Conference of First Ministers on the Constitution (1980); September 8-13, 1980; Ottawa. Charlottetown: Province of Prince Edward Island; 1980; 61 p.

1984. Prince Edward Island. Department of Finance and Tourism. Economics, Statistics and Fiscal Analysis Division. *The importance of equalization to Prince Edward Island.* Charlottetown: Department of Finance and Tourism; 1983; 14 p. (Economic trends; v. 16).

1985. Provincial and Territorial Health Ministers' Conference (1984). *Documents* (Provincial and Territorial Health Ministers' Conference, 1984); April 4, 1984; Ottawa. [Ottawa]: Canadian Intergovernmental Conference Secretariat; 1984; various pagings.

1986. Provincial and Territorial Health Ministers' Conference (1985). *Documents* (Provincial and Territorial Health Ministers' Conference, 1985); September 25-26, 1985; Toronto. [Ottawa]: Canadian Intergovernmental Conference Secretariat; 1985; various pagings.

1987. Provincial-Territorial Conference of Ministers of Social Services (1985). *Documents* (Provincial-Territorial Conference of Ministers of Social Services, 1985); September 17-18, 1985; Ottawa. [Ottawa]: Canadian Intergovernmental Conference Secretariat; 1985; various pagings.

1988. Qu'appelle Evaluation Committee. Reid, Crowther & Partners. *Canada - Saskatchewan Qu'appelle agreement evaluation: final report.* [Regina?]: [s.n.]; 1984; 275 in various pagings. Note: "February, 1984" Includes bibliographical references.

1989. Québec. Ministère des Communications. *Les programmes d'aide: entente auxiliaire Canada-Québec sur le développement des entreprises de communication 1985-1990.* [Québec]: Gouvernement du Québec; 1985; 19 p.

1990. Québec. Ministère des Finances. *Dynamics of finances in Quebec.* [Québec]: Ministère des Finances; 1981. (Québec ministère des Finances direction générale de la politique fiscale\working paper).

1991. Québec. Ministère des Finances. La dynamique des finances publiques au Québec. [Québec]: Gouvernement du Québec, Ministère des Finances; [1981]; 40 p. (Document de travail/Direction générale de la politique fiscale).

1992. Québec. Ministère des Finances. *Fiscal equalization: an important supplement to the provincial tax system.* [Québec]: Ministère des Finances; 1982.

1993. Québec. Ministère des Finances. *The nature and evolution of transfers by the government of Canada to the gouvernement du Quebec: 1972-77 and 1977-82.* [Québec]: Gouvernement du Québec, Ministère des Finances; 1981; 46 p.

1994. Reid, John M. *Notes for an address to the panel of the Canadian Study of Parliament group seminar on First Ministers' Conferences in Halifax 3 May, 1981 by the Honourable John M. Reid M.P. for Kenora-Rainy River.; Federal-provincial conferences: some thoughts on their implications for legislatures, political parties and regionalism; May 30, 1981*; Halifax. [s.l.]: Canadian Study of Parliament Group; 1981.

1995. Resource Task Force on Constitutional Reform; Federation of Canadian Municipalities. *Municipal government in a new Canadian federal system: report of the Resource Task Force on Constitutional Reform, Federation of Canadian Municipalities, Ottawa,* by Edward McWhinney. Ottawa: [Federation of Canadian Municipalities]; 1980; iv, 155 p.

1996. Resource Task Force on Constitutional Reform; Federation of Canadian Municipalities. *Municipal government in the new Canadian federal system: second report,* by Edward McWhinney. Ottawa: Federation of Canadian Municipalities; 1982; ii, 29 p.

1997. Richmond, Dale E. Provincial-municipal tax and revenue sharing: reforms accomplished, 1978 compared with 1971. In: Feldman, Lionel D., ed. *Politics and government of urban Canada.* 4th ed. Toronto: Methuen; 1981: 162-201; xii, 451 p.

1998. Richmond, Dale E. Some common issues in provincial-municipal transfer systems. *Canadian Public Administration*; Summer 1980; 23(2): 252-268.

1999. Ridler, Neil B. Fiscal constraints and the growth of user fees among Canadian municipalities. *Canadian Public Administration*; 1984; 27(3): 429-436.

2000. Robert, Michel. Challenges and choices: implications for fiscal federalism. In: Courchene, Thomas J.; Conklin, David W.; Cook, Gail C.A., eds. *Ottawa and the provinces: the distribution of money and power.* Toronto: Ontario Economic Council; 1985; 1: 22-28; xii, 341 p. (Special research report/Ontario Economic Council).

2001. Robertson, Gordon. Le conflit fédéral-provincial au Canada: raisons et solutions. *Les Cahiers de droit*; 1985; March(1): 57-67.

2002. Robertson, Gordon. Intergovernmental financial relations in Canada and Australia. In: Mathews, Russell, ed. *Public policies in two federal countries: Canada and Australia.* Canberra: Centre for Research on Federal Financial Relations, Australian National University; 1982; 183-187.

2003. Robinson, A. John. An intergovernmental commission for economic policy? In: Bird, Richard M., ed. *Fiscal dimensions of Canadian federalism*. Toronto: Canadian Tax Foundation; 1980: 55-84; v, 151 p. (Financing Canadian federation; v. 4).

2004. Romanow, Roy J,; Ryan, Claude; Stanfield, Robert L. *Ottawa and the provinces : regional perspectives*. Toronto: Ontario Economic Council; [1984]; vi, 45 p. (Federal-provincial relations series).

2005. Romanow, Roy J. Fiscal arrangements: a western perspective. In: Courchene, Thomas J.; Conklin, David W.; Cook, Gail C.A., eds. *Ottawa and the provinces: the distribution of money and power*. Toronto: Ontario Economic Council; 1985; 1: 181-197; xii, 341 p. (Special research report/Ontario Economic Council).

2006. Rosenthal, Donald B. Bargaining analysis in intergovernmental relations. *Publius*; 1980 Summer; 10(3): 5-44.

2007. Rowat, Donald C. A note on the uniqueness of the study of local government. *Canadian Public Administration*; 1983 Summer; 26(3): 441-446.

2008. Roy, Jean Louis. Entre le changement et l'indiscipline. *Les Cahiers de droit*; 1985 March; (1): 69-77.

2009. Rutan, Gerard F. Legislative interaction of a Canadian province and an American state: thoughts upon sub-national cross-border relations. *American Review of Canadian Studies*; 1981; 11(2): 67-79.

2010. Rutan, Gerard F. British Columbia - Washington State intergovernmental interrelations: some findings upon the failure of structure. *American Review of Canadian Studies*; 1985 Spring; 15(1): 97-110.

2011. Ryan, Claude. Federal transfer payments: a Quebec perspective. In: Courchene, Thomas J.; Conklin, David W.; Cook, Gail C.A., eds. *Ottawa and the provinces: the distribution of money and power*. Toronto: Ontario Economic Council; 1985; 1: 198-220; xii, 341 p. (Special research report/Ontario Economic Council).

2012. Ryan, Claude. *Québec d'abord: le PLQ et le projet fédéral de modification constitutionnelle*. [Montréal]: [Parti libéral du Québec]; [1981]; 35 p.

2013. Ryan, Claude. *Quebec first: the PLQ and the federal proposal to amend the Constitution*. [Montreal]: [Liberal Party of Quebec]; [1981]; 35 p.

2014. Soldatos, Panayotis. Les données fondamentales du devenir de la politique étrangère canadienne: essai de synthèse. *Etudes internationales*; 1983 March; 14(1): 5-22.

2015. Sanders, Douglas. *The long road to a fresh start? - the First Ministers' Conference on Aboriginal Rights; April 3, 1983; 20 p.* (Unpublished paper at the Department of Indian Affiars Library, Ottawa).

2016. Saskatchewan. *The future of Canada: a Saskatchewan perspective*. Regina: Government of Saskatchewan; 1980; 10 p.

2017. Saskatchewan. Department of Mineral Resources. *The Canada - Saskatchewan Heavy Oil Agreement*. Regina: Department of Mineral Resources; 1981; 11 p.

2018. Saskatchewan. Office of the Premier. *Speeches and interviews by Hon. Allan Blakeney, Premier of Saskatchewan, in the course of a trip to Ontario and Quebec*. Regina: Government of Saskatchewan; 1980; 144 p.

2019. Saskatchewan. Saskatchewan Finance. *The new fiscal arrangements: Canadians deserve better*. [Regina]: Saskatchewan Finance; 1982; 41 p.

2020. Saunders, Cheryl. *The expiry of the financial agreement*. Canberra: Centre for Research on Federal Financial Relations, Australian National University; 1985; 20 p. (Reprint Series; v. 64).

2021. Savoie, Donald J. L'harmonie fédérale-provinciale est-elle toujours essentielle? *Policy Options*; 1984 November; 5(6): 13-14.

2022. Savoie, Donald J.; Careless, Anthony. *Federal-provincial collaboration: the Canada-New Brunswick General Development Agreement*. Toronto: McGill-Queen's University Press; 1981; 188 p.

2023. Sayeed, Adil. The Canada Assistance Plan: some background. In: Courchene, Thomas J.; Conklin, David W.; Cook, Gail C.A., eds. *Ottawa and the provinces: the distribution of money and power*. Toronto: Ontario Economic Council; 1985; 2: 276-310; 343 p. (Special research report/Ontario Economic Council).

2024. Schlegel, John P. Federalism and Canadian foreign policy. *Round Table*; 1981; 282: 179-192.

2025. Scott, A. D. The evaluation of federal grants. In: Grewal, Bhajan S. [and others], ed. *The economics of federalism*. Canberra: Australian National University; 1980; 291-307 xiii, 432 p.

2026. Scott, A. D. A note on grants in federal countries. In: Bhajan, Grewal S. [and others], ed. *The economics of federalism*. Canberra: Australian National University; 1980: 201-207; xiii, 432 p.

2027. Scott, Anthony. Financing Confederation: introduction. *Canadian Public Policy*; 1982 Summer; 8(3): 283-289.

2028. Scrafton, Derek. Federal urban transport policy formulation in Canada and Australia. In: Mathews, Russell, ed. *Urban federalism: urban studies in a federal context*. Canberra: Centre for Research on Federal Financial Relations, Australian National University; 1981: 95-103 p.

2029. Sewell, D. O.; Slater, D. W. Financing Confederation: rejoinder. *Canadian Public Policy*; 1982 Autumn; 8(4): 625-631.

2030. Shapek, Raymond A. *Managing federalism: evolution and development of the grant-in-aid system*. Charlottesville, Va.: Community Collaborators; 1981; x, 306 p.

2031. Sheppard, Anthony F. Taxation policy and the Canadian economic union. In: Krasnick, Mark, res. coord. *Fiscal federalism*. Toronto: University of Toronto Press; Royal Commission on the Economic Union and Development Prospects for Canada; 1986: 149-210; xvi, 211 p. (The collected research studies; v. 65).

2032. Shere, Waris. *Miracles of survival; Canada and French Canada*. Smithtown, N. Y.: Exposition Press; 1981; viii, 158 p.

2033. Siegel, David. *Federal-provincial diplomacy: re-negotiating EPF-1982*. Toronto: Institute of Public Administration of Canada; [1982]; 4 [12] p. (Case program in Canadian public administration).

2034. Siegel, David. Provincial-municipal relations in Canada: an overview. *Canadian Public Administration*; 1980 Summer; 23(2): 281-317.

2035. Siegel, David. Provincial-municipal relations in Canada: an overview. *Canadian Public Administration*; Summer 1980; 23(2): 281-317.

2036. Simeon, Richard. Federalism in the 1980's. In: Courchene, Thomas J.; Conklin, David W.; Cook, Gail C.A., eds. *Ottawa and the provinces: the distribution of money and power*. Toronto: Ontario Economic Council; 1985; 1: 29-43; xii, 341 p. (Special research report/Ontario Economic Council).

2037. Simeon, Richard. Fiscal federalism in Canada: a review essay. *Canadian Tax Journal*; 1982 January-February; 30(1): 41-51.

2038. Simeon, Richard, res. coord. *Intergovernmental relations*. Toronto: University of Toronto Press; Royal Commission on the Economic Union and Development Prospects for Canada; 1985; xiv, 263 p. (The collected research studies; v. 63).

2039. Simeon, Richard. Intergovernmental relations and the challenges to Canadian federalism. *Canadian Public Administration*; 1980 Spring; 23(1): 14-32.

2040. Simeon, Richard. Natural resource revenues and Canadian federalism: a survey of the issues. *Canadian Public Policy* (Supplement); 1980 February; 6: 182-191.

2041. Simeon, Richard. Some suggestions for improving intergovernmental relations. In: Fox, Paul W., ed. *Politics: Canada*. 5th ed. Toronto: McGraw-Hill Ryerson; 1982: 98-101; 693 p. (McGraw-Hill Ryerson series in Canadian politics).

2042. Simmons, James W. Government and the Canadian urban system: income tax, transfer payments, and employment. *Canadian Geographer*; 1984 Spring; 28(1): 18-45.

2043. Sinha, R. K. *Evolution of fiscal federalism in India*. New Delhi: South Asian Publishers; [1981?]; xii, 253 p.

2044. Sinha, R. K. *Fiscal federalism in India*. New Delhi: South Asian Publishers; c1980; x, 158 p.

2045. Slack, Enid. Local fiscal response to intergovernmental transfers. *Review of Economics and Statistics*; 1980 August; 62(3): 364-70.

2046. Slack, Enid; Crocker, Douglas. The impact of federal-provincial transfers on provincial revenues and expenditures: a review. In: Courchene, Thomas J.; Conklin, David W.; Cook, Gail C.A., eds. *Ottawa and the provinces: the distribution of money and power*. Toronto: Ontario Economic Council; 1985; 2: 311-343; 343 p. (Special research report/Ontario Economic Council).

2047. Slater, David W. *Federal-provincial finances*. Guelph: School of Agricultural Economics and Extension Education, Ontario Agricultural College, University of Guelph; 1982; 28 p.

2048. Social Planning Council of Metropolitan Toronto. *Brief submission to the Parliamentary Task Force on Federal-Provincial Fiscal Arrangements*. [Toronto]: The Council; 1981; 20 p.

2049. Spahn, P. Bernd. *Financing federalism: West German issues and proposals for reform*. Canberra: Centre for Research on Federal Financial Relations, Australian National University; [1981?]; 22 p. (Reprint series; v. 49).

2050. Spector, Norman. Federal-provincial professionalism. *Policy Options*; 1984 November; 5(6): 44-46.

2051. Stanfield, Robert L. Federal transfer payments: centralization or decentralization. In: Courchene, Thomas J. [and others], eds. *Ottawa and the provinces: the distribution of money and power*. Toronto: Ontario Economic Council; 1985; 1: 221-226; xii, 341 p. (Special research report/Ontario Economic Council).

2052. Stevenson, Garth. Political constraints and the province-building objective. *Canadian Public Policy* (Supplement); 1980 February; 6: 265-274.

2053. Stewart, William Alexander. *The impact of federal grants on expenditures of the governments of the Atlantic provinces: an econometric study, 1963-1979* [microfiche]: (M.A.) Dalhousie University; 1983 2 microfiches (130 fr.). Ottawa: National Library of Canada, 1985.

2054. Swainson, Neil A. The provincial-municipal relationship. In: Morley, Terrence J. [and others]. *The reins of power*. Vancouver: Douglas and McIntyre; 1983: 237-270; ix, 342 p.

2055. Szablowski, George J. Treaty-making power in the context of Canadian politics: an exploratory and innovative approach. In: Becton, Clare; MacKay, A. Wayne, res. coords. *Recurring issues in Canadian federalism*. Toronto: University of Toronto Press; Royal Commission on the Economic Union and Development Prospects for Canada; 1986: 145-186; xv, 187 p. (The collected research studies; v. 57).

2056. Tallock, Gordon. Federalism: problems of scale. In: Grewal, Bhajan S. [and others], ed. *The economics of federalism*. Canberra: Australian National University; 1980: 39-49; xiii, 432 p.

2057. Thirsk, Wayne R. Fiscal harmonization in the United States, Australia, West Germany, Switzerland and the EEC. In: Trebilcock, Michael J., ed. *Federalism and the Canadian economic union*. Toronto: Ontario Economic Council; 1983: 424-455; xiv, 560 p. (Ontario Economic Council Research series).

2058. Thomson, Norman J. *Federal equalisation funding of schools in Australia*. Canberra: Centre for Research on Federal Financial Relations, Australian National University; 1985; 14 p. (Reprint series; v. 70).

2059. Trebilcock, Michael J. The politics of positive sum. In: Courchene, Thomas J. [and others], eds. *Ottawa and the provinces: the distribution of money and power*. Toronto: Ontario Economic Council; 1985; 2: 235-250; 343 p. (Special research report/Ontario Economic Council).

2060. Tremblay, André; Turp, Daniel. L'incidence des politiques urbaines sur l'exercice des compétences fédérales et provinciales en matière de gouvernement local. *Revue juridique Thémis*; 1981-82; 16(1-2): 281-321.

2061. Trudeau, Pierre E. Le défi (La réforme des relations fédérales-provinciales). *Les Cahiers de droit*; 1985 March; 26(1): 15-27.

2062. Trudeau, Pierre Elliott. *Statement by the Right Honourable Pierre Elliott Trudeau at the closing of the First Ministers' Conference on the Economy, Ottawa, February 4, 1982*; February 4, 1982; Ottawa. [Ottawa]: Office of the Prime Minister; 1982; 19, 20 p.

2063. Tupper, Allan. *Bill S-31 and the federalism of state capitalism*. Kingston: Institute of Intergovernmental Relations, Queen's University; 1983; ii, 40 p. (Discussion Papers; v. 18).

2064. Twenty-fifth Annual Premiers' Conference (1984). *Documents* (Twenty-fifth Annual Premiers' Conference, 1984); August 19-22, 1984; Charlottetown. [Ottawa]: Canadian Intergovernmental Conference Secretariat; 1984; various pagings.

2065. Twenty-first Annual Premiers' Conference (1980). *Documents* (Twenty-first Annual Premiers' Conference, 1980); August 20-24, 1980; Winnipeg. [Ottawa]: Canadian Intergovernmental Conference Secretariat; 1980; various pagings.

2066. Twenty-fourth Annual Premiers' Conference (1983). *Documents* (Twenty-fourth Annual Premiers' Conference, 1983); August 9-11, 1983; Toronto. [Ottawa[: Canadian Intergovernmental Conference Secretariat; 1983; various pagings.

2067. Twenty-second Annual Premiers' Conference (1982). *Documents* (Second Annual Premiers' Conference, 1982); Victoria. [Ottawa]: Canadian Intergovernmental Conference Secretariat; 1982; various pagings.

2068. Twenty-sixth Annual Premiers' Conference (1985). *Documents* (Twenty-sixth Annual Premiers' Conference, 1985); August 21-22, 1985; St. John's. [Ottawa]: Canadian Intergovernmental Conference Secretariat; 1985; various pagings.

2069. Twenty-third Annual Premiers' Conference (1982). *Documents* (Twenty-third Annual Premiers' Conference, 1982); August 24-28, 1982; Halifax. [Ottawa]: Canadian Intergovernmental Conference Secretariat; 1982; various pagings.

2070. United States. Congress. House. Committee on Government Operations. Intergovernmental Relations and Human Resources Subcommittee. *Current condition of American federalism: hearings before a subcommittee of the Committee on Government Operations, House of Representatives, Ninety-seventh Congress, first session, April 7, 8, 9, 29, 30, May 13, 14, June 17, 18, and October 6, 1981*. Washington, D.C.: U.S. Government Publications Office; 1981; iv, 809 p.

2071. Usher, D. How should the redistributive power of the state be divided between federal and provincial governments? *Canadian Public Policy*; 1980 Winter; 6(1): 16-29.

2072. Vanderkamp, John. Financing Confederation: rejoinder. *Canadian Public Policy*; 1982 Autumn; 8(4): 631-632.

2073. Vanderkamp, John. Financing Confederation: transfers and migration. *Canadian Public Policy*; 1982 Summer; 8(3): 293-297.

2074. Veilleux, Gerard. Intergovernmental Canada: government by conference? A fiscal and economic perspective. *Canadian Public Administration*; 1980 Spring; 23(1): 33-53.

2075. Warhurst, John. Canada's intergovernmental relations specialists. *Australian Journal of Public Administration*; 1983 December; 42(4): 459-481.

2076. Warhurst, John. *Central agencies, intergovernmental managers, and Australian federal-state relations*. Canberra: Centre for Research on Federal Financial Relations, Australian National University; 1983; vi, 27 p. (Occasional paper; 29).

2077. West, Edwin G.; Winer, Stanley L. Will federal centralization help the poor?: *Canadian Public Policy*; 1980 Autumn; 6(4): 662-667.

2078. Western Premiers Conference (1980). *Western Premiers Conference, 1980: communique no.2: Western Premiers' Task Force on Constitutional Trends*; 1980; Lethbridge. [Ottawa]: Canadian Intergovernmental Conference Secretariat; 1980.

2079. Williamson, Richard S. Block grants - a federalist tool. In: Zimmerman, Dierdre A.; Zimmerman, Joseph F., eds. *The politics of subnational governance*. New York: University Press of America; 1983: 11-19.

2080. Wiltshire, Kenneth. Working with intergovernmental agreements - the Canadian and Australian experience. *Canadian Public Administration*; 1980 Fall; 23(3): 353-379.

2081. Woolstencroft, Timothy Bryn. *Intergovernmental emissaries-the provincial guardians of the federal bargain: a case study of Alberta and Ontario* [microfiche]: (M.A.) Queen's University; 1980 3 microfiches (293 fr.). Ottawa: National Library of Canada, 1982. Note: Canadian theses on microfiche.

2082. Wright, Deil Spenser. *Understanding intergovernmental relations*. 2nd ed. Monterey, Cal: Brooks/Cole; c1982; xii, 532 p. (The Brooks/Cole series on public policy).

2083. Young, R.A.; Faucher, Philippe; Blais, André. The concept of province-building: a critique. *Canadian Journal of Political Science*; 1984 December; 17(4): 783-818.

2084. Zimmerman, Dierdre A.; Zimmerman Joseph F., eds. *The politics of subnational governance*. New York: University Press of America; 1983; x, 401 p.

2085. Zukowsy, Ronald James. *Intergovernmental relations in Canada: the year in review 1980*. Kingston: Institute of Intergovernmental Relations, Queen's University; c1981. (2 v.).

5 Policy Issues and Roles

2086. Abele, Frances; Dosman, E. J. Interdepartmental coordination and northern development. *Canadian Public Adminstration*;1981 Fall; 24(3): 428-451.

2087. Abonyi, Arpad; Atkinson, Michael M. Technological innovation and industrial policy: Canada in an international context. In: Atkinson, Michael M.; Chandler, Marsha A, eds. *The politics of Canadian public policy.* Toronto: University of Toronto Press; 1983: 93-126; 286 p. (Studies in Canadian public policy).

2088. Acheson, Keith. Economic regulation in Canada: a survey. In: McFetridge, Donald G., res. coord. *Canadian industrial policy in action.* Toronto: University of Toronto Press, Royal Commission on the Economic Union and Development Prospects for Canada; 1985: 155-193; xvii, 231 p. (The collected research studies; v. 4).

2089. Adams, R. J. The federal government and tripartism. *Industrial Relations*; 1982; 37(3): 606-617.

2090. Advisory Commission on Intergovernmental Relations. *The federal role in the federal system: the dynamics of growth. Public assistance: the growth of a federal function.* Washington D.C.: ACIR; 1980; 123 p.

2091. Advisory Commission on Intergovernmental Relations. *The federal role in the federal system: the dynamics of growth. Intergovernmentalizing the classroom: federal involvement in elementary and secondary education.* Washington D.C.: ACIR; 1981; ix, 81 p. (Commission report; v. A-81).

2092. Advisory Commission on Intergovernmental Relations. *Regulatory federalism: policy, process, impact and reform.* Washington D.C.: ACIR; 1984; x, 326 p. (Commission report; A-95).

2093. Advisory Council for Inter-government Relations. *The provision of services for the aged: a report on relations among governments in Australia.* Canberra: Australian Government Publishing Service; 1983; ix, 206 p. (Relationships Reference; v. 6).

2094. Air Pollution Association and Federation of Associations on the Canadian Environment. *Proceedings: environmental government affairs seminar* (Conference on Environmental Concerns of the 80's); October 12, 1982; Ottawa. [Ottawa]; 1982; 519 p.

2095. Ajao, Ade; Ironside, R.G. Federal Canadian industrial development programs and their implications for Alberta. In: Barr, B.M.; Waters, N.M., eds. *Regional diversification and structural change: proceedings of the Canada-United*

Kingdom symposium on industrial geography; August 1983; Calgary. Vancouver: Tantalus Research; 1984: 222-231. (B.C. Geographical series; 39).

2096. Alberta. *Free trade with the United States: an Alberta perspective.* First Ministers' Conference on the Economy; 1985; Regina. Edmonton: Government of Alberta; 1985; 14 p.

2097. Alberta. *Proposals for an industrial and science strategy for Albertans 1985 to 1990: white paper.* Edmonton: Government of Alberta; 1984; 107 p.

2098. Alberta. *The road to recovery: restoring investor confidence.* (Presented at 23rd Annual Premiers' Conference, Halifax, Nova Scotia). Edmonton: Government of Alberta; 1982 15 p.

2099. Alberta. *Submission to the Committee of Inquiry on Crow Benefit Payment: the Western Grain Transportation Acts.* Edmonton: Government of Alberta; 1984; 25 p.

2100. Alberta. Alberta Economic Development. *Western Grain Transportation Act: Alberta's view.* Edmonton: Alberta Economic Development; 1984; [8] p.

2101. Alberta. Alberta Energy and Natural Resources. *Two perspectives on forestry : national and provincial; excerpts from speeches delivered by F.W. McDougall, Deputy Minister, Renewable Resources, Energy and Natural Resources.* Edmonton: Alberta Energy and Natural Resources; 1983; 27 p.

2102. Alberta. Alberta North Joint Committee. *Canada/Alberta Subsidiary Agreement on Alberta North, April 1, 1977 - March 31, 1983. Provincial Co-ordinator's report to Alberta North Joint Committee.* Edmonton: Alberta Tourism and Small Business, Northern Development Branch; 1984; 33 p.

2103. Alberta. Alberta Social Services and Community Health.; Price Waterhouse Associates. *Interprovincial comparisons: day care facilities, full-day programs: October, 1982.* [Vancouver]: Price Waterhouse Associates; 1982; i v. (various foliations).

2104. Alberta. Alberta Social Services and Community Health.; Price Waterhouse Associates. *Social services & community health : interprovincial comparison : day care facilities : licensed full day program.* Edmonton: Price Waterhouse Associates; 1980; [25] leaves.

2105. Alberta. Energy Resources Conservation Board. *Report on proceeding no. 800065: estimates of ultimate potential and forecasts of attainable productive capacity of Alberta's crude oil and equivalent: supplementary report on impact of the National Energy Program, the federal budget and provincial government announcements on supply forecasts for 1980 to 1990 of crude oil and equivalent, and natural gas.* Calgary: Energy Resources Conservation Board; 1981; various pagings.

2106. Alberta.; Canada. Parliament. House of Commons. Standing Committee on Transport. *Submission to the House of Commons Standing Committee on*

Transport, August 1983: The Western Canada Grain Transportation Act, bill C-155. Edmonton: Government of Alberta; 1983; 10, (9) p.

2107. Alexander, David G. Economic growth in the Atlantic region, 1880-1940. In: Bercuson, David Jay; Buckner, Phillip A., eds. *Eastern and Western perspectives*. Toronto: University of Toronto Press; 1981: 197-227; xi, 227 p.

2108. Alexander, David G. The erosion of social democracy in Canada. In: *idem, Atlantic Canada and Confederation: essays in Canadian political economy*. Toronto: University of Toronto Press; 1983: 106-109; ix, 157 p.

2109. Alexander, David G. Literacy and economic development in nineteenth-century Newfoundland. In: *idem, Atlantic Canada and Confederation: essays in Canadian political economy*. Toronto: University of Toronto Press; 1983: 110-145; ix, 157 p.

2110. Alexander, David G. New notions of happiness: nationalism, regionalism, and Atlantic Canada. In: *idem, Atlantic Canada and Confederation: essays in Canadian political economy*. Toronto: University of Toronto Press; 1983: 79-100; ix, 157 p.

2111. Alexander, David G. The political economy of fishing in Newfoundland. In: *idem*, ed. *Atlantic Canada and Confederation: essays in Canadian political economy*. Toronto: University of Toronto Press; 1983: 32-43; ix, 157 p.

2112. Alexander, David G. *Atlantic Canada and Confederation: essays in Canadian political economy*. Toronto: University of Toronto Press; 1983; ix, 157 p.

2113. Amdur, Reuel S. *Prevention in the Canada Assistance Plan: a likely story: a working paper*. Toronto: Social Planning Council of Metropolitan Toronto; 1980; i, 14 leaves.

2114. Anastasopoulos, Anastasios; Sims, William A. The regional impact of the disintegration of the Canadian common market: the case of Quebec. *Southern Economic Journal*; 1983 January; 49(3): 743-63.

2115. Anastasopoulos, Anastasios; Brault, L.; Sims, William A. The impact on the Quebec economy of a disruption of trade relations between Quebec and its major trading partners. *Canadian Public Policy*; 1980 Autumn; 6(4): 574-83.

2116. Anderson, F. J.; Bonsor, N. C. Regional economic alienation: Atlantic Canada and the West. In: Norrie, Kenneth, res. coord. *Disparities and interregional adjustment*. Toronto: University of Toronto Press; Royal Commission on the Economic Union and Development Prospects for Canada; 1986: 185-221; xiv, 223 p. (The collected research studies; v. 64).

2117. Anderson, F.J. *Natural resources in Canada: economic theory and policy*. Toronto: Methuen; c1985; ix, 301 p.

2118. Anderson, W. J.; Gellner, J. A. Canadian agricultural policy in the export sector. *Canadian Journal of Agricultural Economics* (Proceedings); 1985; 32: 170-185.

2119. Anisman, Philip. The regulation of the securities market and the harmonization of provincial laws. In: Cuming, Ronald C. C., res. coord. *Harmonization of business law in Canada*. Toronto: University of Toronto Press; Royal Commission on the Economic Union and Development Prospects for Canada; 1986: 77-168; xx, 245 p. (The collected research studies; v. 56).

2120. Annual Conference of the Provincial Ministers of Mines, 37th; Mining Association of Canada [pamphlet: 11-49 p.]. *Canadian mining industry and constitutional change: a submission to the Provincial Ministers of Mines; 1980*; Halifax. [s.l.]: The Conference; 1980.

2121. Anonymous. 1983: the year in review. The national view: Canada Health Act looms large. *Canadian Medical Association Journal*; 1984; 130(1): 61-70.

2122. Anonymous. Le Commissaire aux langues officielles présente son dixième rapport. *Vie française*; 1981 April-June; 35(4-6): 4-22.

2123. Anonymous. *Federal and provincial government expenditures to assist and promote rental housing in Canada, 1976-1982*. [Toronto]: [A. Anderson]; 1984; 43 p.

2124. Anonymous. Industrial development in Canada - a panel discussion. *Cost and Management*; 1981 September-October; 55(5): 14-25.

2125. Anonymous. Regulation of Canada's financial markets. *Canadian Business Law Journal*; 1985 December; (1): 48-78.

2126. Asimakopulos, A. Financing Canada's public pensions - who pays?: *Canadian Public Policy*; 1984 June; 10(2): 156-166.

2127. Asimakopulos, A. Public pensions, the federal budget, and discrimination. *Canadian Public Policy*; 1983 March; 9(1): 105-13.

2128. Association of Universities and Colleges of Canada. *Funding Canada's universities in the 1980's : report on the meeting of the Association of Universities and Colleges of Canada*; March 3-4, 1982; Victoria. Ottawa: The Association; 1982; 31 p.

2129. Association of Universities and Colleges of Canada. Annual Meeting. *The management of diminishing resources: Proceedings of the Annual Meeting of the Association of Universities and Colleges*; October 5-7, 1982; Fredericton. Ottawa: The Association; [1982?]; 117 p.

2130. Association of Universities and Colleges of Canada. Research and Analysis Division. *Compendium of university statistics*. Ottawa: The Association; 1983; 8 p.

2131. Association of Universities and Colleges of Canada. Research and Analysis Division. *Compendium of university statistics*. Ottawa: The Association; 1983; 35 p.

2132. Atlantic Provinces Economic Council. *Atlantic Provinces Economic Council - presentation to The House of Commons Standing Committee on Regional Development* [s.l.]: APEC; 1983.

2133. Aucoin, Peter. Federal health care policy. In: Meilicke, Carl A.; Storch, Janet L, eds. *Perspectives on Canadian health and social services policy: history and emerging trends*. Michigan: Health Administration Press; 1980: 224-268; xii, 520 p.

2134. Aucoin, Peter, res. coord. *Regional responsiveness and the national administrative state*. Toronto: University of Toronto Press; Royal Commission on the Economic Union and Development Prospects for Canada; 1985; xv, 119 p. (The collected research studies; 37).

2135. Aucoin, Peter; Bakvis, Herman. Organizational differentiation and integration: the case of regional economic development policy in Canada. *Canadian Public Administration*; 1984 Fall; 27(3): 348-371.

2136. Aucoin, Peter; Bakvis, Herman. Regional responsiveness and government organization: the case of regional economic development policy in Canada. In: Aucoin, Peter, res. coord. *Regional responsiveness and the national administrative state*. Toronto: University of Toronto Press; Royal Commission on the Economic Union and Development Prospects for Canada; 1985: 51-118; xv, 119 p. (The collected research studies; 37).

2137. Aziz, Rashid; Butterfield, David; Kuburski, Atif. Regional equity and efficiency: some experiments for Canada. *Journal of Regional Science*; 1983 August; 23(3): 397-412.

2138. Baggaley, Carman D. *The emergence of the regulatory state in Canada, 1867-1939*. Ottawa: Economic Council of Canada; 1981; x, 290, (5) p. (Technical report; 15).

2139. Bahl, Roy W.; Linn, Johannes F. The assignment of local government revenues in developing countries. In: McLure, Charles E., Jr., ed. *Tax assignment in federal countries*. Canberra: ANU Press; 1983: 177-203; xix, 370 p.

2140. Bailey, Arthur R.; Hull, Douglas G. *The way out: a more revenue-dependent public sector and how it might revitalize the process of governing*. Montreal: Institute for Research on Public Policy; c1980; xxiv, 85 p.

2141. Bajic, Vladimir. Provincial housing policy. In: Jamieson, Barbara, ed. *Governing Nova Scotia: policies, priorities, and the 1984-85 budget*. Halifax: School of Public Administration, Dalhousie University; 1984: 113-126; x, 226 p.

2142. Bakvis, Herman; Mazany, R.L.; Sinclair, A. Energy policy. In: Jamieson, Barbara, ed. *Governing Nova Scotia: policies, priorities, and the 1984-85 budget*.

Halifax: School of Public Administration, Dalhousie University; 1984: 65-79; x, 226 p.

2143. Baldwin, John R. Federal regulation and public policy in the Canadian petroleum industry: 1958-1975. *Journal of Business Administration*; 1983; 13(1).

2144. Baldwin, John R.; Gorecki, Paul K. *The determinants of the Canadian tariff structure before and after the Kennedy round: 1966, 1970.* Ottawa: Economic Council of Canada; 1985; vi, 69 p. (Discussion paper; 280).

2145. Ballantyne, Janet. The changing role of provincial motor fuel tax revenue. *Canadian Tax Journal*; 1980 July-August; 28(4): 529-533.

2146. Bankes, Nigel D. Constitutional problems related to the creation and administration of Canada's national parks. In: Saunders, J. Owen, ed. *Managing natural resources in a federal state.* Toronto: Carswell; 1986: 212-234; vi, 336 p.

2147. Bankes, Nigel D. Saunders, J. Owen. *Public disposition of natural resources: essays from the first Banff Conference on Natural Resources Law; April 12-15, 1983*; Banff. Calgary: Canadian Institute of Resources Law; 1984; xii, 366 p.; 24 cm.

2148. Banting, Keith G. The decision rules: federalism and pension reform. In: Conklin, David W.; Bennett, Jaylynn H.; Courchene, Thomas J., eds. *Pensions today and tomorrow: background studies.* Toronto: Ontario Economic Council; 1984: 189-209; 486 p. (Special research report/Ontario Economic Council).

2149. Banting, Keith G. Institutional conservatism: federalism and pension reform. In: Ismael, Jacqueline S, ed. *Canadian social welfare policy: federal and provincial dimensions.* Kingston: McGill-Queen's University Press; 1985: 48-74; xviii, 187 p. (Canadian public administration).

2150. Banting, Keith G. *The welfare state and Canadian federalism.* Kingston: McGill-Queen's University Press; Institute of Intergovernmental Relations; 1982; xii, 226 p. (Queen's studies on the future of the Canadian communities; v. 3).

2151. Barrett, Gene; Davis, Anthony. Floundering in troubled waters: the political economy of the Atlantic fishery and the Task Force on Atlantic Fisheries. *Journal of Canadian Studies*; 1984 Spring; 19(1): 125-137.

2152. Barry, Leo. Offshore petroleum agreements: an analysis of the Nova Scotian and Newfoundland experience. In: Saunders, J. Owen, ed. *Managing natural resources in a federal state.* Toronto: Carswell; 1986: 177-188; vi, 336 p.

2153. Bartlett, Richard H. Provincial jurisdiction and resource development on Indian reserve lands. In: Saunders, J. Owen, ed. *Managing natural resources in a federal state.* Toronto: Carswell; 1986: 189-211; vi, 336 p.

2154. Barton, Barry. Cooperative management of interprovincial water resources. In: Saunders, J. Owen, ed. *Managing natural resources in a federal state.* Toronto: Carswell; 1986: 235-250; vi, 336 p.

2155. Beach, Charles M. Who will pay for proposed public pension reforms? In: Conklin, David W.; Bennett, Jalynn H.; Courchene, Thomas J, eds. *Pensions today and tomorrow: background studies*. Toronto: Ontario Economic Council; 1984: 210-240; 486 p. (Special research report/Ontario Economic Council).

2156. Begin, M. Health minister Begin comments on proposed Canada Health Act. *Canadian Medical Association Journal*; 1983 March; 128(6): 730-1, 734.

2157. Beigie, Carl. Macroeconomic perspectives of Canada-U.S. trade agreements. *Canada-United States Law Journal*; 1985; 10: 131-136.

2158. Beigie, Carl E.; Hero, Alfred O., Jr., eds. *Natural resources in U.S.-Canadian relations*. Boulder, CO: Westview Press; 1980; xiii, 371 p.

2159. Bélanger, Gérard. Les aspects économiques des programmes de sécurité financière pour les personnes âgées. *Canadian Public Administration*; 1983 Spring; 26(1): 1-15.

2160. Bellan, R.C.; Pope, W.H. *The Canadian economy: problems and options*. Toronto: McGraw-Hill Ryerson; c1981; 394 p.

2161. Belobaba, Edward P. *Products liability and consumer product warranty reform in Canada: the constitutional implications*. Toronto: Consumer and Corporate Affairs Canada; 1981; ii, 38 p.

2162. Bernard, Jean-Thomas. L'évolution de la fiscalité minière fédérale de 1972 à 1978. *L'Actualité économique*; 1980 October-December; 56(4): 597-610.

2163. Bernard, Jean-Thomas. L'exportation d'électricité par le Québec. *Canadian Public Policy*; 1982 Summer; 8(3): 321-333.

2164. Bernard, Jean-Thomas. La rente des ressources naturelles. *Canadian Public Policy*; 1982; 8(3): 297-299.

2165. Bernier, Ivan; Lajoie, Andrée, res. coords. *Consumer protection, environmental law, and corporate power*. Toronto: University of Toronto Press; Royal Commission on the Economic Union and Development Prospects for Canada; 1985; xv, 220 p. (The collected research studies; v. 50).

2166. Berthelet, D. Agriculture Canada policy and expenditure patterns 1868-1983. *Canadian Farm Economics*; 1985; 19(1): 5-15.

2167. Bickerton, James; Gagnon, Alain G. Regional policy in historical perspective: the federal role in regional economic development. *American Review of Canadian Studies*; 1984 Spring; 14(1): 79-92.

2168. Binhammer, H.H.; McDonough, Lawrence Cecil; Lepore, G. *Government grants to private sector firms*. Ottawa: Economic Council of Canada; 1983; iii, 120 p. (Discussion paper; v. 227).

2169. Bird, Richard M. Tax harmonization and federal finance: a perspective on recent Canadian discussion. *Canadian Public Policy*; 1984 September; 10(3): 235-66.

2170. Blackbourn, Anthony; Putnam, Robert G. *The industrial geography of Canada*. Croom Helm Ltd; 1984; 201 p.

2171. Blair, Allan. Capital investment as a vehicle for regional development. *Cost and Management*; 1985 January-February; 59(1): 38-40.

2172. Blais, André. The debate on Canadian industrial policy. In: Blais, André, Res. Coord. *Industrial policy*. Toronto: University of Toronto Press; Royal Commission on the Economic Union and Development Prospects for Canada; 1986: 55-82; xvii, 379 p. (The collected research studies; v. 44).

2173. Blais, André, res. coord. *Industrial policy*. Toronto: University of Toronto Press; Royal Commission on the Economic Union and Development Prospects for Canada; 1986; xvii, 379 p. (The collected research studies; 44).

2174. Blais, André; McRoberts, Kenneth. Public expenditure in Ontario and Quebec, 1950-1980: explaining the differences. *Journal of Canadian Studies*; 1983 Spring; 18(1): 28-53.

2175. Blomqvist, A. G. Political economy of the Canadian welfare state. In: Laidler, David, res. coord. *Approaches to economic well-being*. Toronto: University of Toronto Press; Royal Commission on the Economic Union and Development Prospects for Canada; 1985: 89-136; xix, 249 p. (The collected research studies; 26).

2176. Boadway, Robin. Economic implications of revenue-sharing alternatives. In: Saunders, J. Owen, ed. *Managing natural resources in a federal state*. Toronto: Carswell; 1986: 103-120; vi, 336 p.

2177. Boadway, Robin; Flatters, Frank. The efficiency basis for regional employment policy. *Canadian Journal of Economics*; 1981 February; 14(1): 58-77.

2178. Bon, Daniel L.; Hart, Kenneth D. *Linking Canada's new solitudes: the executive interchange program and business-government relations*. Ottawa: Conference Board of Canada; 1983; xi, 55 p. (Study; 77).

2179. Bonus, John L. Canadian mineral industry in the 1980s - issues and opportunities. *Resources Policy*; 1981 March; 7(1): 58-60.

2180. Boon, John. Telecommunications and the Constitution. *Saskatchewan Law Review*; 1984-85; 49(1): 70-88.

2181. Borins, Sandford F. *The language of the skies: the bilingual air traffic control conflict in Canada*. Kingston: McGill-Queen's University Press; 1983; xvii, 285 p.

2182. Borins, Sandford F. Ottawa's expenditure "envelopes": workable rationality at last? In: Doern, G. Bruce, ed. *How Ottawa spends your tax dollars - 1982*. Toronto: James Lorimer; 1982: 63-86; v, 256 p.

2183. Boucher, Michel. Le régime d'épargne-actions du Québec: mal réellement nécessaire? *Canadian Public Policy*; 1985 June; 11(2): 196-205.

2184. Bourhis, Richard Y. The Charter of the French Language and cross-cultural communication in Montreal. In: *idem*, ed. *Conflict and language planning in Quebec*. London: Multilingual Matters; 1984: 174-204; xvi, 304 p. (Multilingual Matters; v. 5).

2185. Bourhis, Richard Y, ed. *Conflict and language planning in Quebec*. London: Multilingual Matters; 1984; xvi, 304 p. (Multilingual matters; v. 5).

2186. Bourhis, Richard Y. Introduction: language policies in multilingual settings. In: idem. ed. *Conflict and language planning in Quebec*. London: Multilingual Matters; 1984: 1-28; xvi, 304 p. (Multilingual Matters; v. 5).

2187. Bourne, L. S. Regional policy in Canada: an urban system perspective. *Canadian Journal of Regional Science*; 1982 Autumn; 5(2): 283-290.

2188. Bovey, Edmund C. *Ontario universities: options and future*. [Toronto]: Commission on the Future Development of the Universities of Ontario.; Ontario. Ministry of Colleges and Universities; 1984; 64 p.

2189. Bowman, C. Myrna. *Practical tools to improve interprovincial enforcement of maintenance orders after divorce: a study paper*. Ottawa: Law Reform Commission of Canada; 1980; v, 50 p. (Modernization of statutes series).

2190. Boyd, H. J. *Federal roles in wildlife management in Canada*. Forty-fourth North American Wildlife and Natural Resources Conference; 24-28 March 1979; Toronto: Wildlife Management Institute.

2191. Brait, Richard A. The constitutional jurisdiction to regulate the provision of the telephone services in Canada. *Ottawa Law Journal*; 1981 Winter; 13(1): 53-94.

2192. Braithwaite, Carlton. *The impact of investment incentives on Canada's economic growth*. Ottawa: Economic Council of Canada; 1983; ix, 128 p.

2193. Brandon, L.V. *Energy and the environment*. Halifax: Atlantic Provinces Economic Council; 1981; 9 p. (Discussion paper; 1).

2194. Bray, C. E. Agricultural land regulation in several Canadian provinces. *Canadian Public Policy*; 1980 Autumn; 6(4): 591-604.

2195. Brennan, Geoffrey; Buchanan, James. Normative tax theory for a federal polity: some public choice preliminaries. In: McLure, Charles E., Jr. *Tax assignment in federal countries*. Canberra: Centre for Research on Federal Financial Relations, Australian National University; 1983: 52-65; xix, 370 p.

2196. Breton, Albert. Public goods and the stability of federalism. In: Bhajan, Grewal S. [and others], ed. *The economics of federalism*. Canberra: Australian National University; 1980: 155-172; xiii, 432 p.

2197. Breton, Albert. The theory of local government finance and the debt regulation of local governments. In: Grewal, Bhajan S. [and others], ed. *The economics of federalism*. Canberra: Australian National University; 1980: 365-377; xiii, 432 p.

2198. British Columbia. Ministry of Forests; Canada. Canadian Forestry Service. *Canada-British Columbia Forest Resource Development Agreement (1985-1990)*. [s.l.]: Government of British Columbia; Government of Canada; [1985]; 32 p.

2199. Brooks, David B.; Paehlke, Robert C. Canada: a soft path in a hard country. *Canadian Public Policy* ; 1980 Summer; 6(3): 444-53.

2200. Brown, Douglas; Eastman, Julia; Tupper, Allan. *The limits of consultation: a debate among Ottawa, the provinces and the private sector on industrial strategy : a discussion paper*. Kingston: Institute of Intergovernmental Relations, Queen's University; Science Council of Canada; c1981; 195 p. (Discussion paper / Science Council of Canada D81; 1).

2201. Brown, Murray G.; Ruderman, Peter. Health expenditures. In: Jamieson, Barbara. *Governing Nova Scotia: policies, priorities, and the 1984-85 budget*. Halifax: School of Public Administration, Dalhousie University; 1984: 149-161; x, 226 p.

2202. Brown-John, Lloyd. Comprehensive regulatory consultation in Canada's food processing industry. *Canadian Public Administration*; 1985 Spring; 28(1): 70-98.

2203. Brown-John, Lloyd. Consultative regulation. *Policy Options*; 1984 July-August; 5(4): 37-43.

2204. Bryan, Ingrid A. Conference freight rates and eastern Canadian ports. *Canadian Public Policy*; 1984 June; 10(2): 193-200.

2205. Bryden, Kenneth. Public input into policy-making and administration: the present situation and some requirements for the future. *Canadian Public Administration*; 1982 Spring; 25(1): 81-107.

2206. Buchan, Robert J. *Telecommunications regulation and the Constitution*. Montreal: Institute for Research on Public Policy; 1982; xxii, 276 p.

2207. Buchman, James M.; Goetz, Charles J. Efficiency limits of fiscal mobility: an assessment of the Tiebout model. In: Grewal, Bhajan S. [and others], ed. *The economics of federalism*. Canberra: Australian National University; 1980: 71-88; xiii, 432 p.

2208. Burns, R. M. *The acceptable mean: the tax agreements, 1941-1962*. Toronto: Canadian Tax Foundation; 1980; viii, 285 p. (Financing Canadian federation; 3).

2209. Burton, T.L. The promises and problems of coordination in parks development and management. J.G. Nelson; R.D. Needham; S.H. Nelson and R.C. Scace, eds. *The Canadian national parks: today and tomorrow. Conference II: ten years later*. Waterloo: Faculty of Environmental Studies, University of Waterloo; 1979: 313-327.

2210. Butler, Eric D.; Gostick, Ron. *The battle for Canada*. 2nd ed. Flesherton, Ont: Canadian League of Rights; [1980]; 29 p.

2211. Byers, R.B.; Leyton-Brown, David. The strategic and economic implications for the United States of a sovereign Quebec. *Canadian Public Policy*; 1980 Spring; 6(2): 325-341.

2212. Cairns, Robert D. Reform of exhaustible resource taxation. *Canadian Public Policy*; 1985 December; 11(4): 649-658.

2213. Cameron, David M. Financing post-secondary education in Nova Scotia. In: Jamieson, Barbara, ed. *Governing Nova Scotia: policies, priorities, and the 1984-85 budget*. Halifax: School of Public Administration, Dalhousie University; 1984: 181-195; x, 226 p.

2214. Cameron, David M. Postsecondary education: some thoughts on the position of the government of Canada. In: Courchene, Thomas J.; Conklin, David W.; Cook, Gail C.A, eds. *Ottawa and the provinces: the distribution of money and power*. Toronto: Ontario Economic Council; 1985; 1: 315-322; xii, 341 p. (Special research report/Ontario Economic Council).

2215. Cameron, David M. Regional economic disparities: the challenge to federalism and public policy. *Canadian Public Policy*; 1981 Autumn; 7(4): 500-505.

2216. Cameron, David R. A commentary on the Johnson report. In: Noordeh, Ardeshir, ed. *Reforming the financing arrangements for post-secondary education in Canada*. Toronto: Ontario Economic Council; [1985]: 18-25; x, 160 p.

2217. Campbell, A. E. H. Regulations and the orwellian state. *Canadian Public Administration*; 1985 Spring; 28(1): 150-155.

2218. Canada. *Intergovernmental position paper on the principles and framework for regional economic development / by the Government of Canada and the Governments of the Provinces...and the Governments of Yukon and the Northwest Territories*. [Ottawa]: [Government of Canada]; 1985; 17, 19 p.

2219. Canada Studies Foundation. *The challenges of Canada's regional diversity*. Toronto: Canada Studies Foundation; 1981; (134) p. (The Walter L. Gordon lecture series, 1980-81; v. 5).

2220. Canada West Foundation. Special Task Force. *Western Canadian agriculture to 1990*. Canada West Foundation; 1980; xvi, 302 p.

2221. Canada, Department of Indian Affairs and Northern Development. *Report on the nature and cost of the transition to Nunavut*. Ottawa: Department of Indian Affairs and Northern Development; 1984; v, 47 p.

2222. Canada-Manitoba Joint Forest Research Committee. *Forestry research plan for Manitoba 1984-89*. Edmonton: Canadian Forestry Service, Northern Forest Research Centre; 1984; viii, 127 p.

2223. Canada-United States Law Institute. *Conference proceedings: the legal aspects of sectoral integration between the United States and Canada*; April 19-21, 1985; Cleveland. [s.l.]: Canada-United States Law Institute; 1985; 10; 256 p.

2224. Canada. Agriculture Canada; New Brunswick. Agriculture and Rural Development. *Canada-New Brunswick Agri-food Development Subsidiary Agreement 1984-1989*. [Ottawa]: Agriculture Canada; New Brunswick Dept. of Agriculture and Rural Development; [1984]; 34 p.

2225. Canada. Commission on Pacific Fisheries Policy. *Conflict and opportunity: toward a new policy for Canada's pacific fisheries: a preliminary report of The Commission on Pacific Fisheries Policy*, by Peter H. Pearse. Vancouver: The Commission; 1981; 148 p.

2226. Canada. Consultative Task Force on Industrial and Regional Benefits from Major Canadian Projects. *Major Canadian projects: major Canadian opportunities: a report*. Ottawa: The Task Force; 1981; 96 p.

2227. Canada. Department of Agriculture. *Interprovincial barriers to trade in agriculture products*, by E.L. Menzie [Ottawa]: Department of Agriculture; 1980.

2228. Canada. Department of Communications. *Federal-Provincial Conference of Communications Ministers - pre-conference statement by the Honourable Francis Fox, Minister of Communications*; May 20, 1982; Calgary. [Ottawa]: Department of Communications; 1982.

2229. Canada. Department of Consumer and Corporate Affairs. *Interprovincial product liability litigation: jurisdiction, enforcement and choice of law*, by R.J. Sharpe. [Ottawa]: Department of Consumer and Corporate Affairs; 1981.

2230. Canada. Department of Consumer and Corporate Affairs. *Interprovincial product liability litigation: jurisdiction, enforcement and choice of law in Quebec - private international law*, by D. Appel [Ottawa]: Department of Consumer and Corporate Affairs; 1982.

2231. Canada. Department of Employment and Immigration. Task Force on Unemployment Insurance. *Unemployment insurance interprovincial transfers*. [Ottawa]: Department of Employment and Immigration; 1981.

2232. Canada. Department of Energy, Mines and Resources. *The National Energy Program*. Ottawa: Supply and Services Canada; 1980; 115, 127 p.

2233. Canada. Department of Energy, Mines and Resources. Office of Energy Research and Development. *Estimated energy R&D funding by the Governments of the Provinces and Territories in 1978-79, 1979-80, and 1980-81*. [Ottawa]: Energy, Mines, and Resources; [1982]; 70, 3, 34 p.

2234. Canada. Department of External Affairs. *Communications: the Canadian experience*. Ottawa: Department of External Affairs; 1981; 14 p.

2235. Canada. Department of External Affairs. *The French fact in Canada*. Department of External Affairs; 1985; 21 p.

2236. Canada. Department of Finance. *Canada's economic prospects, 1985-1990: the challenge of economic renewal*, by Michael H. Wilson. Ottawa: Department of Finance; 1985; ix, 26, 28, ix p.

2237. Canada. Department of Finance. *The Canadian budgetary process : proposals for improvement*, by Michael H. Wilson. Ottawa: Department of Finance; 1985; v, 36, 39, v p.

2238. Canada. Department of Finance. *The corporate income tax system : a direction for change*, by Michael H. Wilson. Ottawa: Department of Finance; 1985; 50, 55 p.

2239. Canada. Department of Finance. *The current situation and prospects for the Canadian economy in the short and medium term*. [Ottawa]: Department of Finance; [1981]; 30, 30 p.

2240. Canada. Department of Finance. *Economic and fiscal statement*, by Michael H. Wilson. [Ottawa]: Department of Finance; [1984]; 17, 19 p.

2241. Canada. Department of Finance. *Fiscal arrangements in the eighties: proposals of the Government of Canada*, presented by Allan J. MacEachen. [Ottawa]: Department of Finance; 1981; 55 p.

2242. Canada. Department of Finance. *Research and development: tax policies: a paper for consultation*, by the Honourable Marc Lalonde, Minister of Finance. Ottawa: Department of Finance; 1983; 33, 35 p.

2243. Canada. Department of Fisheries and Oceans. *Policy for Canada's Atlantic fisheries in the 1980's: a discussion paper*. Ottawa: Department of Fisheries and Oceans; 1981; 2, v, 60 p.

2244. Canada. Department of Industry Trade and Commerce. *Discussion paper: industrial adjustment policies*. First Ministers' Conference on the Economy; November 27-29, 1978; [Ottawa]; 1978; 21 p. [24 p.].

2245. Canada. Department of Industry, Trade and Commerce; Canada. Department of Regional Economic Expansion. *Industrial and regional development: the proposal* [Ottawa]: Industry, Trade and Commerce; 1983.

2246. Canada. Department of Justice. *Information paper: statute law (Canadian Charter of Rights and Freedoms) amendment bill; equality issues in federal law - a discussion paper* [Ottawa]: Department of Justice; 1985.

2247. Canada. Department of Regional Economic Expansion. *Discussion paper: economic circumstances and medium-term prospects by province.* First Ministers' Conference on the Economy; November 27-29, 1978; Ottawa. [Ottawa]: Canadian Intergovernmental Conference Secretariat; 1978; 89 p. [96 p.].

2248. Canada. Department of Regional Economic Expansion. *Major projects inventory issue 2.* [Ottawa]: Department of Regional Economic Expansion; 1983; 106 p.

2249. Canada. Department of Regional Economic Expansion. *Opportunities for industry and business in Canada; regional development incentives.* Ottawa: DREE; 1981; 28 (28) p.

2250. Canada. Department of Regional Economic Expansion. *Strategic regional development overview - Atlantic region* [Ottawa]: Department of Regional Economic Expansion; 1980.

2251. Canada. Department of Regional Economic Expansion. *Strategic regional development overview - Canada* [Ottawa]: Department of Regional Economic Expansion; 1980.

2252. Canada. Department of Regional Economic Expansion. *Strategic regional development overview - Ontario* [Ottawa]: Department of Regional Economic Expansion; 1980.

2253. Canada. Department of Regional Economic Expansion. *Strategic regional development overview - Quebec* [Ottawa]: Department of Regional Economic Expansion; 1980.

2254. Canada. Department of Regional Economic Expansion. *Strategic regional development overview - western region* [Ottawa]: Department of Regional Economic Expansion; 1980.

2255. Canada. Department of Regional Economic Expansion. *Strategic regional development overview*: Canada. Ottawa: DREE; 1981; 7 (8) p.

2256. Canada. Department of Regional Economic Expansion. *Strategic regional development overview*: Ontario. Ottawa: DREE; 1981; 29 (31) p.

2257. Canada. Department of Regional Economic Expansion. *Strategic regional development overview:* Quebec. Ottawa: DREE; 1981; 28 (32) p.

2258. Canada. Department of Regional Economic Expansion; Organisation for Economic Co-Operation and Development. *Regional policies in Canada.* Paris: OECD; 1980; 80 p.

2259. Canada. Department of Regional Industrial Expansion. *Industrial and regional development program.* Rev. ed. Ottawa: Department of Regional Industrial Expansion; 1984; 9, 9 p.

2260. Canada. Department of Regional Industrial Expansion. *Intergovernmental position paper on the principles and framework for regional economic development* [Ottawa]: Department of Regional Industrial Expansion; 1985.

2261. Canada. Department of the Environment; Federal-Provincial Committee on Air Pollution. *Guidelines for an annual air quality index - report by the Federal-provincial Committee on Air Pollution* [Ottawa]: Department of the Environment; 1980.

2262. Canada. Economic Council of Canada. *Internal migration and fiscal structure (interprovincial migration in Canada)* [Ottawa]: Economic Council of Canada; 1982.

2263. Canada. Energy, Mines and Resources Canada. *The National Energy Program.* [Ottawa]: Energy, Mines and Resources Canada; 1980; 115 p.

2264. Canada. Energy, Mines and Resources Canada. *The National Energy Program: update 1982.* Ottawa: EMR; 1982; vi, 94 p.

2265. Canada. Energy, Mines and Resources Canada. *Nuclear policy review: background papers.* Ottawa: EMR; 1981; 359 p.

2266. Canada. Energy, Mines and Resources Canada. Energy Policy Analysis. *Do governments take too much? an examination of pre and post NEP fiscal regimes.* Ottawa: Energy, Mines and Resources Canada; 1982; 29 p.

2267. Canada. Environment Canada. *Environment Canada and the North: the perceptions, roles and policies of the Department of the Environment regarding development north of 60: discussion paper.* Ottawa: Environment Canada; 1983; xx, 74 p.

2268. Canada. Environment Canada. Initiatives pour un autre developpement: le Canada en 1979: un inventaire des initiatives visant un autre type de developpement pour le Canada: report, by Cathy Starrs. Ottawa: Environment Canada; 1980; ii, 155 p.

2269. Canada. Environment Canada. *Perspectives on economic policy: a discussion paper second draft.* Ottawa: Environment Canada; 1980; 67 p.

2270. Canada. Environment Canada. Corporate Planning Group. *Energy and the environment: environment Canada's energy strategy.* [Ottawa]: Corporate Planning Group; 1983; 9, 39, 10 p.

2271. Canada. Environmental Protection Service. Federal Activities Assessment Branch. *Environmental monitoring of federal and provincial projects: proceedings of a meeting held in Ottawa, January 26, 1982.* Ottawa: Environmental Protection Service; 1983; v, 124, 97, xi p.

2272. Canada. Federal Cultural Policy Review Committee. *Report of the Federal Cultural Policy Review Committee*. [Ottawa]: Supply and Services Canada; 1982; 406 p.

2273. Canada. Federal Cultural Policy Review Committee. *Summary of briefs and hearings*, by Louis Applebaum and Jacques Hébert. [Ottawa]: Supply and Servicesd Canada; 1982; iv, 299 p.

2274. Canada. Federal-Provincial Relations Office. *Canadian Constitution - proposed resolution respecting the Constitution of Canada*. [Ottawa]: Federal-Provincial Relations Office; 1980.

2275. Canada. Federal-Provincial Task Force on Student Assistance. *Report of the Federal-Provincial Task Force on Student Assistance*, by A. Guy. [Ottawa]: The Task Force; 1981.

2276. Canada. Federal-Provincial Task Force on Student Assistance. *Statistical compendium - Federal-Provincial Task Force on Student Assistance*. [Ottawa]: The Task Force; 1980; 4 v.

2277. Canada. Health and Welfare Canada; Federal-Provincial Advisory Committee on Health Manpower. *Provincial, territorial and federal policies on health manpower legislation, 1980*. [Ottawa]: Health and Welfare Canada; [1980?]; v, 75, 81, v p.

2278. Canada. Health Services Review. *Canada's national-provincial health program for the 1980's*, by Emmett M. Hall, Special Commissioner. Ottawa: Department of National Health and Welfare; 1980; 101, 102 p.

2279. Canada. Industry, Trade and Commerce; Canada. Federal-Provincial Relations Office. *Economic mobility in Canada : a comparative study*, by John A. Hayes. [Ottawa]: [Supply and Services Canada]; [1982]; ix, 351 p.

2280. Canada. Inquiry on Federal Water Policy. *Currents of change: final report, inquiry on federal water policy*, by P.H. Pearse et al. [Ottawa]: Inquiry on Federal Water Policy; [1985]; 222 p.

2281. Canada. Inquiry on Federal Water Policy. *Federal-provincial co-operation in water: an exploratory examination*. [Ottawa]: Inquiry on Federal Water Policy; 1985; 48 p. (Research paper; 9).

2282. Canada. Inquiry on Federal Water Policy. *Hearing about water : a synthesis of public hearings of the Inquiry on Federal Water Policy*. Ottawa: Supply and Services Canada; [1985]; 74, 82 p.

2283. Canada. Labour Canada. *March 1982 official languages annual report*. [Ottawa]: Supply and Services Canada; [1982]; 25 p.

2284. Canada. Law Reform Commission. *Practical tools to improve interprovincial enforcement of maintenance orders after divorce* [microform]. [Ottawa]: The

Commission; 1980. (Canada law reform commission modernization of statutes series).

2285. Canada. Mackenzie River Basin Committee. *Mackenzie river basin study report - a report under the 1978-81 Federal-Provincial Study Agreement Respecting the Water and Related Resources of the Mackenzie River Basin* [Ottawa]: Supply and Services Canada; 1981.

2286. Canada. Mineral Development Branch. Regional Development Division. *Federal-Provincial Mineral Development Agreements: annual report 1980-81.* Ottawa: Energy, Mines and Resources; 1981; 13, 13 p.

2287. Canada. Minister for International Trade; Canada. Department of External Affairs. *Canadian trade negotiations: introduction, selected documents, further reading.* Ottawa: Department of External Affairs; 1986; viii, 105 p.

2288. Canada. Ministerial Task Force on Program Review. *Culture and communications,* by Erik Nielsen. Ottawa: Supply and Services Canada; 1986; iii, 429 p.

2289. Canada. Ministerial Task Force on Program Review. *Education and research: a study team report to the Task Force on Program Review,* by Erik Nielsen and Benson A. Wilson. [Ottawa]: The Task Force; 1985; c1986; iii, 311 p.

2290. Canada. Ministerial Task Force on Program Review. *Health and sports program: a study team report to the Task Force on Program Review,* by Erik Nielsen. [Ottawa]: The Task Force; 1985; c1986; iii, 290 p.

2291. Canada. Ministerial Task Force on Program Review. *Natural resources program: from crisis to opportunity,* by Erik Nielsen. Ottawa: Supply and Services Canada; 1986; iii, 319 p.

2292. Canada. Ministerial Task Force on Program Review. *New management initiatives: initial results from the Ministerial Task Force on Program Review,* by Erik Nielsen. Ottawa: Supply and Services; 1985; 131, 141 p.

2293. Canada. Ministerial Task Force on Program Review. *Services and subsidies to business: giving with both hands,* by Erik Nielsen. Ottawa: Supply and Services Canada; 1986; iii, 593 p.

2294. Canada. Ministerial Task Force on Program Review. *Transportation programs,* by Erik Nielsen. Ottawa: Supply and Services; 1986; iii, 386 p.

2295. Canada. Ministry of State for Economic Development. *Notes for an address by the Hon. Donald J. Johnson, Minister of State for Economic and Regional Development and Minister of State for Science and Technology to the Business Council on National Issues, Oct. 13, 1982.* [Ottawa]: The Ministry; 1982.

2296. Canada. Ministry of State for Economic Development. *Notes for an address by the Hon. Donald J. Johnson, Minister of State for Economic and Regional*

Development and Minister of State for Science and Technology to the Canada Club of Toronto; Nov. 8, 1982. [Ottawa]: The Ministry; 1982.

2297. Canada. Ministry of State for Science and Technology. *Discussion paper: industrial research and development.* First Ministers' Conference on the Economy; November 27-29, 1978: Canadian Intergovernmental Conference Secretariat; 1978; 6 p. [8.p.].

2298. Canada. Ministry of State for Science and Technology. *Science, technology and economic development - a working paper.* Federal-Provincial Meeting of Ministers Responsible for Science and Technology; February 4-5, 1985; Calgary. [Ottawa]: Ministry of State for Science and Technology; 1985.

2299. Canada. Ministry of State, Science and Technology. *The Government of Canada's investment in science: an overview of federal science activities, 1982/83.* [Ottawa]: Ministry of State, Science and Technology Canada; 1982; 16, 16 p.

2300. Canada. Ministry of State, Science and Technology. *The Government of Canada's support for technology development.* Ottawa: Ministry of State, Science and Technology; 1983; 19, 23 p.

2301. Canada. Ministry of State, Science and Technology. *Support for technology development: a summary of federal programs and incentives, 1983/84.* [Ottawa]: Ministry of State, Science and Technology; 1983; 19, 23 p.

2302. Canada. Ministry of State, Science and Technology. *Support for technology development: a summary of federal programs and incentives, 1984.* Ottawa: Ministry of State, Science and Technology; 1984; 30, 32 p.

2303. Canada. Multiculturalism Directorate. *Education and cultural and linguistic pluralism: country surveys: Canada for OECD.* Ottawa: The Directorate; 1985; Various pagings.

2304. Canada. National Telecommunications Branch. *Canadian telecommunications: an overview of the Canadian telecommunications carriage industry.* Ottawa: Supply and Services Canada; 1983; 34, (5) p.

2305. Canada. Office of Energy Research and Development. *1983 Guide to research and development activities resulting from the National Energy Program of the Government of Canada.* Ottawa: Energy Mines and Resources; 1984; xiv, 81 p.

2306. Canada. Office of the Commissioner of Official Languages. *Annual report 1982* (Commissioner of Official Languages). Ottawa: Office of the Commissioner; [1983]; 180, 190 p.

2307. Canada. Office of the Commissioner of Official Languages. *Annual report 1984* (Commissioner of Official Languages). Ottawa: Office of the Commissioner; [1985]; 248, 263 p.

2308. Canada. Office of the Commissioner of Official Languages. *Annual report 1985* (Commissioner of Official Languages). Ottawa: Office of the Commissioner; 1986; 238, 258 p.

2309. Canada. Office of the Comptroller General. *Guide on the audit of federal contributions*. [Ottawa]: Treasury Board of Canada, Comptroller General; 1985; 2 v.

2310. Canada. Officer of the Commissioner of Official Languages. *Annual report 1983* (Commissioner of Official Languages). Ottawa: Office of the Commissioner; 1984; 183, 195 p.

2311. Canada. Secretary of State. *Support to education by the Government of Canada*. [Ottawa]: Secretary of State; 1983; 32 (36) p.

2312. Canada. Skill Development Leave Task Force. *Interprovincial standards program - a model of flexibility and cooperation*, by T. Watson. [Ottawa]: The Task Force; 1983.

2313. Canada. Statistics Canada. *International and interprovincial migration in Canada, 1979-80*. Ottawa: Statistics Canada; 1982; 29 p.

2314. Canada. Task Force on Federal Policies and Programs for Technology Development. *Report of the Task Force on Federal Policies and Programs for Technology Development*, by Edward Lumley and Douglas T. Wright. [Ottawa]: Ministry of State, Science and Technology Canada; 1984; ii, 69 p.

2315. Canada. Task Force on Labour Market Development. *Labour market development in the 1980's : a report of the Task Force on Labour Market Development prepared for the Minister of Employment and Immigration as a contribution to a process of consultation with provincial governments and organizations representing different elements of the private sector*. [Ottawa]: Employment and Immigration Canada; 1981; viii, 243 p.

2316. Canada. Task Force on Unemployment Insurance. *Unemployment insurance in the 1980's: a report of the Task Force on Unemployment Insurance prepared for the Minister of Employment and Immigration as a contribution to a process of consultation with provincial governments and organizations representing different elements of the private sector*. [Ottawa]: Employment and Immigration Canada; 1981; vii, 127 p.

2317. Canada. Textile and Clothing Board. *Interim report on a study of the impact of potential free trade in textiles and clothing between Canada and the United States*. Ottawa: The Board; 1983; 13 (15) p.

2318. Canada. Textile and Clothing Board. *Study of the impact of potential free trade in textiles and clothing between Canada and the United States: final report*. Ottawa: The Board; 1984; 89 (98) p.

2319. Canada. Transport Canada. *Discussion paper: transportation and national and regional perspective*. First ministers' Conference on the Economy; November

27-29, 1978: Canadian Intergovernmental Conference Secretariat; 1978; 69 p. (86 p.).

2320. Canadian Arctic Resources Committee. *National and regional interests in the North: third national workshop on people, resources and the environment north of 60*; June 1-3, 1983; Yellowknife. Ottawa: The Committee; 1984; xvii, 758 p.

2321. Canadian Association of Interns and Residents. *Federal-provincial fiscal arrangements: interns' and residents' views: Canadian Association of Interns and Residents.* Canadian Medical Association Journal; 1982 May; 126(10): 1136-1138.

2322. Canadian Association of Statutory Human Rights Agencies Conference (1981). *Documents* (1981 CASHRA Conference); June 1-4, 1981; Windsor. [Ottawa]: Canadian Intergovernmental Conference Secretariat; 1981; various pagings.

2323. Canadian Association of University Teachers. *The funding of Canadian universities: a brief submitted to the Parliamentary Task Force on Federal-Provincial Fiscal Arrangements.* [Ottawa]: The Association; 1981; iii, 32 p.

2324. Canadian Chamber of Commerce; Canada. Ministry of State, Science and Technology. *Research initiatives: a submission to the Minister of State for Science and Technology.* Montreal: The Chamber; 1980; 12 p.

2325. Canadian Conference of the Arts. *More strategy for culture: more proposals for a federal policy for the arts and the cultural industries in Canada.* Ottawa: The Conference; 1981; iv, 140 p.

2326. Canadian Conference of the Arts. *A strategy for culture: proposals for a federal policy for the arts and the cultural industries in Canada.* Ottawa: The Conference; 1980; xiii, 238 p.

2327. Canadian Conference of the Arts. *The third strategy: a Canadian primer of sensible proposals for the solution of insoluble problems,* by Jack Gray and André Fortier. Ottawa: Canadian Conference of the Arts; 1984; xv 112 p.

2328. Canadian Medical Association. *Highlights of CMA brief to the Hall Health Services Review.* Canadian Medical Association Journal; 1980 March; 122(5): 570-578.

2329. Canadian Radio-Television and Telecommunications Commission. *Bibliography of CRTC studies.* Ottawa: CRTC; 1983; 75 (77) p.

2330. Canadian Radio-Television and Telecommunications Commission. *Canadian broadcasting and telecommunications: past experience, future options - a report prepared for the Canadian Radio-Television and Telecommunications Commission.* [Ottawa]: CRTC; 1980.

2331. Canadian Radio-Television and Telecommunications Commission. *The future role of regulation in communications: a call for research proposals.* Ottawa: CRTC; 1983; 7 (7) p.

2332. Cannon, James B. Explaining regional development in Atlantic Canada: a review essay. *Journal of Canadian Studies*; 1984 Fall; 19(3): 65-86.

2333. Cape Breton Advisory Committee. *Towards economic development and productive employment in Cape Breton.* Halifax: The Committee; 1985; 46, (5) p.

2334. Caragata, Patrick James. *Non-fuel minerals and Canadian foreign policy: negotiating from strength and weakness*: University of Toronto; 1981. Dissertation Abstracts International 1982 42 (9) 4137-A.

2335. Carbonneau, C.; Daigneault, A. Les caisses d'épargne et de crédit: agents de développement économique régional. *Ensemble*; 1980; 27(16, special supplement): 1-20.

2336. Carmichael, Edward A. *New stresses on Confederation: diverging regional economies.* Toronto: C.D. Howe Institute; 1986.

2337. Carmichael, Edward A. *Tackling the federal deficit.* Toronto: C.D. Howe Institute; 1984; 88 p. (Observation / C.D. Howe Institute; v. 26).

2338. Carmichael, Edward A. *Time for decisions.* Toronto: C.D. Howe Institute; 1985; 82 p.

2339. Carmichael, Edward A.; Dobson, Wendy. *Achieving a realistic recovery.* Toronto: C.D. Howe Institute; 1983; vi, 65 p. (Policy review and outlook ; 1983).

2340. Carmichael, Edward A.; Herrera, Corina M. *Canada's energy policy, 1985 and beyond.* [Toronto]: C.D. Howe Institute; 1984; 95 p.

2341. Carmichael, Edward A.; Stewart, James K. *Lessons from the National Energy Program.* [Toronto]: C.D. Howe Institute; [1983]; vi, 63 p. (Observation / C.D. Howe Institute; v. 25).

2342. Carter, C.A.; Loynes, R.M.A. The prairie grain industry in western transition. *Canadian Public Policy* (supplement); 1985 July; 11(290-293).

2343. Carter, George E. *The federal impact of financing higher education in Canada.* Canberra: Centre for Research on Federal Financial Relations, Australian National University; 1982; viii, 63 p. (Occasional paper; 25).

2344. Carter, Richard. Le Canada est-il entraîné dans la déréglementation: le cas des communications. *Canadian Public Policy*; 1984 March; 10(1): 10-24.

2345. Carter, Richard. Vers une plus grande décentralisation du financement gouvernemental au Québec. *Canadian Public Administration*; 1985 Spring; 28(1): 47-79.

2346. Cartwright, A. S. Canadian economic outlook. *Vital Speeches*; 1981; 47(14): 439-442.

2347. Cartwright, Donald G. *Official-language populations in Canada: patterns and contacts.* Montreal: Institute for Research on Public Policy; 1980; xxii, 161 p. (Occasional paper).

2348. Cartwright, Donald G. An official-languages policy for Ontario: *Canadian Public Policy*; 1985 Summer; 11: 561-77.

2349. Cartwright, Donald G.; Williams, Colin H. Bilingual districts as an instrument in Canadian language policy: *Transactions of the Institite of British Geographers*; 1982; 7(4): 474-93.

2350. Carty, R. Kenneth; Ward, Peter W., eds. *Entering the eighties: Canada in crisis.* Toronto: Oxford University Press; 1980; 160 p.

2351. Caya, Marcel. The dilemmas of cultural management in a federal state. In: Mathews, Russell, ed. *Public policies in two federal countries: Canada and Australia.* Canberra: Centre for Research on Federal Financial Relations, Australian National University; 1982; 237-244 p.

2352. Cermakian, Jean. Les transports au Québec et l'évolution des relations politiques Québec - Canada: perspectives géographiques. *Cahiers de géographie du Québec*; 1980 April; 24(61): 167-174.

2353. Chambers, E.J.; Dunn, M. James; Gillen, David W.; Tyndall, D. Gordon. Bill C-20: an evaluation from the perspective of current transportation policy and regulatory performance. *Canadian Public Policy*; 1980 Winter; 6(1): 47-62.

2354. Chambers, W. G. *Resource management - Canadian federalism.* American Institute of Mining, Metallurgical and Petroleum Engineers 108th Annual Meeting; 18-22 February 1979; New Orleans, Louisiana. Warrendale, PA: Society of Mining Engineers.

2355. Chandler, Marsha A. The politics of provincial resource policy. In: Atkinson, Michael M.; Chandler, Marsha A., eds. *The politics of Canadian public policy.* Toronto: University of Toronto Press; 1983: 43-68; 286 p. (Studies in Canadian public policy).

2356. Chant, John F.; Dean, James W. An approach to the regulation of banking institutions in a federal state. *Osgoode Hall Law Journal*; 1982 December; 20(4): 721-744.

2357. Charney, J. I. The offshore jurisdiction of the states of the United States and the provinces of Canada -- a comparison. *Ocean Development and International Law*; 1983; 12(3-4): 301-335.

2358. Chow, Garland. How much longer can we live with regulation of Canada's trucking industry? *Canadian Business Review*; 1983 Spring; 10(1): 45-52.

2359. Cihlar, J. *The transfer of federal technology to the provinces: proceedings of a workshop*; November 20-21, 1980; Ottawa. Ottawa: Canada Centre for Remote Sensing; [1980?]; 162 p.

2360. Clark, T. C. Federal governments and university science research: a comparison of practices in the United States and Canada, 1970-1979. *Canadian Public Policy*; 1980 Spring; 6(2): 342-51.

2361. Clarke, Larry P. The role of governments in changing government-industry relations. *Business Quarterly* (Special Supplement); 1985 Summer; 50(2): 70-74.

2362. Clements, D.J.; Carter, C.A. *Nontariff barriers to interprovincial trade in swine.* Winnipeg: Department of Agricultural Economics and Farm Management, Faculty of Agriculture; 1984; vii, 86 p. (Extension Bulletin).

2363. Coffey, J. Edwin. Is Quebec medicare really a model for Canada? *Canadian Medical Association Journal*; 1984 June; 130(2): 1602-1604.

2364. Coffey, William J,; Polèse, Mario, eds. *Still living together: recent trends and future directions in Canadian regional development.* Montreal: Institute for Research on Public Policy; 1987; xxx, 459 p.

2365. Coffey, William J.; Polèse, Mario. Local development - conceptual bases and policy implications. *Regional Studies*; 1985; 19(2): 85-93.

2366. Coleman, William D. The class bases of language policy in Quebec, 1949-1983. In: Gagnon, Alain G., ed. *Quebec state and society.* Toronto: Methuen; 1984: 388-409; ix, 438 p.

2367. Coleman, William D. A comparative study of language policy in Quebec: a political economy approach. In: Atkinson, Michael M.; Chandler, Marsha A., eds. *The politics of Canadian public policy.* Toronto: University of Toronto Press; 1983: 21-42; 286 p. (Studies in Canadian public policy).

2368. Collishaw, Neil E. Historique de l'évolution des modes de financement des services de santé au Canada. *L'Actualité économique*; 1980 April-June; 56(2): 154-163.

2369. Commission on the Future Development of the Universities of Ontario. *Ontario universities 1984: issues and alternatives : background data.* Toronto: The Commission; 1984; 65 p.

2370. Conférence canadienne des arts. *La culture, secteur de pointe du développement canadien: perspectives pour aborder l'ère des loisirs.* [Ottawa]: The Conference; 1982; 28 p.

2371. Conférence canadienne des arts. *Perspectives pour l'élaboration d'une politique culturelle, stratégie II: nouvelle contribution à la formulation d'une politique fédérale sur les arts et les industries culturelles au Canada.* Ottawa: The Conference; 1981; v, 149 p.

2372. Conklin, David W.; Courchene, Thomas J., eds. *Deficits: how big and how bad?* Toronto: Ontario Economic Council; 1983; 361 p. (Special research report/Ontario Economic Council).

2373. Conklin, David W.; Courchene, Thomas J., eds. *Ontario universities: access, operations, and funding.* Toronto: Ontario Economic Council; 1985; xiv, 467 p. (Special research report / Ontario Economic Council).

2374. Conklin, David W.; Bennett, Jaylynn H.; Courchene, Thomas J., eds. *Pensions today and tomorrow: background studies.* Toronto: Ontario Economic Council; 1984; 486 p. (Special research report/Ontario Economic Council).

2375. Conseil de planification et de développement du Québec. *Le point sur la situation énergétique: internationale, canadienne, québécoise:* rapport au Conseil de planification et de développement du Québec: 30 juin 1982, by Antoine Ayoub. [Québec]: Gouvernement du Québec, Conseil de planification et de développement du Québec; [1982]; 91 p. (Collection études et recherches).

2376. Constantinou, Stavros. A crow in search of a nest. *Canadian Business Review*; 1983 Summer; 10(2): 56-60.

2377. Conway, J. F. The politics of health care in Canada. *Hospital Trustee*; 1981; 5(3): 6-8.

2378. Copes, P. Fish and the public interest: the problem in Newfoundland. In: Lorimer, R.; McMullin, S.E, eds. *Canada and the sea.* Willowdale: Association for Canadian Studies; 1980: 103-113.

2379. Copes, Parsival. The evolution of marine fisheries policy in Canada. Chapter 10. *Journal of Business Administration*; 1980; 11(1-2): 125-148.

2380. Copes, Parsival. Fisheries management on Canada's Atlantic coast: economic factors and socio-political constraints. *Canadian Journal of Regional Science*; 1983 Spring; 6(1): 1-32.

2381. Copes, Parsival. Implementing Canada's marine fisheries policy: objectives, hazards and constraints. *Maritime Policy*; 1982; 6(3): 219-235.

2382. Copithorne, Lawrence. *Richesses naturelles et disparités régionales.* [Ottawa]: Conseil économique du Canada; 1980; 277 p.

2383. Copithorne, Lawrence; MacFadyen, Alan; Bell, Bruce. Revenue sharing and the efficient valuation of natural resources. *Canadian Public Policy* (supplement); 1985 July; 11: 465-478.

2384. Copplestone, Glen Howard. *Implications of Canadian oil tax policies: University of Western Ontario*; 1984. Dissertation Abstracts International 45 (1): 242-A.

2385. Côté, Francois Bernard. Du langage législatif au Canada ou de la difficulté de parler la même langue avec des mots différents. *Revue du barreau de Québec*; 1986 March-April; (2): 302-307.

2386. Cottrill, A. Peckford speaks for Newfoundland. *Offshore Engineer*; 1983: 36-37.

2387. COU Special Committee on Macro-Indicators. *Ontario universities statistical compendium : 1970-71 to 1979-80. part a: macro-indicators.* Toronto: Council of Ontario Universities; 1981; v, 58 p.

2388. COU Special Committee on Macro-Indicators. *Ontario universities statistical compendium : 1970-71 to 1980-81. part b: supporting data.* Toronto: Council of Ontario Universities; 1982; (8) p.

2389. COU Special Committee on Macro-Indicators. *Ontario universities statistical compendium : 1970-71 to 1981-82, part a: macro-indicators.* Toronto: Council of Ontario Universities; 1983; 60 p.

2390. COU Special Committee on Macro-Indicators. *Ontario universities statistical compendium : 1970-71 to 1982-83, part a: macro-indicators.* Toronto: Council of Ontario Universities; 1984; 58 p.

2391. Council of Maritime Premiers. Committee on Research and Development. *Technological innovation, an industrial imperative: report of the Council of Maritime Premiers on research and development.* Halifax: The Council; 1981; 85 p.

2392. Council of Ministers of Education, Canada. *The state of minority language education in the ten provinces of Canada: a report.* Toronto: The Council; 1978; 241 (246) p.

2393. Council of Ontario Universities. *Federal-provincial relations and support for universities.* Toronto: Council of Ontario Universities; 1982; iv, 83 p.

2394. Council of Ontario Universities. *Universities and the future of Ontario: a foundation on which to build: response of the Council of Ontario Universities to the preliminary report of the Committee on the Future Role of Universities in Ontario.* Toronto: The Council; 1981; iv, 48 p.

2395. Council of Ontario Universities. *Universities: the sleeper in federal-provincial relations.* [Toronto]: Council of Ontario Universities; 1985. (Council of Ontario universities briefing notes; v. 14).

2396. Council of Ontario Universities. Committee on Operating Grants. *Brief to the Ontario Council on University Affairs : a future of lost opportunities?* Toronto: Council of Ontario Universities; 1981; v, 68 p.

2397. Council of Ontario Universities. Research Division. *The financial position of universities in Ontario : some relevant data* / prepared by the research division of the Council of Ontario Universities. Toronto: Council of Ontario Universities; 1985; v, 49 p.

2398. Council of Ontario Universities; Commission on the Future Development of the Universities of Ontario. *Continuity and renewal: the demands of excellence: a response to the discussion paper of the Commission on the Future Development of the Universities of Ontario, "Ontario universities 1984 : issues and alternatives".* Toronto: The Council; 1984; viii, 70, (85) p.

2399. Council of Ontario Universities; Ontario Council on University Affairs. *Once more, with feeling: brief to the Ontario Council on University Affairs.* Toronto: Council of Ontario Universities; 1982; xi, 5 p.

2400. Courchene, Thomas J. A market perspective on regional disparities. *Canadian Public Policy*; 1981 Autumn; 7(4): 506-18.

2401. Courchene, Thomas J. Regions, transfers and growth. *Canadian Business Review*; 1981 Spring; 8(1): 6-12.

2402. Courchene, Thomas J. Towards a protected society: the politicization of economic life. *Canadian Journal of Economics*; 1980 November; 13(4): 556-77.

2403. Courchene, Thomas J. Analytical perspectives on the Canadian economic union. In: Trebilcock, Michael J., ed. *Federalism and the Canadian economic union*. Toronto: Ontario Economic Council; 1983: 51-110; xiv, 560 p. (Ontario Economic Council Research Studies).

2404. Courchene, Thomas J. The citizen and the state: a market perspective. In: Lermer, George, ed. *Probing leviathan: an investigation of government in the economy*. Vancouver: Fraser Institute; 1984: 39-55; xv, 223 p.

2405. Courchene, Thomas J. *Federalism and the Canadian economic union*. Toronto: University of Toronto Press. Published for the Ontario Economic Council; 1983.

2406. Courchene, Thomas J. The market system in the age of entitlements. *Business Quarterly* (Special Supplement); 1985 Summer; 50(2): 75-81.

2407. Courchene, Thomas J.; Norrie, K.H. *Reaction, the National Energy Program*. [Vancouver]: Fraser Institute; 1981; xviii, 144 p.

2408. Courville, Leon; De Fontenay, Alain; Dobell, Rodney, eds. *Economic analysis of telecommunications: theory and applications*; March 4-6, 1981; Montreal. Amsterdam: Elsevier Science Publishing; 1983; xv, 413 p.

2409. Couzin, Robert. Divying up Canada's petrodollars. *Canadian Business Review*; 1980 Spring; 7(1): 18-21.

2410. Cox, Joseph C. The interprovincial and international impact of federal grants to provincial governments: evidence from the Canadian federation. *Public Finance*; 1981; 36(2): 214-28.

2411. Cox, Joseph C. The interindustry impact of provincial fiscal response to federal grants. *Canadian Journal of Regional Science*; 1983 Autumn; 6(2): 185-206.

2412. Crandall, R.H. Government intervention: the PIP grant accounting controversy. *Cost and Management*; 1983; 57(5): 55-59.

2413. Crane, David. *Controlling interest: the Canadian gas and oil stakes*. Toronto: McClelland and Stewart; 1982; 336 p.

2414. Crispo, John. An "industrial strategy" for Canada. *Cost and Management*; 1981 July-August; 554(4): 5-8.

2415. Crispo, John. *National consultation: problems and prospects.* Toronto: C.D. Howe Institute; 1984; 44 p. (Policy commentary / C.D. Howe Institute; 5).

2416. Crowley, R. W. A new power focus in Ottawa: the Ministry of State for Economic and Regional Development. *Optimum*; 1982; 132(2): 5-16.

2417. Dacks, Gurston. The politics of development in Canada's North. *Current History*; 1984 May; 83(493): 220-224, 226.

2418. Dales, John H. Distortions and Dissipations. *Canadian Public Policy*; 1983 June; 9(2): 257-63.

2419. Daly, Donald J. The continuing debate about freer trade and its effects: a comment. *Canadian Public Policy* (supplement); 1982 October; 8: 444-450.

2420. Daly, Michael J. The role of government tax transfer programs and the structure of personal income taxation in Canada's retirement income system. *Canadian Tax Journal*; 1980 March-April; 28(2): 145-163.

2421. Daneau, Marcel. Les pêches maritimes: répartition et fédéralisme nouveaux. Canadian Public Policy; 1985 March; 11(1): 111-112.

2422. Daneau, Marcel. *Le Québec et ses pêches maritimes: une analyse des politiques et des programmes.* Québec: Département d'économique, Faculté des sciences sociales, Université Laval; 1984; 185 p.

2423. Daneau, Marcel. *Les relations Québec-Canada en matière de pêches maritimes.* Québec: Départment d'économique, Faculté des sciences sociales, Université Laval; c1984; 46 p. (Cahier; v. 8420).

2424. Daneau, Marcel. Réorganisation des pêcheries dans les Maritimes. *Policy Options*; 1984 July-August; 5(4): 35-36.

2425. Dar, R.K. The role of states in the Indian planning system. In: Mathews, Russcll, *Regional disparities and economic development.* Canberra: Centre for Research on Federal Financial Relations, Australian National University; 1981; 99-142 p.

2426. Darling, Howard. *The politics of freight rates.* Toronto: McClelland and Stewart; 1980; viii, 258 p.

2427. Davis, Bruce W. Federalism and environmental politics: an Australian overview. In: Mathews, Russell, ed. *Federalism and the environment.* Canberra: Centre for Research on Federal Financial Relations, Australian National University; 1985; 1-11 p.

2428. Davis, Christine K. *Accessibility to Ontario universities* / prepared by Christine K. Davis on behalf of Commission on the Future Development of the Universities of Ontario. Toronto: Council of Ontario Universities; 1984; viii, 102 p.

2429. Davis, William G. *A blueprint for economic recovery: Conference of First Ministers on the Economy*; February 2-3, 1982; Ottawa. Ottawa: Queen's Printer; 1982; 24, vi p.

2430. Davis, William G. *Economic transformation: a new priority for employment and human resources* (25th Annual Premiers' Conference); 1984; Charlottetown. Toronto: Office of the Premier; 1984; 16 p.

2431. de Pouvourville, Gerard; Renaud, Marc. Hospital system management in France and Canada: national pluralism and provincial centralism. *Social Science and Medicine*; 1985; 20(2): 153-166.

2432. de Vries, John; Vallee, Frank G. *Language use in Canada*. Ottawa: Statistics Canada; 1980; 176 p. (Census analytical study Ottawa).

2433. de Wilde, James. *Modern capitalist planning and Canadian federalism the case of high-technology industries* [microfiche]: (Ph.D) McGill University; 1979 4 microfiches (390 fr.). Ottawa: National Library of Canada, Canadian theses on microfiche.

2434. Delorme, Francois. *Selective economic subsidization and stablization policy in an inflationary environment: a dynamic aggregative model*. Ottawa: Economic Council of Canada; 1983; vii, 56 p. (Discussion paper / Economic Council of Canada; 238).

2435. Denny, M.; Fuss, M.; May, J.D. Intertemporal changes in regional productivity in Canadian manufacturing. *Canadian Journal of Economics*; 1981 August; 14(3): 390-408.

2436. Denton, Frank T.; Spencer, Byron G. Population aging and future health costs in Canada. *Canadian Public Policy*; 1983 June; 9(2): 155-156.

2437. Denton, Frank T.; Robb, A. Leslie; Spencer, Byron G. *The future financing of the Canada and Quebec pension plans : some alternative possibilities*. [Ottawa]: [Economic Council of Canada]; 1980; 40 p.

2438. DeVoretz, Don; Schwindt, Richard. *Harvesting Canadian fish and rents: a partial review of the report of the Commission on Canadian Pacific Fisheries Policy*. Marine Resource Economics; 1985; 1(4): 347-67.

2439. Doering, Ronald L. Natural resource jurisdiction and political development in the North: the case of Nunavut. In: *National and regional interests in the North: Third National Workshop on People, Resources and the Environment North of 60*; 1-3 June 1983. Ottawa: Canadian Arctic Resources Committee; 1984: 117-131.

2440. Doern, G. Bruce. Energy expenditures and the NEP; controlling the energy leviathan. In: Maslove, Allan M., ed. *How Ottawa spends, 1984: the new agenda*. Toronto: Methuen; 1984: 31-78; 334 p.

2441. Doern, G. Bruce. Energy, mines and resources, the energy ministry and the National Energy Program. In: *idem. How Ottawa spends your tax dollars: federal priorities - 1981*. Toronto: James Lorimer; 1981: 56-89; 303 p.

2442. Doern, G. Bruce. *Government intervention in the Canadian nuclear industry*. Montreal: Institute for Research on Public Policy; 1980; xxi, 203 p.

2443. Doern, G. Bruce, ed. *How Ottawa spends: the liberals, the opposition and federal priorities -1983*. Toronto, James Lorimer. 1983; 244 p.

2444. Doern, G. Bruce. Liberal priorities 1982: the limits of scheming virtuously. In: *idem*, ed. *How Ottawa spends your tax dollars - 1982*. Toronto: James Lorimer; 1982: 1-36; v, 256 p.

2445. Doern, G. Bruce. The liberals and the opposition: ideas, priorities and the imperatives of governing Canada in the 1980's. In: *idem*, ed. *How Ottawa spends: the liberals, the opposition and federal priorities - 1983*. Toronto: James Lorimer; 1983: 1-36; 244 p.

2446. Doern, G. Bruce. The mega-project episode and the formulation of Canadian economic development policy. *Canadian Public Administration*; 1983 Summer; 26(2): 219-238.

2447. Doern, G. Bruce. *The peripheral nature of scientific and technological controversy in federal policy formation*. Ottawa: Science Council of Canada; c1981; 108 p. (Science council of Canada. Background study; 46).

2448. Doern, G. Bruce. The politics of Canadian economic policy: an overview. In: *idem. The politics of economic policy*. Toronto: University of Toronto Press; Royal Commission on the Economic Union and Development Prospects for Canada; 1985: 1-109; xv, 306 p. (The collected research studies; 40).

2449. Doern, G. Bruce, res. coord. *The politics of economic policy*. Toronto: University of Toronto Press; Royal Commission on the Economic Union and Development Prospects for Canada; 1985; xv, 306 p. (The collected research studies; 40).

2450. Doern, G. Bruce. Priorities and priority setting in the Trudeau era: the political problems of doing first things first. In: *idem*, ed. *How Ottawa spends: the liberals, the opposition and federal priorities - 1983*. Toronto: James Lorimer; 1983: 66-92; 244 p.

2451. Doern, G. Bruce. Spending priorities: the liberal view. In: *idem. How Ottawa spends your tax dollars: federal priorities - 1981*. Toronto: James Lorimer; 1981: 1-55; 303 p.

2452. Doern, G. Bruce; Morrison, Robert W. *Canadian nuclear policies: proceedings of a conference on Canadian nuclear policy*. Montreal: Institute for Research on Public Policy; 1980; xvi, 326 p.

2453. Doern, G. Bruce; Phidd, Richard W. *Canadian public policy: ideas, structure, process.* Toronto: Methuen; 1983; 624 p.

2454. Doern, G. Bruce; Toner, Glen. Energy budgets and Canadian oil and gas interests. In: Maslove, Allan M., ed. *How Ottawa spends, 1985: sharing the pie.* Toronto: Methuen; 1985: 58-89; 184 p.

2455. Doern, G. Bruce; Toner, Glen. *The politics of energy: the development and implementation of the NEP.* Toronto: Methuen; 1985; xvii, 523 p.

2456. Doern, Russell. *The battle over bilingualism: the Manitoba language question, 1983-85.* Winnipeg: Cambridge Publishers; 1985; 227 p;

2457. Doody, C. William; Leblanc, Fernand E. *Report of the Standing Senate Committee on National Finance: federal government support for technological advancement: an overview.* [Ottawa]: Supply and Services Canada; 1984; 50 (50) p.

2458. Dorcey, Anthony H.J. Techniques for joint management of natural resources: getting to yes. In: Saunders, J. Owen, ed. *Managing natural resources in a federal state.* Toronto: Carswell; 1986: 14-32; vi, 336 p.

2459. Douglas, Gordon W.; Battle, Ellen F. *Energy and regional investment in Canada.* Calgary: Canadian Energy Research Institute; 1983; ix, 114 p. (Study/Canadian Energy Research Institute; 17).

2460. Douglas, Gordon W.; MacMillan, James A. *Interregional economic impacts of the Alberta Alsands project.* Calgary: Canadian Energy Research Institute; [1982]; x, 78 p.

2461. Douglas, Gordon W.; MacMillan, James A. *Significance of interregional feedbacks for Canadian and regional energy policy decisions.* Calgary: Canadian Energy Research Institute; 1982; ii, 10 p. (Discussion paper / Canadian Energy Research Institute; v. 82).

2462. Doutriaux, Jérôme; Crener, Maxime A. Le rôle du gouvernement dans la vie économique canadienne (1ière partie). *Cost and Management*; 1981 November-December; 55(6): 26-31.

2463. Doutriaux, Jérôme; Crener, Maxime, A. Le rôle du gouvernement dans la vie économique canadienne (2ième partie). *Cost and Management*; 1982 January-February; 56(1): 24-29.

2464. Due, John F. Accepted v. Controversial sales tax structures - Switzerland, Australia, New Zealand, Canada. *Australian Tax Forum*; December 1984; 1(4): 363-77.

2465. Dufour, Jean-Marie; Vaillancourt, Francois. *Provincial and federal sales taxes: evidence of their effect and prospect for change.* Montréal: Départment de science économique et Centre de recherche en développement économique, Université de Montréal; [1981?]; 49 p.

2466. Dugas, Clermont. *Les régions périphériques: défi au développement du Québec*. Sillery: Presses de l'Université du Québec; 1983; xvii, 253 p.

2467. Duhamel, Roger. La francophonie en pleine tourmente. *L'Action nationale*; 1983 October; 73(2): 127-133.

2468. Duhamel, Roger. L'offensive d'Ottawa se poursuit. *L'Action nationale*; 1984 September; 74(1): 55-61.

2469. Dupuis, Lionel Alain. *Le domaine des activités aéroportuaires et la compétence constitutionnelle en aéronautique* [microfiche]: (L.L.M.) McGill University; 1981; 3 microfiches (260 IM.). Ottawa: Bibliothèque nationale du Canada, 1983.

2470. Dvorak, P.; Zuk, W.M. *Regulatory control of x-ray hazards in Canada - an integrated federal-provincial approach. International symposium on radiological protection - advances in theory and practices*; June 6-11, 1982; Inverness, Scotland. Berkeley, UK: Society for Radiological Protection; 1982; v. 2.

2471. Dwivedi, O.P. *Resources and the environment: policy perspectives for Canada*. Toronto: McClelland and Stewart; c1980; 346 p. ; 23 cm.

2472. Dyck, Rand. The Canada Assistance Plan: the ultimate in federalism. In: Meilicke, Carl A.; Storch, Janet L., eds. *Perspectives on Canadian health and social services policy: history and emerging trends*. Michigan: Health Administration Press; 1980: 115-130; xii, 520 p.

2473. Dymond, W.A. Canada-U.S. trade options: a view from the Canadian side. In: David G. Meany, ed. *Proceedings: the legal aspects of sectoral integration between the United States and Canada*; April 19-21, 1985; Cleveland: Canada-United States Law Institute; 1985: 27-34; 256 p.

2474. Dymond, W.A. Canada-U.S. trade options: a view from the Canadian side. *Canada-United States Law Journal*; 1985; 10: 27-34.

2475. Earp, Alan. Canadian universities and the current crisis in intergovernmental relations. In: Mathews, Russell, ed. *Public policies in two federal countries: Canada and Australia*. Canberra: Centre for Research on Federal Financial Relations, Australian National University; 1982; 191-196 p.

2476. Ebert, David G. Provincial governments and university relations: a Canadian perspective. *Journal of Education Administration and History*; 1984; 16(2): 45-53.

2477. Ecole nationale d'administration publique; Centre d'études politiques et administratives du Québec. *La décentralisation--un effritement de l'état ou un enrichissement démocratique: actes du colloque tenu les 30 mai et 1er juin 1984*, Manoir du lac Delage, Ville du lac Delage. Sainte-Foy: Le Centre; 1984; 315 p. (Collection Bilans et Perspectives; v. 5).

2478. Economic Council of Canada. *Connections: an energy strategy for the future*. Ottawa: The Council; 1985; x, 20 p.

2479. Economic Council of Canada. *Eighteenth annual review 1981: room for manoeuvre*. Hull: The Council; 1981; vi, 130 p.

2480. Economic Council of Canada. *Intervention and efficiency: a study of government credit and credit guarantees to the private sector*. Ottawa: The Council; 1982; 186 p.

2481. Economic Council of Canada. *Lean times: policies and constraints: Economic Council of Canada nineteenth annual review 1982*. Ottawa: The Council; 1982; xiv, 115 p.

2482. Economic Council of Canada. *Reforming regulation*. Ottawa: The Council; 1981; xii, 157 p.

2483. Economic Council of Canada. Regional disparities in Canada. In: Fox, Paul W., ed. *Politics: Canada*. Toronto: McGraw-Hill Ryerson; 1982: 146-155; 693 p.

2484. Economic Council of Canada. *Room for manoeuvre*. Ottawa: Economic Council of Canada; 1981; vi, 134 p.

2485. Economic Council of Canada. *Steering the course : twenty-first annual review, 1984*. Ottawa: The Council; 1984; x, 121 p.

2486. Economic Council of Canada. *Strengthening growth: options and constraints: Economic Council of Canada twenty-second annual review, 1985*. Ottawa: Economic Council of Canada; 1985; x, 158 p.

2487. Economic Council of Canada. Western transition. *Au Courant*; 1984; 5(2): 1-17.

2488. Empey, W. F. The impact of higher energy prices In Canada. *Canadian Public Policy*; 1981 Winter; 7(1): 18-35.

2489. Enemark, Tex. A federal-provincial affairs perspective. *Canadian Public Policy*; 1982 Winter; 8(1): 40-44.

2490. Esman, Milton J. The politics of official bilingualism in Canada. *Political Science Quarterly*; 1982 Summer; 97: 233-53.

2491. Ethier, Mirielle. Regional grievances: the Quebec case. In: Norrie, Kenneth, res. coord. *Disparities and interregional adjustment*. Toronto: University of Toronto Press; Royal Commission on the Economic Union and Development Prospects for Canada; 1986: 159-184; xiv, 223 p. (The collected research studies; 64).

2492. Ethier, Mirielle. Survey of pension issues. In: Vaillancourt, François, res. coord. *Income distribution and economic security in Canada*. Toronto: University of Toronto Press; Royal Commission on the Economic Union and Development Prospects for Canada; 1985: 215-250; xv, 321 p. (The collected research studies; 1).

2493. Evans, John R. Funding of education and research in Canada's universities. In: Noordeh, Ardeshir, ed. *Reforming the financing arrangements for post-secon-*

dary education in Canada. Toronto: Ontario Economic Council; [1985]: 40-46; x, 160 p.

2494. Evans, Robert G. Health care in Canada: patterns of funding and regulation. *Journal of Health Politics, Policy and Law*; 1983; 8(1): 1-43.

2495. Evans, Robert G. *Strained mercy: the economics of Canadian health care*. [Toronto]: Butterworth; 1984; xvi, 390 p.

2496. Everett, Douglas D.; Leblanc, Fernand E. *Report of the Standing Senate Committee on National Finance on Government Policy and Regional Development*. [Ottawa]: The Committee; 1982; 156 p.

2497. Falcone, David; VanLoon, Richard J. Public attitudes and intergovernmental shifts in responsibility for health program: paying the piper without calling the tune? In: Kornberg, Allan; Clarke, Harold D., eds. *Political support in Canada: the crisis years*. Durham, N.C.: Duke University Press; 1983: 225-251; xvi, 463 p. (Duke University Center for International Studies publications).

2498. Federal Business Development Bank. *ABC 1984: assistance to business in Canada: a handbook of federal assistance programs, including a supplement of provincial/territorial programs*. 3rd ed. Ottawa: FBDB; 1984; 10 v.

2499. Federal-Provincial Committee of Criminal Justice Officials; Canada. Solicitor General Canada. *Report to Deputy Ministers of Justice, Deputy Attorneys General and Deputy Solicitors General ...with respect to the McDonald commission report*. [Ottawa]: [Communication Division, Solicitor General of Canada]; 1983; 138 p.

2500. Federal-Provincial Conference of First Ministers on the Economy. *Co-operation for economic expansion, by the Honourable Frank S. Miller, Premier of Ontario*; 1985; Regina. Toronto: Office of the Premier; 1985; 16 p.

2501. Federal-Provincial Conference of First Ministers on the Economy (1985). *Manitoba position paper on: fiscal arrangements for health and higher education programs* (Federal-Provincial Conference of First Ministers on the Economy, 1985); 1985; Halifax. [Winnipeg]: Manitoba; 1985; 1 v. Note: various pagings.

2502. Federal-Provincial Task Force on Student Assistance. *Report of the Federal-Provincial Task Force on Student Assistance*, by A.J.Y. Guy and G.T. Rayner. [Toronto]: Council of Ministers of Education, Canada; 1981; 229 p.

2503. Federal-Provincial Task Force on the Use of Satellites in Education. *Final report of the Federal-Provincial Task Force on the Use of Satellites in Education*. [Ottawa]: The Task Force; 1981.

2504. Federal-Provincial Working Group on Wastewater Disinfection. *Municipal wastewater disinfection in Canada: need and application: a report of the Working Group on Wastewater Dinsinfection to the Federal-Provincial Advisory Committee on Environmental and Occupational Health*. Ottawa: Health and Welfare Canada; [1984]; xv, 117 p.

2505. Feehan, James P. Provincial government taxation of clothing and footwear: revenue and equity aspects. *Canadian Public Policy*; 1985 March; 11(1): 26-39.

2506. Feldman, Elliot J.; Feldman, Lily Gardner. The impact of federalism on the organization of Canadian foreign policy. *Publius*; 1984 Fall; 14(4): 33-59.

2507. Feldman, Elliot J.; Milch, Jerome; Slann, Martin. *The politics of Canadian airport development: lessons for federalism*. Durham, N.C.: Duke University Press; 1983; 261 pp. (Duke press policy series; 47).

2508. Ferris, J.S.; Plourde, C.G. Labor mobility, seasonal unemployment insurance, and the Newfoundland inshore fishery. *Canadian Journal of Economics*; 1982 August; 15(3): 426-41.

2509. Finkelstein, N. Constitutional law - Section 91(2) of the Constitution Act, 1867 - competition legislation. *Canadian Bar Review*; 1984 June; 62(2): 182-196.

2510. Finkle, Peter Z.R. Canadian environmental law in the eighties: problems and perspectives. *Dalhousie Law Journal*; 1983 April; 7(2): 257-276.

2511. Finlayson, Jock A. Canadian international economic policy: context, issues and a review of some recent literature. In: Stairs, Denis; Winham, Gilbert R., res. coord. *Canada and the international political economic environment*. Toronto: University of Toronto Press; Royal Commission on the Economic Union and Development Prospects for Canada; 1985: 9-84; xvii, 151 p. (The collected research studies; 28).

2512. Flatters, F.R.; Lipsey, R.G. *Common ground for the Canadian common market economic, regional, interprovincial*. [s.l.]: Institute for Research on Public Policy; 1983.

2513. Flatters, Frank; Henderson, Vernon; Mieszkowski, Peter. Public goods, efficiency and regional fiscal equalization. In: Grewal, Bhajan S. [and others], ed. *The economics of federalism*. Canberra: Australian National University; 1980: 89-104; xiii, 432 p.

2514. Foot, David K. *Canada's population outlook: demographic futures and economic challenges*. Toronto: J. Lorimer; 1982; xxvii, 268 p. (The Canadian Institute for Economic Policy series).

2515. Foot, David K.; Milne, William J. *Public policies and interprovincial migration in Canada: an econometric analysis*. Toronto: University of Toronto. Institute for Policy Analysis; 1981; 38 p. (Working paper series; 8126).

2516. Forget, Claude E. Educational policy goals for Canada: major trade-offs and other issues. In: Courchene, Thomas J.; Conklin, David W.; Cook, Gail C.A., eds. *Ottawa and the provinces: the distribution of money and power*. Toronto: Ontario Economic Council; 1985; 1: 299-314; xii, 341 p. (Special research report/Ontario Economic Council).

2517. Fortier, D'Iberville. Les droits linguistiques canadiens en évolution. *Les Cahiers de droit*; 1986 March; (1): 227-238.

2518. Fortin, Bernard. Income security in Canada. In: Vaillancourt, François, res. coord. *Income distribution and economic security in Canada*. Toronto: University of Toronto Press; Royal Commission on the Economic Union and Development Prospects for Canada; 1985: 153-186; xv, 321 p. (The collected research studies; v. 1).

2519. Fortin, Bernard. La sécurité du revenu au Québec: un bilan. *Canadian Public Policy*; 1984 December; 10(4): 446-458.

2520. Fortin, Luc; Winn, Conrad. Communications and culture: evaluating an impossible portfolio. In: Doern, Bruce G., ed. *How Ottawa spends: the liberals, the opposition and federal priorities -1983*. Toronto: James Lorimer; 1983: 208-232; 244 p.

2521. Fortin, Pierre. *The comparative size of the federal and provincial budgets and economic stabilization*. Ottawa: Economic Council of Canada; 1982; 24 p. (Discussion paper).

2522. Fortin, Pierre. *Provincial involvement in regulating the business cycle : justification, scope, and terms*. Ottawa: Economic Council of Canada; 1982; iv, 40 p. (Discussion paper / Economic Council of Canada; 213).

2523. Foster, Peter. *The sorcerer's apprentices: Canada's super-bureaucrats and the energy mess*. Toronto: Collins; 1982; 287 p.

2524. Fowler, David J.; Gordon, Myron J. The effect of public initiatives on drug prices in Canada. *Canadian Public Policy*; 1984; 10(1): 64-73.

2525. French, Richard D. *How Ottawa decides: planning and industrial policy-making 1968-1980*. Toronto: J. Lorimer; 1980; x, 190 p. (The Canadian Institute for Economic Policy series).

2526. French, Richard D.; Van Loon, Richard J. *How Ottawa decides: planning and industrial policy making 1968-1984*. 2nd ed. Toronto: J. Lorimer; 1984; xvi, 225 p. (The Canadian Institute for Economic Policy series).

2527. Fry, Earl H. *The role of state and provincial governments in Canada-U.S. sectoral integration*. Canada-United States Law Journal (Proceedings: the legal aspects of sectoral integration between the United States and Canada, April 19-21, 1985); Cleveland: Canada-United States Law Institute; 1985: 169-184; 256 p.

2528. Fry, Earl H. The role of state and provincial governments in Canada-U.S. sectoral integration. *Canada-United States Law Journal*; 1985; 10: 169-188.

2529. Fry, Earl H. The role of subnational governments in sectoral integration. *Canada-United States Law Journal*; 1985; 10: 189-196.

2530. Gagnon, Alain G.; Montcalm, Mary Beth. From heartland to periphery: the effects of capitalist restructuring in Quebec. *IDS Bulletin Institute of Development Studies*; 1985; 16(2): 23-27.

2531. Galligan, Brian. Federalism and resource development in Australia and Canada. *Australian Quarterly*; 1982; 54(3): 236-251.

2532. Gardner, Peter. Regional development and optimal management of the Prince Edward Island lobster fishery. *Canadian Journal of Regional Science*; 1984 Autumn; 7(2): 227-249.

2533. Gates, Paul W.; Gates, Lillian F. Canadian and American land policy decisions, 1930. *Western Historical Quarterly*; 1984; 15(4): 389-405.

2534. Geekie, D.A. A new federal-provincial agreement for health-care financing? *Canadian Medical Association Journal*; 1981 May; 124(10): 1343.

2535. Gellman, D.D.; Lachaine, R.; Law, M.M. The Canadian approach to health policies and programs. In: Meilicke, Carl A.; Storch, Janet L., eds. *Perspectives on Canadian health and social services policy: history and emerging trends*. Michigan: Health Administration Press; 1980: 280-292; xii, 520 p.

2536. Genest, Jean. Le dernier rapport du Conseil de planification et de développement du Québec. *L'Action national*; 1984 March; 73(7): 591-593.

2537. Ghiz, Joseph A. Constitutional impasse over oil and gas: is further decentralization compatible with nationhood? *University of New Brunswick Law Journal*; 1982: 43-67.

2538. Gill, Robert M. Billingualism in New Brunswick and the future of l'Acadie. *American Review of Canadian Studies*; 1980 Autumn; 10(2): 56-74.

2539. Gill, Robert M. Federal and provincial language policy in Ontario and the future of Franco-Ontarians. *American Review of Canadian Studies*; 1983 Spring; 13(1): 13-43.

2540. Gill, Robert M. Federal, provincial and local language legislation in Manitoba and the Franco-Manitobans. *American Review of Canadian Studies*; 1982 Spring; 12(1): 30-52.

2541. Gill, Robert M. Language policy in Saskatchewan, Alberta, and British Columbia and the future of French in the West. *American Review of Canadian Studies*; 1985 Spring; 15(1): 16-37.

2542. Gillespie, W. Irwin. The department of finance and PEMS: increased influence or reduced monopoly power? In: Maslove, Allan M., ed. *How Ottawa spends, 1984: the new agenda*. Toronto: Methuen; 1984: 189-214; 334 p.

2543. Gillespie, W. Irwin. Tax reform: the battlefield, the strategies, the spoils. *Canadian Public Administration*; 1983 Summer; 26(2): 182-202.

2544. Gillies, James M. *Where business fails: business-government relations at the federal level.* Montreal: Institute for Research on Public Policy; 1981; xii, 172 p.

2545. Gilmore, W. C. The Newfoundland continental shelf dispute in the Supreme Court of Canada. *Maritime Policy*; 1984; 8(4): 323-329.

2546. Gilmore, W. C. Newfoundland offshore mineral rights. *Maritime Policy*; 1983; 7(3): 175-196.

2547. Gilson, J.Clayton. The Agricultural Task Force report - the benefit of hindsight. *Canadian Journal of Agricultural Economics*; 1980 July; 28(2): 1-10.

2548. Globerman, Steve. Canada's Foreign Investment Review Agency and the direct investment process in Canada. *Canadian Public Administration*; 1984 Fall; 27(3): 313-328.

2549. Goldberg, Michael A.; Mark, Jonathan H. The roles of government in housing policy: a Canadian perspective and overview. *Journal of the American Planning Association*; 1985; 51(1): 34-42.

2550. Goldstein, Jonah. Communication, property rights and broadcasting vouchers. *Canadian Public Policy*; 1982 Winter; 8(1): 45-56.

2551. Goldstein, Walter. Canada's constitutional crisis: the uncertain development of Alberta's energy resources. *Energy Policy*; 1981 March; 9(1): 4-13.

2552. Goodermote, Dean; Mancke, Richard B. Nationalizing oil in the 1970s. *Energy Journal*; 1983 October; 4(4): 67-80.

2553. Goodman, Millie; Gurney, Mary; Perry, David B. Provincial budget roundup - 1981. *Canadian Tax Journal*; 1981 May-June; 29(3): 327-351.

2554. Goodman, Millie; Gurney, Mary; Perry, David B. Provincial budget roundup - 1983. *Canadian Tax Journal*; 1983 July-August; 31(4): 615-652.

2555. Gordon, Roger H. An optimal taxation approach to fiscal federalism. In: McLure, Charles E. (Jr.), ed. *Tax assignment in federal countries.* Canberra: ANU Press; 1983: 26-51; xix, 370 p.

2556. Graham, John. Funding of universities in Canada. In: Courchene, Thomas J.; Conklin, David W.; Cook, Gail C.A., eds. *Ottawa and the provinces: the distribution of money and power.* Toronto: Ontario Economic Council; 1985; 1: 323-334; xii, 341 p. (Special research report/Ontario Economic Council).

2557. Graham, John F. Financing elementary and secondary education. In: Jamieson, Barbara, ed. *Governing Nova Scotia: policies, priorities and the 1984-85 budget.* Halifax: School of Public Administration, Dalhousie University; 1984: 129-149; x, 226 p.

2558. Graham, W.C. Government procurement policies: GATT, the EEC, and the United States. In: Trebilcock, Michael J., ed. *Federalism and the Canadian economic union.* Toronto: Ontario Economic Council; 1983: 355-393; xiv, 560 p. (Ontario Economic Council Research Studies).

2559. Granatstein, J. L. Free trade between Canada and the United States: the issue that will not go away. In: Stairs, Denis; Winham, Gilbert R., res. coords. *The politics of Canada's economic relationship with the United States.* Toronto: University of Toronto Press; Royal Commission on the Economic Union and Development Prospects for Canada; 1985: 11-54; xix, 207 p. (The collected research studies; 29).

2560. Grant, E. Kenneth; Joseph, Alun E. The spacial aspects and regularities of multiple interregional migration within Canada: evidence and implications. *Canadian Journal of Regional Science*; 1983 Spring; 6(1): 75-95.

2561. Grant, John. Foreign investment: turning off and turning on. *Canadian Public Policy*; 1983 March; 9(1): 32-36.

2562. Green, Christopher. Agricultural marketing boards in Canada: an economic and legal analysis. *University of Toronto Law Journal*; 1983; 33: 407-433.

2563. Greene, Stephen; Keating, Thomas. Domestic factors and Canada-United States fisheries relations. *Canadian Journal of Political Science*; 1980 December; 13(4): 731-750.

2564. Grenier, Gilles. Health care costs in Canada: past and future trends. In: Vaillancourt, François, res. coord. *Income distribution and economic security in Canada.* Toronto: University of Toronto Press; Royal Commission on the Economic Union and Development Prospects for Canada; 1985: 251-282; xv, 321 p. (The collected research studies; 1).

2565. Grewal, Bhajan Singh. *Equalization techniques for school finance: an evaluation.* Canberra: Centre Research on Federal Financial Relations, Australian National University; 1981; viii, 52 p. (Occasional paper; 20).

2566. Grey, Rodney de C. Some issues in Canada-US trade relations. Canadian Public Policy; 1982 October; 8: 451-456.

2567. Gross, Paul F. The political economy of urban health policy. In: Mathews, Russell, ed. *Urban federalism: urban studies in a federal context.* Canberra: Centre for Research on Federal Financial Relations, Australian National University; 1981; 122-141 p.

2568. Grossman, Larry. Interprovincial barriers. *Vital Speeches*; 1980; 46(20): 627-630.

2569. Grube, John. Une sécurité sociale bien de chez nous. *L'Action nationale*; 1980 May; 69(9): 690-706.

2570. Grubel, Herbert. The costs of Canada's social insurance programs. In: Lermer, George, ed. *Probing leviathan: an investment of government in the economy.* Toronto: Fraser Institute; 1984: 59-85; xv, 223 p.

2571. Guest, Dennis. Social policy in Canada. *Social Policy and Administration*; 1984 Summer; 18(2): 130-147.

2572. Haack, Richard; Hughes, D. R.; Shapiro, R. G. *The splintered market: barriers to interprovincial trade in Canadian agriculture.* Toronto: J. Lorimer; Canadian Institute for Economic Policy; 1981; xv, 72 p. (The Canadian Institute for Economic Policy series).

2573. Haase, Gordon. A provincial perspective for jurisdiction. In: McPhail, T.; Hamilton, S., eds. *Proceedings of communication in the 80's*; April 29-May 1, 1984; Calgary: 13-21; vii, 162 p.

2574. Hallett, William D. *A history of federal government involvement in the development of sport in Canada, 1943-1979* [microfiche]: (Ph.D.) University of Alberta; 1981; 13 microfiches (1206 fr.). Ottawa: National Library of Canada, 1984.

2575. Hamelin, Louis-Emond. Managing Canada's North: challenges and opportunities - rapporteurs summary and comments. *Canadian Public Administration*; 1984 Summer; 27(2): 165-181.

2576. Hamilton, Colleen; Whalley, John. Regional considerations and Canadian trade policies: summary of the proceedings of a research symposium. In: Whalley, John, res. coord. *Canada-United States free trade.* Toronto: University of Toronto Press; Royal Commission on the Economic Union and Development Prospects for Canada; 1985: 295-312; xi, 374 p. (The collected research studies; v. 11).

2577. Handler, W. Why the Canada Health Act? *Health Management Forum*; 1984; 5(2): 27-35.

2578. Hardy, André; Piette, Jacques. *Le contentieux fédéral/provincial sur la compétence en communication.* Québec: Gouvernement du Québec, Ministère des Communications; 1983; 75 p. (Le Québec et les communications).

2579. Haritos, Z.; Elliott, A. Canadian transportation regulation: trends and issues. *Transportation*; 1983; 12(1): 3-20.

2580. Harling K. F; Thompson, R. L. The economic effects of intervention in Canadian agriculture. *Canadian Journal of Agricultural Economics*; 1983 July; 31(2): 153-173.

2581. Harris, Richard G. *Trade, industrial policy and international competition.* Toronto: University of Toronto Press; Royal Commission on the Economic Union and Development Prospects for Canada; 1985; xvii, 167 p. (The collected research studies; v. 13).

2582. Harris, Richard G.; Cox, David. *Trade, industrial policy, and Canadian manufacturing.* Toronto: Ontario Economic Council; 1984; 209 (122) p. (Ontario Economic Council research studies; 31).

2583. Harris, Stuart; Perkins, Frances. Federalism and the environment: economic aspects. In: Mathews, Russel, ed. *Federalism and the environment.* Canberra: Centre for Research on Federal Financial Relations, Australian National University; 1985; 35-46 p.

2584. Harrison, Peter; Parkes, J.G.Michael. *Coastal zone management in Canada.* Coastal Zone Management Journal; 1983; 11(1-2): 1-11.

2585. Hart, Michael M. Canada's economic development policies: constraints and opportunities. In: Hart, Michael M. *Canadian economic development and the international trading system.* Toronto: University of Toronto Press; Royal Commission on the Economic Union and Development Prospects for Canada; 1985: 53-81; xvi, 156 p. (The collected research studies; 53).

2586. Hart, Michael M. *Canadian economic development and the international trading system.* Toronto: University of Toronto Press; Royal Commission on the Economic Union and Development Prospects for Canada; 1985; xvi, 156 p. (The collected research studies; v. 53).

2587. Hart, Michael M. *Some thoughts on Canada-United States sectoral free trade.* Montreal: Institute for Research on Public Policy; 1985; xiii, 54 p. (Essays in international economics).

2588. Harvey, David R. *Christmas turkey or prairie vulture?: an economic analysis of the Crow's Nest Pass grain rates.* Montreal: Institute for Research on Public Policy; 1980.

2589. Hastings, J.E.F. Federal-provincial insurance for hospital and physician's care in Canada. In: Meilicke, Carl A.; Storch, Janet L., eds. *Perspectives on Canadian health and social services policy: history and emerging trends.* Michigan: Health Administration Press; 1980: 198-219; xii, 520 p.

2590. Hatcher, G. H. Access to medical care and the remuneration of physicians. Justice Hall's report on Canada's National Provincial Health Program for the 1980s. *Lancet;* 1981; 1(8230): 1143-1146.

2591. Haughey, Douglas J.; Liddle, Robert T. *The implications of Canadian natural gas deregulation.* Calgary: Canadian Energy Research Institute; 1985; viii, 97 p. (Working paper / Canadian Energy Research Institute; 85-1).

2592. Hawkes, David C.; Pollard, Bruce G. *The medicare debate in Canada: the politics of new federalism.* Publius; 1984 Summer; 14(3): 183-198.

2593. Hayes, John A. *Economic mobility in Canada: a comparative study.* Ottawa: Supply and Services Canada; 1982; ix, 351 p.

2594. Helliwell, John F. Canadian energy pricing. *Canadian Journal of Economics;* 1981 November; 14(4): 577-95.

2595. Helliwell, John F. Energy in Canada. *Current History;* 1980; 79(460): 125-128, 149-150.

2596. Helliwell, John F. Taxation of oil and gas revenues of four countries: Canada. *Energy Journal*; 1982 April; 3(2): 20-31.

2597. Helliwell, John F. *The distribution of energy revenues within Canada: functional or factional federalism?* Vancouver: University of British Columbia, Dept. of Economics; 1980; 32; 3 p. (Resources paper).

2598. Helliwell, John F. Trade policies for natural gas and electricity. In: Ontario Economic Council. *Energy policies for the 1980's: an economic analysis.* Toronto: Ontario Economic Council; 1980; 2: 1-53; 168 p. (Special research report/Ontario Economic Council).

2599. Helliwell, John F. *Using Canadian oil and gas revenues in the 1980's: provincial and federal perspectives.* Vancouver: University of British Columbia, Dept. of Economics; 1980; 32, 4 p. (Resource paper).

2600. Helliwell, John F.; McRae, Robert N. The national energy conflict. *Canadian Public Policy*; 1981 Winter; 7(1): 15-23.

2601. Helliwell, John F.; McRae, Robert N. Resolving the energy conflict: from the National Energy Program to the energy agreements. *Canadian Public Policy*; 1982 Winter; 8(1): 14-23.

2602. Helliwell, John F.; Scott, Anthony. *Canada in fiscal conflict: resources and the West.* [Vancouver]: Pemberton Securities; c1981; 80 p.

2603. Helliwell, John F.; Boothe, Paul M.; McRae, Robert N. Stabilization, allocation and the 1970s, oil price shocks. *Scandinavian Journal of Economics*; 1982; 84(2): 259-88.

2604. Helliwell, John F.; MacGregor, Mary E.; Plourde, André. Changes in Canadian energy demand, supply, and policies, 1974-1986. *Natural Resources Journal*; 1984 April; 24(2): 297-324.

2605. Helliwell, John F.; MacGregor, Mary E.; Plourde, Andre. Energy policy and industrial activity: a reply. *Canadian Public Policy*; 1984 December; 104: 476-80.

2606. Helliwell, John F.; MacGregor, Mary E.; Plourde, Andre. The National Energy Program meets falling world oil prices. *Canadian Public Policy*; 1983 September; 9(3): 284-296.

2607. Hepworth, Philip H. Trends in provincial social service department expenditures 1963-1982. In: Ismael, Jacqueline S., ed. *Canadian social welfare policy: federal and provincial dimensions.* Kingston: McGill-Queen's University Press; 1985: 139-172; xviii, 187 p. (Canadian public administration).

2608. Hewison, G. A national fishery policy for Canada: dream or debacle. In: Lorimer, R.; McMullin, S.E, eds. *Canada and the sea.* Willowdale: Association for Canadian Studies; 1980: 87-93.

2609. Higgins, Benjamin. Economic development and regional disparities: a comparative study of four federations. In: Mathews, Russell, ed. *Regional disparities and economic development.* Canberra: Centre for Research on Federal Financial Relations, Australian National University; 1981; 21-80.

2610. Hindley, M. Patricia. *The tangled net: basic issues in Canadian communications.* Vancouver: Douglas & McIntyre; [1980]; xiv, 178 p.

2611. Hodgins, Barbara. *Where the economy and the Constitution meet in Canada.* Montreal: C.D. Howe Institute; 1981; iv, 53 p.

2612. Hooker, C.A. *Energy and the quality of life: understanding energy policy.* Toronto: University of Toronto Press; c1981; ix, 283 p.

2613. Houle, François. Stratégie économique et restructuration de l'Etat au Canada. *Politique*; 1983; 3: 63-87.

2614. Howard, John L.; Stanbury, W.T. Measuring leviathan: the size, scope and growth of governments in Canada. In: Lermer, George, ed. *Probing leviathan: an investigation of government in the economy.* Vancouver: The Fraser Institute; 1980: 87-110; xv, 223 p.

2615. Hubley, R. Why Canadianize the oil industry? *Canadian Business Review*; 1982 Spring; 9(1): 15-19.

2616. Hudon, Raymond. *De la gérance de l'intégration continentale au redéploiement de l'économie canadienne politiques économiques et constitutionnelles des années soixante-dix au Canada* [microfiche]: (Ph.D.) Queen's University; 1982; 9 microfiches (828 IM.). Ottawa: Bibliothèque nationale du Canada, 1984.

2617. Hum, Derek. *Federalism and the poor: a review of the Canada Assistance Plan.* Toronto: Ontario Economic Council; c1982; vi, 111 p. (Policy study series (Ontario Economic Council)).

2618. Hum, Derek. The working paper, the Canada Assistance Plan, and provincial response in income supplementation. In: Ismael, Jacqueline S., ed. *Canadian social welfare policy: federal and provincial dimensions.* Kingston: McGill-Queen's University Press; 1985: 120-138; xviii, 187 p. (Canadian public administration).

2619. Hunt, Constance D. Management of federal petroleum lands in Canada. In: Saunders, J. Owen, ed. *Managing natural resources in a federal state.* Toronto: Carswell; 1986; 121-138 vi, 336 p.

2620. Hunter, David. Federal-provincial responses to the management of the Niagara River. In: Saunders, J. Owen, ed. *Managing natural resources in a federal state.* Toronto: Carswell; 1986: 285-294; vi, 336 p.

2621. Interdepartmental Task Force on Land-Use Policy. *Land use in Canada: the report of the Interdepartmental Task Force on Land-use Policy,* by L.C. Munn. Hull: Land Directorate, Environment Canada; 1980; vii, 51 p.

2622. Intergovernmental Task Force on Land Use Policy; Canada. Department of the Environment. *Land use in Canada: the report of the Intergovernmental Task*

Force on Land-Use Policy, by L.C. Munn [Ottawa]: Supply and Services Canada; 1980.

2623. Interprovincial Task Force on Social Security. *Income security in Canada: report*. [Ottawa]: [Canadian Intergovernmental Conference Secretariat]; 1980; xi, 147 p.

2624. Islam, Muhammed N. The efficiency of interprovincial migration in Canada, 1961-1978. *Regional Science and Urban Economics*; 1983 May; 13(2): 231-49.

2625. Ismael, Jacqueline S., ed. *Canadian social welfare policy: federal and provincial dimensions*. Kingston: McGill-Queen's University Press; 1985; xviii, 187 p. (Canadian public administration).

2626. Ivany, J. W. George. *Federal-provincial relations: education Canada*. Toronto: Ontario Institute for Studies in Education; 1981; x, 150 p. (Symposium series).

2627. Ivany, J.W. George; Manley-Casimir, Michael E., eds. *Federal-provincial relations: education Canada*. Toronto: Ontario Institute for Studies in Education Press; 1981; x, 150 p. (Symposium series / the Ontario Institute for Studies in Education; v. 14).

2628. Jackson, Edgar L.; Foster, Leslie T. *Energy attitudes and policies*. Victoria: Dept. of Geography, University of Victoria; [1980?]; ix, 193 p. (Cornett occasional papers; v. 2).

2629. Jagoe, E.H.M.; Fiander, A.D. *Assessment of the impact of the National Energy Program on the long-haul freight movements from the maritime provinces, prepared for Transport Canada, strategic planning group*. [Fredericton]: ADI Limited; 1982; 7 (290) p.

2630. James F. Hickling Management Consultants Ltd.; Canada. Dept. of Regional Industrial Expansion. *Transportation and regional industrial expansion: users' perspective on issues for the 1980s: final report*. Ottawa: DRIE; 1984; 2 v.

2631. James, L. R. Will deregulation give business more influence over governmnent decision-makers? *Canadian Business Review*; 1985 Spring; 12(1): 35-39.

2632. Jamieson, Barbara; Amirkhalkhali, Saleh. Taxes, transfers, and deficit financing: seeking the appropriate balance. In: Jamicson, Barbara, ed. *Governing Nova Scotia: policies, priorities, and the 1984-85 budget*. Halifax: School of Public Administration, Dalhousie University; 1984: 21-50; x, 226 p.

2633. Janisch, H.; Kurisaki, Y. Reform of telecommunications regulation in Japan and Canada. *Telecommunications Policy*; 1985; 9(1): 31-40.

2634. Jansen, Janni Margaretha. Regional socio-economic development: the case of fishing in Atlantic Canada. Rutgers University; 1981. Dissertation Abstracts International 42 (1): 302 pp.

2635. Jenkin, Michael. *The challenge of diversity: industrial policy in the Canadian federation.* Ottawa: Science Council of Canada; 1983; 214 p. (Background study; v. 50).

2636. Johannson, P. Roff; Thomas J.C. A dilemma of nuclear regulations in Canada: political control and public confidence. *Canadian Public Policy;* 1981 Summer; 7(3): 433-43.

2637. Johnson, A. W. *Giving greater point and purpose to the federal financing of post-secondary education and research in Canada.* Ottawa: Secretary of State; 1985; xi, 55 p.

2638. Johnson, Susan. *Fiscally-induced interprovincial migration in Canada* [microfiche]: (M.A.) University of Alberta; 1982; 2 microfiches (138 fr.). Ottawa: National Library of Canada, 1984.

2639. Johnston, Richard. *Public opinion and public policy in Canada.* Toronto: University of Toronto Press, Royal Commission on the Economic Union and Development Prospects for Canada; 1986; xviii, 244 p. (The collected research studies; 35).

2640. Julien, Pierre-André. Les avantages économiques de la récupération des pouvoirs dans les domaines de la monnaie. *L'Action nationale;* 1982 January; 71(5): 515-527.

2641. Julien, Pierre-André. La centralisation des politiques économiques au Canada et l'économie. *L'Action nationale;* 1981 September; 71(1): 51-55.

2642. Julien, Pierre-André. Responsabilité et coopération doivent être les nouvelles prémisses de développement régional. *L'Action nationale;* 1982 May-June; 71(9-10): 965-972.

2643. Jump, G.V. Financing public pensions: some capital market implications. In: Conklin, David W.; Bennett, Jalynn H.; Courchene, Thomas J., eds. *Pensions today and tomorrow: background studies.* Toronto: Ontario Economic Council; 1984: 295-326; 486 p. (Special research report/Ontario Economic Council).

2644. Jump, Gregory V. On interpreting simulations with a macroeconometric model: comment: the impact of higher energy prices in Canada. *Canadian Public Policy;* 1981 Winter; 7(1): 35-38.

2645. Kane, T. Gregory. *Consumers and the regulators: intervention in the federal regulatory process.* Montreal: Institute for Research on Public Policy; 1980; xvii, 123 p.

2646. Kane, T. Gregory; Elliott, Stikeman. Keynote address - the constitutional basis for jurisdiction: evolving federal and provincial rules. In: McPhail, T.; Hamilton, S., eds. *Proceedings of Communication in the 80's;* April 28-May 1, 1984. Calgary: University of Calgary: 1-13; vii, 162 p.

2647. Kapsalis, Constantine. Block-funding and provincial spending on social programs. *Canadian Tax Journal*; 1982 March-April; 30: 219-227.

2648. Kearney, Richard C.; Garey, Robert B. American federalism and the management of radioactive wastes. In: Wright, Deil S.; White, Harvey L., eds. *Federalism and intergovernmental relations*. Washington: American Society for Public Administration; 1984: 302-323; 333 p.

2649. Kellough, Howard J.; McQuillan, Peter E. Provincial taxation differences and the private corporation. *Canadian Tax Foundation*; 1983 November: 749-791.

2650. Kelly, Brian. *Environment Canada's options for intervention in energy: a report prepared for the Energy Branch, Corporate Planning Group, Environment Canada*. Ottawa: Marbeck Resource Consultants Ltd; 1983; x, 180 p.

2651. KenAgra Management Services; Alberta. Alberta Economic Development. *Major government programs affecting the competitive position of provincial livestock industries in British Columbia, Alberta, Saskatchewan, Manitoba, Ontario, and Quebec, prepared for Alberta Economic Development*. Edmonton: KenAgra Management Services; [1981]; 2 v.

2652. Kernaghan, Kenneth. Politics, public administration and Canada's aging population. *Canadian Public Policy*; 1982 Winter; 8(1): 69-79.

2653. Kernaghan, Kenneth. Representative and responsive bureaucracy: implications for Canadian regionalism. In: Aucoin, Peter, res. coord. *Regional responsiveness and the national administrative state*. Toronto: University of Toronto Press; Royal Commission on the Economic Union and Development Prospects for Canada; 1985: 1-50; xv, 119 p. (The collected research studies; v. 37).

2654. Kernaghan, Kenneth. Universities and government. *Optimum*; 1981; 12(4): 29-40.

2655. Kierans, Eric. Quest for community. *Journal of Business Administration*; 1984-1985; 15: 23-41.

2656. Kirby, M.J.L. *Navigating troubled waters: a new policy for the Atlantic fisheries. Report of the Task Force on Atlantic Fisheries*. Ottawa: Supply and Services Canada; 1982; 393 p. Note: French ed. also available.

2657. Kirby, Michael J.L. Restructuring the Atlantic fishery: a case study in business-government relations. *Business Quarterly* (Special Supplement); 1985 Summer; 50(2): 115-118.

2658. Knight, David B. Regionalisms, nationalisms, and the Canadian state. *Journal of Geography*; 1984 September-October; 83(5): 212-220.

2659. Knuttila, K.M.K.; McCrome, J.N. National policy and prairie agrarian development: a reassessment. *Canadian Review of Sociology and Anthropology*; 1980 August; 17(3): 263-272.

2660. Knuttila, Kenneth Murray. *The impact of the western Canadian agrarian movement on federal government policy, 1900-1930: an assessment and analysis* [microfiche]: (Ph.D.) University of Toronto; 1982; 3 microfiches (278 fr.). Ottawa: National Library of Canada, 1984.

2661. Kovacs, Jerry D. Managing Alberta water: the decision-making process. *Resources Policy*; 1982 December; 8(4): 316-319.

2662. Krasnick, Mark, res. coord. *Perspectives on the Canadian economic union.* Toronto: University of Toronto Press; Royal Commission on the Economic Union and Development Prospects for Canada; 1986; xvi, 271 p. (The collected research studies; 60).

2663. Kresl, Peter Karl. Quebec turns to technology. *American Review of Canadian Studies*; 1983 Summer; 13(2): 11-28.

2664. Krishnan, P. *Linguistic dispersal in Canada 1951-1976.* Edmonton: University of Alberta, Dept. of Sociology; 1981; 20 p. (Discussion paper / Population Research Laboratory, University of Alberta; 27).

2665. Kucharczyk, John. Student aid, federal-provincial relations, and university finance. *Journal of Canadian Studies*; 1984; 19(3): 87-98.

2666. Kwon, O. Yul. Neutral taxation and provincial mineral royalties: the Manitoba metallic minerals and Saskatchewan uranium royalties. *Canadian Public Policy*; 1983 June; 9(2): 189-199.

2667. Lacasse, Jean-Paul. Oil and gas revenue sharing: beyond legal foundations and constraints. In: Saunders, J. Owen, ed. *Managing natural resources in a federal state.* Toronto: Carswell; 1986: 73-83; vi, 336 p.

2668. Lacer, James. The three-sided struggle for power in shaping Canada's petroleum policy. *Journal of Business Administration*; 1983; 13(1): 191-199.

2669. Lacroix, Robert; Rabeau, Yves. *Politiques nationales, conjonctures régionales: la stabilisation économique.* Montréal: Presses de l'Université de Montréal; 1981; 199 p.

2670. Laidler, David, res. coord. *Approaches to economic well-being.* Toronto: University of Toronto Press; Royal Commission on the Economic Union and Development Prospects for Canada; 1985; xix, 249 p. (The collected research studies; 26).

2671. Lambert, Ronald D.; Curtis, James E. Opposition to multiculturalism among Quebecois and English-Canadians: *Canadian Review of Sociology and Anthropology*; 1983 May; 20(2): 193-207.

2672. Lander, J.B.; Hecht, A. *Regional development in Ontario: federal and provincial involvement.* Marburg/Lahn: Selbstverlag des Geographischen Institutes der Universitat Marburg; 1980; 146 p.

2673. Lang, Graeme. Regional variations in worksharing: the case of Newfoundland. Canadian Public Policy; 1985 March; 11(1): 54-63.

2674. Langford, John W. Transport Canada and the transport ministry: the attempt to retreat to basics. In: Doern, Bruce G., ed. *How Ottawa spends your tax dollars - 1982*. Toronto: James Lorimer; 1982: 147-172; v, 256 p.

2675. Lapointe, F. Regional development in Quebec; intervention by the federal and provincial governments. *Geoscope*; 1979 December; 11(1): 39-86.

2676. Laporte, Pierre E. Status language planning in Quebec: an evaluation. In: Bourhis, Richard Y., ed. *Conflict and language planning in Quebec*. London: Multilingual Matters; 1984: 53-80; xvi, 304 p. (Multilingual matters; 5).

2677. Larin, Gilles-N.; Racette, Jean-Pierre. Etude de l'incidence des dépenses fiscales sur l'équité du système fiscal canadien au cours d'un cycle de vie. *Canadian Tax Journal*; 1984 November-December; 32(6): 1096-1116.

2678. Larter, Sylvia; Cheng, Maisy. *Bilingual education and bilingualism: a review of research literature*. Toronto: Board of Education, Research Dept.; 1984; iii, 169 p.

2679. Laskin, John B. Personal mobility in the United States and the EEC. In: Trebilcock, Michael J., ed. *Federalism and the Canadian economic union*. Toronto: Ontario Economic Council; 1983: 456-498; xiv, 560 p. (Ontario Economic Council research series).

2680. Lattimore, Ralph; Weedle, Stephanie. *The "world price" impact of multilateral free trade in dairy products*. Ottawa: Agriculture Canada; 1981; 18 p. (Economic working papers / agriculture Canada).

2681. Laxer, James. *Canada's economic strategy*. Toronto: McClelland and Stewart; 1981; 202 p.

2682. Laxer, James. *Oil and gas: Ottawa, the provinces, and the petroleum industry*. Toronto: J. Lorimer; 1983; 221 p. (The Canadian issues series).

2683. Leach, Richard H. *Whatever happened to urban policy? A comparative study of urban policy in Australia, Canada and the United States*. Canberra: Centre for Research on Federal Financial Relations, Australian National University; 1985; ix, 134 p. (Research monograph; 40).

2684. Leavy, James. *La clause de commerce et l'intégration économique*. Montréal: Editions Thémis; 1982; xiii, 356 p.

2685. Leclerc, Wilbrod. The crow should go. *Policy Options*; 1984 January-February; 5(1): 45-48.

2686. Lemieux, Vincent; Turgeon, Jean. La décentralisation: une analyse structurale. *Canadian Journal of Political Science*; 1980 December; 13(4): 691-710.

2687. Lermer, George, ed. *Probing leviathan: an investigation of government in the economy*. Vancouver: The Fraser Institute; 1984; xv, 223 p.

2688. Lermer, George; Stanbury, W.T. Measuring the cost of redistrubuting income by means of direct regulation. *Canadian Journal of Economics*; 1985 February; 18(1): 190-207.

2689. Leslie, Peter M. *Canadian universities 1980 and beyond: enrolment, structural change, and finance*. Ottawa: Association of Universities and Colleges of Canada; 1980; xii, 446 p. (AUCC policy studies; 3).

2690. Leslie, Peter M. Financing techniques, good and bad. In Conklin, David W.; Courchene, Thomas J., eds. *Ontario universities: access, operations and funding*. Toronto: Ontario Economic Council; 1985: 303-335; xiv, 467 p.

2691. Leslie, Peter M. Fiscal transfers for post-secondary education: some comments on the Johnson report. In: Noordeh, Ardeshir, ed. *Reforming the financing arrangements for post-secondary education in Canada*. Toronto: Ontario Economic Council; [1985]: 3-17; x, 160 p.

2692. Lesser, Barry. Regional development matters. *Policy Options*; 1983 November; 4(4): 27-29.

2693. Lester, John. The impact of higher energy prices in Canada: Comment. *Canadian Public Policy*; 1981 Winter; 7(1): 52-58.

2694. Lindenfield, Rita. Hospital insurance in Canada: an example in federal-provincial relations. In: Meilicke, Carl A.; Storch, Janet L., eds. *Perspectives on Canadian health and social services policy: history and emerging trends*. Michigan: Health Administration Press; 1980: 166-182; xii, 520 p.

2695. Lindquist, Evert A. *Consultation and budget secrecy: reforming the process of creating revenue budgets in the Canadian Federal Government*. Ottawa: Conference Board of Canada; 1985; xxii, 90 p.

2696. Lindsey, Edward H. Jr. Linguistic minority educational rights in Canada: an international and comparative perspective. *Georgia Journal of International and Comparative Law*; 1983 Spring; 13(2): 515-547.

2697. Linton, A. L.; Naylor, D. Problems of health care in Canada. *Medical Journal of Australia*; 1985; 142(10): 556-558.

2698. Lipsey, Richard G. Can the market economy survive? In: Lermer, George, ed. *Probing leviathan: an investigation of government in the economy*. Vancouver: The Fraser Institute; 1984: 3-37; xv, 223 p.

2699. Lister, Ross. Agricultural development agreements in the Maritimes from a farm management perspective (Proceedings). *Canadian Journal of Agricultural Economics*; 1983; 31: 39-43.

2700. Lithwick, N. H. *Canadian regional policy: undisciplined experimentation*. *Canadian Journal of Regional Science*; 1982 Autumn; 5(2): 275-281.

2701. Lithwick, N. H. Regional policy: a matter of perspectives. *Canadian Journal of Regional Science*; 1982 Autumn; 5(2): 353-363.

2702. Lithwick, N. Harvey. The decline and fall of the housing market. In: Maslove, Allan M., ed. *How Ottawa spends, 1985: sharing the pie*. Toronto: Methuen; 1985: 30-57; 184 p.

2703. Lithwick, N. Harvey. Federal government regional economic development policies: an evalvative survey. In: Norrie, Kenneth, res. coord. *Disparities and interregional adjustment*. Toronto: University of Toronto Press; Royal Commission on the Economic Union and Development Prospects for Canada; 1986: 109-157; xiv, 223 p. (The collected research studies; 64).

2704. Lithwick, N. Harvey. Regional policy: the embodiment of contradictions. In: Doern, G. Bruce, ed. *How Ottawa spends your tax dollars - 1982*. Toronto: James Lorimer; 1982: 131-146; v, 256 p.

2705. Lithwick, N. Harvey; Devlin, John. Economic development policy: a case study in underdeveloped policy making. In: Maslove, Allan M., ed. *How Ottawa spends, 1984: the new agenda*. Toronto: Methuen; 1984: 122-166; 334 p.

2706. Lucas, Alastair R. The harmonization of federal and provincial environmental policies: the changing legal and policy framework. In: Saunders, J. Owen, ed. *Managing natural resources in a federal state*. Toronto: Carswell; 1986: 33-51; vi, 336 p.

2707. Macdonald, Donald S. Canadian industrial policy objectives and article III of GATT: national ambitions and international obligations. *Canadian Business Law Journal*; 1982 August; 6(4): 385-407.

2708. Macdonald, Donald S. An overview of the prospects for sectoral integration: the view from Canada. In: David G. Meany, ed. *Proceedings: the legal aspects of sectoral integration between the United States and Canada*; April 19-21, 1985; Cleveland: Canada-United States Law Institute; 1985: 3-12; 256 p.

2709. Macdonald, Donald S. An overview of the prospects for sectoral integration: the view from Canada (Conference: The legal aspects of sectoral integration between the United States and Canada, Cleveland, April 19-21, 1985). *Canada-United States Law Journal*; 1985; 10: 3-12.

2710. Macdonald, Roderick A. Understanding regulation by regulations. In: Bernier, Ivan; Lajoie, Andée, res. coords. *Regulations, crown corporations and administrative tribunals*. Toronto: University of Toronto Press; Royal Commission on the Economic Union and Development Prospects for Canada; 1985: 81-154; xvii, 202 p. (The collected research studies; 48).

2711. Macdonald, Wendy. *Constitutional change and the mineral industry in Canada*. Kingston: Institute for Intergovernmental Relations and Centre for Resource Studies, Queen's University; 1980; viii, 73 p. (Working paper).

2712. MacEachen, Allan J. *Federal-provincial fiscal arrangements in the eighties: a submission to the parliamentary Task Force on the Federal-Provincial Fiscal Arrangements.* Ottawa: Department of Finance Canada; 1981; 89 p.

2713. MacLaren, Roy. Canadian views on the U.S. government reaction to the National Energy Program. *Canadian Public Policy* (supplement); 1982 October; 8: 493-97.

2714. Maclennan, Rod J. *Report of the Royal Commission on Post-Secondary Education, Province of Nova Scotia.* [Halifax]: The Commission; 1985; xxiii, 269 p.

2715. MacMillan, C. Michael. Henri Bourassa on the defence of language rights. *Dalhousie Review*; 1982-83; 62(3): 413-430.

2716. Macnaughton, Bruce D.; Winn, Conrad J. Economic policy and electoral self interest: the allocations of the Department of Regional Economic Expansion. *Canadian Public Policy*; 1981 Spring; 7(2): 318-27.

2717. MacNevin, Alex Stanley. *Fiscal integration and subcentral public sector inducements to Canadian interprovincial migration* [microfiche]: (Ph.D.) McMaster University; 1984 3 microfiches (231 fr.). Ottawa: National Library of Canada, 1985.

2718. Magnet, Joseph Eliot. Les écoles et la constitution. *Les Cahiers de droit*; 1983 March; (1): 145-155.

2719. Magor, Murray C. *The language of education in Quebec: a study of Bill 101 in terms of constitutional and natural law* [microfiche]: (M.A.) McGill University; 1982 2 microfiches (114 fr.). Ottawa: National Library of Canada, 1985.

2720. Mahon, Rianne. Unravelling Canada's textile policy. In: Maslove, Allan M., ed. *How Ottawa spends, 1985: sharing the pie.* Toronto: Methuen; 1985: 90-113; 184 p.

2721. Mallea, John. Minority language education in Quebec and anglophone Canada. In: Bourhis, Richard Y., ed. *Conflict and language planning in Quebec.* London: Multilingual Matters; 1984: 222-261; xvi, 304 p. (Multilingual matters; 5).

2722. Manga, Pran. Preserving Medicare: the Canada Health Act. *Perception*; 1984 January-February; 7: 12-15.

2723. Manitoba. Department of Finance. *Manitoba's capital project proposals to the Government of Canada*, by Honourable Vic Schroeder, Minister of Finance. [Winnipeg]: [Department of Finance]; [1983]; 18 p.

2724. Mansell, R. L. Texas and Alberta: a comparison of regional economies. *Texas Business Review*; 1981 November-December; 55(6): 241-247.

2725. Mansell, Robert L.; Copithorne, Lawrence. Canadian regional economic disparities: a survey. In: Norrie, Kenneth, res. coord. *Disparities and interregional ad-*

justment. Toronto: University of Toronto Press; Royal Commission on the Economic Union and Development Prospects for Canada; 1986: 1-51; xiv, 223 p. (The collected research studies; v. 64).

2726. Mansfield, E.; Switzer, L. Effects of federal support on company-financed R and D: the case of energy. *Management Science*; 1984 May; 30(5): 562-571.

2727. Marr, William.; McCready, Douglas.; Millerd, Frank. Canadian internal migration of medical personnel. *Growth and Change*; 1981 July; 12(3): 32-40.

2728. Marr, William; Whitney, Wayne. The changing pattern of differential regional growth in Canada, 1951-1961 and 1961-1971. *Nebraska Journal of Economics and Business*; 1983 Winter; 22(1): 29-43.

2729. Marston, Geoffrey. The Newfoundland offshore jurisdictional dispute: a postscript. *Journal of World Trade Law*; 1985 July-August; (4): 423-425.

2730. Martin, Fernand. Canadian regional policy: an overview. *Canadian Journal of Regional Science*; 1982 Autumn; 5(2): 267-274.

2731. Martin, J.C. Canada Health Act--the debate continues. *Hospital Trustee*; 1984; 8(2): 4-5.

2732. Maslove, Allan M.; Prince, Michael J.; Doern, G. Bruce. *Federal and provincial budgeting*. Toronto: University of Toronto Press; Royal Commission on the Economic Union and Development Prospects for Canada; 1986; xvi, 262 p. (The collected research studies; 41).

2733. Maslove, Allan M., ed. *How Ottawa spends, 1984: the new agenda*. Toronto: Methuen; 1984; 334 p.

2734. Maslove, Allan M., ed. *How Ottawa spends, 1985: sharing the pie*. Toronto: Methuen; 1985; 184 p.

2735. Maslove, Allan M. Ottawa's new agenda: the issues and the constraints. In: Maslove, Allan M., ed. *How Ottawa spends, 1984: the new agenda*. Toronto: Methuen; 1984: 1-30; 334 p.

2736. Maslove, Allan M. Tax expenditures, tax credits and equity. In: Doern, Bruce G., ed. *How Ottawa spends your tax dollars: federal priorities - 1981*. Toronto: James Lorimer; 1981: 232-254; 303 p.

2737. Matheson, Duncan. Clarifying social welfare. *Policy Options*; 1983 July; 4(4): 26-29.

2738. Mathews, Russell. *The case for indirect taxation*. Canberra: Centre for Research on Federal Financial Relations, Australian National University; 1983; 26 p. (Reprint Series; v. 54).

2739. Mathews, Russell. *Changing the tax mix: federalism aspects*. Canberra: Centre for Research on Federal Financial Relations, Australian National University; 1985; 25 p. (Reprint Series; v. 63).

2740. Mathews, Russell, ed. *Federalism and the environment*. Canberra: Centre for Research on Federal Financial Relations, Australian National University; 1985; ix, 67 p.

2741. Mathews, Russell. *Fiscal equalization in transport*. Canberra: Centre for Research on Federal Financial Relations, Australian National University; 1984; v, 27 p. (Occasional paper; 32).

2742. Mathews, Russell. *Public policies in two federal countries: Canada and Australia*. Canberra: Centre for Research on Federal Financial Relations, Australian National University; 1982; xxx, 298 p.

2743. Mathews, Russell, ed. *Regional disparities and economic development*. Canberra: Centre for Research on Federal Financial Relations, Australian National University; 1981; xx, 254 p.

2744. Mathews, Russell. *The structure of taxation*. Canberra: Centre for Research on Federal Financial Relations, Australian National University; 1980; 44 p. (Reprint series; 34).

2745. Mathews, Russell. *Tax effectiveness and tax equity in federal countries*. Canberra: Centre for Research on Federal Financial Relations, Australian National University; 1983; 26 p. (Reprint Series; v. 51).

2746. Matthews, R. Class interests and role of the state in the development of Canada's east coast fishery. In: Lorimer, R.; McMullin, S.E, eds. Canada and the sea. Willowdale: Association for Canadian Studies/L'Association des Etudes Canadiennes; 1980: 115-124.

2747. Matthews, Ralph. Two alternative explanations of the problem of regional dependency in Canada. *Canadian Public Policy*; 1981 Spring; 7(2): 268-83.

2748. Matthews, Roy A.; McCulla, D.J. *Structural change and industrial policy: the redeployment of Canadian manufacturing, 1960-80*. Ottawa: Economic Council of Canada; 1985; vii, 70 p.

2749. Maxwell, Judith; Pestieau, Caroline. *Economic realities of contemporary Confederation*. [Montreal]: C.D. Howe Research Institute; [1980]; vi, 131 p.

2750. McAllister, Ian, ed. *Regional development and the European Community : a Canadian perspective*. Montreal: Institute for Research on Public Policy; 1982; xviii, 243 p.

2751. McAllister, James A. The fiscal analysis of policy outputs. *Canadian Public Administration*; 1980 Fall; 23(3): 458-486.

2752. McArthur, D. *Analysis of public responses to the report of the Federal-Provincial Task Force on Student Assistance*. [s.l.]: Council of Ministers of Education; 1981.

2753. McCallum, John. Government deficits: historical analysis and present policy alternatives. In: Conklin, David W.; Courchene, Thomas J., eds. *Deficits: how big and how bad?* Toronto: Ontario Economic Council; 1983: 284-322; 361 p. (Special research report/Ontario Economic Council).

2754. McCallum, John S. The empirical impact of changes in government on bond yields: the Canadian provincial experience. *Journal of Bank Research*; 1981 Winter; 11(4): 254-47.

2755. McCorquodale, Susan. The management of a common property resource: fisheries policy in Atlantic Canada. In: Atkinson, Michael M.; Chandler, Marsha A., eds. *The politics of Canadian public policy*. Toronto: University of Toronto Press; 1983: 151-172; 286 p. (Studies in Canadian public policy).

2756. McCrorie, J. N.; Knuttila, Murray. National policy and agrarian development: a reassessment. *Canadian Review of Sociology and Anthropology*; 1980 August; 17(3).

2757. McDougall, Ian. *Marketing Canada's energy: a strategy for security in oil and gas*. Toronto: James Lorimer; 1983; xiii, 148 p. (The Canadian Institute for Economic Policy series).

2758. McDougall, John N. Natural resources and national politics: a look at three Canadian resource industries. In: Doern, G. Bruce, res. coord. *The politics of economic policy*. Toronto: University of Toronto Press; Royal Commission on the Economic Union and Development Prospects for Canada; 1985: 163-219; xv, 306 p. (The collected research studies; 40).

2759. McEwan, E. D. The realities of Medicare. *Health Management Forum*; 1980; 1(1): 32-49.

2760. McFetridge, Donald G. Research and development expenditures. In: Doern, Bruce G., ed. *How Ottawa spends your tax dollars: federal priorities - 1981*. Toronto: James Lorimer; 1981: 225-279; 303 p.

2761. McGinnis, Janice P. Dickin. *From health to welfare: federal government policies regarding standards of public health for Canadians, 1919-1945* [microfiche]: (Ph.D.) University of Alberta; 1980; 4 microfiches (347 fr.). Ottawa: National Library of Canada, 1981.

2762. McKercher, William. Government and the drive towards centralized control (business caught in the middle). *Business Quarterly*; 1980 Winter; 45(4): 37-43.

2763. McKinsey, Lauren S. Détente in Canada's energy war. *American Review of Canadian Studies*; 1982 Spring; 12(1): 98-119.

2764. McLaren, D. J. Earth science and federal issues. *Geoscience Canada*; 1981 September; 8(3): 106-12.

2765. McLarty, R.A. Government of Canada policies for regional development. In: Mathews, Russell, ed. *Regional disparities and economic development*. Canberra: Centre for Research on Federal Financial Relations, Australian National University; 1981; 81-98 p.

2766. McLure, Charles E., Jr. Assignment of corporate income taxes in a federal system. In: idem, ed. *Tax assignment in federal countries.* Canberra, Aus.: ANU Press; 1983: 101-128; xix, 370 p.

2767. McLure, Charles E., Jr., ed. *Tax assignment in federal countries.* Canberra: Centre for Research on Federal Financial Relations, Australian National University; 1983; xix, 370 p.

2768. McLure, Charles E.; Mieszkowski, Peter M. *Fiscal federalism and the taxation of natural resources.* Toronto: Lexington Books; c1983; viii, 260 p.

2769. McMillan, Melville L. Local fiscal reform in Alberta? - a review and assessment of the report of Alberta's Provincial-Municipal Finance Council. *Canadian Tax Journal*; 1980 March-April; 28(2): 164-179.

2770. McMillan, Melville L. L'Ouest en transition: l'avenir économique de l'Ouest canadien: introduction. *Canadian Public Policy* (supplement); 1985 July; 11: 275-282.

2771. McMillan, Melville L. Western transition: the economic future of the West: introduction. *Canadian Public Policy* (supplement); 1985 July; 11: 268-274.

2772. McMillan, Melville L. *Natural resource prosperity: boon or burden for Canadian federalism?* Canberra: Centre for Research on Federal Financial Relations, Australian National University; 1981; 25 p. (Reprint Series; v. 41).

2773. McMillan, Melville L.; Norrie, Kenneth H. Province-building vs. a rentier society. *Canadian Public Policy* (supplement); 1980 February; 6: 213-20.

2774. McNiven, J. D. Regional development policy in the next decade. *Canadian Journal of Regional Science*; 1986; 9(1): 79-88.

2775. McPhail, T.; Hamilton, S., eds. *Proceedings of communication in the 80's: major issues*; April 29-May 1, 1984; Calgary. [Calgary]: University of Calgary; [1984]; vii, 162 p.

2776. McQueen, David. One piece of a larger problem: The Economic Council on regulation. *Canadian Business Law Journal*; 1982 October; 7(1): 73-100.

2777. McQuillan, P. Working with Canada's statutory and discretionary industrial and petroleum assistance programs. *Bulletin for International Fiscal Documentation*; 1982; 36(8-9): 375-385.

2778. McRae, James J. An empirical measure of the influence of transportation costs on regional income. *Canadian Journal of Economics*; 1981 February; 14(1): 155-163.

2779. McRae, Robert N. A major shift in Canada's energy policy: impact of the National Energy Program. *Journal of Energy and Development*; 1982 Spring; 7(2): 173-98.

2780. Meekison, J. Peter. Getting off the playing field as a major player. In: Noordeh, Ardeshir, ed. *Reforming the financing arrangements for post-secondary education in Canada*. Toronto: Ontario Economic Council; [1985]: 85-95; x, 160 p.

2781. Meekison, J. Peter. Negotiating the revenue-sharing agreements. In: Saunders, J. Owen, ed. *Managing natural resources in a federal state*. Toronto: Carswell; 1986: 84-102; vi, 336 p.

2782. Meerman, Jacob. Are public goods public goods? *Public Choice*; 1980; 35(1): 45-57.

2783. Meilicke, Carl A.; Storch, Janet L., eds. *Perspectives on Canadian health and social services policy: history and emerging trends*. Michigan: Health Administration Press; 1980; xii, 520 p.

2784. Melvin, James R. The regional economic consequences of tariffs and domestic transportation costs. *Canadian Journal of Economics*; 1985 May; 18(2): 237-257.

2785. Melvin, James R. Political structure and the pursuit of economic objectives. In: Trebilcock, Michael J., ed. *Federalism and the Canadian economic union*. Toronto: Ontario Economic Council; 1983: 111-158; xiv, 560 p. (Ontario Economic Council research studies).

2786. Melvin, James R. The regional impact of tariffs. In: Whalley, John, res. coord. *Canada-United States free trade*. Toronto: University of Toronto Press; Royal Commission on the Economic Union and Development Prospects for Canada; 1985: 313-324; xi, 374 p. (The collected research studies; 11).

2787. Mendelson, Michael. Rationalization of income security in Canada. In: Courchene, Thomas J. [and others], eds. *Ottawa and the provinces: the distribution of money and power*. Toronto: Ontario Economic Council; 1985; 1: 229 252; xii, 341 p. (Special research report/Ontario Economic Council).

2788. Menzie, E.L. *Interprovincial barriers to trade in agricultural products*. Ottawa: Agriculture Canada; 1981; 43 p. (Economic working papers).

2789. Merkin, William S. An overview of the prospects for sectoral integration: the view from the United States (Conference: The legal aspects of sectoral integration between the United States and Canada, Cleveland, April 19-21, 1985). *Canada-United States Law Journal*; 1985; 10: 13-18.

2790. Metropolitan Toronto. Social Planning Council. *Brief submission to the Parliamentary Task Force on Federal-Provincial Fiscal Arrangements*. Toronto: Social Planning Council; 1981.

2791. Mieszkowski, Peter. Energy policy, taxation of natural resources, and fiscal federalism. In: McLure, Charles E., Jr., ed. *Tax assignment in federal countries*. Canberra: ANU Press; 1983: 129-149; xix, 370 p.

2792. Miller, Donna J. Regulatory reform in Manitoba: a blueprint for change. *Manitoba Law Journal*; 1986; 15(2): 219-230.

2793. Miller, F. C.; Wallace, D. J. The feasibility of regionally differentiated fiscal policies: some further results. *Canadian Journal of Regional Science*; 1983 Autumn; 6(2): 259-279.

2794. Mills, K.E.; Percy, M.B.; Wilson, L.S. The influence of fiscal incentives on interregional migration: Canada 1961-78. *Canadian Journal of Regional Science*; 1983 Autumn; 6(2): 207-230.

2795. Milne, William J. *The regional economy of Canada: environment, economic adjustment and barriers to interprovincial trade.* [Toronto]: Institute for Policy Analysis, University of Toronto; [1983]; 257 p.

2796. Mitchell, B. The natural resources development debate in Canada. *Geoforum*; 1981; 12(3): 227-236.

2797. Mitchell, B.; King, P. Resource conflict, policy change and practice in Canadian fisheries management. *Geoforum*; 1984; 15(3): 419-432.

2798. Mitchell, Bruce; Sewell, W.R. Derrick. *Canadian resource policies: problems and prospects.* Toronto: Methuen; 1981; viii, 294 p.

2799. Monière, Denis. La dynamique de l'inégalité économique au Canada. *L'Action nationale*; 1983 September; 73(1): 42-54.

2800. Monière, Denis. Questions sur le libre-échange. *L'Action nationale*; 1985 December; 75(4): 331-334.

2801. Montmarquette, Claude; Dallaire, Claude. Le rendement des obligations provinciales de l'incertitude politique: une analyse de séries chronologiques. *L'Actualité économique*; 1980 July-September; 56(3): 388-403.

2802. Moore, Milton. Some proposals for adapting federal-provincial financial agreements to current conditions. *Canadian Public Administration*; 1981 Summer; 24(2): 232-256.

2803. Morici, Peter. U.S.- Canada full trade discussions: what are the issues? *American Review of Canadian Studies*; 1985 Autumn; 15(3): 311-323.

2804. Morin, Rosaire. L'épargne au Québec. *L'Action nationale*; 1982 May-June; 71(9-10): 973-1031.

2805. Morin, Rosaire. L'épargne au Québec. *L'Action nationale*; 1984 March; 73(7): 625-640.

2806. Morneau, François. Capital et question nationale. *L'Action nationale*; 1983 March; 72(7): 630-642.

2807. Morneau, François. Le patronat et la question nationale. *L'Action nationale*; 1980 October; 60(2): 110-128.

2808. Morrow, J.B. National fisheries policy: the perspective of industry. In: Lorimer, R.; McMullin, S.E, eds. *Canada and the sea.* Willowdale: Association for Canadian Studies; 1980: 95-101.

2809. Moscovitch, Allan; Drover Glenn, eds. *Inequality: essays on the political economy of social welfare.* Toronto: University of Toronto Press; 1981; ix, 386 p. (Studies in the political economy of Canada).

2810. Moull, William D. Constitutional aspects of bank regulation - silence on the green line. *Canadian Business Law Journal;* 1985 February; 10(1): 71-79.

2811. Moull, William D. Natural resources: the other crisis in Canadian federalism. *Osgoode Hall Law Journal;* 1980 March; 18(1): 1-48.

2812. Moull, William D. Pricing Alberta's gas: cooperative federalism and the resource amendment. *Alberta Law Review;* 1984 Fall; 22(3): 348-362.

2813. Moull, William D. Mineral taxation in Saskatchewan under the new Constitution. In: Bartlett, Richard, ed. *Mining law in Canada.* Saskatoon: Law Society of Saskatchewan; 1984: 221-231.

2814. Mulder, Nick. Freight transportation issues. *Canadian Business Review;* 1980 Autumn; 7(3): 22-28.

2815. Mullan, David J. Administrative tribunals: their evolution in Canada from 1945 to 1984. In: Bernier, Ivan; Lajoie, Andrée, res. coords. *Regulations, crown corporations and administrative tribunals.* Toronto: University of Toronto Press; Royal Commission on the Economic Union and Development Prospects for Canada; 1985: 155-201; xvii, 202 p. (The collected research studies; 48).

2816. Mulvaney, J. M. *Canadian approach - federal and provincial.* 73rd Annual Air Pollution Control Association Meeting & Exhibition; 22-27 June 1980; Montreal, Canada. Pittsburgh: Air Pollution Control Association.

2817. Munro, Gordon R. *Fisheries, extended jurisdiction and the economics of common property resources.* Vancouver: University of British Columbia, Dept. of Economics; 1981; 32 p. (Resources paper; 71).

2818. Munton, D. *Political, bureaucratic and legal solutions and constraints in environmental policy: a comment on Kirby, Pross and Lax;* September 14-16, 1979; Halifax. Halifax: Institute of Resource and Environmental Studies; 1981: 193-197.

2819. Murphy, Larry J. Adapting Canadian energy policy to changing world energy trends. *Canadian Business Review;* 1983 Spring; 10(1): 32-39.

2820. Murray, Catherine A. *Managing diversity: federal-provincial collaboration and the Committee on Extension of Services to Northern and Remote Communities.* Kingston: Institute of Intergovernmental Relations, Queen's University; 1983; xii, 173 p.

2821. Murray, V. V.; McMillan, C. J. Business-government relations in Canada: a conceptual map. *Canadian Public Administration;* 1983 Summer; 26(4): 591-609.

2822. Musgrave, Richard A. Who should tax, where and what? In: McLure, Charles, E., Jr. *Tax assignment in federal countries*. Canberra: Centre for Research on Federal Financial Relations, Australian National University; 1983: 20-25; xix, 370 p.

2823. Nagy, Gretchen E. Sagebrush and snowshoes: the struggle for natural resource control in the United States and Canada. *Law and Contemporary Problems*; 1981 Summer; 44(3): 247-276.

2824. *National and regional interests in the North*. Third workshop on people, resources, and the environment north of 60; June 1-3, 1983; Yellowknife. Ottawa: Canadian Arctic Resources Committee; 1984; xvii, 758 p.

2825. National Education and the Law Conference (1981). *Constitutional law, protection of individual rights: papers presented at the second National Education and the Law Conference, held at the University of Saskatchewan, under the aegis of the Department of Educational Administration*, by Joseph F. Pyra; May 11-13, 1981; Saskatoon. Saskatoon: The Department; 1982; 285 p.

2826. National Union of Students. *From the perspective of equity - response to the report of the Federal-Provincial Task Force on Student Assistance*. [s.l.]: National Union of Students; 1981.

2827. Needham, H. G. Historical perspectives on the federal-provincial split in jurisdiction in corrections. *Canadian Journal of Criminology*; 1980; 22(3): 298-306.

2828. Neil, W. *Canada - U.S. trade policy issues: sectoral free trade discussions*. [Ottawa]: Canada. Parliament. Library. Research Branch; 1984. (Current issues system review; v. 84-11).

2829. Neill, Robin F. Nationalism, nationalization, and social communications: an economic perspective on the Canadian case. *Canadian Review of Studies in Nationalism*; 1980; 7(1): 72-86.

2830. Nelles, H.V. Canadian energy policy, 1945-1980: a federalist perspective. In: Carty, R. Kenneth; Ward, W. Peter, eds. *Entering the eighties: Canada in crisis*. Toronto: University of Toronto Press; 1980: 91-119; 160 p.

2831. Nemetz, Peter N. An energy policy of British Columbia. *B.C. Studies*; 1982 Spring; 53: 3-27.

2832. Nemetz, Peter N. *Resource policy: international perspectives*. Montreal: Institute for Research on Public Policy; 1980; xliv, 371 p.

2833. New Brunswick. *Meeting the challenge of the eighties: an economic development strategy for New Brunswick*. Fredericton: Government of New Brunswick; [1980?]; 42 (48) p.

2834. New Brunswick. Department of Justice. *Official languages policy of the Department of Justice.* Fredericton: Government of New Brunswick; 1984; 11 (11) p.

2835. New Brunswick. Department of Justice. *Summary response to report and recommendation on the integration of the two official languages: justice services.* [Fredericton]: Government of New Brunswick; 1983; 87 (87) p.

2836. New Brunswick. Provincial Advisory Committee on Official Languages. *Report: towards equality of official languages in New Brunswick: a summary.* Fredericton: The Committee; 1984; 12 (12) p.

2837. New Brunswick. Study Group on the Official Languages. *Towards the equality of the official languages in New Brunswick: summary report.* Fredericton: Cabinet Secretariat, Official Languages Branch; 1982; 125 (123) p.

2838. Newfoundland Information Services. *Managing all our resources: a development plan for Newfoundland and Labrador, 1980-85.* St. John's: Newfoundland Information Services; 1980; xii, 160 p.

2839. Newfoundland. Department of Fisheries and Oceans. *Agreement between Government of Canada and the Government of Newfoundland and Labrador concerning the restructuring of the Newfoundland fishery.* St. John's: Department of Fisheries and Oceans; 1983; 16 p.

2840. Newfoundland. Petroleum Directorate. *An analysis of the impact of a Nova Scotia type offshore agreement on Newfoundland.* [St. John's]: The Directorate; 1982; 11, 45, (35) p.

2841. Newfoundland. Petroleum Directorate. Economics Unit. *Economic analysis of the Hibernia discovery and the related provincial and federal positions.* [St. John's]: Economics Unit, Petroleum Directorate; 1980; 53 leaves. (Special report / Petroleum Directorate; PD 80-1).

2842. Newfoundland. Petroleum Directorate. Economics Unit. *Effects of the federal energy policy on oil and gas exploration and production offshore Newfoundland and Labrador.* St. John's: Economics Unit, Petroleum Directorate; 1981; 74 p.

2843. Nielsen, Arne [and others]. Contrasting policy reactions: a reader's guide. *Canadian Public Policy* (supplement); 1985 July; 11: 383-396.

2844. Nielsen, Erick; Bruk, John. *Natural resources program: from crisis to opportunity: a study team report to the Task Force on Program Review.* Ottawa: The Task Force; 1985; iii, 319 p.

2845. Nixon .A.J. *Natural gas pricing in Canada: an economic analysis.* Calgary: Canadian Energy Research Institute; 1981; xiv, 116 p. (Working paper / Canadian Energy Research Institute; 81-2).

2846. Noam, Eli M. Government regulation of business in a federal state: allocation of power under deregulation. *Osgoode Hall Law Journal*; 1982 December; 20(4): 762-779.

2847. Noordeh, Ardeshir, ed. *Reforming the financing arrangements for post-secondary education in Canada*. Toronto: Ontario Economic Council; [1985]; x, 160 p.

2848. Norrie, Kenneth H., res. coord. *Disparities and interregional adjustment*. Toronto: University of Toronto Press; Royal Commission on the Economic Union and Development Prospects for Canada; 1986; xiv, 223 p. (The collected research studies; 64).

2849. Norrie, Kenneth H. Not much to crow about: a primer on the statutory grain freight rate issue. *Canadian Public Policy*; 1983 December; 9(4): 434-445.

2850. Norrie, Kenneth H. *Energy, Canadian federalism and the West*. Edmonton: University of Alberta. Department of Economics; 1982. (University of Alberta Dept. of Economics research paper; 08).

2851. Norrie, Kenneth H. A regional economic overview of the West since 1945. In: Rasporich, A.W., ed. *The making of the modern West*. Calgary: University of Calgary Press; 1984: 63-78.

2852. Norrie, Kenneth H.; Percy, Michael. *Economic rents, province-building, and interregional adjustment: a two-region general equilibrium analysis*. Ottawa: Economic Council of Canada; [1983]; vi, 47 p. (Discussion paper, Economic Council of Canada; 230).

2853. Norrie, Kenneth H.; Percy, Michael. *Energy price increases, economic rents, and industrial structure in a small regional economy*. Ottawa: Economic Council of Canada; 1982; v, 103 p.

2854. Norrie, Kenneth H.; Percy, Michael. *Westward shift and interregional adjustment: a preliminary assessment*. Ottawa: Economic Council of Canada; 1981; x, 141 p. (Discussion paper / Economic Council of Canada; 201).

2855. Norrie, Kenneth H.; Percy, Michael B. Freight rate reform and regional burden: a general equilibrium analysis of western freight rate proposals. *Canadian Journal of Economics*; 1983 May; 16(2): 325-349.

2856. Nova Scotia. *Canada-Nova Scotia Agreement on Offshore Oil and Gas Resource Management and Revenue Sharing*. [Halifax]: Province of Nova Scotia; 1982; 35 (26) p.

2857. Nova Scotia. Department of Development. *Building competitiveness: a white paper on economic development: province of Nova Scotia*. [Halifax]: Department of Development; 1984; 35 p.

2858. Nova Scotia. Department of Municipal Affairs. *Financial assistance programs for Nova Scotia municipalities, 1984-85*. Halifax: Department of Municipal Affairs; [1984]; vi, 69 p.

2859. Nowlan, David M.; Bellaire, Richard L., eds. *Financing Canadian universities: for whom and by whom?: papers and perspectives from a conference held in Toronto on March 3, 1981*. Toronto: Institute for Policy Analysis; [1981]; viii, 244 p.

2860. Nowotny, Ewald. Tax assignment and revenue sharing in the federal republic of Germany and Switzerland. In: McLure, Charles E., Jr., ed. *Tax assignment in federal countries*. Canberra: ANU Press; 1983: 260-292; xix, 370 p.

2861. O'Donnell, Margaret. An inquiry into provincial jurisdiction over uranium development in Saskatchewan. *Saskatchewan Law Review*; 1983-84; 48(2): 293-324.

2862. O'Donoghue, Leslie. *Federal-provincial tax collection agreements : recent provincial complaints*. [Edmonton]: [s.n.]; 1985; 15, (3) p.

2863. O'Shea, Kevin D. *Public diplomacy and federal-provincial negotiations: the cable negotiations 1970-1976* [microfiche]: (M.A.) McGill University; 1979 2 microfiches (150 fr.). Ottawa: National Library of Canada, 1982.

2864. Oksanen, E. H.; Williams, J. R. Industrial location and inter-industry linkages. *Empirical Economics*; 1984; 9(3): 139-50.

2865. Olewiler, Nancy D. *The regulation of natural resources in Canada: theory and practice*. [Ottawa]: Economic Council of Canada; 1981; iii, 81 p. (Technical report; v. 4).

2866. Ontario Advisory Council on Senior Citizens. *Guide to intergovernmental programs*. [Ottawa]: The Council; 1982.

2867. Ontario Economic Council. *Energy policies for the 1980's: an economic analysis*. Toronto: Ontario Economic Council; 1980; 2 v. (Special research report).

2868. Ontario Economic Council. *Inflation and the taxation of personal investment income : an Ontario Economic Council position paper on the Canadian 1982 reform proposals*. Toronto: The Council; c1982; 33 p. (Special research report / Ontario Economic Council).

2869. Ontario Energy and Agriculture Policy Committee. *Energy and agriculture: report of the Ontario Energy and Agricultural Policy Committee. vol. 1: summary and recommendations*. Toronto: The Committee; 1981; 49 p.

2870. Ontario Federation of Students. *The many answers to restraint*, by Mark Rosenfeld. Toronto: Ontario Federation of Students; 1981; 19 p.

2871. Ontario Federation of Students. *Swimming against the current: a brief to the Federal-Provincial Task Force on Student Assistance*. Toronto: The Federation; 1980; 43, 3p.

2872. Ontario. Ministry of Colleges and Universities. *Brief to the Federal-Provincial Task Force on Student Assistance.* [Toronto]: Ministry of Colleges and Universities; 1980.

2873. Ontario. Ministry of Colleges and Universities. Tripartite Committee on Interprovincial Comparisons. *Interprovincial comparisons of university financing - third report on the Tripartite Committee on Interprovincial Comparisions,* by P. Stenton. [Toronto]: Ministry of Colleges and Universities; 1981.

2874. Ontario. Ministry of Colleges and Universities. Tripartite Committee on Interprovincial Comparisons. *Interprovincial comparisons of university financing - third report of the Tripartite Committee on Interprovincial Comparisons.* [Toronto]: Ministry of Colleges and Universities; 1982.

2875. Ontario. Ministry of Colleges and Universities. Tripartite Committee on Interprovincial Comparisons. *Interprovincial comparisons of university financing - sixth report of the Tripartite Committee on Interprovincial Comparisons.* [Toronto]: Ministry of Colleges and Universities; 1985.

2876. Ontario. Ministry of Colleges and Universities. Tripartite Committee on University Affairs. *Interprovincial comparisons of university financing - fifth report of the Tripartite Committee on Interprovincial Comparisons,* by P. Stenton. [Toronto]: Ministry of Colleges and Universities; 1984.

2877. Ontario. Ministry of Industry and Tourism. *Interprovincial economic cooperation - towards the development of a Canadian common market.* [Toronto]: Ministry of Industry and Tourism; 1981.

2878. Ontario. Ministry of Industry and Trade. Innovation and Technology Division. *The technology challenge: Ontario faces the future: a discussion paper.* Toronto: Ministry of Industry and Trade; 1984; xxviii, 284 p.

2879. Ontario. Ministry of Intergovernmental Affairs. *Challenges facing governments in the 1980's - notes for remarks by the Honourable Thomas L. Wells, Minister of Intergovernmental Affairs and Government House Leader to the U. of T./Manulife Business Conference.* [Toronto]: Ministry of Intergovernmental Affairs; 1983.

2880. Ontario. Ministry of Transportation and Communications. *Final argument...before the Canadian Radio-television and Telecommunications Commission in the matter of interexchange voice competition and related issues.* Toronto: Ministry of Transportation and Communications; 1984.

2881. Ontario. Ministry of Transportation and Communications. Communications Division. *The privatization of Teleglobe Canada: issues and concerns.* Toronto: Ontario Ministry of Transportation and Communications, Communications Division; 1985; 15 p.

2882. Ontario. Ministry of Treasury and Economics. *Canadian and provincial industrial policies, strategy debates since 1970: a bibliography.* Monticello, Ill: Vance Bibliographies; [1985]; 28 p. (Public administration series; P 1807).

2883. Ontario. Ministry of Treasury and Economics. *Notes for remarks by the Hon. Frank S. Miller, Treasurer of Ontario and Minister of Economics to the Financial Executives Institute Pension Conference on the Federal-Provincial Dialogue on Pension Reform*, by F.S. Miller; Nov. 17, 1981; [s.l.]. Toronto: Ministry of Treasury and Economics; 1981.

2884. Organisation for Economic Co-operation and Development. *Regional policies in Canada.* Paris: OECD; 1980; 80 p.

2885. Owram, D. *The economic development of western Canada: an historical overview.* Ottawa: Economic Council of Canada; 1982; iv, 60 p. (Discussion paper / Economic Council of Canada; v. 219).

2886. Paehlke, R. Canadian nuclear policies. *Canadian Public Policy*; 1981; 7(2): 360-361.

2887. Paikin, Marnie. Other sources of financing for post-secondary education and research in Canada. In: Noordeh, Ardeshir, ed. *Reforming the financing arrangements for post-secondary education in Canada.* Toronto: Ontario Economic Council; [1985]: 99-113; x, 160 p.

2888. Pal, Leslie A. The fall and rise of developmental uses of UI funds. *Canadian Public Policy*; 1983 March; 9(1): 81-93.

2889. Pal, Leslie A. The finance view: the case of unemployment insurance, 1970-1978. *Canadian Tax Journal*; 1985 July-August; 33(4): 786-801.

2890. Pal, Leslie A. Federalism, social policy, and the Constitution. In: Ismael, Jacqueline S., ed. *Canadian social welfare policy: federal and provincial dimensions.* Kingston: McGill-Queen's University Press; 1985: 1-20; xviii, 187 p. (Canadian public administration).

2891. Parenteau, Roland. Le cadre historique et institutionnel des sociétés d'Etat au Québec. *Annals of Public and Co-operative Economy*; 1983 March; 54(1): 57-72.

2892. Paterson, Robert K. Do unto others: the extraterritorial reach of regulatory legislation in Canada. *Canadian Business Law Journal*; 1980 December; 5(1): 114-128.

2893. Patry, Réjean M, ed. *La législation linguistique fédérale.* Québec: Conseil de la langue française; 1981; 108 p. (Documentation du Conseil de la langue française; v. 6).

2894. Patton, Donald J. The evolution of Canadian federal mineral policies. In: Beigie, Carl E.; Hero, Alfred O., Jr., eds. *Natural resources in U.S.-Canadian relations.* Boulder, CO: Westview Press; 1980; 1: 203-246; xii, 371 p.

2895. Pauly, Mark V. Optimality, 'public' goods, and local governments: a general theoretical analysis. In: Grewal, Bhajan S. [and others], ed. *The economics of federalism*. Canberra: Australian National University; 1980: 139-153; xiii, 432 p.

2896. Pauwels, Jacques R. FIRA: instrument of regulation or vote-maximization? *Osgoode Hall Law Journal*; 1985 Spring; 23(1): 131-170.

2897. Pearse, P.H.; Bertrand, F.; Maclaren, J.W. *Currents of change: final report of the Inquiry on Federal Water Policy*. Ottawa: Environment Canada; 1985; 222 p.

2898. Pederson, K. George. The fourth revolution: which side are we on? In: Noordeh, Ardeshir, ed. *Reforming the financing arrangements for post-secondary education in Canada*. Toronto: Ontario Economic Council; [1985]; c]: 29-39; x, 160 p.

2899. Penny, Michael; Trebilcock, Michael J.; Laskin, John B. Existing and proposed constitutional constraints on provincially induced barriers to economic mobility in Canada. In: Trebilcock, Michael J., ed. *Federalism and the Canadian economic union*. Toronto: Ontario Economic Council; 1983: 501-54; xiv, 560 p. (Ontario Economic Council research studies).

2900. Pentland, Charles. North American integration and the Canadian political system. In: Stairs, Denis; Winham, Gilbert R., res. coords. *The politics of Canada's economic relationship with the United States*. Toronto: University of Toronto Press; Royal Commission on the Economic Union and Development Prospects for Canada; 1985: 95-125; xix, 207 p. (The collected research studies; v. 29).

2901. Percy, David R. Legal and jurisdictional aspects of interbasin transfers. *Canadian Water Resources Journal*; 1981; 6(2): 1-12.

2902. Perry, David B. The escalating costs of education. *Canadian Tax Journal*; 1983 September-October; 31(5): 879-890.

2903. Perry, David B. The national accounts budgets by province, 1983. *Canadian Tax Journal*; 1985 September-October; 33(5): 1068-1079.

2904. Perry, David B. Provincial variation in the distribution of personal income tax. *Canadian Tax Journal*; 1981 May-June; 29(3): 401-405.

2905. Perry, David B. Restraint in government (federal, provincial, and local government revenue and spending trends, 1965-1981). *Canadian Tax Journal*; 1982 May-June; 30: 468-473.

2906. Perry, David B.; Gurney, Mary P. Provincial budget roundup, 1984 - part 1. *Canadian Tax Journal*; 1984 March-April; 32(2): 310-326.

2907. Perry, David B.; Gurney, Mary P. Provincial budget roundup, 1984 - part 2. *Canadian Tax Journal*; 1984 May-June; 32(3): 510-528.

2908. Perry, David B.; Treff, Karin. Provincial budget roundup, 1985 - part 1. *Canadian Tax Journal*; 1985 March-April; 33(2): 319-329.

2909. Perry, David B.; Treff, Karin. Provincial budget roundup, 1985 - part 2. *Canadian Tax Journal*; 1985 May-June; 33(3): 511-527.

2910. Perry, David B.; Treff, Karin. Provincial budget roundup, 1985 - part 3. *Canadian Tax Journal*; 1985 November-December; 33(6): 1193-1200.

2911. Peterson, David. *Canada's trading relationships in a changing world.* 26th Annual Premier's Conference; 21-22 August, 1985; St. John's. Ottawa: Canadian Intergovernmental Conference Secretariat; 1985; 17 p.

2912. Phillips, Paul A. *Regional disparities*: Toronto; J. Lorimer; c1982; 167 p.

2913. Pinfold, Thomas; Verma, Bharti. *Federal flows in the Nova Scotia economy.* Halifax: Institute of Public Affairs, Dalhousie University; 1981; vi, 54 p. (Occasional paper; v. 5).

2914. Pinto, Marina. *Federalism and higher education: the Indian experience.* Bombay: Orient Longman; 1984; xiii, 250 p.

2915. Pitfield, P. Michael. Closing the government-business gap. *Canadian Business Review*; 1984 Summer; 11(2): 21-24.

2916. Poetschke, T. Community dependence on fishing in the Atlantic provinces. *Canadian Journal of Regional Science*; 1984; 7(2): 211-227.

2917. Polèse, Mario. Regional disparity, migration and economic adjustment: a reappraisal. *Canadian Public Policy*; 1981 Autumn; 7(4): 519-25.

2918. Poulain, Michel. L'analyse spatiale d'une matrice de migration interne: l'exemple des migrations interprovinciales de six provinces du Canada pour les périodes 1956-1961, 1966-1971 et 1971-1976. *Cahiers québécois de démographie*; 1982; 11(1): 47-68.

2919. Power, M. L.; Martin, J. C. Government policy: the present context of financial support. *Hospital Trustee*; 1980; 4(5): 4-6.

2920. Powrie, T.L. Taxation and energy. In: Ontario Economic Council. *Energy policies for the 1980's: an economic analysis.* Toronto: Ontario Economic Council; 1980: 73-101; 176 p. (Special research report/Ontario Economic Council).

2921. Pratt, Larry. Whose oil is it? In: Pratt, Larry; Stevenson, Garth, eds. *Western separatism: myths, realities and dangers.* Edmonton: Hurtig Publishers; 1981: 155-172; 255 p.

2922. Prebble, Peter. Interjurisdictional problems in the area of uranium mining. In: Duncan, Linda F., ed. *Environmental enforcement: proceedings of the National Conference on the Enforcement of Environmental Law*; October 1984; Edmonton. Edmonton: Environmental Law Centre; 1985; pp. 36-39.

2923. Preston, R.S.; Eyford, B.L.; Saiyed, H.M. *An essay on revenue and spending elasticities by level of government: an analysis using Candide model 2.0.* Ottawa: Economic Council of Canada; 1981; xv, 134 p. (Discussion paper / Economic Council of Canada; 199).

2924. Prévost, Paul. Du développement coopératif au développement régional. *L'Actualité économique*; 1981 July-September; 57(3): 290-307.

2925. Prince Edward Island. Department of Finance and Tourism. Economic, Statistics and Fiscal Analysis Division. *Provincial government finance: a historical perspective*. Charlottetown: Department of Finance and Tourism; 1985; 14 p. (Economic trends; 25).

2926. Prince, Michael J. Startling facts, sobering truths, and sacred trust: pension policy and the Tories. In: Maslove, Allan M., ed. *How Ottawa spends, 1985: sharing the pie*. Toronto: Methuen; 1985: 114-161; 184 p.

2927. Prince, Michael J. Whatever happened to compassion? liberal social policy 1980-84. In: Maslove, Allan M., ed. *How Ottawa spends, 1984: the new agenda*. Toronto: Methuen; 1984: 79-121; 334 p.

2928. Prince, Michael J.; Doern, G. Bruce. *Federal policy and the role of public enterprise in the mining sector*. Kingston: Centre for Resource Studies, Queen's University; 1984; vi, 47 p.

2929. Prince, Michael J.; Doern, G. Bruce. *The origins of public enterprise in the Canadian mineral sector : three provincial case studies: a study*. Kingston: Queen's University, Centre for Resource Studies; c1985; xii, 131 p. (Working paper / Centre for Resource Studies; 33).

2930. Prince, Michael J.; Rice, James J. Department of National Health and Welfare: the attack on social policy. In: Doern, G. Bruce, ed. *How Ottawa spends your tax dollars: federal priorities - 1981*. Toronto: James Lorimer; 1981: 90-119; 303 p.

2931. Pritchard, J. Robert S.; Benedickson, Jamie. Securing the Canadian economic union: federalism and internal barriers to trade. In: Trebilcock, Michael J., ed. *Federalism and the Canadian economic union*. Toronto: Ontario Economic Council; 1983: 3-50; xiv, 560 p. (Ontario Economic Council research studies).

2932. Pross, A. Paul. The fishery: Ali versus Frazier. In: Jamieson, Barbara, ed. *Governing Nova Scotia: policies, priorities, and the 1984-85 budget*. Halifax: School of Public Administration, Dalhousie University; 1984: 81-108; x, 226 p.

2933. Provincial Conference on the Economy. *Meeting the challenge of change: conference report*; 1985; Halifax. Halifax: The Conference; 1985; 1 v. Note: Various pagings.

2934. Provincial Ministers of Finance and Treasurers. *Federal proposal to reduce health and post-secondary education financing*. Toronto: Ontario Ministry of Treasury and Economics; 1983; 7, 9 p.

2935. Purvis, Douglas D.; Chambers, Frances, eds. *The Canadian balance of payments: perspectives and policy issues : the first John Deutsch Round Table on economic policy.* Montreal: Institute for Research on Public Policy; 1983; xvi, 256 p.

2936. Purvis, Douglas D.; Smith, Constance. Fiscal policy in Canada: 1963-84. In: Sargent, John, res. coord. *Fiscal and monetary policy.* Toronto: University of Toronto Press; Royal Commission on the Economic Union and Development Prospects for Canada: 1-42; xviii, 339 p. (The collected research studies; 21).

2937. Québec. *Charter of the french language: Bill no. 101, with regulations.* 2nd ed. Don Mills: CCH Canadian; 1980; 89 (91) p.

2938. Québec. *Le virage technologique: bâtir le Québec, phase 2: programme d'action économique 1982-1986.* [Québec]: Gouvernement du Québec, Développement économique; 1982; 248 p.

2939. Québec. Assemblée nationale. *Les défis de l'aménagement,* by Normand Alexandre and Denis Vaugeois. [Québec]: Assemblée nationale du Québec; 1982; 368 p.

2940. Québec. Conseil de la langue française. Effets démolinguistiques de l'article 23 du projet fédéral de Charte canadienne des droits et libertés. [Québec]: Conseil de la langue française; [1981]; ii, 37 p. (Notes et documents / Conseil de la langue française; 8).

2941. Québec. Conseil de la langue française. *L'état de la langue française au Québec: bilan et prospective.* Québec: Conseil de la langue française; 1983; 4 v.

2942. Québec. Conseil de la langue française. *La qualité de la langue après la loi 101: actes du colloque, Québec, 30 septembre-3 octobre 1979.* Québec: Gouvernement du Québec; 1980; 244 p. (Documentation du Conseil de la langue française; 3).

2943. Québec. Direction générale de l'urbanisme et de l'aménagement du territoire. *Répertoire des informations du gouvernement du Québec en matière d'aménagement du territoire.* [Québec]: [Gouvernement du Québec]; 1983; 352 p.

2944. Québec. Ministère des Finances. *Les préférences fiscales du régime d'imposition au Canada.* [Québec]: Gouvernement du Québec, Ministère des Finances; [1981]; 70 p. (Document de travail / Direction générale de la politique fiscale).

2945. Québec. Secrétariat à l'aménagement. *Aménager l'avenir: les orientations du gouvernement en matière d'aménagement du territoire.* [Québec]: [Gouvernement du Québec]; 1983; 126 p.

2946. Quinn, John. Federalism and foreign economic relations. *Canada-United States Law Journal;* 1985; 10: 197-224.

2947. Quinn, John J. Federalism and foreign economic relations. In: David G. Meany, ed. *Proceedings: the legal aspects of sectoral integration between the United States and Canada*; April 19-21, 1985; Cleveland: Canada-United States Law Institute; 1985: 197-220; 256 p.

2948. Quinn, John J., res. coord. *The international legal environment*. Toronto: University of Toronto Press; Royal Commission on the Economic Union and Development Prospects for Canada; 1986: xviii, 270 p. (The collected research studies; 52).

2949. Quinn, John J. The international legal environment: an overview. In: Quinn, John J., res. coord. *The international legal environment*. Toronto: University of Toronto Press; Royal Commission on the Economic Union and Development Prospects for Canada; 1986: 1-13; xviii, 270 p. (The collected research studies; 52).

2950. Rabeau, Yves. Regional stabilization in Canada. In: Sargent, John, res. coord. *Fiscal and monetary policy*. Toronto: University of Toronto Press; Royal Commission on the Economic Union and Development Prospects for Canada; 1986: 151-197; xviii, 339 p. (The collected research studies; 21).

2951. Rafati, Mohammad Reza. *Exchange rate risk and the long term borrowing behaviour of Canadian provincial governments and private corporations under different exchange rate regimes*. Queen's University Kingston; 1980. Dissertation Abstracts International 41 (5).

2952. Ravault, René-Jean. *Perceptions de deux solitudes: étude sur les relations entre les deux communautés de langues officielles du Nouveau-Brunswick*. Québec: Centre international de recherche sur le bilinguisme, Université Laval; iii, 101 p.

2953. Reed, F. L. C. *The role of the federal government in forestry: forestry program, the University of Alberta, 5 March, 1980*. [Edmonton]: [Department of Forest Science]; 1980; [8] 22 p. (Forestry industry lecture series).

2954. Reisman, Simon. Canada-United States trade at the crossroads: options for growth. *Canadian Business Review*; 1985 Autumn; 12(3): 17-23.

2955. Reschenhaler, G. B.; Stanbury, W. T. Deregulating Canada's airlines: grounded by false assumptions. *Canadian Public Policy*; 1983 June; 9(2): 210-222.

2956. Richardson, Jack; Docwra, G.E.; Kolsen, H.M. *The Inter-State Commission and Australian transport*. Canberra: Centre for Research on Federal Financial Relations, Australian National University; 1984; v, 27 p. (Occasional paper; 34).

2957. Richeson, David E. Canadian government involvements in telegraphic communication in western Canada. *Journal of the West*; 1984; 23(4): 11-18.

2958. Ridler, Neil B. Some economic implications of the projected age structure of Canada: A reply. *Canadian Public Policy*; 1980 Summer; 6(3): 546-48.

2959. Ritchie, Gordon. Government aid to industry: a public sector perspective. *Canadian Public Administration*; 1983 Spring; 26(J1): 36-46.

2960. Roberts, C. A. Some reflections on the role of the government of Canada in the provision of health services. *Psychiatric Journal of the University of Ottawa*; 1980; 5(3): 153-159.

2961. Roberts, J. Industrial development in Canada. *Cost and Management*; 1981 September-October; 55(5): 4-7.

2962. Robertson, E. J. Developing the West's manufacturing potential: the role of provincial governments. *Canadian Public Policy* (supplement); 1985 July; 11: 335-338.

2963. Robertson, Gordon. Public policy and business: some of the problems of the eighties. *Business Quarterly* (Special Supplement); 1985 Summer; 50(2): 66-69.

2964. Robillard, Jean-D. La bataille des gens de l'air. *L'Action nationale*; 1983 October; 73(2): 149-158.

2965. Robillard, Jean-D. La bataille des gens de l'air (2e partie). *L'Action nationale*; 1983 November; 73(3): 259-271.

2966. Robillard, Jean-D. La bataille des gens de l'air (fin). *L'Action nationale*; 1983 December; 73(4): 353-365.

2967. Robillard, Jean-D. Le commissaire aux langues et ses rapports. *L'Action nationale*; 1983 March; 72(7): 611-620.

2968. Robillard, Jean-D. La farce du bilinguisme. *L'Action nationale*; 1982 November; 72(3): 253-264.

2969. Robillard, Jean-D. Le grand jeu du bilinguisme. *L'Action nationale*; 1982 December; 72(4): 365-374.

2970. Robillard, Jean-D. La langue française au Québec. *L'Action nationale*; 1982 May-June; 71(9-10): 939-957.

2971. Robinson, Chris; Tomes, Nigel. Self-selection and interprovincial migration in Canada. *Canadian Journal of Economics*; 1982 August; 15(3): 474-502.

2972. Robinson, Christopher M. G. F.; Tomes, Nigel. *Self-selection and interprovincial migration in Canada*. London: Department of Economics, University of Western Ontario; 1980; 38 p. (Research report).

2973. Robinson, Ira M.; Webster, Douglas R. Regional planning in Canada: history, practice, issues, and prospects. *Journal of the American Planning Association*; 1985; 51(1): 23-33.

2974. Robinson, John Bridger. Pendulum policy: natural gas forecasts and Canadian energy policy, 1969-1981. *Canadian Journal of Political Science*; 1983 June; 16(2): 299-319.

2975. Rodgers-Magnet, Sanda; Magnet, Joseph Eliot. Mobility rights: personal mobility and the Canadian economic union. In: Krasnick, Mark, res. coord. *Perspectives on the Canadian economic union*. Toronto: University of Toronto

Press; Royal Commission on the Economic Union and Development Prospects for Canada; 1986: 195-270; xvi, 271 p. (The collected research studies; v. 60).

2976. Rodwin, Victor G. *The health planning predicament: France, Quebec, England, and the United States.* Berkeley: University of California Press; 1984; 293 p.

2977. Roe, Eric R.; Toogood, John D. The revenue budgetary process. In: Jamieson, Barbara, ed. *Governing Nova Scotia: policies, priorities, and the 1984-85 budget.* Halifax: School of Public Administration, Dalhousie University; 1984: 209-225; x, 226 p.

2978. Romanow, Roy. Politics and health: cooperative spirit is essential. *Hospital Trustee*; 1985; 9(4): 5-9.

2979. Rousseau, Henri-Paul. The Dome syndrome: the debt overhanging Canadian government and business. *Canadian Public Policy*; 1983 March; 9(1): 37-52.

2980. Le Roy, Donald J.; Dufour, Paul. *Partners in industrial strategy: the special role of the provincial research organizations.* Ottawa: Science Council of Canada; 1983; 146 p. (Background study; 51).

2981. Roy, Léonard. Le Conseil de planification et de développement du Québec. *L'Action nationale*; 1984 March; 73(7): 594-624.

2982. Roy, Léonard. Edouard Montpetit et le régionalisme. *L'Action nationale*; 1983 January; 72(5): 409-417.

2983. Roy, Nicolas. *Mobility of capital in the Canadian economic union.* Toronto: University of Toronto Press; Royal Commission on the Economic Union and Development Prospects for Canada; 1986; xv, 111 p. (The collected research studies; v. 66).

2984. Roy, Noel; Schrank, William E.; Tsoa, Eugene. The Newfoundland groundfishery: some options for renewal. *Canadian Public Policy*; 1982 Spring; 8(2): 222-38.

2985. Royal Commission on the Economic Union and Development Prospects for Canada. *Challenges and choices.* Ottawa: The Commission; 1984; 80 p.

2986. Rubinfield, Daniel L. Tax assignment and revenue sharing in the United States. In: McLure, Charles E., Jr., ed. *Tax assignment in federal countries.* Canberra: ANU Press; 1983: 205-233; xix, 370 p.

2987. Rueggeberg, Harriet; Thompson, Andrew R. *Resource management boundary problems: a paper prepared for the Western Constitutional Forum (WCF).* Yellowknife: WCF; 1984; 111 p.

2988. Ruthven, Carol Lynn. *Managing oil and natural gas law, policy and intergovernmental relations in the Canadian and American West* [microfiche]: (M.A.) Queen's University; 1981 2 microfiches (189 fr.). Ottawa: National Library of Canada, 1983.

2989. Safarian, A.E. *Ten markets or one?: regional barriers to economic activity in Canada*. Toronto: Ontario Economic Council; 1980; iv, 19 p. (Ontario Economic Council. Discussion paper series).

2990. Sahir, A. H.; Seaborne, A. A. Economic diversification in the Canadian prairies: myth or reality? *Prairie Forum*; 1982 Spring; 7(1): 91-94.

2991. Salter, L.; Slaco, D. *Use of a regulatory tribunal as an inquiry: the satellite case before the Canadian Radio-Television and Telecommunications Commission*. [Ottawa]: Science Council of Canada; 1982. (Science Council of Canada manuscript report).

2992. Saltman, Lorne. Recent tax developments in Canada. *International Business Lawyer*; 1982 June; 10(6): 195-198.

2993. Sargent, John, res. coord. *Fiscal and monetary policy*. Toronto: University of Toronto Press; Royal Commission on the Economic Union and Development Prospects for Canada; 1986; xviii, 339 p. (The collected research studies; v. 21).

2994. Saskatchewan. *Partnership for progress: working together to build a stronger tomorrow*. Regina: Queen's Printer; 1985; 31 p.

2995. Saskatchewan. *The road out of recession: an alternative economic policy for Canadians*; 1982; Saskatoon. Regina: Government of Saskatchewan; 1982; 15 p.

2996. Saskatchewan. *Transportation overview*. Regina: Queen's Printer; 1984; 15 p.

2997. Saunders, J. Owen. Canadian federalism and international management of natural resources. In: *idem.*, ed. *Managing natural resources in a federal state*. Toronto: Carswell; 1986: 267-284; vi, 336 p.

2998. Saunders, J. Owen. Good federalism, bad federalism: managing our natural resources. In: *idem.*, ed. *Managing natural resources in a federal state*. Toronto: Carswell; 1986: ix,-1; vi, 336 p.

2999. Saunders, J. Owen. *Managing natural resources in a federal state: essays from the second Banff Conference on Natural Resources Law*; 1985; Banff. Toronto: Carswell; 1986; xviii, 336 p.

3000. Saunders, J. Owen; Gault, Townsend. The National Energy Program and the pursuit of claims under international law. *Newsletter of the Canadian Institute of Resources Law*; 1982 May; 1: 1-2.

3001. Saunders, Ronald J. Continentalism and economic nationalism in the manufacturing sector: seeking middle ground. *Canadian Public Policy* (supplement); 1982 October; 8: 463-479.

3002. Savoie, Donald J. Cash incentives versus tax incentives for regional-development - issues and considerations. *Canadian Journal of Regional Science*; 1985 Spring; 8(1): 1-15.

3003. Savoie, Donald J. The toppling of DREE and prospects for regional economic development. *Canadian Public Policy*; 1984 September; 10(3): 328-337.

3004. Savoie, Donald J. The General Development Agreement approach and the bureaucratization of provincial governments in the Atlantic provinces. *Canadian Public Administration*; 1981 Spring; 24(1): 116-132.

3005. Sayeed, Adil. Tax-transfer benefits for the elderly. In: Conklin, David W. [and others], eds. *Pensions today and tomorrow: background studies.* Toronto: Ontario Economic Council; 1984: 241-282; 486 p. (Special research report/Ontario Economic Council).

3006. Scarfe, Brian L. The federal budget and energy program. *Canadian Public Policy*; 1981 Winter; 7(1): 1-14.

3007. Scarfe, Brian L. Financing oil and gas exploration and development activity. *Canadian Public Policy* (supplement); 1985 July; 11: 402-406.

3008. Scarfe, Brian L. The new oil price scenario and the Chretien - Zaozirny agreement: a comment. *Canadian Public Policy*; 1984 September; 10(3): 340-46.

3009. Scarfe, Brian L. Prospects and policies for western Canadian growth. *Canadian Public Policy* (supplement); 1985 July; 11: 361-364.

3010. Scarfe, Brian L.; Rilkoff, Edwin W. *Financing oil and gas exploration and development activity.* Ottawa: Economic Council of Canada; 1984; viii, 106 p. (Discussion paper / Economic Council of Canada; 274).

3011. Scarlett, M. J. Coastal land use under the impact of offshore oil development in Newfoundland: some implications of public policy. *Coastal Zone Management Journal*; 1983; 11(1-2): 133-148.

3012. Schrecker, Ted. The mobilization of bias in closed systems: environmental regulation in Canada. *Journal of Business Administration*; 1984-1985; 15: 43-63.

3013. Schultz, Richard J. Federalism and telecommunications: multiplication, division and sharing. *Osgoode Hall Law Journal*; 1982 December; 20(4): 745-761.

3014. Schultz, Richard J. *Delegation and cable distribution systems: a negative assessment.* Kingston: Institute of Intergovernmental Relations, Queen's University; 1981; 15 p. (Discussion papers).

3015. Schultz, Richard J. *Federalism, bureaucracy and public policy: the politics of highway transport regulation.* Toronto: Institute of Public Administration of Canada; 1980; xv, 228 p. (Canadian public adminstration series).

3016. Schultz, Richard J. *Recent developments in federal-provincial liaison.* Montreal: Centre for the Study of Regulated Industries, McGill University; 1980; 32 p.

3017. Schultz, Richard J. Regulation as a Maginot Line: confronting the technological revolution in telecommunications. *Canadian Public Administration*; 1983 Summer; 26(2): 203-218.

3018. Schultz, Richard J. Regulatory agencies. In: Whittington, Michael J.; Williams, Glen, eds. *Canadian politics in the 1980's*. Toronto: Methuen 1981: 313-324; xiv, 336 p.

3019. Schultz, Richard J.; Alexandroff, Alan. *Economic regulation and the federal system*. Toronto: University of Toronto Press; Royal Commission on the Economic Union and Development Prospects for Canada; 1985; xv, 187 p. (The collected research studies; 42).

3020. Schultz, Richard J.; Brown-John, Lloyd. *Federalism and the regulatory process*. Toronto: Butterworth for Institute for Research on Public Policy; 1979; 92 p.

3021. Schuster, J. Mark Davidson. *Supporting the arts: an international comparative study, Canada, federal republic of Germany, France, Italy, Great Britain, Netherlands, Sweden, United States*. [Washington]: Policy and Planning Division, National Endowment for the Arts; 1985; 107 p.

3022. Schwartz, Mildred A. *The environment for policy-making in Canada and the United States*. [Montreal]: C.D. Howe Institute; 1981; ix, 178 p. (Canada-U.S. prospects; v. 9).

3023. Schwartz, S.L.; Fuller, J.D.; Ziemba, W.T. Long-run effects of the Canadian national energy agreements. *Energy Journal*; 1985 January; 6(1): 63-77.

3024. Schwartz, Warren F. Regulation of industrial subsidies in the EEC, the United States, and GATT. In: Trebilcock, Michael J., ed. *Federalism and the Canadian economic union*. Toronto: Ontario Economic Council; 1983: 394-423; xiv, 560 p. (Ontario Economic Council research studies).

3025. Schweitzer, Thomas T. *Migration and a small long-term econometric model of Alberta*. Ottawa: Economic Council of Canada; 1982; vii, 163 p. (Discussion paper / Economic Council of Canada; 221).

3026. Schweitzer, Thomas T. *Old myths and new choices: railway freight rates and western economic development*. Ottawa: Economic Council of Canada; 1984; 102 p.

3027. Science Council of Canada. *Canadian industrial development: some policy directions*. Ottawa: Science Council of Canada; 1984; 83 p. (Science Council of Canada report; 37).

3028. Scott, Anthony. *Divided jurisdiction over natural resource revenues*. Kingston: Institute of Intergovernmental Relations, Queen's University; 1980; 17 [6] p. (Discussion papers).

3029. Scott, Anthony. Regulation and the location of jurisdictional powers: the fishery. *Osgoode Hall Law Journal*; 1982 December; 20(4): 780-805.

3030. Scott, Anthony; Neher, Philip A. *The public regulation of commercial fisheries in Canada*. Ottawa: Economic Council of Canada; 1981; x, 76 p.

3031. Senécal, A.J. The growing role of the Quebec state in language corpus planning. *American Review of Canadian Studies*; 1983 Summer; 13(2): 52-63.

3032. Shaffer, Ed. The political economy of oil in Alberta. In: Leadbeater, David, ed. *Essays on the political economy of Alberta*. Toronto: New Hogtown Press; 1984: 174-191; xvii, 222 p.

3033. Sharpe, Robert J. *Interprovincial product liability litigation*. Toronto: Butterworths; 1982; xxi, 145 p.

3034. Shaw, R. P. Fiscal vs traditional market variables in inter-metropolitan migration in Canada - 1956-1981. *Population Index*; 1985; 51(3): 452.

3035. Shaw, R.P. Fiscal versus traditional market variables in Canadian migration. *Journal of Political Economy*; 1986; 94(3): 648-666.

3036. Shearer, Ronald A. Regionalism and international trade policy. In: Whalley, John, res. coord. *Canada-United States free trade*. Toronto: University of Toronto Press; Royal Commission on the Economic Union and Development Prospects for Canada; 1985: 325-368; xi, 374 p. (The collected research studies; v. 11).

3037. Sheikh, Munir A.; Grady, Patrick; Lapointe, P.H. The effectiveness of fiscal policy in a Keynesian-monetarist model of Canada. *Empirical Economics*; 1983; 8(3-4): 139-68.

3038. Shepherd, John R. Government aid to industry: a private sector perspective. *Canadian Public Administration*; 1983 Spring; 26(1): 47-56.

3039. Shepperd, John J. *The transition to reality: directions for Canadian industrial strategy*. Ottawa: Canadian Institute for Economic Policy; 1980; 42 p. (Industrial strategy series).

3040. Shifrin, Leonard. Income security: the rise and stall of the federal role. In: Ismael, Jacqueline S., ed. *Canadian social welfare policy: federal and provincial dimensions*. Kingston: McGill-Queen's University Press; 1985: 21-28; xviii, 187 p. (Canadian public administration).

3041. Sidor, Nick. *Consumer policy in the Canadian federal state*. Kingston: Institute of Intergovernmental Relations, Queen's University; c1984; 87 p. (Discussion paper).

3042. Silzer, Nola; Krasnick, Mark. The free flow of goods in the Canadian economic union. In: Krasnick, Mark, res. coord. *Perspectives on the Canadian economic union*. Toronto: University of Toronto Press; Royal Commission on the Economic Union and Development Prospects for Canada; 1986: 155-194; xvi, 271 p. (The collected research studies; 60).

3043. Sims, W. A.; Smith, J.B. *The impact of environmental regulation on productivity growth*. Ottawa: Economic Council of Canada; [1983]; vii, 101 p. (Discussion paper 241).

3044. Sinclair, P. *The state goes fishing: the emergence of public ownership in the Newfoundland and fishing industry*. St. John's: Institute Social and Economic Research; 1985; 39 p.

3045. Skogstad, Grace. The Farm Products Marketing Agencies Act: a case study of agricultural policy. *Canadian Public Policy*; 1980 Winter; 6(1): 89-100.

3046. Slack, Enid. The implications of federalism for postsecondary education. In: Conklin, David W.; Courchene, Thomas J., eds. *Ontario universities: access, operations and funding*. Toronto: Ontario Economic Council; 1985: 362-375; xiv, 467 p.

3047. Slater, David W. The Newfoundland reference: an update. *Business Quarterly* (Special Supplement); 1985 Summer; 50(2): 90-92.

3048. Slater, David W. Public support of postsecondary education. In: Courchene, Thomas J.; Conklin, David W.; Cook, Gail C.A., eds. *Ottawa and the provinces: the distribution of money and power*. Toronto: Ontario Economic Council; 1985; 1: 287-298; xii, 341 p. (Special research report/Ontario Economic Council).

3049. Slater, David W. Reforming Canada's financial institutions. *Canadian Business Review*; 1985 Winter; 12(4): 14-18.

3050. Smit, B.; Johnston, T. Public policy assessment: evaluating objectives of resource policies. *Professional Geographer*; 1983; 35(2): 172-178.

3051. Smit, Hans. The relevance of the EEC experience to additional prospective sectoral integration between Canada and the United States. *Canada-United States Law Journal*; 1985; 10: 53-60.

3052. Smith, M. E. The role of federal laboratories in technological development of Canadian industry. *Journal of Canadian Studies*; 1982-83 Winter; 17(4): 10-19.

3053. Smythe, Elizabeth. *From FIRA to Investment Canada: Canadian foreign investment regime change and the world economy* [Photocopy]. Annual meeting of the Canadian Political Science Association; June 6-8, 1986; Winnipeg; [1986]; 52 p.

3054. Social Science Federation of Canada. *Principles and mechanisms for the financing of university education and research in Canada: brief submitted to the House Committee on Federal-Provincial Fiscal Arrangements on behalf of the Social Science Federation of Canada*. [Ottawa]: The Federation; 1981; 30 p.

3055. Soderstrom, Lee. The Canadian experience (Regulating health care: the struggle for control). *Proceedings of the Academy of Political Science*; 1980; 33(4): 224-238.

3056. Soderstrom, Lee. Extra-billing and cost-sharing. *Canadian Public Policy*; 1981 Winter; 7(1): 103-107.

3057. Somers, E. *Drinking water in Canada: "the federal perspective"*. Environmental government affairs seminar, proceedings, environmental concerns of the 80's; October 12-15, 1982; Ottawa. [Ottawa]: Air Pollution Control Association and Federal Association Canadian Environment; 1982; 430-437.

3058. Spicer, Keith. Une étude claire et objective sur la querelle des gens de l'air. *L'Action nationale*; 1983 October; 73(2): 159-162.

3059. Splane, Richard B. Social welfare development in Alberta: the federal-provincial interplay. In: Ismael, Jacqueline S., ed. *Canadian social welfare policy: federal and provincial dimensions*. Kingston: McGill-Queen's University Press; 1985: 173-187; xviii, 187 p. (Canadian public administration).

3060. St-Hilaire, France; Whalley, John. Reforming taxes: some problems of implementation. In: Laidler. David, res. coord. *Approaches to economic well-being*. Toronto: University of Toronto Press; Royal Commission on the Economic Union and Development Prospects for Canada; 1985: 195-224; xix, 249 p. (The collected research studies; 26).

3061. Stabler, J. C.; Olfert, M. R. Gaslight follies: The political economy of the western Arctic. *Canadian Public Policy*; 1980 Spring; 6(2): 374-388.

3062. Stagemann, K. *Domestic monopoly as a domestic distortion under free trade conditions*. Kingston: Queen's University. Institute for Economic Research; 1980. (Queen's University Institute for Economic Research discussion paper; v. 379).

3063. Stager, P.; Proulx, P.; Walsh, B.; Fudakowski, T. Bilingualism in Canadian air-traffic control. *Canadian Journal of Psychology*; 1980; 34(4): 346-358.

3064. Stairs, Denis; Winham, Gilbert R., res. coords. *Canada and the international political economic environment*. Toronto: University of Toronto Press; Royal Commission on the Economic Union and Development Prospects for Canada; 1985; xvii, 151 p. (The collected research studies; v. 28).

3065. Stairs, Denis; Winham, Gilbert R., res. coords. *The politics of Canada's economic relationship with the United-States*. Toronto: University of Toronto Press; Royal Commission on the Economic Union and Development Prospects for Canada; 1985; xix, 207 p. (The collected research studies; 29).

3066. Stairs, Denis; Winham, Gilbert R. The politics of Canada's economic relationship with the United States: an introduction. In: idem., res. coords. *The politics of Canada's economic relationship with the United States*. Toronto: University of Toronto Press; Royal Commission on the Economic Union and Development Prospects for Canada; 1985: 1-10; xix, 207 p. (The collected research studies; 29).

3067. Stanbury, W. T.; Lermer, G. Regulation and the redistribution of income and wealth. *Canadian Public Administration*; 1983 Fall; 26(3): 378-401.

3068. Stanbury, W.T. *Government regulation: scope, growth, process*. Montreal: Institute for Research on Public Policy; 1980; xxviii, 267 p.

3069. Stanbury, W.T.; Thompson, Fred. *Regulatory reform in Canada*. Montreal: Institute for Research on Public Policy; 1982; vi, 139 p.

3070. Stanbury, W.T.; Gorn, Gerald J.; Weinberg, Charles B. Federal advertising expenditures. In: Doern, G. Bruce, ed. *How Ottawa spends: the Liberals, the opposition and federal priorities - 1983*. Toronto: James Lorimer; 1983: 133-172; 244 p.

3071. Stevenson, Colin P. A new perspective on environmental rights after the Charter. *Osgoode Hall Law Journal*; 1983 September; 21(3): 390-421.

3072. Stevenson, Garth. The process of making mineral resource policy in Canada. In: Beigie, Carl E.; Hero, Alfred O., Jr., eds. *Natural resources in U.S.-Canadian relations*. Boulder, CO: Westview Press; 1980; 1: 167-202; xiii, 371 p.

3073. Stevenson, H. Michael; Williams, A. Paul. Physicians and medicare: professional ideology and Canadian health care policy. *Canadian Public Policy*; 1985 September; 11(3): 504-521.

3074. Stock, Robert. *Monitoring migration in the prairie provinces: administrative data sources and methodologies*. Regina: Canadian Plains Research Center, University of Regina; 1981; viii, 101 p. (Canadian plains reports; 5).

3075. Stoddart, Greg L. Rationalizing the health-care system. In: Courchene, Thomas J. [and others], eds. *Ottawa and the provinces: the distribution of money and power*. Toronto: Ontario Economic Council; 1985; 2: 3-39; 343 p. (Special research report/Ontario Econcomic Council).

3076. Stone, Frank. The framework and process of Canada-United States trade liberalization. *Canada-United States Law Journal*; 1985; 10: 119-126.

3077. Stone, Frank. Implementation of sectoral integration. *Canada-United States Law Journal*; 1985; 10: 245-250.

3078. Strachan, W. R. The development of Canadian energy policy 1970-1982: one man's view. *Journal of Business Administration*; 1983-1984; 14: 143-162.

3079. Strain, Frank. *Fiscal federalism and the welfare state: a theory applied in an examination of federal provincial fiscal arrangements affecting education* [microfiche]: (Ph.D.) University of Manitoba; 1985 4 microfiches (358 fr.). Ottawa: National Library of Canada, 1985.

3080. Sultan, Ralph G. M. Canada's recent experiment in the repatriation of American capital. *Canadian Public Policy* (supplement); 1982 October; 8: 498-504.

3081. Susman, Paul; Kresl, Peter Karl. The probable impact of offshore oil and gas exploration and Newfoundland's underdevelopment. *American Journal of Canadian Studies*; 1982 Fall; 12(3): 46-60.

3082. Sutherland, S.L. The justice portfolio: social policy through regulation. In: Doern, Bruce G., ed. *How Ottawa spends: the Liberals, the opposition and federal priorities - 1983*. Toronto: James Lorimer; 1983: 173-207; 244 p.

3083. Swaigen, John; Boyden, Ernest D. Federal regulation of nuclear facilities in Canada: better safe than sorry. *Saskatchewan Law Review*; 1980-81; 45(1): 53-81.

3084. Swan, N. M. Competing models of western growth continued specialization in resources or greater diversification. *Canadian Public Policy* (supplement); 1985 July; 11: 283-289.

3085. Swan, Neil; Slater, David W. Reflections on western transition. *Canadian Public Policy* (supplement); 1985 July; 11: 365-370.

3086. Swanick, Eric L, ed. *Bilingualism in the federal Canadian public service*. Monticello, Ill.: Vance Bibliographies; 1980; 6 p. (Public administration series; P-425).

3087. Swimmer, Eugene. "Six and five". In: Maslove, Allan M., ed. *How Ottawa spends, 1984: the new agenda*. Toronto: Methuen; 1984: 240-281; 334 p.

3088. Tardi, Gregory. The appointment of federal regulatory commissioners: a case study of the CRTC. *Canadian Public Administration*; 1981 Winter; 24(4): 587-595.

3089. Task Force on Northern Conservation, 1984. *Report of the Task Force on Northern Conservation*. Ottawa: Department of Indian Affairs and Northern Development; 1984; 48 p.

3090. Taylor, Don M.; Dube-Simard, Lise. Language planning and intergroup relations: anglophone and francophone attitudes towards the Charter of the French Language. In: Bourhis, Richard Y., ed. *Conflict and language planning in Quebec*. London: Multilingual Matters; 1984: 148-173; xvi, 304 p. (Multilingual matters; v. 5).

3091. Taylor, James R. Communication technologies, regional identity, and Canadian dualism. In: Westfall, William, ed. *Perspectives on regions and regionalism in Canada*. Ottawa: Association for Canadian Studies; 1983: 106-115; 137 p.

3092. Tepperman, Lorne. *The social costs of rapid turnover: patterns of migration to Alberta in the 1970s*. Toronto: Centre for Urban and Community Studies, University of Toronto; 1983; 21 p. (Research paper; 143).

3093. Tetley, William. Language and education rights in Quebec and Canada (a legislative history and personal political diary). *Law and Contemporary Problems*; 1982 Autumn; 45(4): 177-219.

3094. Thain, D. H. The key issues in federal government-business relations. *Business Quarterly* (Special Supplement); 1982 October: 106-118.

3095. Thibault, J. Laurent. The Economic Council's assessment, and the future. *Canadian Public Policy*; 1982 Winter; 8(1): 35-39.

3096. Thirsk, Wayne R. Interprovincial trade and the welfare effects of marketing boards. In: Krasnick, Mark, res. coord. *Perspectives on the Canadian economic union*. Toronto: University of Toronto Press; Royal Commission on the Economic Union and Development Prospects for Canada; 1986: 1-33; xvi, 271 p. (The collected research studies; 60).

3097. Thirsk, Wayne R. Tax assignment and revenue sharing in Canada. In: McLure, Charles E., Jr. *Tax assignment in federal countries*. Canberra: Centre for Research on Federal Financial Relations, Australian National University; 1983: 234-250; xix, 370 p.

3098. Thirsk, Wayne R. Tax harmonization and its importance in the Canadian federation. In: Bird, Richard M., ed. *Fiscal dimensions of Canadian federalism*. Toronto: Canadian Tax Foundation; 1980: 118-142. (Financing Canadian federation; 4).

3099. Thomas, R. M, ed. *Politics and education: cases from eleven nations*. Oxford: Pergamon Press; 1983; xiii, 301 p.

3100. Thompson, Donald N. The Canadian pharmaceutical industry: a business-government failure. *Business Quarterly* (Special Supplement); 1983 Summer; 48(2): 120-124.

3101. Thorburn, Hugh G. The politics of economic development in Canada. *Queen's Quarterly*; 1983; 90(1): 138-150.

3102. Thorburn, Hugh G. *Planning and the economy: building federal-provincial consensus*. Toronto: J. Lorimer; Canadian Institute for Economic Policy; 1984; xv, 253 p. (The Canadian Institute for Economic Policy series).

3103. Thur, Livia M., ed. *Energy policy and federalism*. Toronto: Institute of Public Administration; 1981; xii, 182 p.

3104. Tiebout, Charles M. A pure theory of local expenditures. In: Grewal, Bhajan S. [and others], ed. *The economics of federalism*. Canberra: Australian National University; 1980: 59-70; xiii, 432 p.

3105. Toner, Glen; Bregha, Francois. The political economy of energy. In: Whittington, Michael J.; Williams, Glen, eds. *Canadian politics in the 1980's*. Toronto: Methuen; 1981: 1-26; xiv, 336 p.

3106. Trebilcock, Michael J. *The political economy of economic adjustment*. Toronto: University of Toronto Press; Royal Commission on the Economic Union and Development Prospects for Canada; 1986; xx, 366 p. (The collected research studies; 8).

3107. Trebilcock, Michael J. Provincially induced barriers to trade in Canada: a survey. In: *idem.*, ed. *Federalism and the Canadian economic union*. Toronto: Ontario Economic Council; 1983: 243-352; xiv, 560 p. (Ontario Economic Council Research studies).

3108. Treff, Karin F. Provincial estimates for 1984-85. *Canadian Tax Journal*; 1984 September-October; 32(5): 1003-1012.

3109. Tremblay, Rodrigue. *The regional impact in Canada of free trade*. Montreal: Université de Montréal; [1985?]; 22 p. (Cahier; 8510).

3110. Tripartite Committee on Interprovincial Comparisons; Council of Ontario Universities. *Interprovincial comparisons of university financing: third report of the Tripartite Committee on Interprovincial Comparisons, December, 1981*. [Toronto]: [Council of Ontario Universities]; 1981; 35 p.

3111. Tripartite Committee on Interprovincial Comparisons; Council of Ontario Universities. *Interprovincial comparisons of university financing: fourth report*. Toronto: Ontario Ministry of Colleges and Universities; 1982; 36 p.

3112. Tripartite Committee on Interprovincial Comparisons; Council of Ontario Universities. *Interprovincial comparisons of university financing: fifth report of the Tripartite Committee on Interprovincial Comparisons*. Toronto: Ontario Ministry of Colleges and Universities; 1984; 36 p.

3113. Tripartite Committee on Interprovincial Comparisons; Council of Ontario Universities. *Interprovincial comparisons of university financing: sixth report of the Tripartite Committee on Interprovincial Comparisons, May 1985*. [Toronto]: Ontario Ministry of Colleges and Universities; 1985; 35 p.

3114. Tripartite Committee on Interprovincial Comparisons; Council of Ontario Universities. *Interprovincial comparisons of university financing: seventh report of the Tripartite Committee on Interprovincial Comparisons*. [Toronto]: Ontario Ministry of Colleges and Universities; [1986]; 35 p.

3115. Trithart, Elroy C. *An assessment of DREE involvement in the manufacturing sector of the Saskatchewan economy* (M.A. thesis): University of Regina; 1983.

3116. Trudel, Pierre. Certaines garanties du pluralisme dans la réglementation canadienne de la radiodiffusion. Etudes canadiennes; 1982; 12: 5-40.

3117. Tupper, Allan. *Public money in the private sector: industrial assistance policy and Canadian federalism*. Kingston: Institute of Intergovernmental Relations, Queen's University; 1982; x, 135 p. (Queen's studies on the future of the Canadian communities).

3118. Turner, Jeff. Canadian regulation of foreign direct investment. *Harvard International Law Journal*; 1983 Winter; 23(2): 333-356.

3119. Tyrchniewicz, E. W. Western grain transportation initiatives: where do we go from here? *Canadian Journal of Agricultural Economics*; 1984 July; 32(2): 253-268.

3120. Vaillancourt, François. Financing local authorities in Québec - the reform of Bill 57. *Canadian Tax Journal*; 1980 May-June; 28(3): 274-288.

3121. Vaillancourt, François, res. coord. *Income distribution and economic security in Canada*. Toronto: University of Toronto Press; Royal Commission on the Economic Union and Development Prospects for Canada; 1985; xv, 321 p. (The collected research studies; 1).

3122. Vaillancourt, François. Income distribution and economic security in Canada: an overview. In: idem., res. coord. *Income distribution and economic security in Canada*. Toronto: University of Toronto Press, Royal Commission on the Economic Union and Development Prospects for Canada; 1985: 1-76; xv, 321 p. (The collected research studies. 1).

3123. Van Loon, Richard. Rapporteur's remarks (OEC seminar on giving greater point and purpose to the federal financing of post-secondary education and research in Canada). In: Noordeh, Ardeshir, ed. *Reforming the financing arrangements for post-secondary education in Canada*. Toronto: Ontario Economic Council; [1985]: 115-141; x, 160 p.

3124. Vanderkamp, John. The efficiency of the interregional adjustment process. In: Norrie, Kennth, res. coord. *Disparities and interregional adjustment*. Toronto: University of Toronto Press; Royal Commission on the Economic Union and Development Prospects for Canada; 1986: 53-108; xiv, 223 p. (The collected research studies; 64).

3125. VanderZwaag, David. Canadian fisheries management: a legal and administrative overview. *Ocean Devevelopment and International Law Journal*; 1983 Spring; 13(2): 171-211.

3126. Vomberg, E. M. Regulating the transportation of dangerous goods. *Alberta Law Review*; 1983 Summer; 21(3): 488-517.

3127. Voyer, Roger; Murphy, Mark G. *Global 2000: Canada: a view of Canadian economic development prospects, resources and the environment*. Toronto: Pergamon Press; 1984; xii, 164 p.

3128. Wagner, Richard E. Optimality in local debt limitation. In: Grewal, Bhajan S. [and others], ed. *The economics of federalism*. Canberra: Australian National University; 1980: 351-363; xiii, 432 p.

3129. Wahby, Mandy J. Petroleum taxation and efficiency: the Canadian system in question. *Journal of Energy and Development*; 1983 Autumn; 9(1): 111-127.

3130. Walker, Beverly Jane. *The effects of federal provincial negotiations upon cable regulation in Manitoba and Saskatchewan* [M.A. thesis]: Simon Fraser University; 1984.

3131. Walters, Vivienne. State, capital, and labour: the introduction of federal provincial insurance for physician care in Canada. *Canadian Review of Sociology and Anthropology*; 1982 May; 19(2): 157-172.

3132. Wansbrough, J.C.C. Financial market deregulation: prospects and challenges. *Canadian Business Review*; 1985 Autumn; 12(3): 28-30.

3133. Warhurst, John. *State governments and Australian tariff policy*. Canberra: Centre for Research on Federal Financial Relations, Australian National University; 1980; ix, 89 p. (Research monograph; 33).

3134. Warner, Morton. Governments and health care in Canada: the sharing of cost and control. *Journal of Contemporary Business*; 1980; 9(4): 111-125.

3135. Waters, W. G. Transportation policies and the western transition. *Canadian Public Policy* (supplement); 1985 July; 11: 339-343.

3136. Watkins, G.C.; Waverman, L. Canadian natural gas export pricing behaviour. *Canadian Public Policy* (supplement); 1985 July; 11: 414-426.

3137. Watkins, Mel. The case against United States-Canada free trade. In: David G. Meany, ed. *Proceedings: the legal aspects of sectoral integration between the United States and Canada*; April 19-21, 1985; Cleveland: Canada-United States Law Institute; 1985: 89-96; 256 p.

3138. Watkins, Mel. The case against United States-Canada free trade. *Canada-United States Law Journal*; 1985; 10: 89-96.

3139. Watson, William G. Health care and federalism. In: Courchene, Thomas J. [and others], eds. *Ottawa and the provinces: the distribution of money and power*. Toronto: Ontario Economic Council; 1985; 2: 40-49; 343 p. (Special research report/Ontario Economic Council).

3140. Watson, William G. *A primer on the economics of industrial policy*. Toronto: Ontario Economic Council; 1983; ix, 113 p. (Policy study series / Ontario Economic Council).

3141. Waverman, Leonard. *The process of telecommunications regulation in Canada*. Ottawa: Economic Council of Canada; 1982; xv, 220, 106 p. (Working paper / Economic Council of Canada; 28).

3142. Waverman, Leonard. The visible hand: the pricing of Canadian oil resources. In: Ontario Economic Council. *Energy policies for the 1980's: an economic analysis*. Toronto: Ontario Economic Council; 1980; 1: 25-72; 176 p. (Special research report/Ontario Economic Council).

3143. Weaver, Clyde. *Regional development and the local community: planning, politics, and social context*. Toronto: Wiley; 1984; x, 205 p.

3144. Weaver, Clyde; Gunton, Thomas I. From drought assistance to megaprojects: fifty years of regional theory and policy in Canada. *Canadian Journal of Regional Science*; 1982 Spring; 5(1): 5-38.

3145. Weeks, E.P.; Mazany, L. *The future of the Atlantic fisheries*. Montreal: Institute for Research on Public Policy; 1983; vii, 112 p.

3146. Weeks, E.P.; Sommerville, A. *The future of the Atlantic fisheries. Interim report*. Montreal: Institute for Research on Public Policy; 1982; 70 p.

3147. Wellar, Barry S, ed. *National and regional economic development strategies: perspectives on Canada's problems and prospects: colloquium proceedings.* Ottawa: University of Ottawa Press; 1981; xiii, 179 p. (Occasional papers / Department of Geography, University of Ottawa; v. 5).

3148. Weller, Geoffrey R. *Common problems, alternative solutions: a comparison of the Canadian and American health systems* [Photocopy]. Annual meeting of the American Political Science Association; Aug.30-Sept.2, 1984; Washington; c[1984]; 29 p.

3149. Weller, Geoffrey R. The determinants of Canadian health policy. *Journal of Health Politics, Policy and Law*; 1980 Fall; 5(3): 405-418.

3150. Weller, Geoffrey R.; Pranlal, Manga. The development of health policy in Canada. In: Atkinson, Michael M.; Chandler, Marsha A., eds. *The politics of Canadian public policy.* Toronto: University of Toronto Press; 1983: 223-246; 286 p. (Studies in Canadian public policy).

3151. Weller, Geoffrey R.; Pranlal, Manga. The push for reprivatization of health care services in Canada, Britain, and the United States. *Journal of Health Politics, Policy and Law*; 1983 Fall; 8(3): 485-518.

3152. West, Edwin G. The universal student grant option in the federal financing of post-secondary education. In: Noordeh, Ardeshir, ed. *Reforming the financing arrangements for post-secondary education in Canada.* Toronto: Ontario Economic Council; [1985]: 65-81; x, 160 p.

3153. Western Premiers' Conference (1985). *Western Canadian trade objectives for the next decade*; 1985; Grande Prairie. [Ottawa]: Canadian Intergovernmental Conference Secretariat; 1985; 21 p.

3154. Whalley, John, res. coord. *Canada-United States free trade.* Toronto: University of Toronto Press; Royal Commission on the Economic Union and Development Prospects for Canada; 1985; xi, 374 p. (The collected research studies; v. 11).

3155. Whalley, John. The impact of federal policies on interprovincial activity. In: Trebilcock, Michael J., ed. *Federalism and the Canadian economic union.* Toronto: Ontario Economic Council; 1983: 201-242; xiv, 560 p. (Ontario Economic Council Research studies).

3156. Whalley, John. Induced distortions of interprovincial activity: an overview of issues. In: Trebilcock, Michael J., ed. *Federalism and the Canadian economic union.* Toronto: Ontario Economic Council; 1983: 161-200; xiv, 560 p. (Ontario Economic Council Research Studies).

3157. Whalley, John [and others]. *Canadian trade policies and the world economy.* Toronto: University of Toronto Press; Royal Commission on the Economic Union and Development Prospects for Canada; 1985; xv, 147 p. (The collected research studies; v. 9).

3158. Whittington, Michael S. Canada's North in the eighties. In: Whittington, Michael S.; Williams, Glen, eds. *Canadian politics in the 1980's.* Toronto: Methuen; 1981: 48-67; xiv, 336 p.

3159. Whyte, John D. Issues in Canadian federal-provincial cooperation. In: Saunders, J. Owen, ed. *Managing natural resources in a federal state.* Toronto: Carswell; 1986: 322-336; vi, 336 p.

3160. Wietfeldt, Richard A. The role of the state in retirement income policy: some fundamental considerations. In: Conklin, David W. [and others], eds. *Pensions today and tomorrow: background studies.* Toronto: Ontario Economic Council; 1984: 445-453; 486 p. (Special research report/Ontario Economic Council).

3161. Wilby, J. *Revenue implications of offshore oil under different taxation and profit-sharing regimes: the case of Hibernia.* Ottawa: Economic Council of Canada; 1981; 105 p. (Discussion paper / Economic Council of Canada; 197).

3162. Wildavsky, Aaron. From chaos comes opportunity: the movement toward spending limits in American and Canadian budgeting. *Canadian Public Administration*; 1983 Summer; 26(2): 163-181.

3163. Wildsmith, B. H. Federal, provincial, and municipal government in aquaculture. In: *Proceedings of the national aquaculture conference -- strategies for aquaculture development in Canada*; 10 July, 1983; St. Andrews. [Ottawa]: Canada. Department of Fisheries and Oceans; 1984: 104-112.

3164. Wilhelm, Hughes. La politique énergétique canadienne et les provinces de l'Atlantique. *Etudes canadiennes*; 1982; 13: 63-80.

3165. Wilkie, J. Scott. The Radio Reference and onward: exclusive federal jurisdiction over general content in broadcasting. *Osgoode Hall Law Journal*; 1980 March; 18(1): 49-86.

3166. Wilkinson, Bruce W. Canada-US free trade and some options. *Canadian Public Policy* (supplement); 1982 October; 8: 428-439.

3167. Wilkinson, Bruce W. Canada-US trade policy relations. *Canadian Public Policy*; 1984 March; 10(1): 96-103.

3168. Williams, Alan. The optimal provision of public goods in a system of local government. In: Grewal, Bhajan S. [and others], ed. *The economics of federalism.* Canberra: Australian National University; 1980: 111-129; xiii, 432 p.

3169. Williams, Glen. Trade promotion and Canada's industrial dilemma: the demise of the Department of Industry, Trade and Commerce. In: Doern, G. Bruce, ed. *How Ottawa spends your tax dollars - 1982.* Toronto: James Lorimer; 1982: 115-130; v, 256 p.

3170. Willsmith, Bruce H. Fisheries harmonization and the economic union. In: Krasnick, Mark, res. coord. *Case studies in the division of powers.* Toronto: University of Toronto Press; Royal Commission on the Economic Union and Development Prospects for Canada; 1986; 203-268 xvii, 269 p. (The collected research studies; 62).

3171. Willson, Bruce F. An assessment of the national energy program 1980. *Journal of Business Administration*; 1982; 13(1): 29-56.

3172. Wilson, Barry. *Beyond the harvest: Canadian grain at the crossroads.* Saskatoon: Western Producer Prairie Books; 1981; 289 p.

3173. Wilson, Bruce F. *The energy squeeze: Canadian policies for survival.* Toronto: J. Lorimer, Canadian Institute for Economic Policy; 1980; xiv, 144 p. (The Canadian Institute for Economic Policy series).

3174. Wilson, L.S. The socialization of medical insurance in Canada. *Canadian Journal of Economics*; 1985 May; 18(2): 355-376.

3175. Wilson, T.A. Energy policy; overview and macroeconomic implications. In: Ontario Economic Council. *Energy policies for the 1980's: an economic analysis.* Toronto: Ontario Economic Council; 1980; 1: 1-24; 176 p. (Special research report/Ontario Economic Council).

3176. Wilson, Thomas A.; Macgregor, Mary E. The 1985 federal budget: macroeconomic and fiscal effects. *Canadian Public Policy*; 1985 September; 11(3): 602-616.

3177. Winer, Stanley L. Some evidence on the effect of the separation of spending and taxing decisions. *Journal of Political Economy*; 1983 February; 91(1): 126-40.

3178. Winer, Stanley L.; Gauthier, Denis. *Internal migration and fiscal structure: an econometric study of the determinants of interprovincial migration in Canada.* Ottawa: Economic Council of Canada; 1982; viii, 98 p.

3179. Winer, Stanley L.; Gauthier, Denis. *Interprovincial migration data: a supplement to "internal migration and fiscal structure".* [Ottawa]: Economic Council of Canada; 1982.

3180. Wirick, R.G. Fiscal policy 'crowding out' of private investment in an open economy: the case of Canada. In: Conklin, David W.; Courchene, Thomas J., eds. *Deficits: how big and how bad?* Toronto: Ontario Economic Council; 1983: 215-283; 361 p. (Special research report/Ontario Economic Council).

3181. Wirick, Ronald G. Prospects for the world petroleum market and implications for Canadian policy. *Canadian Public Policy*; 1982 Autumn; 8(4): 534-53.

3182. Wojciechowski, Margot J. *Mineral policy update 1983: policy and program changes affecting the Canadian mineral industry.* Kingston: Queen's University, Centre for Resource Studies; 1984; xiv, 74 p.

3183. Wolff, Alan W. The case for a U.S.- Canada free trade agreement. *Canada-United States Law Journal*; 1985; 10: 225-234.

3184. Wolff, Alan W. The case for a U.S.-Canada free trade agreement. In: David G. Meany, ed. *Proceedings: the legal aspects of sectoral integration between the United States and Canada*; April 19-21, 1985; Cleveland: Canada-United States Law Institute; 1985: 225-234; 256 p.

3185. Wonder, Edward. The U.S. government response to the Canadian National Energy Program. *Canadian Public Policy* (supplement); 1982 October; 8: 480-93.

3186. Wonnacott, Paul; Wonnacott, Ronald J. Free trade between the United States and Canada: fifteen years later. *Canadian Public Policy* (supplement); 1982 October; 8: 412-427.

3187. Wonnacott, Ronald J. *Canada-United States free trade: problems and opportunities*. Toronto: Ontario Economic Council; 1985; 30 p. (Special research report / Ontario Economic Council Canadian trade at a crossroads series).

3188. Wonnacott, Ronald J. *Selected new developments in international trade theory*. Montreal: Institute for Research on Public Policy; 1984; xxi, 40 p. (Essays in international economics).

3189. Wonnacott, Ronald J.; Wonnacott, Paul. Towards free trade between Canada and the United States. *Canadian Business Review*; 1985 Autumn; 12(3): 12-16.

3190. Woodcock, George. *Strange bedfellows: the state and the arts in Canada*. Vancouver: Douglas & McIntyre; 1985; 207 p.

3191. Woodrow, R. Brian. *Conflict over communications policy: a study of federal-provincial relations and public policy*. [Montreal]: C. D. Howe Institute; 1980; vi, 76 p. (Policy commentary).

3192. Woolfson, Peter. Language in Quebec: legal and societal issues. *American Review of Canadian Studies*; 1983 Summer; 13(2): 42-51.

3193. Wrage, Peter. The effects of internal migration on regional wage and unemployment disparities in Canada. *Journal of Regional Science*; 1981 February; 21(1): 51-63.

3194. Wyman, Kenneth. The role of regulatory agencies in today's communications environment. In: McPhail, T.; Hamilton, S., eds. *Proceedings of communication in the 80's*; April 29-May 1, 1984; Calgary: 55-59; vii, 162 p.

3195. Yergeau, Pierre. Les subventions fédérales à la recherche scientifique et technologique. *L'action Nationale*; 1982 December; 71(4): 415-418.

3196. Young, Walter D. The voices of democracy: politics and communications in Canada. *Canadian Journal of Political Science*; 1981 December; 14(4): 683-700.

3197. Yudelman, D. Canadian mineral policy debated: industry reaction to a major federal initiative. *Resources Policy*; 1984 December; 10(4): 269-285.

3198. Yukon. Department of Economic Development. *Economic development strategy for Yukon for the 1980's - draft.* Whitehorse: Department of Economic Development; 1983; 131 p.

3199. Zaharko, Janice. *Procedures for transferring to British Columbia the federal government's interest in offshore oil and gas* [microfiche]: (LL.M.) University of British Columbia; 1980 3 microfiches (271 fr.). Ottawa: National Library Of Canada, 1982.

3200. Zines, Leslie. The environment and the Constitution. In: Mathews, Russell, ed. *Federalism and the environment.* Canberra: Centre for Research on Federal Financial Relations, Australian National University; 1985; 13-29 p.

6 Politics and Government

3201. Abele, Frances; Dickerson, Mark O. The 1982 plebiscite on division of the Northwest Territories: regional government and federal policy. *Canadian Public Policy*; 1985 March; 11(1): 1-15.

3202. Alberta. Alberta Federal and Intergovernmental Affairs. *A provincially-appointed senate: a new federalism for Canada. Alberta government discussion paper on strengthening western representation in national institutions.* [Edmonton]: FIGA; 1982; 28 p.

3203. Alberta. Legislative Assembly. Select Special Committee on Senate Reform. *Report of the Alberta Select Special Committee on Senate Reform. Strengthening Canada: reform of Canada's Senate*, by Dennis Anderson. Edmonton: Government of Alberta; 1985; iii, 263 p.

3204. Anderson, Jim. The municipal government reform movement and Alberta. In: Leadbeater, David, ed. *Essays on the political economy of Alberta*. Toronto: New Hogtown Press; 1984: 138-164; xvii, 222 p.

3205. Antoft, Kell. Municipal finance. In: Jamieson, Barbara, ed. *Governing Nova Scotia: policies, priorities, and the 1984-85 budget*. Halifax: School of Public Administration, Dalhousie University; 1984: 197-208; x, 226 p.

3206. Archibald, Clinton. Corporatist tendencies in Quebec. In: Gagnon, Alain G, ed. *Quebec state and society*. Toronto: Methuen; 1984: 353-364; ix, 438 p.

3207. Association des manufacturiers canadiens. Les rouages du gouvernement. Toronto: The Association; [1981?]; 47 p.

3208. Atkinson, Michael M. Parliamentary government in Canada. In: Whittington, Michael J.; Williams, Glen, eds. *Canadian politics in the 1980's*. Toronto: Methuen; 1981: 260-274; xiv, 336 p.

3209. Atkinson, Michael M.; Chandler, Marsha A, eds. *The politics of Canadian public policy*. Toronto: University of Toronto Press; 1983; vi, 286 p. (Studies in Canadian Public Policy).

3210. Aubin, Paul. *Bibliographie de l'histoire du Québec et du Canada, 1966-1975*; avec la collaboration de Paul-André Linteau. Québec: Institut québécois de recherche sur la culture; 1981; 2 v. (xxiii, 1430 p.).

3211. Aucoin, Peter, res. coord. *Institutional reforms for representative government*. Toronto: University of Toronto Press; Royal Commission on the Economic Union and Development Prospects for Canada; 1985; xv, 161 p. (The collected research studies; v. 38).

3212. Aucoin, Peter, res. coord. *Party government and regional representation in Canada*. Toronto: University of Toronto Press; Royal Commission on the Economic Union and Development Prospects for Canada; 1985; xv, 161 p. (The collected research studies; 36).

3213. Aucoin, Peter. Regionalism, party and national government. In: *idem*, res. coord. *Party government and regional representation in Canada*. Toronto: University of Toronto Press; Royal Commission on the Economic Union and Development Prospects for Canada; 1985: 137-160; xv, 161 p. (The collected research studies; v. 36).

3214. Banting, Keith G., res. coord. *State and society: Canada in comparative perspective*. Toronto: University of Toronto Press; Royal Commission on the Economic Union and Development Prospects for Canada; 1986; xiii, 131 p. (The collected research studies; v. 31).

3215. Beaudoin, Gérald-A. Quebec's propositions [La réforme de la Chambre des communes]. *Les Cahiers de droit*; 1985 March; 26(1): 143-160.

3216. Beaudoin, Gérald-A. La réforme des institutions centrales: quelques jalons. *Les Cahiers de droit*; 1984 March; 25(1): 173-188.

3217. Beck, J. M. *Howe and the enactment of the B.N.A. Act: the final disillusionment of a statesman of empire*. Nova Scotia Historical Society Collections; 1980; 40: 7-30.

3218. Bell, Joel. Government oil companies: "quo-vadis"? Journal of Business Administration; 1983; 13(1): 99-126.

3219. Bernier, Ivan; Lajoie, Andrée, res. coords. *Regulations, crown corporations and administrative tribunals*. Toronto: University of Toronto Press; Royal Commission on the Economic Union and Development Prospects for Canada; 1985; xvii, 202 p. (The collected research studies; 48).

3220. Berthiaume, Jean-Luc; Boivin, Marc. *La réforme municipale du gouvernement du Québec: une analyse de la décentralisation*. Péribonka, Québec: The Authors; 1983; 151 p.

3221. Bertrand, Guy. Le Livre beige et le pouvoir d'urgence. *L'Action nationale*; 1980 October; 60(2): 129-140.

3222. Birch, Anthony H. Political authority and crisis in comparative perspective. In: Banting, Keith, res. coord. *State and society: Canada in comparative perspective*. Toronto: University of Toronto Press; Royal Commission on the Economic Union and Development Prospects for Canada; 1986: 87-130; xiii, 131 p. (The collected research studies; 31).

3223. Blake, Donald E. The consistency of inconsistency: party identification in federal and provincial politics. *Canadian Journal of Political Science*; 1982 December; 15(4): 691-710.

3224. Boardman, Anthony; Eckel, Catherine; Linde, Mari-Ann; Vining, Aidan. An overview of mixed enterprises in Canada. *Business Quarterly* (Special Supplement); 1983 Summer; 48(2): 101-107.

3225. Bolduc, Roch. Incidences du rôle accru de l'Etat sur la démocratie locale. *Canadian Public Administration*; 1980 Summer; 23(1): 60-75.

3226. Bothe, Michael. Le Bundesrat: la protection des intérêts des Länder selon la Loi fondamentale allemande. (La réforme du sénat). *Les Cahiers de droit*; 1985 March; 26(1): 93-109.

3227. Bothwell, Robert; Drummond, Ian; English, John. *Canada since 1945: power, politics, and provincialism.* Toronto: University of Toronto Press; 1981; ix, 489 p.

3228. Boyer, J. Patrick. *Lawmaking by the people : referendums and plebiscites in Canada.* Toronto: Butterworths; c1982; xxxii, 304 p.

3229. Boyer, J. Patrick. *Political rights: and the legal framework of elections in Canada.* Toronto: Butterworths; c1981; xxiv, 348 p.

3230. Bradbury, John H. State corporations and resource based development in Quebec, Canada: 1960-1980. *Economic Geography*; 1982 January; 58(1): 45-61.

3231. Brooks, Stephen. The state as entrepreneur: from CDC to CDIC. *Canadian Public Administration*; 1983 Winter; 26(4): 525-543.

3232. Buckner, Phillip A.; Frank, David Alexander. *Atlantic Canada after Confederation: the Acadiensis reader.* Fredericton: Acadiensis Press; 1985; 2; 386 p.

3233. Buckner, Phillip A.; Frank, David Alexander. *Atlantic Canada before Confederation: the Acadiensis reader.* Fredericton: Acadiensis Press; 1985; 1; 355 p.

3234. Butler, Dan; Macnaughton, Bruce D. Public sector growth in Canada: issues, explanations and implications. In: Whittington, Michael J.; Williams, Glen, eds. *Canadian politics in the 1980's.* Toronto: Methuen; 1981: 84-107; xiv, 336 p.

3235. Cairns, Alan C. The constitutional, legal, and historical background. In: Penniman, Howard R, ed. *Canada at the polls, 1979-1980.* Washington: American Enterprise Institute for Public Policy; 1981: 1-23; xii, 426 p. (At the polls studies/AEI; 345).

3236. Cairns, Rosemary; Desarmia, Robert. Western Arctic Constitutional Conference: a look at political development. *The North*; 1982; 29(1): 2-5.

3237. Canada. *Reference texts: systems of government, economic associations-- and how they work.* [Ottawa]: Supply and Services Canada; 1984; v, 39 p.

3238. Canada. Privy Council. *Guide to Canadian ministries since Confederation: July 1, 1967 - February 1, 1982.* Ottawa: Government of Canada, Privy Council Office; [1982]; viii, 326 p.

3239. Cassidy, Michael. Crown corporations and the Canadian legislatures - a vain search for accountability. *Parliamentarian*; 1982 July; 63(3): 129-137.

3240. Chandler, Marsha A. State enterprise and partisanship in provincial politics. *Canadian Journal of Political Science*; 1982 December; 15(4): 711-740.

3241. Channing, J.G. *The effects of transition to Confederation on public administration in Newfoundland.* Toronto: Institute of Public Administration of Canada; c1982; xi, 107 p. (Monographs on Canadian public administration; v. 7).

3242. Chorney, Harold; Hansen, Phillip. Neo-conservatism, social democracy and 'province building': the experience of Manitoba. *Canadian Review of Sociology and Anthropology*; 1985; 22(1): 1-29. Note: Language: English.

3243. Churchill, Gordon. Deux nations or one Canada: John Diefenbaker at the 1967 Conservative Convention. *Canadian Historical Review*; 1983; 64(4): 597-624.

3244. Clarke, Harold D.; Campbell, Colin; Quo, F.Q.; Goddard, Arthur, eds. *Parliament, policy and representation.* Toronto: Methuen; xxv, 325 p.

3245. Clarke, Harold D.; Jenson, Jane; Leduc, Lawrence; Pammett, Jon. Voting behaviour and the outcome of the 1979 federal election: the impact of leaders and issues. *Canadian Journal of Political Science*; 1982 September; 15(3): 517-552.

3246. Clarke, Harold D.; Kornberg, Allan; Stewart, Marianne C. Parliament and political support in Canada. *American Political Science Review*; 1984 June; 78(2): 452-469.

3247. Clyne, J.V. Reforming Parliament. *Policy Options*; 1983 November; 4(4): 13-16.

3248. Collins, A. F. The Alberta Heritage Savings Trust Fund: an overview of the issues. *Canadian Public Policy* (supplement); 1980 February; 6: 158-65.

3249. Cross, Jack L. *Guide to Canadian ministries since Confederation, July 1, 1867-February 1, 1982.* [Ottawa]: Government of Canada, Privy Council Office; c1982; ix, 326 p.

3250. Crowley, R. W. The design of government policy agencies: do we learn from experience? *Canadian Journal of Regional Science*; 1982 Spring; 5(1): 103-123.

3251. d'Aquino, Thomas; Doern, G. Bruce; Blair, Cassandra. *Parliamentary democracy in Canada.* Toronto: Methuen; c1983; xiii, 130 p.

3252. Dacks, Gurston. *A choice of futures: politics in the Canadian North.* Toronto: Methuen; c1981; ix, 226 p.

3253. Dickerson, Mark O. Commentary: *The Drury Report and political development in the N.W.T.* Arctic; 1982 December; 35(4): 457-464.

3254. Dion, Léon. Les enjeux de la réforme du Sénat. *Les Cahiers de droit*; 1984 March; 25(1): 189-208.

3255. Dobell, Bill. A second chamber for regions. *Policy Options*; 1983 November; 4(4): 16-18.

3256. Doern, G. Bruce, ed. *How Ottawa spends your tax dollars - 1982*. Toronto: James Lorimer; 1982; v, 256 p.

3257. Doern, G. Bruce, ed. *How Ottawa spends your tax dollars: federal priorities - 1981*. Toronto: James Lorimer; 1981; 303 p.

3258. Doerr, Audrey D. *The machinery of government in Canada*. Toronto: Methuen; ix, 223 p.

3259. Dua, B. D. Federalism or patrimonialism: the making and unmaking of chief ministers in India. *Asian Survey*; 1985; 25(8): 793-804.

3260. Duhamel, Roger. Le Sénat canadien refait toilette. *L'Action nationale*; 1984 April; 73(8): 735-739.

3261. Elford, E. Craig; Stanbury, W. T. Mixed enterprises in Canada. In: McFetridge, Donald G., res. coord. *Canadian industry in transition*. Toronto: University of Toronto Press; Royal Commission on the Economic Union and Development Prospects for Canada; 1986: 261-303; xviii, 388 p. (The collected research studies; v. 2).

3262. Fleming, Robert J.; Mitchinson, J. Thomas, eds. *Canadian legislatures: the 1981 comparative study*. Toronto: Office of the Assembly; 1981; 131 p.

3263. Forsey, Eugene A. The Canadian Senate. *Parliamentarian*; 1982 October; 63(4): 270-276.

3264. Forsey, Eugene A.; Schull, Joseph. *How Canadians govern themselves*. rev ed. Ottawa: Government of Canada; c1982; 45 (53) p.

3265. Franks, C.E.S. Plus ca change, plus c'est la meme chose: reflections on the Canadian general elections of 1984. *American Review of Canadian Studies*; 1986 Spring; 16(1): 1-16.

3266. Frith, Royce. Senators by election. *Policy Options*; 1983 May-June; 4(3): 26-29.

3267. Fulton, Jane. Suasion as a governing instrument. In: Maslove, Allan M., ed. *How Ottawa spends, 1984: the new agenda*. Toronto: Methuen; 1984: 282-324; 334 p.

3268. Funston, Bernard W. The Northwest Territories and its future constitutional and political development: an examination of the Drury Report. *Polar Record*; 1982 May; 21(131): 117-25.

3269. Galligan, Brian. An elected Senate for Canada? The Australian model. *Journal of Canadian Studies*; 1985-86 Winter; 20(4): 77-98.

3270. Garant, Patrice. Crown corporations: instruments of economic intervention. In: Bernier, Ivan; Lajoie, Andrée, res. coords. *Regulations, crown corporations and administrative tribunals*. Toronto: University of Toronto Press; Royal Commission on the Economic Union and Development Prospects for Canada; 1985: 1-79; xvii, 202 p. (The collected research studies; 48).

3271. Garrod, Stan. *Confederation*. Toronto: Fitzhenry and Whiteside; 1982; 96 p. (Growth of a nation series).

3272. Gibbins, Roger. *Senate reform: moving towards the slippery slope*. Kingston: Institute of Intergovernmental Relations, Queen's University; c1983; 51 p. Note: Discussion papers.

3273. Godbois, Albert. Provincial venture corporations: a progress report. *Cost and Management*; 1984 November-December; 58(6): 5-14.

3274. Grafftey, Howard. Government and business: the caisse de dépôt et placement du Québec: understanding the Quebec background. *Business Quarterly* (Special Supplement); 1983 Summer; 48(2): 107-110.

3275. Graham, K.A.; McAllister, A.B.; George, M.E. *Local and regional government in the Northwest Territories*. Kingston: Institute of Local Government, Queen's University; 1980; 69 p.

3276. Grasham, W.E.; Alain, Jean-Marc. *Canadian public administration: bibliography. Supplement 4, 1979-1982*. Toronto: Institute of Public Administration of Canada; c1985; xv, 269 p.

3277. Grasham, W.E.; Julien, Germain. *Canadian public administration: bibliography. supplement 3, 1976-1978*. Toronto: Institute of Public Administration of Canada; c1980; xiii, 131 p.

3278. Gravel, Robert. *La création des municipalités régionales de comté et la décentralisation gouvernementale: analyse et évaluation*. Québec: Ecole nationale d'administration publique; 1983; 234 p.

3279. Gravel, Robert; Robitaille, Denis. *Les MRC et la décentralisation: conception de l'aménagement et extension des compétences*. Sainte-Foy: Ecole nationale d'administration publique; 1985; vi, 30 p.

3280. Gwyn, Richard. *The 49th paradox: Canada in North America*. Toronto: McClelland and Stewart; 1985; 362 p.

3281. Hamelin, Louis-Edmond. *La gestion du nord canadien: défis et perspectives d'avenir*. Institute of Public Administration of Canada. National Seminar (16th); 1983; Minaki. Toronto: Institute of Public Administration of Canada; c1984; 149-254 p.

3282. Heintzman, R. The political culture of Quebec, 1840-1960. *Canadian Journal of Political Science*; 1983 March; 16(1): 3-59.

3283. Hilborn, John. Reform needs reasoning. *Policy Options*; 1984 September; 5(5): 49-52.

3284. Hiller, J.K.; Neary, Peter. *Newfoundland in the nineteenth and twentieth centuries: essays in interpretation.* Toronto: University of Toronto Press; c1980; viii, 289 p.

3285. House, J.D. Premier Peckford, petroleum policy, and popular politics in Newfoundland and Labrador. *Journal of Canadian Studies*; 1982 Summer; 17(2): 12-31.

3286. Hudon, Raymond. Polarization and depolarization of Quebec political parties. In: Gagnon, Alain G., ed. *Quebec state and society.* Toronto: Methuen; 1984: 314-330; ix, 438 p.

3287. Huffman, K. J.; Langford, J. W.; Neilson, W. A. W. Public enterprise and federalism in Canada. In: Simeon, Richard, res. coord. *Intergovernmental relations.* Toronto: University of Toronto Press; Royal Commission on the Economic Union and Development Prospects for Canada; 1985: 131-178; xiv, 263 p. (The collected research studies; 63).

3288. Jamieson, Barbara, ed. *Governing Nova Scotia: policies, priorities and the 1984-85 budget.* Halifax: School of Public Administration, Dalhousie University; 1984; x, 226 p.

3289. Johnson, Richard. Federal and provincial voting: contemporary patterns and historical evolution. In: Elkins, David J.; Simeon, Richard, eds. *Small worlds: provinces and parties in Canadian political life.* Toronto: Methuen; 1980: 131-178; xvi, 316 p.

3290. Kernaghan, Kenneth. *Canadian public administration: discipline and profession.* Toronto: Butterworths; c1983; 270 p.

3291. Kerr, Donald C., ed. *Western Canadian politics: the radical tradition.* Edmonton: NeWest Institute for Western Canadian Studies; 1981; 118 p.

3292. Kirby, Michael J.L. Shaping the government of the 80's. *Optimum*; 1980; 11(2): 7-15.

3293. Klass, Gary Martin. *The dynamics of politics and policy in American states and Canadian provinces.* State University of New York; 1980. Dissertation Abstracts International 41 (6).

3294. Knopff, Rainer. *In defense of liberal democracy: an inquiry into the philosophical premises underlying French-Canadian liberalism's battle with theocracy and nationalism* [microfiche]: (Ph.D.) University of Toronto; 1981 5 microfiches (453 fr.). Ottawa: National Library of Canada, 1981.

3295. Kornberg, Allan. *Representative democracy in the Canadian provinces.* Prentice-Hall; 1982; xii, 292 p.

3296. Kornberg, Allan; Clarke, Harold D., eds. *Political support in Canada: the crisis years.* Durham, N.C.: Duke University Press; 1983; xvi, 463 p.

3297. Lammers, William W.; Nyomarkay, Joseph L. The Canadian cabinet in comparative perspective. *Canadian Journal of Political Science*; 1982 March; 15(1): 29-48.

3298. Landry, Réjean. *Introduction à l'analyse des politiques*. Québec: Presses de l'Université Laval; 1980; xviii, 384 p.

3299. Lane, Alexander E.A. *Charte de la confédération canadienne*. [Ottawa]: Leat Pub; [1983?]; 42 (42) p.

3300. Laucke, Sir Condor. The Australian Senate. *Parliamentarian*; 1982 October; 63(4): 253-261.

3301. Laux, Jeanne Kirk. Public enterprises and Canadian foreign economic policy. *Publius*; 1984 Fall; 14(4): 61-80.

3302. Leadbeater, David, ed. *Essays on the political economy of Alberta*. Toronto: New Hogtown Press; 1984; xvii, 222 p.

3303. Legare, Anne. Quebec: one of many roads toward change? In: Gagnon, Alain G., ed. *Quebec state and society*. Toronto: Methuen; 1984: 113-123; ix, 438 p.

3304. Lemieux, Vincent. La Chambre des communes, le système électoral et l'usage du référendum. *Les Cahiers de droit*; 1985 March; 26(1): 175-186.

3305. Lijphart, Arend. Language, religion, class and party choice: Belgium, Canada, Switzerland and South Africa compared. In: Rose, Richard, ed. *Electoral participation: a comparative analysis*. London: Sage Publications; 1980: 283-328; 358 p.

3306. MacDonald, L. Ian. *From Bourassa to Bourassa: a pivotal decade in Canadian history*. [Montreal]: Harvest House; 1984; 324 p.

3307. MacEwen, Grant. The birth of twin provinces. *Beaver*; 1980 Summer; 311(1): 10-19.

3308. Mackenzie, David Clark. *Canada and the entrance of Newfoundland into Confederation, 1939-1949* [microfiche]: (Ph.D.) University of Toronto; 1983 5 microfiches (454 fr.). Ottawa: National Library of Canada, 1985.

3309. Macleod, Malcolm. *Nearer than neighbours: Newfoundland and Canada before Confederation*. St. John's: H. Cuff Publications; 1982; 64 p.

3310. Mallory, J. R. *The structure of Canadian government*. Rev ed. Toronto: Gage; 1984; viii, 472 p.

3311. Mallory, J.R. Parliament in the eighties. In: Carty, R. Kenneth; Ward, W. Peter, eds. *Entering the eighties: Canada in crisis*. Toronto: University of Toronto Press; 1980: 120-135; 160 p.

3312. Manzer, Ronald. *Public policies and political development in Canada*. Toronto: University of Toronto Press; 1985; x, 240 p.

3313. Maslove, Allan M. The public pursuit of private interests. In: Maslove, Allan M., ed. *How Ottawa spends, 1985: sharing the pie*. Toronto: Methuen; 1985: 1-29; 184 p.

3314. McCann, Phillip. *Confederation revisited: new light on British policy*. [St John's]: [s.n.]; [1983]; 24 leaves.

3315. McCready, John. *Political ideology and social policy: expenditure and revenue in three Canadian provinces, 1947-60*: University of Toronto; 1983. Dissertation Abstracts International1984 44(9): 2888-A.

3316. McRoberts, Kenneth; Posgate, Dale. *Quebec: social change and political crisis*. Rev. ed. Toronto: McClelland and Stewart; 1980; x, 325 p. (Canada in transition series).

3317. Mercer, John; Goldberg, Michael A. The fiscal condition of American and Canadian cities. *Urban Studies*; 1984 August; 21(3): 233-43.

3318. Mishler, William; Clarke, Harold D, eds. *Representative democracy in the Canadian provinces*. Scarborough: Prentice-Hall; 1982; xii, 292 p.

3319. Molot, Maureen Cippel; Williams, Glen. A political economy of continentalism. In: Whittington, Michael J.; Williams, Glen, eds. *Canadian politics in the 1980's*. Toronto: Methuen; 1981: 68-83; xiv, 336 p.

3320. Moore, Mike; Vanderhaden, Gary. Northern problems or Canadian opportunities. *Canadian Public Administration*; 1984 Summer; 27(2): 182-187.

3321. Neary, Peter. Newfoundland's union with Canada, 1949: conspiracy of choice? *Acadiensis*; 1983 Spring; 12(2): 110-119.

3322. Niosi, Jorge. The rise of French-Canadian capitalism. In: Gagnon, Alain G., ed. *Quebec state and society*. Toronto: Methuen; 1984: 186-200; ix, 438 p.

3323. Northwest Territories. *Aboriginal peoples and political institutions: the experience and direction in Canada's Northwest Territories*, by Hon. Dennis Patterson. Yellowknife: Government of the Northwest Territories; March 1984; 23 p.

3324. Northwest Territories. *Report of the Special Committee on the Impact of Division of the Northwest Territories*, by P.C. Fraser, Chairman. Yellowknife: Northwest Territories Legislative Assembly; October, 1981.

3325. Northwest Territories. Department of Information. *Position of the Legislative Assembly on constitutional development in the Northwest Territories*. [Yellowknife]: Government of the Northwest Territories; 1982.

3326. Northwest Territories. Legislative Assembly Special Committee on Constitutional Development in the Northwest Territories. *Guaranteed representation of aboriginal peoples in institutions of public government*, by Marc S. Malone. Yellowknife: Government of the Northwest Territories; 1983; 134 p.

3327. Nunavut Constitutional Forum. *Nunavut*. [s.l.]: Nunavut Constitutional Forum; 1983; 64 p.

3328. Nunavut Constitutional Forum. *Nunavut Constitutional Forum Workshop with regional councils*; September 9, 1984. Cambridge Bay, N.W.T.: Nunavut Constitutional Forum; 17 p.

3329. Olive, D. Ontario's smarter idea. *Canadian Business*; 1983; 56(3): 95-99.

3330. Ollivant, Simon. *Canada, how powerful an ally?* London, Ont: Institute for the Study of Conflict; 1984; 20 p. (Conflict studies).

3331. Ontario. Commission on Election Contribution and Expenses. *Canadian election reform: dialogue on issues and effects*. Toronto: Commission on Election Contributions and Expenses; [1982]; 282 p.

3332. Ontario. Commission on Election Contributions and Expenses. *Parliamentary pay issues: a framework for discussion, September 1981*. Toronto: Commission on Election Contributions and Expenses; [1981?]; ii, 153 p.

3333. Patenaude, Pierre. La réforme de la Chambre des communes: introduction. *Les Cahiers de droit*; 1985 March; 26(1): 141-142.

3334. Pelletier, Réjean. Du modèle australien au modèle canadien. *Les Cahiers de droit*; 1985 March; 26(1): 111-124.

3335. Pelletier, Réjean. Political parties and the state since 1960. In: Gagnon, Alain G., ed. *Quebec state and society*. Toronto: Methuen; 1984: 331-352; ix, 438 p.

3336. Pelletier, Réjean. La réforme du Sénat canadien à la lumière d'expériences étrangères. *Les Cahiers de droit*; 1984 March; 25(1): 209-226.

3337. Polèse, Mario. Concentration et déconcentration des administrations publiques: une analyse de la structure spatiale de l'administration fédérale canadienne. *Annals of Public and Cooperative Economy*; 1980; 51(1/2): 123-148.

3338. Powrie, T. L.; Scarfe, B. L. The optimal savings question: an Alberta perspective. *Canadian Public Policy*; 6 (Supplement): 166-176.

3339. Pratt, Larry. Petro-Canada: tool for energy security or instrument of economic development. In: Doern, G. Bruce, ed. *How Ottawa spends your tax dollars - 1982*. Toronto: James Lorimer; 1982: 87-114; v, 256 p.

3340. Pratt, Larry. The political economy of province-building: Alberta's development strategy, 1971-1981. In: Leadbeater, David, ed. *Essays on the political economy of Alberta*. Toronto: New Hogtown Press; 1984: 194-220; xvii, 222 p.

3341. Preece, Rod. The political wisdom of Sir John A. Macdonald. *Canadian Journal of Political Science*; 1984 September; 17(3): 459-488.

3342. Preston, Richard A.; Briggs, E. Donald; Kornberg, Allan; Clarke, Harold D. *Political support in Canada: the crisis years: essays in honor of Richard A. Preston*. Durham, N.C.: Duke University Press; 1983; xi, 463 p.

3343. Prichard, J. Robert S.; Trebilcock, Michael J. Crown corporations in Canada: the choice of instrument. In: Atkinson, Michael M.; Chandler, Marsha A., eds. *The politics of Canadian public policy*. Toronto: University of Toronto Press; 1983: 199-222; 286 p. (Studies in Canadian public policy).

3344. Prince Edward Island. Department of Finance. Planning & Statistics Division. *The growth of the government sector of Prince Edward Island*. Charlottetown: Department of Finance; 1981; 13 p. (Economic trends; v. 6).

3345. Prince, Michael J. The Tories and the NDP: alternative governments or ad hoc advocates? In: Doern, G. Bruce, ed. *How Ottawa spends: the Liberals, the opposition and federal priorities - 1983*. Toronto: James Lorimer; 1983: 37-65; 244 p.

3346. Pross, A. Paul. Parliamentary influence and the diffusion of power. *Canadian Journal of Political Science*; 1985 June; 18(2): 235-266.

3347. Rémillard, Gil. Quelques propositions. *Les Cahiers de droit*; 1985 March; 26(1): 125-139.

3348. Resnick, Phillip. *Parliament vs. people: an essay on democracy and Canadian political culture*. Vancouver: New Star Books; 1984; ii, 120 p.

3349. Richard, Laurence. *Il était une fois le Québec: d'hier à aujourd'hui, condensé de l'histoire du Québec dans la confédération*. [Montréal]: Québécor; [1980]; 72 p.

3350. Roberts, John. *Agenda for Canada: towards a new liberalism*. Toronto: Lester & Orpen Dennys; 1985; 239 p.

3351. Robertson, Gordon. New hope for federalism. *Policy Options*; 1984 March; 5(2): 8-11.

3352. Robertson, Gordon. *Northern provinces: a mistaken goal*. Montreal: Institute for Research on Public Policy; 1985; xx, 77 p.

3353. Rose, Richard, ed. *Electoral participation: a comparative analysis*. London: Sage Publications; 1980; 358 p.

3354. Rowat, Donald C. The centralizing effect of recent local government reorganizations. *Planning and Administration*; 1983; 10(2): 64-67.

3355. Rowat, Donald Cameron, ed. *Provincial policy-making: comparative essays*. Ottawa: Dept. of Political Science, Carleton University; 1981; 409 p.

3356. Royal Commission on the Economic Union and Development Prospects for Canada. *Report of the Royal Commission on the Economic Union and Development Prospects for Canada*. Toronto: University of Toronto Press; Royal Commission on the Economic Union and Development Prospects for Canada; 1985; 3; 3 v.

3357. Royal Commission on the Economic Union and Development Prospects for Canada. *Research for the Commission on Canada's future*. Toronto: University of Toronto Press; Royal Commission on the Economic Union and Development Prospects for Canada; 1984; 58 (60) p.

3358. Ruff, Norman J. British Columbia and Canadian federalism. In: Morley, Terrence J. [and others]. *The reins of power*. Vancouver: Douglas and McIntyre; 1983: 271-305; ix, 342 p.

3359. Russell, Peter H. The Supreme Court and federal-provincial relations: the political use of legal resources. *Canadian Public Policy*; 1985 June; 11(2): 161-170.

3360. Ryerson, Stanley B. Disputed claims: Quebec/Canada. In: Gagnon, Alain G., ed. *Quebec state and society*. Toronto: Methuem; 1984: 59-68; ix, 438 p.

3361. Ryerson, Stanley B. *French Canada: a study in Canadian democracy*. Toronto: Progress Books; 1980; 254 p.

3362. Saskatchewan. *An act to repeal the Department of Intergovernmental Affairs Act: chapter 8, 1983*. [Regina]: [Queen's Printer]; [1983]; 1 p. Note: Assented to April 29, 1983.

3363. Saskatchewan. Saskatchewan Intergovernmental Affairs. *Annual report for the year ending March 31, 1982*. Regina: Government of Saskatchewan; 1982; 15 p.

3364. Saskatchewan. Saskatchewan Intergovernmental Affairs. *Annual report for the year ending March 31, 1983*. [Regina]: Government of Saskatchewan; [1983]; 15 p.

3365. Savoie, Donald J. Government decentralization: a review of some management considerations. *Canadian Public Administration*; 1985 Fall; 28(3): 440-446.

3366. Scarfe, Brian L. Redistributing elected Senate seats for regional balance. *Canadian Public Policy*; 1984 June; 10(2): 245-246.

3367. Shackleton, Lord; Clark, George. The role of second chambers: the report of a study group of the Commonwealth Parliamentary Association. *Parliamentarian*; 1982 October; 63(4): 199-252.

3368. Simeon, James C. *The federal government's policy and expenditure management system: bureaucratic perceptions of expenditure control, accountability and improved decision-making* [microfiche]: (Ph.D.) York University; 1985 5 microfiches (394 fr.). Ottawa: National Library of Canada, 1985.

3369. Simeon, Richard; Blake, Donald E. Regional preferences: citizens' views of public policy. In: Elkins, David J.; Simeon, Richard, eds. *Small worlds: provinces and parties in Canadian political life*. Toronto: Methuen; 1980: 77-105; xvi, 316 p.

3370. Simeon, Richard; Elkins, David J. Provincial political cultures in Canada. In: idem., eds. *Small worlds: provinces and parties in Canadian political life.* Toronto: Methuen; 1980: 31-76; xvi, 316 p.

3371. Simeon, Richard; Miller, Robert. Regional variations in public policy. In: Elkins, David J.; Simeon, Richard, eds. *Small worlds: provinces and parties in Canadian political life.* Toronto. Methuen: 1980: 242-284; xvi, 316 p.

3372. Skogstad, Grace. Interest groups, representation and conflict management in the Standing Committees of the House of Commons. *Canadian Journal of Political Science*; 1985 December; 18(4): 739-772.

3373. Slatter, Frans F.; Law Reform Commission of Canada. *Parliament and administrative agencies.* Ottawa: Supply and Services Canada; 1982; 154 p. (Adminstrative law series).

3374. Smiley, Donald V. Central institutions. In: Beck, Stanley M.; Bernier, Ivan, eds. *Canada and the new Constitution: the unfinished agenda.* Montreal: Institute for Research on Public Policy; 1983; 1: 19-90; xii, 399 p.

3375. Smiley, Donald V. *An elected Senate for Canada?: clues from the Australian experience.* Kingston: Institute of Intergovernmental Relations, Queen's University; 1985; iv, 75 p. (Discussion papers).

3376. Smiley, Donald V. Reflections on cultural nationhood and political community in Canada. In: Carty, R. Kenneth; Ward, W. Peter, eds. *Entering the eighties: Canada in crisis.* Toronto: University of Toronto Press; 1980: 20-45; 160 p.

3377. Smith, David E. Party government, representation and national integration in Canada. In: Aucoin, Peter, res. coord. *Party government and regional representation in Canada.* Toronto: University of Toronto Press; Royal Commission on the Economic Union and Development Prospects for Canada; 1985: 1-68; xv, 161 p. (The collected research studies; 36).

3378. Smith, David E. Political culture in the West. In: Bercuson, David Jay; Buckner, Phillip A., eds. *Eastern and western perspectives.* Toronto: University of Toronto Press; 1981: 169-182; xi, 227 p.

3379. Smith, David E. *The regional decline of a national party: Liberals on the prairies.* Toronto: University of Toronto Press; 1981; xviii, 188 p. (Canadian government series; 21).

3380. Smith, Dennis. Political parties and the survival of Canada. In: Carty, R. Kenneth; Ward, W. Peter, eds. *Entering the eighties: Canada in crisis.* Toronto: University of Toronto Press; 1980: 136-148; 160 p.

3381. Solomon, Peter H., Jr. Government officials and the study of policy-making. *Canadian Public Administration*; 1983 Fall; 26(3): 420-440.

3382. Sproule-Jones, Mark. Institutions, constitutions, and public policies: a public-choice overview. In: Atkinson, Michael M.; Chandler, Marsha A., eds. *The politics of Canadian public policy.* Toronto: University of Toronto Press; 1983: 127-150; 286 p. (Studies in Canadian public policy).

3383. Stanfield, Robert L. *National political parties and regional diversity: notes for the Kenneth R. MacGregor lecture, Queen's University, Monday, February 25, 1985.* Kingston: Institute of Intergovernmental Relations, Queen's University; 1985; ii, 17 p. (Discussion papers).

3384. Stewart, Ian. Of customs and coalitions: the formation of Canadian federal parliamentary alliances. *Canadian Journal of Political Science*; 1980; 13(3): 451-479.

3385. Sutherland, S.L.; Doern, G. Bruce. *Bureaucracy in Canada: control and reform.* Toronto: University of Toronto Press; Royal Commission on the Economic Union and Development Prospects for Canada; 1985; xix, 230 p. (The collected research studies; 43).

3386. Swimmer, Gene. Labour Canada: a department "of" labour or "for" labour? In: Doern, G. Bruce, ed. *How Ottawa spends your tax dollars: federal priorities - 1981.* Toronto: James Lorimer; 1981: 148-183; 303 p.

3387. Tanguay, Brian. Concerted action in Quebec, 1976-1983: dialogue of the deaf. In: Gagnon, Alain G., ed. *Quebec state and society.* Toronto: Methuen; 1984: 365-386; ix, 438 p.

3388. Tremblay, Arthur. Commentaires sur le rapport du Comité mixte spécial sur la réforme du Sénat. *Les Cahiers de droit*; 1985 March; 26(1): 83-92.

3389. Trofimenkoff, Susan Mann. *The dream of nation: a social and intellectual history of Quebec.* Toronto: MacMillan of Canada; 1982; 344 p.

3390. Tupper, Allan; Doern, G. Bruce. Understanding public corporations in Canada. *Canadian Business Review*; 1982 Autumn; 9(3): 33-39.

3391. Vaillancourt, Jean-Guy. The political economy of Quebec: a selective annotated bibliography. In: Gagnon, Alain G., ed. *Quebec state and society.* Toronto: Methuen; 1984: 427-438; ix, 438 p.

3392. Van Loon, Richard. Ottawa's expenditure process, four systems in search of co-ordination. In: Doern, G. Bruce, ed. *How Ottawa spends: the Liberals, the opposition and federal priorities.* 1983 ed. Toronto: James Lorimer; 1983: 93-120; 244 p.

3393. Verney, Douglas V. *Three civilizations, two cultures, one state: Canada's political traditions.* Durham N.C.: Duke University Press; 1985; xiii, 454 p. (Duke University Center for International Studies publication).

3394. Vining, Aidan R. Provincial ownership of government enterprise in Canada. *Annals of Public and Co-operative Economy*; March 1983; 54(1): 35-55.

3395. Walsh, Bren. *More than a poor majority: the story of Newfoundland's Confederation with Canada.* St. John's: Breakwater; 1985; 332 p.

3396. Ward, Norman. One prairie province: historical and political perspectives. In: Fox, Paul W., ed. *Politics: Canada*. 5th ed. Toronto: McGraw-Hill Ryerson; 1982: 140-145; 693 p.

3397. Weller, G. R. Local government in the Canadian provincial North. *Canadian Public Administration*; 1981 Spring; 24(1): 44-72.

3398. Western Constitutional Forum. *Chronological notes on the Western Constitutional Forum of the constitutional alliance of the Northwest Territories*. [Yellowknife]: Western Constitutional Forum; 1984.

3399. Western Constitutional Forum. *Division of the Northwest Territories*. [Yellowknife]: Western Constitutional Forum; 1985.

3400. Western Constitutional Forum. *Information pamphlets relating to constitutional development and division of the Northwest Territories*. Yellowknife: Western Constitutional Forum; 1984; 12 pamphlets.

3401. Western Constitutional Forum. *Partners for the future: a selection of papers related to constitutional development in the western Northwest Territories*. [Yellowknife]: Western Constitutional Forum; 1984-85; 1v.

3402. Western Constitutional Forum. *Responses to the Royal Commission on the Economic Union and Development Prospects for Canada's recommendations on the North*. Future Directions of Canada Conference; November 1, 1985; Ottawa; 10 p.

3403. Western Constitutional Forum. *The Western Arctic Constitutional Forum: an overview*. Yellowknife: Western Constitutional Forum; October, 1984.

3404. Western Constitutional Forum; Legislative Assembly Special Committee on *Constitutional Development*. *Regional government*. Yellowknife: Western Constitutional Forum; 1983; xii, 142 p.

3405. Whitaker, Reginald. The Liberal party and the Canadian state. *Acadiensis*; 1982 Autumn; 12(1): 145-163.

3406. Whitaker, Reginald. The Quebec cauldron: a recent account. In: Gagnon, Alain G., ed. *Quebec state and society*. Toronto: Methuen; 1984: ix,438 p.

3407. Whitaker, Reginald A. The Quebec cauldron. In: Whittington, Michael J.; Williams, Glen, eds. *Canadian politics in the 1980's*. Toronto: Methuen; 1981: 27-47; xiv, 336 p.

3408. White, Randall. *Ontario, 1610-1985: a political and economic history*. Toronto: Dundurn Press; 1985; 352 p. (Ontario Heritage Foundation local history series; v. 1).

3409. Whittington, M. S. *Territorial bureaucracy: trends in public administration in the Northwest Territories*. Canadian Public Administration; 1984 Summer; 27(2): 242-252.

3410. Whittington, Michael S.; Williams, Glen, eds. *Canadian politics in the 1980's*. Toronto: Methuen; 1981; xiv, 336 p.

3411. Wilson, Keith; Macdonald, John A. *John A. Macdonald and Confederation*. Agincourt: Book Society of Canada; 1983; 84 p. (We built Canada).

3412. Wood, David. *The Lougheed legacy*. Toronto: Key Porter Books; 1985; 250 p.

3413. Woods, Seumas. Towards a more federal parliament. *Saskatchewan Law Review*; 1983-84; 48(1): 91-116.

3414. Woodside, Kenneth. The political economy of policy instruments: tax expenditures and subsidies in Canada. In: Atkinson, Michael M.; Chandler, Marsha A., eds. *The politics of Canadian public policy*. Toronto: University of Toronto Press; 1983: 173-198; 286 p. (Studies in Canadian public policy).

3415. Yukon. Department of Economic Development and Intergovernmental Relations. *Yukon Indian people and the one government system*. Whitehorse: Government of the Yukon; May, 1983; 12 p.

3416. Yurko, William J.; Pratt, David S. *Renewed federalism: structural reform of the Canadian Senate*. Canada: s.n.; 1982; 179 p.

3417. Ziller, Gebhard. The Bundesrat of the Federal Republic of Germany. *Parliamentarian*; 1982 October; 63(4): 277-280.

3418. Zussman, David. The image of the public service in Canada. *Canadian Public Administration*; 1982 Spring; 25(1): 63-80.

Author Index

Abel, Albert S 637

Abele, Frances 231, 2086, 3201

Abizadeh, Sohrab 1405

Abonyi, Arpad 2087

Aboriginal Rights and Constitutional Development Secretariat 232

Acheson, Keith 2088

Ackerman, Bruce A 638

Adam, G.S 639

Adams, E. Kathleen 1

Adams, R. J 2089

Adshead, Gordon 233

Advisory Commission on Intergovernmental Relations (United States) 2-10, 1407-14, 2090-2

Advisory Council for Inter-Goverment Relations (Australia) 11, 1415-1426, 2093

Ahana, Daniel U 12

Air Pollution Association and Federation of Associations on the Canadian Environment 2094

Aitken, Don 13

Ajao, Ade 2095

Alain, Jean-Marc 3276

Albert, Alan Dale 640

Albert, Lionel 590

Alberta 641-4, 1427, 1553, 1554, 2096-9, 2106

Alberta Federation of Metis Settlement Associations 234

Alberta. Alberta Economic Development 2100, 2651

Alberta. Alberta Energy and Natural Resources 2101

Alberta. Alberta Federal and Intergovernmental Affairs 1428-1433, 1526, 3202

Alberta. Alberta North Joint Committee 2102

Alberta. Alberta Social Services and Community Health 2103, 2104

Alberta. Alberta Tourism and Small Business 1524, 1525

Alberta. Energy Resources Conservation Board 2105

Alberta. Legislative Assembly. Select Special Committee on Senate Reform 3203

Alberta. Legislative Assembly. Special Select Committee on Constitutional Matters 1211

Alberta. Premier 1434

Albinski, Henry S 645

Alexander, David G 235, 236, 2107-12

Alexandroff, Alan 3019

Allen, J. Garfield 646, 647

Allen, Patrick 424

Amdur, Reuel S 2113

Amirkhalkhali, Saleh 2632

Anastasopoulos, Anastasios 2114, 2115

Anderson, D.L 1435

Anderson, Ellen 237

Anderson, F. J 2116, 2117

Anderson, Jim 3204

Anderson, W. J 2118

Angers, François Albert 238-241, 424, 576

Anisman, Philip 2119

Annual Conference of New England Governors and Eastern Canadian Premiers (10th, 1982) 1436

Annual Conference of New England Governors and Eastern Canadian Premiers (11th, 1983) 1437

Annual Conference of New England Governors and Eastern Canadian Premiers (12th, 1984) 1438

Annual Conference of New England Governors and Eastern Canadian Premiers (13th, 1985) 1439

Annual Conference of the Provincial Ministers of Mines, 37th 2120

Annual Interprovincial Conference of Ministers with Responsibility for Northern Development (1981) 1440-8

Annual Premiers' Conference (22nd, 1981) 1449

Annual Premiers' Conference (23rd, 1982) 1450

Antoft, Kell 3205

Appel, David 1451

Apps, Eric 650

Arbess, Daniel J 651

Archer, Keith 1050, 1051

Archibald, Clinton 3206

Arès, Richard 243, 652

Armour, Leslie 244

Armstrong, Christopher 14, 1452, 1453

Arnopoulos, Sheila M 245, 246

Arsenault, Pierre 653

Asch, Michael I 247

Asimakopulos, A 2126, 2127

Aspaturian, Vernon V 15

Asplund, C. T 654

Assemblée constitutionnelle du Nunavut 655

Assemblée des évêques du Québec 656

Assembly of First Nations 248, 249

Association canadienne des sociologues et anthropologues de langue française 250

Association canadienne-française de l'Ontario 657

Association des manufacturiers canadiens 3207

Association for Canadian Studies 251

Association of Metis and Non-Status Indians of Saskatchewan 658

Association of Universities and Colleges of Canada 2128, 2129

Association of Universities and Colleges of Canada. Research and Analysis Division 2130, 2131

Atkinson, Michael M 2087, 3208, 3209

Atlantic Provinces Economic Council 2132

Atlantic Provinces Economic Union 252

Aubin, Paul 3210

Aucoin, Peter 2133-6, 3211-3

Auld, D. A. L 1454-9

Aziz, Rashid 2137

Baar, Carl 1162

Bergeron, Gérard 272-4, 690, 1469, 1470

Beriault, Yves 1471

Bernard, Jean Thomas 2162-4

Bernier, Ivan 28, 680, 691, 692, 693, 2165, 3219

Bernier, Jacques 275

Berry, J.W 448

Berthelet, D 2166

Berthiaume, Jean-Luc 3220

Berton, Pierre 276

Bertrand, F 2897

Bertrand, Guy 1472, 3221

Berube, A 694

Berube, Guylaine 1270

Bickerton, James 2167

Bilodeau, Roger 277

Binavince, Emilio S 695, 995

Binette, Denis 278

Binhammer, H.H 2168

Birch, Anthony H 3222

Bird Quinney, Henry 571

Bird, Richard M 1474, 1475, 2169

Bird, Roland 279

Bissonnette, Lise 1476

Blache, Pierre 696

Black, Edwin R 697

Blackbourn, Anthony 2170

Blackburn, V.C 1477

Blair, Allan 2171

Blair, Cassandra 3251

Blair, D.G 698, 699

Blair, Philip M 29

Blais, André 2083, 2172-4

Blake, Donald E 3223, 3369

Blakeney, Allan E 700, 701

Blanchard, René 280, 702, 703

Bliss, Michael 704

Block, W 705

Blom, Joost 706

Blomqvist, A. G 2175

Boadway, Robin 707, 1478-84, 2176, 2177

Boardman, Anthony 3224

Boily, Robert 30

Boismenu, Gérard 281

Boisvert, David 282

Boisvert, Michel 31

Boivin, Marc 3220

Bolaria, B. Singh 475

Boldt, Menno 283-6, 477-9

Bolduc, Roch 3225

Bon, Daniel L 2178

Bonet, Luciano 88

Bonsor, N. C 2116

Bonus, John L 2179

Boogman, J. C 32

Boon, John 2180

Boothe, Paul M 2603

Bordeleau, A.G 708

Borins, Sandford F 2181, 2182

Bossuyt, Marc 709

Bothe, Michael 3226

Bothwell, Robert 3227

Boucher, Michel 2183

Bourassa, Robert 1485

Bourgault, Pierre 287, 288

Bourhis, Richard Y 2184-6

Bourne, L. S 2187

Bourque, Gilles 289

Butterfield, David 2137

Byers, R.B 2211

Cahow, Clark R 724, 725

Cairns, Alan C 42, 43, 301, 726-31, 3235

Cairns, Robert D 732, 733, 2212

Cairns, Rosemary 3236

Caldwell, Gary 302, 303

Calgary. Corporate Resource Department 1504

Cameron, David M 304, 734, 1505, 1506, 2213-5

Cameron, David R 2216

Cameron, Kenneth D 1507

Campbell, A. E. H 2217

Campbell, Colin 3244

Canada 735-51, 1508, 1553-69, 2218, 3237

Canada Advisory Council on the Status of Women 1509

Canada Studies Foundation 2219

Canada West Foundation. Special Task Force 2220

Canada-Manitoba Joint Forest Research Committee 2222

Canada-United States Law Institute 2223

Canada. Ministry of State for Economic and Regional Development 1510

Canada. Agriculture Canada 2224

Canada. Bureau des revendications des Autochtones 322

Canada. Canadian Forestry Service 1512, 2198

Canada. Canadian Unity Information Office 44-6, 305, 752-5

Canada. Commission on Pacific Fisheries Policy 2225

Canada. Consultative Task Force on Industrial and Regional Benefits from Major Canadian Projects 2226

Canada. Department of Agriculture 1513, 2227

Canada. Department of Communications 2228

Canada. Department of Consumer and Corporate Affairs 2229, 2230

Canada. Department of Employment and Immigration. Task Force on Unemployment Insurance 2231

Canada. Department of Energy, Mines and Resources 2232

Canada. Department of Energy, Mines and Resources. Office of Energy Research and Development 2233

Canada. Department of External Affairs 2234, 2235, 2287

Canada. Department of Finance 1514-7, 2236-42

Canada. Department of Fisheries and Oceans 306, 1518, 2243

Canada. Department of Indian Affairs and Northern Development 307-9, 756-8, 2221

Canada. Department of Industry, Trade and Commerce 2244, 2245, 2279

Canada. Department of Justice 311, 759-71, 2246

Canada. Department of Regional Economic Expansion 1496, 1519-23, 2245, 2247-58

Canada. Department of Regional Industrial Expansion 1524-6, 2259, 2260, 2630

Canada. Department of the Environment 2261, 2622

Federal-Provincial Fiscal Arrangements 1532

Canada. Parliament. House of Commons. Special Committee on Indian Self-Government 312, 320

Canada. Parliament. House of Commons. Standing Committee on Finance, Trade and Economic Affairs 1511

Canada. Parliament. House of Commons. Standing Committee on Transport 2106

Canada. Parliament. House of Commons. Task Force on Federal-Provincial Fiscal Arrangements 1550

Canada. Parliament. Library. Research Branch 785, 786

Canada. Parliament. Senate. Standing Committee on Legal and Constitutional Affairs 787

Canada. Parliament. Special Joint Committee on the Constitution Canada 618, 720, 788-96, 1186

Canada. Prime Minister 321, 797-803, 1551

Canada. Privy Council 3238

Canada. Public Works Canada 1552

Canada. Secretary of State 804, 805, 2311

Canada. Skill Development Leave Task Force 2312

Canada. Special Representative for Constitutional Development in the Northwest Territories 806

Canada. Solicitor General Canada 2499

Canada. Statistics Canada 2313

Canada. Supreme Court 807-12

Canada. Task Force on Federal Policies and Programs for Technology Development 2314

Canada. Task Force on Labour Market Development 2315

Canada. Task Force on Unemployment Insurance 2316

Canada. Textile and Clothing Board 2317, 2318

Canada. Transport Canada 2319

Canadian Arctic Resources Committee 322, 2320

Canadian Association of Interns and Residents 2321

Canadian Association of Statutory Human Rights Agencies Conference (1981) 2322

Canadian Association of Statutory Human Rights Agencies Conference (1982) 813

Canadian Association of University Teachers 1544, 2323

Canadian Bar Association 814

Canadian Bar Association of Ontario (Continuing Legal Education) 323

Canadian Chamber of Commerce 2324

Canadian Conference of the Arts 2325-7

Canadian Federal-Provincial Task Force on Justice for Victims of Crime 816

Canadian Human Rights Commission 817

Canadian Human Rights Foundation 788

Canadian Intergovernmental Conference Secretariat 818, 1570

Canadian Labour Congress 1571

Clark, Gordon L 1579

Clark, T. C 2360

Clarke, Harold D 126, 335, 467, 3244-6, 3296, 3318, 3342

Clarke, J 835

Clarke, Larry P 2361

Claydon, John 836

Cleland, Mike 1580

Clement, Wallace 336, 337

Clements, D.J 2362

Cleroux, Richard 338

Clift, Dominique 245, 246, 339, 340

Close, D 837

Clyne, J.V 3247

Coffey, J. Edwin 2363

Coffey, William J 2364, 2365

Coffin, Marie-Claire L 838

Cohen, Maxwell 839

Cole, Richard L 51

Coleman, William D 341-3, 2366, 2367

Collins, A. F 3248

Collins, John 52

Collishaw, Neil E 2368

Colvin, Eric 344, 840

Commission on the Future Development of the Universities of Ontario 2369, 2398

Committee for Original Peoples' Entitlement 317, 318

Committee of Social Planning Councils 1545

Communist Party of Canada 841

Conférence canadienne des arts 2370, 2371

Conference of Ministers of Finance and Provincial Treasurers (5th, 1968) 1581

Conference of New England Governors and Eastern Canadian Premiers (1982) 1582

Conference of Provincial Ministers of Mines (41st, 1984) 1583

Conference of the Council of Ministers Responsible for Transportation and Highway Safety 1584

Conference of the Council of Provincial and Territorial Attorneys General 1585

Conference of the Provincial Council of Attorneys General and Ministers of Justice (1981) 1586

Conference of the Provincial Council of Attorneys General and Ministers of Justice (1983) 1587

Conklin, David W 1588, 1601, 2372-4

Conklin, Francis 842

Conklin, William E 843

Conseil de la langue française 844

Conseil de la vie française 345

Conseil de planification et de développement du Québec 2375

Conseil pour l'unité canadienne 845

Constantinou, Stavros 2376

Constitutional Alliance of the Northwest Territories 847, 1208

Continuing Committee of Ministers on the Constitution 848-78, 1303

Conway, J.F 346-49, 2377

Cook, Gail 1588, 1601

Cook, Ramsay 350

Coolican, Murray 351, 352

Cooper, Barry F 353, 354

Davis, William G 898-904, 1608, 2429, 2430

Dawson, D 905

Daynes, Byron W 138

Days, Drew S. III 906

de Bellefeuille, Pierre 268, 1611

de Brou, David 362

de Fontenay, Alain 2408

de Grandpré, Louis-Philippe 907

de Mestral, A.L.C 908

de Montigny, Yves 721, 912, 913

de Pouvourville, Gerard 2431

de Vries, John 2432

de Wilde, James 2433

Dean, James M 1609, 1610

Dean, James W 2356

Decision-Canada (Association) 363

Delisle, Carole 465

Dellinger, Walter 909, 910

Delmartino, Frank 54

Delorme, François 2434

Delperee, Francis 911

Dembkowski, Harry E 55

Dempsey, Hugh A 364

Denny, M 2435

Denton, Frank T 1612, 2436, 2437

Denton, Geoffrey 41

Desarmia, Robert 3236

Desbarats, Peter 365

Desrosiers, Danielle 233

Deutsch, Antal 1613, 1614

Devlin, John 2705

DeVoretz, Don 2438

Dick, Ronald S 366

Dickerson, Mark O 3201, 3253

Dickinson, I.S 914, 915

Diep, Bich Ngoc 367

Dion, Léon 368, 3254

Divay, Gérard 1615

Dobell, A. R 1616

Dobell, Bill 3255

Dobell, Peter C 369, 916

Dobell, Rodney 1617, 2408

Dobson, Wendy 2339

Docwra, G.E 2956

Doering, Ronald L 370, 2439

Doern, G. Bruce 2440-55, 2732, 2928, 2929, 3251, 3256, 3257, 3385, 3390

Doern, Russell 2456

Doerr, Audrey D 56, 917, 3258

Dolan, Michael B 1618

Doody, C. William 2457

Doody, Michael R 918

Dorcey, Anthony H.J 2458

Dorff, Robert H 203

Dorion, Henri 919

Dosman, E. J 2086

Dostaler, Gilles 289

Douglas, Colin 920

Douglas, Gordon W 2459-61

Doutriaux, Jérôme 2462, 2463

Dowd, Kevin 1619

Driben, Paul 371

Driedger, Elmer A 921, 922

Driedger, Leo 372, 373

Drouilly, Pierre 255

Drover, Glenn 2809

Drummond, Ian 3227

Drury, C.M 923

Dua, B.D 57, 3259

Dube-Simard, Lise 3090

Duchacek, Ivo D 58-60, 1620

Due, John F 2464

Dufour, Jean-Marie 1884, 2465

Dufour, Paul 2980

Dugas, Clermont 2466

Duhamel, Roger 374, 924, 1621, 2467, 2468, 3260

Dunbar, Laurence J.E 893

Dunn, M. James 2353

Dunn, Sheilagh M 61, 1622, 1623

Duplé, Nicole 925-27

Dupras, Martin 375

Dupras, Pierre 375

Dupré, J. Stephan 62, 734, 1624-25

Dupuis, Lionel Alain 2469

Dussault, René 978

Dvorak, P 2470

Dwivedi, O.P 2471

Dyck, Rand 2472

Dymond, W.A 2473, 2474

Earp, Alan 2475

Eastman, Julia 2200

Ebert, David G 2476

Eberts, Mary 673, 928, 929

Eckel, Catherine 3224

Ecole nationale d'administration publique 2477

Economic Council of Canada 1626, 1627, 2478-87

Eden, L.B 1455, 1459

Edinger, Elizabeth 930, 931

Ehrlich, Stanislaw 63

Elazar, Daniel J 64-71, 932, 933, 1628

Elford, E Craig 3261

Elkins, David J 376, 377, 3370

Elliot, Jean Leonard 378

Elliot, Robin 934

Elliott, A 2579

Elliott, Stikeman 2646

Elman, Bruce P 1150, 1151

Else-Mitchell, R 935, 1926

Elton, David K 379

Emerson, David, L 1629

Emery, Georges 936

Empey, W. F 2488

En Lutte (Organisation) 380

Enemark, Tex 2489

Engelen, E 381

Engelmann, Frederick C 72, 382

English, John 3227

Epstein, Leon D 73

Esman, Milton J 74, 2490

Esterbauer, Fried 75

Ethier, Mirielle 2491, 2492

Evans, John R 2493

Evans, Robert G 2494, 2495

Everett, Douglas D 2496

Eyford, B.L 2923

Fairley, H. Scott 937-40

Falcone, David 2497

Falconer, P 383

Fashler, Robert 941

Faucher, Philippe 2083

Federal Business Development Bank 2498

Federal-Provincial Advisory Committee on Health Manpower 2277

Federal-Provincial Committee of Criminal Justice Officials 2499

Federal-Provincial Meeting on Aboriginal Constitutional Matters (1984) 1790

Federal-Provincial Task Force on Justice for Victims of Crime 942

Federal-Provincial Task Force on Student Assistance 2502

Federal-Provincial Task Force on the Uniform Rules of Evidence 943

Federal-Provincial Task Force on the Use of Satellites in Education 2503

Federal-Provincial Trade Ministers Conference 1791

Federal-Provincial Working Group on Wastewater Disinfection 2504

Federal-Provincial-Territorial Conference of Ministers of Consumer and Corporate Affairs (1985) 1792

Federal-Provincial-Territorial Conference of Ministers of Housing 1793

Federal-Provincial-Territorial Conference of Ministers of Housing (1985) 1794

Federal-Provincial-Territorial Conference of Ministers of Tourism 1795

Federal-Provincial-Territorial Conference of Ministers Responsible for Social Services 1796

Federal-Provincial-Territorial Conference of Ministers Responsible for Social Services (1985) 1797

Federal-Provincial-Territorial Conference of Ministers Responsible for the Status of Women (1983) 1798-800

Federal-Provincial-Territorial Conference of Ministers Responsible for the Status of Women (1984) 1801, 1802

Federal-Provincial-Territorial Meeting of Ministers and Deputy Ministers Responsible for Indian Affairs 1803

Federal-Provincial-Territorial Meeting of Ministers Responsible for the Status of Women (1985) 1804

Federal-Provincial-Territorial Ministerial Conference on Human Rights 1805

Federal-Provincial-Territorial Ministerial Conference on Human Rights (1983) 1806

Fédération des groupes ethniques du Québec 384

Federation of Canadian Municipalities 796, 1807, 1995, 1996

Federation of Canadian Municipalities. Resource Task Force on Constitutional Reform 944, 945

Feehan, James P 2505

Feldman, Elliot J 385, 1808, 2506, 2507

Feldman, Lily Gardner 2506

Feldman, Lionel D 1809, 1810

Ferland, Marc 386

Ferris, J.S 2508

Fiander, A.D 2629

Finkelstein, N 2509

Finkle, Peter Z.R 2510

Finlayson, Jock A 2511

Fitzmaurice, John 387

Flanagan, Thomas 388

Flatters, Frank 1479-82, 1484, 2177, 2512, 2513

Flavelle, L 946

Fleming, Robert J 3262

Fletcher, Frederick J 1816

Flowers, Mary Kathryn 389

Ghent, Jocelyn 1825

Ghiz, Joseph A 2537

Gibbins, Roger 84, 406-14, 524, 547, 548, 963, 3272

Gibson, Dale 415, 416, 964-70

Gilbert, Christopher David 971

Gill, Robert M 2538-41

Gillen, David W 2353

Gillespie, W. Irwin 2542, 2543

Gillies, James M 2544

Gilmore, W. C 2545, 2546

Gilson, J. Clayton 2547

Ginger, Laura 138

Gingras, François-Pierre 417, 418

Girotti, Fiorenzo 88

Giroux, Jean-Baptiste 972-5, 1826

Gitelman, Zvi 85

Glendening, Parris N 86

Globerman, Steve 2548

Godbois, Albert 3273

Goddard, Arthur 3244

Godin, Gerald 419

Goetz, Charles J 2207

Gold, Alan D 976

Gold, Marc 977

Gold, Marc E 978

Goldberg, Michael A 2549, 3317

Goldstein, Jonah 2550

Goldstein, Walter 2551

Golembiewski, Robert T 87

Goodermote, Dean 2552

Goodman, Millie 2553, 2554

Gordon, Myron J 2524

Gordon, Roger H 2555

Gorecki, Paul K 2144

Gorn, Gerald J 3070

Gostick, Ron 2210

Gotlieb, Marc J 1827

Gould, G.P 954

Grady, Patrick 3037

Grafftey, Howard 3274

Graham, John F 1828, 2556, 2557

Graham, Katherine A 420, 979, 1810, 3275

Graham, W.C 2558

Granatstein, J.L 2559

Grant, E. Kenneth 2560

Grant, John 2561

Grasham, W.E 3276, 3277

Gravel, Robert 3278, 3279

Gray, M.F 980

Graziano, Luigi 88

Great Britain. Parliament. House of Commons 981

Great Britain. Parliament. House of Commons. Foreign Affairs Committee 982

Green, Christopher 2562

Green, L.C 983-5

Greene, Jack P 89

Greene, Stephen 2563

Greilsammer, Ilan 90

Grencer, Gilles 421

Grenier, Gilles 2564

Grewal, Bhajan Singh 91-3, 1473, 2565

Grey, Julius H 986

Grey, Rodney de C 2566

Griffin, Anne 422

Groenewegen, Peter 1829

Gross, Paul F 2567

Grossman, Larry 2568

Grube, John 423, 424, 1830, 2569

Grubel, Herbert G 987, 2570

Guest, Dennis 2571

Guillaume, Pierre 425

Gummer, Burton 371

Gunther, Richard 988

Gunton, Thomas I 3144

Gurney, Mary P 2553, 2554, 2906, 2907

Gwyn, Richard 3280

Haack, Richard 2572

Haase, Gordon 2573

Hadfield, Brigid 989

Hahn, Randolph 990

Haider, Donald H 94

Hallett, William D 2574

Hamelin, Louis-Emond 2575, 3281

Hamilton, Colleen 2576

Hamilton, Richard 426

Hamilton, S 2775

Handler, W 2577

Hansen, Phillip 3242

Hanson, Russell 95

Hardy, Andre 2578

Hari, Ram 96

Haritos, Z 2579

Harling, K.F 2580

Harrington, Denise 427

Harris, Richard G 2581, 2582

Harris, Stuart 2583

Harrison, Peter 2584

Harrison, Rowland J 991

Hart, Kenneth D 2178

Hart, Michael M 2585-7

Hartle, Douglas G 1831

Hartley, Trevor C 97

Harvey, David R 2588

Harvey, Fernand 428

Harvey, Julien 992

Harvey, Pierre 429

Hastings, J.E.F 2589

Hatcher, G. H 2590

Hatfield, Richard 993

Haughey, Douglas J 2591

Hawkes, David C 430, 431, 2592

Hawkins, Freda 432

Hawkins, Robert B., Jr 98

Hayes, John A 2593

Head, J. G 1832

Hecht, A 2672

Heintzman, R 3282

Helliwell, John F 994, 1833, 2594-606

Helms, Andrea R.C 149

Henderson, Gordon F 995

Henderson, James Youngblood 671

Henderson, Vernon 2513

Henderson, William B 433, 996

Hepworth, Philip H 2607

Herber, Bernard P 1834

Hero, Alfred O., Jr 1835, 2158

Herrera, Corina M 2340

Herriges, Guy M 997

Herron, David R 99

Hettich, W 100

Heureux, Jacques 1836

Hewison, G 2608

Hiemstra, John L 101

Higgins, Benjamin 2609

Hilborn, John 3283

Hiller, J.K 102, 3284

Hindley, M. Patricia 2610

Hodge, William C 103, 998

Hodgins, Barbara 2611

Hogg, Peter W 999-1014

Holdsworth, Deryck 434

Holloway, Kaye 435

Homes, Jean 104

Hooker, C.A 2612

Horth, Camille 1015

Hosek, Chaviva 1016

Houle, François 2613

House, J.D 3285

House, Peter W 105

Hovius, Berend 1017, 1018

Howard, C 1019, 1837

Howard, John L 2614

Howard, Lawrence C 106

Howitt, Arnold M 107

Hubley, R 2615

Hudon, Raymond 108, 1020, 2616, 3286

Hudson, Richard 1405

Hueglin, Thomas O 109, 110

Huffman, K.J 3287

Hughes, D.R 2572

Hughes, Patricia 1021

Hull, Douglas G 2140

Hum, Derek 1838, 2617, 2618

Hunt, Constance D 664, 2619

Hunt, Wayne Austin 1839

Hunter, David 2620

Hunter, J.S.H 1840

Huon de Kermadec, Jean-Michel 111

Huppe, Luc 1022

Hurley, John 1023

Hutcheson, John 112

Hutton, Brian 1024

In Struggle 436, 437

Inions, Noella J 1025

Institute of Intergovernmental Relations, Queen's University 438-40

Interdepartmental Task Force on Land-Use Policy 2621

Intergovernmental Conference on Acid Rain (1985) 1841

Intergovernmental Conference on Local Government Information Development 1842

Intergovernmental Task Force on Land Use Policy 2622

Interprovincial Conference of Agriculture Ministers 1843

Interprovincial Conference of Ministers and Deputy Ministers of Agriculture 1844-6

Interprovincial Conference of Ministers and Deputy Ministers of Agriculture (1984) 1847

Interprovincial Conference of Ministers and Deputy Ministers of Agriculture (1985) 1848

Interprovincial Conference of Ministers of Agriculture 1849, 1850

Interprovincial Conference of Ministers of Communications 1851

Interprovincial Conference of Ministers of Culture and Historical Resources 1852

Interprovincial Conference of Ministers of Health 1853, 1854

Li, Peter S 475

Liddle, Robert T 2591

Lieberman, Michael 1088

Light, Alfred R 135

Lijphart, Arend 136, 3305

Linde, Mari-Ann 3224

Lindenfield, Rita 2694

Lindquist, Evert A 2695

Lindsey, Edward H. Jr 2696

Linn, Johannes F 2139

Linton, A. L 2697

Lipsey, Richard G 2152, 2698

Lister, Ross 2699

Lithwick, N. Harvey 476, 2700-5

Little Bear, Leroy 286, 477-9

Lluelles, Didier 1089

Loeb-Mayer, Nicole 50

Long, J.A 283-6, 477-9

Louder, Dean R. 480

Loughlin, John 137

Lovrich, Nicholas P., Jr 138

Low, D. Martin 1090

Lowe, Carl 139

Lower, Arthur 1900

Lowi, Theodore J 140

Loynes, R.M.A 2342

Lucas, Alistair R 1091-3, 2706

Lupul, Manoly R 481

Luther, Richard 141

Lutz, Donald S 142, 1094

Lyon, J.N 1095

Lyon, Noel 482, 1096

Lysyk, K 1097

Macdonald, Donald S 2707-9

Macdonald, H. Ian 1901

Macdonald, John A 3411

MacDonald, L. Ian 3306

Macdonald, R.A 1098-1100

Macdonald, Roderick A 2710

Macdonald, Wendy 2711

MacEachen, Allan J 1902, 2712

MacEwen, Grant 3307

MacFadyen, Alan 2383

MacGregor, Mary E 2604-6, 3176

MacGuigan, Mark 1101-4

MacKay, A. Wayne 24, 143, 682, 1105-7

Mackay, Jacques 483

Mackenzie, David Clark 3308

MacKinnon, Frank 484, 1108

MacLaren Plansearch Ltd 1903

Maclaren, J.W 2897

MacLaren, Roy 2713

Maclean, J. Angus 1109, 1110

Maclennan, Rod J 2714

Macleod, Malcolm 3309

MacMillan, C. Michael 2715

MacMillan, James A 2460, 2461

Macnaughton, Bruce D 2716, 3234

MacNevin, Alex Stanley 2717

MacPherson, James C 1111-4

Maffini, G 1115

Magnet, Joseph Eliot 485, 1116-20, 2718, 2975

Magnusson, Warren 1904

Magor, Murray C 2719

Mahon, Rianne 2720

Mair, Nathan H 486

Mallea, John 2721

Mallet, Pascal 487

Malloch, Lesley 488

Mallory, J.R 1121-3, 1905, 3310, 3311

Malone, S. Marc 1124, 1125

Mancke, Richard B 2552

Manga, Pran 2722

Manitoba 1126, 1555-61, 1906-8

Manitoba. Court of Appeal 1127

Manitoba. Department of Energy and Mines 1909

Manitoba. Department of Finance 1910, 2723

Manitoba. Department of the Attorney-General 1128

Manitoba. Department of the Attorney General 812

Manitoba. Municipal Planning Branch. Northern Planning Section 1911

Manitoba. Premier 1129

Manitowabi, Mark 489

Manley-Casimir, Michael E 2627

Mann, F 1130, 1131

Manning, Morris 1132

Mansell, Robert L 2724, 2725

Mansfield, E 2726

Many Fingers, Wallace 490

Manzer, Ronald 3312

Maps, Thomas W 1133

Marchak, Patricia 491-3

Marchant, C. Kenneth 494

Mark, Jonathan H 2549

Markusen, Ann R 1912

Marr, William 2727, 2728

Marshall, Geoffrey 1134-7

Marston, Geoffrey 2729

Martin, A.W 144

Martin, Fernand 2730

Martin, J. C 2731, 2919

Martin, Maedythe J 1138

Martin, Robert 1018

Marvin Shaffer & Associates Ltd 1139

Marx, Herbert 830

Mascotto, Jacques 1140

Maskell, C.A 1913

Maslove, Allan M 2732-6, 3313

Mason, Michael D 495

Matheson, Duncan 2737

Mathews, Russell 93, 145-7, 1473, 1914-26, 2738-45

Matthews, Ralph 496, 497, 2746, 2747

Matthews, Roy A 2748

Mawhood, Philip 148

Maxwell, Judith 2749

May, J.D 2435

Mazany, L 3145

Mazany, R.L 2142

McAllister, A.B 420, 979, 3275

McAllister, Ian 2750

McAllister, James A 2751

McArthur, D 2752

McBeath, Gerald A 149

McCallum, John S 2753, 2754

McCann, Phillip 3314

McConnell, W.H 498, 1083, 1141-3

McCorquodale, Susan 2755

McCready, Douglas 2727

McCready, John 3315

McCrome, J.N 2659

McCrorie, J.N 2756

McCue, Harvey 499

McCulla, D.J 2748

McDonald, David C 1144

McDonald, Susan A 1145

McDonough, Lawrence Cecil 2168

McDougall, Ian 1091, 2757

McDougall, John N 2758

McEvoy, J 1146, 1147

McEwan, E.D 2759

McFadden, M 1927

McFetridge, Donald G 2760

McGinnis, Janice P. Dickin 2761

McGraw, Donna 1138

McInnes, Simon 500-2

McKercher, William R 1148, 1149, 2762

McKinsey, Lauren S 503, 2763

McLaren, D.J 2764

McLaren, Richard 1386

McLarty, R.A 150, 1928, 1929, 2765

McLellan, A. Anne 1150, 1151

McLure, Charles E., Jr 2766-8

McMillan, C.J 2821

McMillan, Melville L 1891, 1892, 1930, 1931, 2769-73 2773

McMurtry, R. Roy 1152, 1153

McNeil, Kent 504, 1154

McNiven, J.D 2774

McPhail, T 2775

McQueen, David 2776

McQuillan, P 2777

McQuillan, Peter E 2649

McRae, James J 2778

McRae, Robert N 2600-3, 2779

McRoberts, Kenneth 151, 2174, 3316

McWhinney, Edward 505, 1155-9

Meekison, J. Peter 1160, 1161, 1932, 2780, 2781

Meerman, Jacob 2782

Meeting of Federal-Provincial Ministers on Grain Handling and Transportation (1980) 1933

Meeting of the Continuing Committee of Ministers on the Constitution (1980) 1934-6

Meeting of the Council of Provincial Energy Ministers (1983) 1937

Meeting of the Interprovincial Sport and Recreation Council (1983) 1938

Meeting of the Interprovincial Sport and Recreation Council (1985) 1939

Meilicke, Carl A 2783

Melnyk, George 506

Melvin, James R 1599, 2784-6

Mendelson, Michael 2787

Menzie, E.L 2788

Mercer, John 3317

Merkin, William S 2789

Metropolitan Toronto. Social Planning Council 2790

Mieszkowski, Peter M 2513, 2768, 2791

Milch, Jerome 1808, 2507

Millar, Perry S 1162

Miller, Donna J 2792

Miller, F.C 2793

Miller, Robert 3371

Miller, Robert F 152

Millerd, Frank 2727

Milligan, S.M 498

Milloy, John S 507

Mills, K.E 2794

Milne, David 1163

Native Council of Canada. Métis and Non-Status Indian Constitutional Review Commission 523

Naylor, D 2697

Neary, Peter 1187, 3284, 3321

Needham, H.G 2827

Neher, Philip A 3030

Neil, W 2828

Neill, Robin F 2829

Neilson, William A.W 1188, 3287

Nelles, H.V 2830

Nelson, Ralph C 601

Nemetz, Peter N 2831, 2832

Nesgos, Peter D 1189

Neuberger, Benjamin 157

Nevitte, Neil 385, 417, 418, 524, 525

New Brunswick 2833

New Brunswick. Advisory Council on the Status of Women 1190

New Brunswick. Agriculture and Rural Development 2224

New Brunswick. Department of Finance 1945

New Brunswick. Department of Fisheries 1518

New Brunswick. Department of Justice 2834, 2835

New Brunswick. Department of Natural Resources 1512

New Brunswick. Provincial Advisory Committee on Official Languages 2836

New Brunswick. Study Group on the Official Languages 2837

Newfoundland 1946

Newfoundland Information Services 2838

Newfoundland. Court of Appeal 1191

Newfoundland. Department of Finance 1947

Newfoundland. Department of Fisheries and Oceans 2839

Newfoundland. Department of Inter-governmental Affairs 1192

Newfoundland. Department of Justice 812

Newfoundland. Petroleum Directorate 2840

Newfoundland. Petroleum Directorate. Economics Unit 2841, 2842

Newfoundland. Premier 1193, 1948

Newton, Robert D 158

Nielsen, Arne 2843

Nielsen, Erick 2844

Niosi, Jorge 3322

Nixon A.J 2845

Noam, Eli M 2846

Noordeh, Ardeshir 2847

Norrie, Kenneth H 159, 160, 526, 707, 1949, 1950, 2407, 2773, 2849-55

Northwest Territories 527, 1194, 1208, 3323, 3324

Northwest Territories. Aboriginal Rights and Constitutional Development Secretariat 528, 1195-7

Northwest Territories. Department of Information 1951, 3325

Northwest Territories. Economic Development Agreement Secretariat 1952

Northwest Territories. Energy, Mines and Resources Secretariat 1953

Northwest Territories. Executive Committee 1198

Northwest Territories. Legislative Assembly 1199, 1200

Northwest Territories. Legislative Assembly. Special Committee on Constitutional Development 1201-7, 3326

Norton, Derek G 1931

Nouailhat, Yves-Henri 1209

Nova Scotia 2856

Nova Scotia. Department of Development 2857

Nova Scotia. Department of Development. Federal-Provincial Development Agreements Branch 1954

Nova Scotia. Department of Municipal Affairs 2858

Nova Scotia. House of Assembly. Select Committee on Constitutional Matters 1210, 1211

Nova Scotia. Intergovernmental Affairs 1955

Nowlan, David M 2859

Nowotny, Ewald 2860

Nuechterlein, Donald E 161

Nunavut Constitutional Forum 1212, 1213, 3327, 3328

Nurgitz, Nathan 1214

Nussli, Kurt 125

Nyomarkay, Joseph L 3297

O'Donnell, Margaret 2861

O'Donoghue, Leslie 2862

O'Grady, William D 529

O'Neill, Louis 530

O'Reilly, James O 1215

O'Shea, Kevin D 2863

Oates, Wallace E 1486

Odjig, Alfred 531

Oksanen, E.H 2864

Olewiler, Nancy D 2865

Olfert, M.R 3061

Olive, D 3329

Olling, R.D 1216, 1217

Ollivant, Simon 3330

Olson, Mancur, Jr 1956

Ontario 1218, 1562

Ontario Advisory Council on Senior Citizens 2866

Ontario Council on University Affairs 2399

Ontario Economic Council 2867, 2868

Ontario Energy and Agriculture Policy Committee 2869

Ontario Federation of Students 2870, 2871

Ontario Welfare Council 1545, 1957

Ontario. Commission on Election Contribution and Expenses 3331

Ontario. Commission on Election Contributions and Expenses 3332

Ontario. Legislative Assembly. Select Committee on Constitutional Reform 1219-21

Ontario. Ministry of Colleges and Universities 2872

Ontario. Ministry of Colleges and Universities. Tripartite Committee on Interprovincial Comparisons 2873-5

Ontario. Ministry of Colleges and Universities. Tripartite Committee on University Affairs 2876

Ontario. Ministry of Industry and Tourism 1961, 2877

Ontario. Ministry of Industry and Trade. Innovation and Technology Division 2878

Ontario. Ministry of Intergovernmental Affairs 1222-7, 1962-6, 2879

Ontario. Ministry of Labour 1228

Ontario. Ministry of the Attorney General 1229, 1230

Ontario. Ministry of Transportation and Communications 2880

Ontario. Ministry of Transportation and Communications. Communications Division 2881

Ontario. Ministry of Treasury and Economics 1967, 2882, 2883

Ontario. Ministry of Treasury and Economics. Intergovernmental Finance Policy Branch 1958-60, 1968

Ontario. Premier 1969

Ontario. Provincial Secretariat for Resources Development, Native Affairs 532

Opekokew, Delia 533

Orban, Edmond 162, 534, 1231, 1232

Organisation for Economic Co-Operation and Development 2258, 2884

Ornstein, Michael D 535, 536

Orridge, Andrew W 537

Ostrom, Vincent 163, 164

Ouellette, Yves 1233, 1970

Owram, Doug 538, 2885

Oyovbaire, S. Egite 165

Pacific Rim Metropolitan Conference 1971

Paehlke, Robert C 2199, 2886

Paikin, Marnie 2887

Pal, Leslie A 1175, 2888-90

Palmer, Kenneth T 166

Pammelt, Jon H 467, 3245

Paquet, Gilles 393

Paquette, Gilbert 539

Parenteau, Roland 2891

Parkes, J.G. Michael 2584

Parti libéral du Canada. Commission constitutionnelle 1234

Parti libéral du Québec. Commission constitutionnelle 1235

Parti nationaliste 540

Parti québécois 541

Parti québécois. Permanence nationale 542

Patenaude, Pierre 3333

Paterson, Robert K 2892

Patience, Allan 167

Patry, Réjean M 2893

Pattakos, Alex N 166

Patton, Donald J 2894

Paul, Victor, C.A 1236

Pauly, Mark V 2895

Pauwels, Jacques R 2896

Pearse, P.H 2897

Peckford, A. Brian 1972, 1973

Pederson, K. George 2898

Peiris, G.L 1237

Pelletier, Benoit B 1238

Pélletier, Gérard 543

Pelletier, Réjean 274, 544, 3334-6

Pelot, Bernard J 1239

Penny, Michael 2899

Pentland, Charles 28, 2900

Penton, M. James 1240

Pépin, Gilles 1241-3

Percy, David R 2901

Percy, Michael B 526, 545, 1949, 1950, 2794, 2852-5

Provincial Conference on the Economy 2933

Provincial Ministers of Finance and Treasurers 2934

Provincial-Territorial Conference of Ministers of Social Services (1985) 1987

Purvis, Douglas D 2935, 2936

Putnam, Robert D 132

Putnam, Robert G 2170

Puxley, Peter 551

Pye, A. Kenneth 1254, 1255

Qu'appelle Evaluation Committee. Reid, Crowther & Partners 1988

Québec 1256, 1257, 2937, 2938

Quebec Liberal Party 1258

Quebec Liberal Party. Policy Commission 1259

Québec. Assemblée nationale 553, 2939

Québec. Assemblée nationale. Commission permanente de la présidence du conseil, de la constitution et des affaires intergouvernementales 1260

Québec. Conseil de la langue française 2940-2

Québec. Cour d'appel 1261

Quebec. Department of Justice 812

Québec. Direction générale de l'urbanisme et de l'aménagement du territoire 2943

Québec. Ministère des Affaires intergouvernementales 1262

Québec. Ministère des Communications 1263, 1989

Québec. Ministère des Finances 1990-3, 2944

Québec. Secrétariat à l'aménagement 2945

Quinn, John J 2946-9

Quo, F.Q 3244

Rabeau, Yves 393, 2669, 2950

Racette, Jean-Pierre 2677

Radkowski-Harmstone, Teresa 1264

Rafati, Mohammad Reza 2951

Rakove, Jack 170

Ralph Hedlin Associates 554

Ramet, Pedro 171

Rath, Sharada 172

Ravault, René-Jean 2952

Ray, D.I 555

Raynauld, André 173

Reagan, Michael D 174

Reed, F.L.C 2953

Reeves, Mavis Mann 86

Reeves, William 556

Regan, Gerald A 1265

Regenstreif, Peter 131

Reid, John M 1994

Reilly, Wayne G 557

Reisman, Simon 2954

Reitz, Jeffrey G 294

Rémillard, Gil 175, 176, 1266-71, 3347

Renaud, Marc 2431

Reschenhaler, G.B 2955

Resnick, Phillip 3348

Resource Task Force on Constitutional Reform 1995, 1996

Review Committee on Newfoundland Legislation 1272

Rhéaume, Gilles 558

Rydon, Joan 185

Ryerson, Stanley B 3360, 3361

Sabetti, Filippo 186, 187, 1291-3

Safarian, A.E 2989

Sahir, A.H 2990

Saiyed, H.M 2923

Saldatos, Panayotis 2014

Salter, L 2991

Saltman, Lorne 2992

Sanders, Douglas 583, 584, 1294-6, 2015

Sanguin, André-Louis 188, 189

Sanzone, John G 174

Sargent, John 2993

Saskatchewan 1297, 1298, 1303, 1553, 2016, 2994-6, 3362

Saskatchewan. Advisory Council on the Status of Women 1299

Saskatchewan. Department of Justice 1301

Saskatchewan. Department of Mineral Resources 2017

Saskatchewan. Legislative Assembly 1302

Saskatchewan. Premier 2018

Saskatchewan. Saskatchewan Finance 2019

Saskatchewan. Saskatchewan Intergovernmental Affairs 1300, 3363, 3364

Saunders, C.A 1019

Saunders, Cheryl 1304, 1305, 2020

Saunders, J. Owen 664, 2147, 2997-3000

Saunders, Ronald J 3001

Savoie, Donald J 2021, 2022, 3002-4, 3365

Saxenian, Annalee 1912

Sayeed, Adil 1619, 2023, 3005

Scarfe, Brian L 3006-10, 3338, 3366

Scarlett, M. J 3011

Scharpf, Fritz Wilhelm 190

Schechter, Stephen L 191-3, 1306

Schlegel, John P 2024

Schmeiser, Douglas A 1307-9

Schrank, William E 2984

Schrecker, Ted 3012

Schuetz, C.F 585

Schull, Joseph 3264

Schultz, Richard J 3013-20

Schuster, J. Mark Davidson 3021

Schwartz, Bryan 586, 587, 1310

Schwartz, Mildred A 72, 3022

Schwartz, S.L 3023

Schwartz, Warren F 3024

Schweitzer, Thomas T 3025, 3026

Schwindt, Richard 2438

Science Council of Canada 3027

Scott, A.D 2025, 2026

Scott, Anthony 33, 1311, 1833, 2027, 2602, 3028-30

Scott, Graham 588

Scott, Jeffrey 167

Scott, Stephen A 1312-8

Scrafton, Derek 2028

Seaborne, A.A 2990

Seagram Company 589

Sedler, Robert A 1319

Segal, Hugh 1214

Segre, Dan 194

Seifried, N.R.M 595

Semkow, Brian 1320

Snell, James G 1342-4

Soberman, Daniel A 28, 1345

Social Planning Council of Metropolitan Toronto 2048

Social Science Federation of Canada 3054

Soderlund, Walter C 601

Soderstrom, Lee 3055, 3056

Soldatos, P 602

Solomon, Peter H., Jr 3381

Somers, E 3057

Sommerville, A 3146

Soucy, Pierre Yves 1140

Spahn, P. Bernd 2049

Spector, Norman 2050

Spencer, Byron G 1612, 2436, 2437

Spicer, Keith 603, 3058

Splane, Richard B 3059

Sproule-Jones, Mark 1346, 1347, 3382

St-Hilaire, France 3060

Stabler, J.C 3061

Stagemann, K 3062

Stager, P 3063

Stairs, Denis 1348, 3064-6

Stanbury, W.T 2614, 2688, 2955, 3067-70, 3261

Stanfield, Robert L 1349, 2004, 2051, 3383

Steger, Wilbur A 105

Stein, Michael B 1350

Steiner, Jürg 203

Stenburg, Carl W 204

Stephen, N 1351

Stephen, Ninian 1352

Stevenson, Colin P 3071

Stevenson, Donald W 821

Stevenson, Garth 205, 206, 550, 604, 605, 1353, 1354, 2052, 3072

Stevenson, H. Michael 535, 536, 3073

Stever, James A 27

Stewart, Ian 3384

Stewart, James K 2341

Stewart, Marianne C 126, 335, 3246

Stewart, William Alexander 2053

Stewart, William H 207

Stewart, William L 208

Stienstra, Deborah 606

Stock, Robert 3074

Stoddart, Greg L 3075

Stone, Dennis 1355

Stone, Frank 3076, 3077

Storch, Janet L 2783

Strachan, W.R 3078

Strain, Frank 3079

Strayer, Barry L 1356, 1357

Sturm, Albert L 1358

Subramaniam, V 209

Sultan, Ralph G.M 3080

Susman, Paul 3081

Sutherland, S.L 3082, 3385

Swaigen, John 3083

Swainson, Donald 607

Swainson, Neil A 2054

Swan, John 1359

Swan, N.M 3084

Swan, Neil 3085

Swanick, Eric L 3086

Swimmer, Eugene 3087, 3386

Swindon, Hubert 608

Swinton, Katherine 1360

Switzer, L 2726

Symons, T.H.B 609

Szablowski, George J 2055

Taebel, Delbert A 51

Tallock, Gordon 2056

Tanguay, Brian 3387

Tardi, Gregory 3088

Tarnopolsky, Walter S 1361-70

Task Force on Northern Conservation, 1984 3089

Taylor, Charles 610

Taylor, Donald M 611, 3090

Taylor, James R 3091

Taylor, John F.A 210

Tennant, Paul 612

Tepperman, Lorne 3092

Tetley, William 1371, 3093

Thain, D.H 3094

Theauvette, Carole 1372

Thériault, Léon 613

Thibault, J. Laurent 3095

Thirsk, Wayne R 1460, 2057, 3096-8

Thomas J.C 2636

Thomas, Paul 1838

Thomas, R.M 3099

Thompson, Andrew R 941, 2987

Thompson, Donald N 3100

Thompson, Fred 3069

Thompson, R.L 2580

Thomson, Norman J 2058

Thorburn, Hugh G 211, 3101, 3102

Thur, Livia M 3103

Tiebout, Charles M 3104

Tomes, Nigel 2971, 2972

Tomlin, Brian W 1618

Toner, Glen 2454, 2455, 3105

Toogood, John D 2977

Tournon, Jean 53

Trebilcock, Michael J 212, 2059, 2899, 3106, 3107, 3343

Treff, Karin 2908-10, 3108

Trela, Irene 631

Tremblay, André 1373, 2060

Tremblay, Arthur 3388

Tremblay, Guy 1374-6

Tremblay, Marc-Adélard 614

Tremblay, Rodrigue 3109

Tripartite Committee on Interprovincial Comparisons 3110-4

Trithart, Elroy C 3115

Trofimenkoff, Susan Mann 3389

Trudeau, Pierre E 213, 2061, 2062

Trudel, Pierre 1089, 3116

Tschaeni, Hanspeter 1377

Tsoa, Eugene 2984

Tupper, Allan 214, 615, 2063, 2200, 3117, 3390

Turgeon, Jean 2686

Turner, Jeff 3118

Turp, Daniel 1378, 2060

Twenty-fifth Annual Premiers' Conference (1984) 2064

Twenty-first Annual Premiers' Conference (1980) 2065

Twenty-fourth Annual Premiers' Conference (1983) 2066

Twenty-second Annual Premiers' Conference (1982) 2067

Twenty-sixth Annual Premiers' Conference (1985) 2068

Twenty-third Annual Premiers' Conference (1982) 2069

Tyndall, D. Gordon 2353

Tyrchniewicz, E.W 3119

Union bolchévique du Canada 616

Union of New Brunswick Indians 617

Union of Nova Scotia Indians 618

United States. Congress. House. Committee on Government Operations. 2070

Usher, D 2071

Vadeboncoeur, Pierre 619

Vaillancourt, François 2465, 3120-2

Vaillancourt, Jean-Guy 3391

Vaillancourt, Yves 386

Valaskakis, Kimon 620, 621

Valentine, Victor F 294

Vallee, Frank G 2432

Vallieres, Pierre 622

Valpy, Michael 1323

van der Plaat, G.N 32

Van Loon, Richard 2497, 2526, 3123, 3392

Vanderhaden, Gary 3320

Vanderkamp, John 2072, 2073, 3124

VanderZwaag, David 3125

Vaughan, Frederick 1344

Veilleux, Gerard 2074

Verma, Bharti 2913

Verney, Douglas V 215, 3393

Villemaire, Carmen 521

Vining, Aidan R 3224, 3394

Vipond Robert C 1379, 1380

Vomberg, E.M 3126

von Beyme, Klaus 216

VonRiekhoff, Harald 1618

Voyer, Roger 3127

Waddell, Eric 480, 623

Wade, Mason 513

Wagenberg, Ronald H 601

Wagner, Richard E 1502, 3128

Wah-Shee, James J 624, 1381

Wahby, Mandy J 3129

Walker, Beverly Jane 3130

Walker, David B 217, 218

Wallace, D.J 2793

Wallace, Donald C 1816

Waller, Harold M 187

Walpole, F. Kim 1355

Walsh, B 3063

Walsh, Bren 3395

Walsh, Sandra A 1382

Walters, Vivienne 3131

Wansbrough, J.C.C 3132

Ward, Norman 3396

Ward, Peter W 2350

Wardhaugh, Ronald 625

Warhurst, John 2075, 2076, 3133

Warner, Morton 3134

Waters, W.G 3135

Watkins, G.C 3136

Watkins, Mel 3137, 3138

Watson, William G 1383, 1384, 3139, 3140

Watts, Ronald L 201, 219

Waverman, Leonard 3136, 3141, 3142

Weaver, Clyde 3143, 3144

Weaver, Sally M 626-8

Webster, Douglas R 2973

Weedle, Stephanie 2680

Bibliography

Title Index

The 1982 plebiscite on division of the Northwest Territories: regional government and federal policy 3201

The 1983 Constitutional Accord on Aboriginal Rights 314

The 1983 Constitutional record on aboriginal rights 756

1983 Guide to research and development activities resulting from the National Energy Program of the Government of Canada 2305

1983: the year in review. The national view: Canada Health Act looms large 2121

The 1985 federal budget: macroeconomic and fiscal effects 3176

The 49th paradox: Canada in North America 3280

ABC 1984: assistance to business in Canada: a handbook of federal assistance programs, including a supplement of provincial-territorial programs 2498

Aboriginal nationhood, the northern challenge and the construction of Canadian unity 515

Aboriginal peoples and political change in the North Atlantic area 445

Aboriginal peoples and political institutions: the experience and direction in Canada's Northwest Territories 3323

Aboriginal peoples and the Constitution 583

Aboriginal peoples, international law and the Canadian Charter of Rights and Freedoms 983

Aboriginal rights and constitutional development in the Northwest Territories 1198

Aboriginal rights in Canada 531

Aboriginal rights in the constitutional process 572

Aboriginal rights, the Constitution and the Marshall court 1023

Aboriginal rights, treaty rights, and human rights: indian tribes and "constitutional renewal" 671

Aboriginal self-government in Australia and Canada 518

Aboriginal self-government: a discussion paper in preparation for the 1984 First Ministers' Conference on Aboriginal and Treaty Rights 532

Aboriginal self-government: rights of citizenship and access to governmental services 482

Aboriginal self-government: what does it mean? 430

Aboriginal title, rights and the Canadian Constitution 444

Absence of juridiction: a perspective 1100

Acadians of Canada: the difficulties of a minority within a minority 585

Acadiens, droits linguistiques rapatriement de la constitution 425

The acceptable mean: the tax agreements, 1941-1962 2208

Accepted v. controversial sales tax structures - Switzerland, Australia, New Zealand, Canada 2464

Access to medical care and the remuneration of physicians. Justice Hall's report on Canada's national provincial health program for the 1980s 2590

Accessibility to Ontario universities 2428

L'accident et la nécessité 924

Accord constitutionnel: projet canadien de repatriement de la constitution 735

Achieving a realistic recovery 2339

An Act to Amend the Constitutional Questions Act: chapter 31, 1983-84 1297

An Act to Amend the Federal-Provincial Fiscal Arrangements and Established Programs Financing Act, 1977 and to Provide for Payments to Certain Provinces 1538

An Act to Repeal the Department of Intergovernmental Affairs Act: Chapter 8, 1983 3362

L'action de nos sociétés nationales face à une constitution antinationale 280

Adapting Canadian energy policy to changing world energy trends 2819

Adieu la France, salut l'Amérique 465

Administering the new federalism 27

Administration of justice: an introduction 1011

Administrative criteria for the allocation of functions between levels of government in a federation 226

Administrative federalism 158

Administrative tribunals: their evolution in Canada from 1945 to 1984 2815

Aeronautics law and the Canadian Constitution 1189

L'affaire Riel 558

Les affaires extérieures: la perspective juridique 691

After the referenda: the future of ethnic nationalism in Britain and Canada 562

Afterward: steps in the study of American political culture 64

Agenda for American federalism: restoring confidence and competence: the federal role in the federal system: the dynamics of growth 2

Agenda for Canada: towards a new liberalism 3350

An agenda-setting study of the coverage of the 1981 constitutional debate: a comparison 838

Agreement between Government of Canada and the Government of Newfoundland and Labrador concerning the restructuring of the Newfoundland fishery 2839

And no one cheered: federalism, democracy and the Constitution Act 668

Anglo-Quebec: demographic realities and options for the future 302

Les années d'impatience, 1950-1960 543

Annual report 1982 (Commissioner of Official Languages) 2306

Annual report 1983 (Commissioner of Official Languages) 2310

Annual report 1984 (Commissioner of Official Languages) 2307

Annual report 1984, part iv: the minority challenge - extract 319

Annual report 1985 (Commissioner of Official Languages) 2308

Annual report April 1, 1982 to March 31, 1983 (British Columbia. Ministry of Intergovernmental Affairs) 1491

Annual report April 1, 1983 to March 31, 1984 (British Columbia. Ministry of Intergovernmental Affairs) 1492

Annual Report April 1, 1984 to March 31, 1985 (British Columbia. Ministry of Intergovernmental Affairs) 1493

Annual report for the year ending March 31, 1982 (Saskatchewan Intergovernmental Affairs) 3363

Annual report for the year ending March 31, 1983 (Saskatchewan Intergovernmental Affairs) 3364

Appeals by the Provinces of Canada to the Attorney General of Canada 807

L'application de la Charte canadienne des droits et libertés aux rapports de droit privé 1089

Applying the Charter 1273

The appointment of federal regulatory commissioners: a case study of the CRTC 3088

An approach to the regulation of banking institutions in a federal state 2356

Approaches to a fiscal theory of political federalism 1942

Approaches to economic well-being 2670

The appropriate fiscal transfer to the Northwest Territories: a structure 1609

Are public goods public goods? 2782

Arguments for Maritime union 252

L'article 7 de la Charte - toujours énigmatique après 18 mois de jurisprudence 958

L'article 7 de la Charte canadienne des droits et libertés et les principes de justice fondamentale 925

L'article 96 de la Loi constitutionnelle de 1867 959

Les aspects économiques des programmes de sécurité financière pour les personnes âgées 2159

Aspects of the Constitutional debate: 1981 835

Aspects of the flexibility of Canadian federalism 44

Assam's attitude to federalism 168

Assessing the economic evidence ("Power shift west: myth or reality?") 545

Assessing the policy and operational implications of state constitutional change 1251

An assessment of DREE involvement in the manufacturing sector of the Saskatchewan economy 3115

Assessment of the impact of the National Energy Program on the long-haul freight movements from the Maritime provinces, prepared for Transport Canada, Strategic Planning Group 2629

An assessment of the National Energy Program 1980 3171

An assessment of the probable impact of aboriginal self-government in Canada 412

Assignment of corporate income taxes in a federal system 2766

The assignment of local government revenues in developing countries 2139

At doctrine's twilight: the structure of Canadian federalism 154

Atlantic Canada after Confederation: the Acadiensis reader 3232

Atlantic Canada and Confederation: essays in Canadian political economy 2112

Atlantic Canada before Confederation: the Acadiensis reader 3233

Atlantic Canada: the constitutional offshore regime 1146

Atlantic Provinces Economic Council - presentation to the House of Commons Standing Committee on Regional Development 2132

An Atlantic region political culture: a chimera 263

Au pays de Riel (2e partie) 567

Au pays de Riel (3e partie) 568

Au-delà du Parti québécois: lutte nationale et classes populaires 329

Australian federalism and nationalism: historical notes 144

Australian federalism system 104

Australian federalism, future tense 167

Australian housing policy and intergovernmental relations 1415

The Australian Loan Council and intergovernmental relations 1416

The Australian Loan Council: co-ordination of public debt policies in a federation 1914

Australian national government 887

Australian politics in a federal context 13

Australian processes for constitutional amendment 935

The Australian Senate 3300

Austrian experiences in utilizing federalism to conciliate ethnic minorities 75

Authority relations and legitimacy: a conflict analysis of Quebec nationalism 389

Les avantages économiques de la récupération des pouvoirs dans les domaines de la monnaie 2640

Awakening the slumbering giant: intergovernmental relations and federal grant law 1406

L'axe Québec - Etats-Unis 1472

Background information on equalization 1910

Background material prepared for the Canada West Foundation presented to the Special Joint Committee of the Senate and of the House of Commons on the Constitution of Canada November 25, 1980 789

The background of the Articles of Confederation 89

Banzhaf's power index and Canada's constitutional amending formula: a comment on Kilgour's analysis 1164

Bare bones: putting flesh on the skeleton of American federalism 224

Bargaining analysis in intergovernmental relations 2006

La bataille des gens de l'air 2964

La bataille des gens de l'air (2e partie) 2965

La bataille des gens de l'air (fin) 2966

Bâtir le Nunavut; un document de travail accompagné de propositions en vue d'une constitution de l'Arctique 655

Bâtisseur de pays: la pensée de Francois-Albert Angers 424

The battle for Canada 2210

The battle over bilingualism: the Manitoba language question, 1983-85 2456

Belgium: a regional state or a federal state in the making? 54

Beyond jurisdiction: judicial review and the Charter of Rights 1028

Beyond the B.N.A. Act: amendment and patriation 1134

Beyond the harvest: Canadian grain at the crossroads 3172

Bibliographie de l'histoire du Québec et du Canada, 1966-1975 3210

Bibliography of CRTC studies 2329

Biennial report of activities, April 1982-April 1984: The James Bay and Northern Quebec Agreement (chapter 22): Environmental Quality Act (chapter II) 315

Bilingual districts as an instrument in Canadian language policy 2349

Bilingual education and bilingualism: a review of research literature 2678

Bilingualism in Canadian air-traffic control 3063

Bilingualism in New Brunswick and the future of l'acadie 2538

Bilingualism in the federal Canadian public service 3086

Bill C-20: an evaluation from the perspective of current transportation policy and regulatory performance 2353

Bill S-31 and the federalism of state capitalism 2063

The birth of twin provinces 3307

Le Bloc populaire canadien and the origins of french-canadian neo-nationalism, 1942-48 264

Block grants - a federalist tool 2079

Block-funding and provincial spending on social programs 2647

A blueprint for economy recovery 1969

Bold statescraft, questionable jurisprudence 1287

Bora Laskin and federalism 1360

Brief - submitted by the National Indian Brotherhood to the Task Force on Federal-Provincial Fiscal Arrangements 1539

Brief presented to the Special Joint Committee on the Constitution - Saskatchewan.; patriation and amendment of the Constitution of Canada 790

Brief submission to the Parliamentary Task Force on Federal-Provincial Fiscal Arrangements 2048, 2790

Brief to the Federal-Provincial Task Force on Student Assistance 2872

Brief to the Ontario Council on University Affairs : a future of lost opportunities? 2396

Brief to the Select Committee on Foreign Affairs, House of Commons - subject: the legal and constitutional responsibilities of the Parliament of the United Kingdom with respect to the proposed Constitution Act, 1980 1193

Brief to the Special Joint Committee of the Senate and the House of Commons on the Constitution of Canada 788

Brief to the Special Joint Committee of the Senate and the House of Commons on the Constitution of Canada - Union of British Columbia Municipalities 791

Brief to the Special Joint Committee of the Senate and the House of Commons on the Constitution of Canada - Federation of Canadian Municipalities 796

Bringing all of New Brunswick laws into conformity with section 15 of the Canadian Charter of Rights and Freedoms 1190

Bringing home Canada's Constitution - Saskatchewan's position 1302

British Columbia - Washington State intergovernmental interrelations: some findings upon the failure of structure 2010

British Columbia and Canadian federalism 3358

British Columbia's constitutional proposals presented to the First Ministers' Conference on the Constitution October, 1978 719

British North America at Confederation: a study, prepared for the Royal Commission on Dominion-Provincial Relations 1602

Broken promises: the aboriginal constitutional conferences 954

The buckskin curtain: a discussion paper on aboriginal rights in the Constitution 1239

Building competitiveness: a white paper on economic development: province of Nova Scotia 2857

Building Nunavut: a working document with a proposal for an Arctic Constitution 1212

Building Nunavut: today and tomorrow 1213

The Bundesrat of the Federal Republic of Gernmany 3417

Le Bundesrat: la protection des intérêts des Länder selon la Loi fondamentale allemande 3226

Bureaucracy in Canada: control and reform 3385

Business law implications of the Canadian Charter of Rights and Freedoms 1176

Business-government relations in Canada: a conceptual map 2821

C.C.U. and the Constitution - the position of the Council for Canadian Unity concerning the proposed resolution on the Constitution 882

Le cadre historique et institutionnel des societés d'Etat au Québec 2891

Les caisses d'épargne et de crédit: agents de développement économique régional 2335

Les calculs stratégiques derrière le "Canada Bill" 1067

Can the market economy survive? 2698

Canada - notwithstanding: the making of the Constitution, 1976-1982 1281

The Canada Act 1982 1248

The Canada Act 1982 - some facts and comments 665

Canada and Quebec, past and future: an essay 1069

Canada and the burden of unity 1468

Canada and the Constitution 1979-1982: patriation and the Charter of Rights 1155

Canada and the constitutional question 1970-1980: themes and variations 1216

Canada and the entrance of Newfoundland into Confederation, 1939-1949 3308

Canada and the international political economic environment 3064

Canada and the new Constitution: the unfinished agenda 680

Le Canada après le référendum au Québec 602

Canada as a bicommunal polity 133

Canada as a family: Ontario responses to the Quebec independence movement 517

The Canada Assistance Plan: some background 2023

The Canada Assistance Plan: the ultimate in federalism 2472

Canada's new Charter of Rights 999

Canada's new Constitution - some personal reminiscences, impressions and feelings 1222

Canada's new Constitution: the struggle for human rights 952

Canada's new equalization program: description and evaluation 1592

Canada's North in the eighties 3158

Canada's population outlook: demographic futures and economic challenges 2514

Canada's recent experiment in the repatriation of American capital 3080

Canada's trading relationships in a changing world 2911

Canada, how powerful an ally? 3330

Le Canada, pourquoi l'impasse? 435

Canada-Alberta cooperation on native (Indian-Metis) development: memorandum of understanding 1554

Canada-Alberta Subsidiary Agreement on Northern Development 1524

Canada-Alberta Subsidiary Agreement on Northern Development between the Government of Canada, presented by the Minister of Regional Industrial Expansion and the Government of the Province of Alberta, represented by the Minister of Tourism and Small Business 1525

Canada-British Columbia Forest Resource Development Agreement (1985-1990) 2198

Canada-British Columbia Subsidiary Agreement on Intensive Forest Management 1496

Canada-Manitoba Mineral Development Agreement, 1984/89. Sector "A" geoscientific activities: progress report, 1984/1985 1909

Canada-Manitoba Northlands Agreement 1981-82 progress report: northern planning program 1911

Canada-Manitoba Subsidiary Agreement on Churchill 1555

Canada-Manitoba Subsidiary Agreement on Communications and Cultural Enterprises 1556

Canada-Manitoba Subsidiary Agreement on Transportation Development 1557

Canada-Manitoba Subsidiary Agreement on Urban Bus Industrial Development 1558

Canada-New Brunswick Agri-food Development Subsidiary Agreement 1984-1989 2224

Canada-New Brunswick Subsidiary Agreement on Fisheries Development under the Economic and Regional Development Agreement 1518

Canada-Newfoundland Rural Development Subsidiary Agreement Regional Development Programs 1519

Comparison of the role of the Supreme Court in Canada and the United States: a one-day conference 648

Compendium of university statistics 2130, 2131

Competing models of western growth: continued specialization in resources or greater diversification 3084

Compliance of Saskatchewan laws with Canadian Charter of Rights and Freedoms: discussion paper 1301

Comprehensive regulatory consultation in Canada's food processing industry 2202

Concentration et déconcentration des administrations publiques: une analyse de la structure spatiale de l'administration fédérale canadienne 3337

The concept of economic union in international and constitutional law 28

The concept of province-building: a critique 2083

Concepts of federalism 207

Concerted action in Quebec, 1976-1983: dialogue of the deaf 3387

La conclusion et la mise en oeuvre des traités dans le fédéralisme allemand 228

Condition of contemporary federalism: conflicting theories and collapsing constraints 3

Confederation 3271

Confederation and federal liberty 66

Confederation as a world example 1399

Confederation betrayed 635

The Confederation debate: the Constitution in crisis 1217

Confederation or western independence? 455

Confederation revisited: new light on British policy 3314

La "confédération" engloutie parmi les convulsions de reptiles 972

Confederation, unitary system federation; federalism throughout the world; the Common Market and the Canadian experience; aspects of the flexibility of Canadian federalism 45

Confederation: a new nationality 704

Conference freight rates and eastern Canadian ports 2204

Conflict and language planning in Quebec 2185

Conflict and opportunity: toward a new policy for Canada's pacific fisheries: a preliminary report of the Commission on Pacific Fisheries Policy 2225

Conflict management in the Canadian federal system 1905

Conflict of laws and constitutional law - extraterritorial provincial legislation 706

Conflict of taste and conflict of claim in federal countries 153

Constitutional law - federal power to amend the Constitution of Canada - reform of the Senate 1003

Constitutional law - Section 91(2) of the Constitution Act, 1867 - competition legislation 2509

Constitutional law of Canada 1013

Constitutional law of Canada: cases, notes, and materials 1118, 1119

Constitutional law of Canada; Canada Act 1982 annotated (combined ed.) 1014

Constitutional law: patriation of Canadian Constitution - Canada Act, 1982, ch. 11, incorporating the Constitution Act, 1982; Reference re Amendment of the Constitution of Canada, 125 D.L.R.3d 1 (1981) 640

Constitutional law: rearranging the administration of criminal justice 1245

Constitutional law: the doctrines of colorability and extra-territoriality 930

The constitutional misfire of 1982 1070

Constitutional patriation as prologue: phase two constitution-making and reform of federal institutions 1157

The constitutional patriation project, 1980-82 1158

Constitutional politics and the legacy of the provincial rights movement in Canada 1379

Constitutional politics and the West 963

The constitutional position of local government in Canada 966

Constitutional powers: cases on the separation of powers and federalism 18

Constitutional problems related to the creation and administration of Canada's national parks 2146

Constitutional procedure and the reform of the Supreme Court of Canada 1079

Constitutional protection of individual rights in Canada: the impact of the new Canadian Charter of Rights and Freedoms 1319

Constitutional reform 1004

Constitutional reform 1980 754

Constitutional reform Canadian-style: an economic perspective 707

Constitutional reform in Canada 1005

Constitutional reform in Switzerland: task distribution, political ideas and financial interests 125

Constitutional reform of the judicial branch: symbolic vs. operational considerations 1283

Constitutional reform: Canadian issues 1349

The constitutional right of Indian self-government 522

The constitutional rights of the aboriginal peoples of Canada 1154

Constitutional rights: extinguishment or entrenchment 447

The constitutional situation of the Nigerian states 1030

The constitutional status of the press in Canada 639

Constitutional theory and the Martland-Richie dissent 1095

The constitutional, legal, and historical background 3235

Constitutionalism, citizenship and society in Canada 731

The constitutionality of the Carriage by Air Act in Canada: Marier v. Air Canada 960

Constitutionally speaking - published by the Department of the Attorney-General to inform Manitobans about proposed constitutional amendments 1128

Les constitutions américaines et l'expérience canadienne 955

Constitutions of Canada: federal and provincial 747

Contraintes de la double légitimité 334

Consultation and budget secrecy: reforming the process of creating revenue budgets in the Canadian federal government 2695

The consultation process: prospects for 1987 and beyond 1617

Consultative regulation 2203

Consumer policy in the Canadian federal state 3041

Consumer protection, environmental law, and corporate power 2165

Consumers and the regulators: intervention in the federal regulatory process 2645

Contemporary Canadian politics 645

Contemporary western alienation: an option profile 379

Le contentieux fédéral/provincial sur la compétence en communication 2578

Continentalism and economic nationalism in the manufacturing sector: seeking middle ground 3001

Continuing Canadian constitutional dilemmas: essays on the constitutional history, public law and federal system of Canada 1083

The continuing debate about freer trade and its effects: a comment 2419

Continuity and renewal: the demands of excellence: a response to the discussion paper of the Commission on the Future Development of the Universities of Ontario, "Ontario universities 1984: issues and alternatives" 2398

Contrasting policy reactions: a reader's guide 2843

A contribution to the class and region debate 491

The control of natural resources through the trade and commerce power and proprietary rights 723

Le contrôle de la constitutionnalité des lois au lendemain de la Loi constitutionnelle de 1982 1270

Controlling interest: the Canadian gas and oil stakes 2413

Cooperative management of interprovincial water resources 2154

The determinants of the Canadian tariff structure before and after the Kennedy round: 1966, 1970 2144

Determining disrepute: opinion polls and the Canadian Charter of Rights and Freedoms 967

Deux nations or one Canada: John Diefenbaker at the 1967 Conservative convention 3243

Deux pays pour vivre: un plaidoyer 565

Deux questions au parti libéral 290

Developing the West's manufacturing potential: the role of provincial governments 2962

The development of American state Constitutions 1358

The development of Canadian energy policy 1970-1982: one man's view 3078

The development of health policy in Canada 3150

The development of Nigerian federalism 12

Developments in administrative law: the 1982-83 term 1182

Developments in constitutional law: the 1978-79 term 1111

Developments in constitutional law: the 1979-80 term 1112

Developments in constitutional law: the 1980-81 term 1097

Developments in constitutional law: the 1982-83 term 1393

Developments in constitutional law: the 1983-84 term 939

Le développement d'initiative locale 1615

Devolution as a political process: the case of Italy 132

Devolution or federalism?: options for a United Kingdom 41

The dilemma of nuclear regulations in Canada: political control and public confidence 2636

The dilemmas of cultural management in a federal state 2351

Discovering and developing English-Canadian nationalism in Quebec 303

Discussion paper on major bilateral issues: Canada - Newfoundland 1948

Discussion paper on the Denendeh government proposal 232

Discussion paper: economic circumstances and medium-term prospects by province 2247

Discussion paper: industrial adjustment policies 2244

Discussion paper: industrial research and development 2297

Discussion paper: transportation and national and regional perspective 2319

Disparities and interregional adjustment 2848

Disputed claims: Quebec/Canada 3360

Economic analysis of the Hibernia discovery and the related provincial and federal positions 2841

Economic and fiscal statement 2240

Economic and Regional Development Agreements - backgrounder 1510

The Economic Council's assessment, and the future 3095

Economic criteria for the assignment of functions in a federal system 91

Economic development and regional disparities: a comparative study of four federations 2609

The economic development of Western Canada: an historical overview 2885

Economic development policy: a case study in underdeveloped policy making 2705

Economic development strategy for Yukon for the 1980's - draft 3198

Economic diversification in the Canadian prairies: myth or reality? 2990

The economic effects of intervention in Canadian agriculture 2580

The economic geography of Prairie Canada in regional perspective 256

Economic growth in the Atlantic region, 1880-1940 2107

Economic implications of revenue-sharing alternatives 2176

Economic integration, national policies and the rationality of regional separatism 546

Economic management and the division of powers 885

Economic mobility in Canada: a comparative study 2593

Economic peripheralization and Quebec unrest 401, 402

Economic policy and electoral self interest: the allocations of the Department of Regional Economic Expansion 2716

Economic realities of contemporary Confederation 2749

Economic regulation and the British North America Act: Labatt Breweries and other constitutional imbroglios 1113

Economic regulation and the federal system 3019

Economic regulation in Canada: a survey 2088

Economic rents, province-building, and interregional adjustment: a two-region general equilibrium analysis 2852

The economics of a separate West 526

The economics of Constitution making 1384

The economics of federalism 93

Ecrits polémiques 287

Edouard Montpetit et le régionalisme 2982

Energy policy and industrial activity: a reply 2605

An energy policy of British Columbia 2831

Energy policy, taxation of natural resources, and fiscal federalism 2791

Energy policy; overview and macroeconomic implications 3175

Energy price increases, economic rents, and industrial structure in a small regional economy 2853

Energy revenues: consequences for the rest of Canada 1599

The energy squeeze: Canadian policies for survival 3173

Energy, Canadian federalism and the West 2850

Energy, Mines and Resources, the energy ministry and the National Energy Program 2441

Enfin, le livre blanc 404

The enforcement of the Canadian Charter of Rights and Freedoms: an analysis of section 24 1151

Enforcing the Charter: some thoughts on an appropriate and just standard for judicial review 940

English Canadian nationalists and the Canadian character 1957-1974 473

The English fact in Quebec 245

Les enjeux de la réforme du Sénat 3254

Entering the eighties: Canada in crisis 2350

Entre le changement et l'indiscipline 2008

Entrenchment by executive action: a partial solution to "legislative override" 1313

The entrenchment of a Bill of Rights 1309

Entrenchment revisited: the effect of the Canadian Charter of Rights and Freedoms 1307

The environment and the Constitution 3200

Environment Canada and the North: the perceptions, roles and policies of the Department of the Environment regarding development north of 60: discussion paper 2267

Environment Canada's options for intervention in energy: a report 2650

The environment for policy-making in Canada and the United States 3022

Environmental issues 1574

Environmental monitoring of federal and provincial projects 2271

L'épargne au Québec 2804

Equality issues in federal law: a discussion paper 766

Equality rights and the Canadian Charter of Rights and Freedoms 673

The equality rights in the Canadian Charter of Rights and Freedoms 1363

Federal government regional economic development policies: an evalvative survey 2703

Federal government response on land claims policies and processes 310

The federal government's policy and expenditure management system: bureaucratic perceptions of expenditure control, accountability and improved decision-making 3368

Federal governments and university science research: a comparison of practices in the United States and Canada 2360

Federal grants to states 1926

Federal health care policy 2133

Federal ideas in contemporary Ireland 52

The federal impact of financing higher education in Canada 2343

Federal Indian policy and Indian self-government in Canada: an analysis of a current proposal 479

Federal policy and the role of public enterprise in the mining sector 2928

Federal policy-making for Métis and non-status Indians in the context of native policy 628

Federal principles of organization and ethnic communities 163

Federal proposal to reduce health and post-secondary education financing 2934

Federal-provincial financial equalization and the Canadian Constitution 1455

Federal regulation and public policy in the Canadian petroleum industry: 1958-1975 2143

Federal regulation of nuclear facilities in Canada: better safe than sorry 3083

The federal role in the federal system: the dynamics of growth. Intergovernmentalizing the classroom: federal involvement in elementary and secondary education 2091

The federal role in the federal system: the dynamics of growth. Hearings on the federal role 1407

The federal role in the federal system: the dynamics of growth. Public assistance: The growth of a federal function 2090

Federal roles in wildlife management in Canada 2190

Federal sales tax reform in Canada: some parallels with Australia 1886

Federal states and federal societies, with special reference to Canada 199

Federal transfer payments: a Quebec perspective 2011

Federal transfer payments: centralization or decentralization 2051

Federal urban transport policy formulation in Canada and Australia 2028

A federal view of consultation 1897

Federal, provincial and local language legislation in Manitoba and the franco-Manitobans 2540

Federal, provincial, and municipal government in aquaculture 3163

The federal government and tripartism 2089

A federal-provincial affairs perspective 2489

Federal-provincial co-operation in water: an exploratory examination 2281

Federal-provincial collaboration: the Canada-New Brunswick general development agreement 2022

Federal-provincial conditional transfers: from cost-sharing to block funding 1929

The Federal-Provincial Conference of First Ministers, 1960-1976 1839

Federal-Provincial Development Agreements Branch: a status report 1954

Federal-provincial diplomacy: re-negotiating EPF-1982 2033

Federal-provincial discussions raise some key issues 1770

Federal-provincial finances 2047

Federal-Provincial First Ministers' Conferences, 1906-1985 1570

Federal-Provincial Fiscal Arrangements and Federal Post-Secondary Education and Health Contributions Act, 1977: B1976-77, C.10 amended by 1980-81-82-82, CC. 46, 48, 94, 121; 1984, CC. 6, 13, 3 1508

Federal-provincial fiscal arrangements and the search for fiscal equity through reformulation of the equalization program 1605

The federal-provincial fiscal arrangements for 1982-87 1976

Federal-provincial fiscal arrangements in the eighties : a submission to the Parliamentary Task Force on the Federal-Provincial Fiscal Arrangements 1546

Federal-provincial fiscal arrangements, 1982-1987 1945

Federal-provincial fiscal arrangements: interns' and residents' views: 2321

Federal-provincial fiscal issues in Canada 1901

Federal-provincial fiscal relations: an historical perspective 1885

Federal-provincial fiscal relations: some background 1619

Federal-provincial implications of various concepts of Indian sclf-government 1943

Federal-provincial insurance for hospital and physician's care in Canada 2589

Federal-provincial Mineral Development Agreements: annual report 1980-81 2286

Federal-provincial professionalism 2050

Federal-provincial relations and support for universities 2393

Federal-provincial relations and the making of public policy in Canada: a review of case studies 1816

Federal-provincial relations: education Canada 2626, 2627

Government of Canada policies for regional development 2765

The Government of Canada's investment in science: an overview of federal science activities, 1982/83 2299

The Government of Canada's support for technology development 2300

Government officials and the study of policy-making 3381

Government oil companies: "quo-vadis"? 3218

Government policy: the present context of financial support 2919

Government procurement policies: GATT, the EEC, and the United States 2558

Government regulation of business in a federal state: allocation of power under deregulation 2846

Government regulation: scope, growth, process 3068

Government response to representations for change to the proposed resolution respecting the Constitution of Canada 775

Governments and health care in Canada: the sharing of cost and control 3134

The governors' push for emergency energy powers 135

Le grand jeu du bilinguisme 2969

Group rights individual rights in the Charter: the special cases of natives and quebecois 519

The growing role of the Quebec state in language corpus planning 3031

The growth of government transfer payments to individuals 1977

The growth of the government sector of Prince Edward Island 3344

Guaranteed representation of aboriginal peoples in institutions of public government: constitutional development in the western Northwest Territories 1124

La guerre de la centralisation 423

La guide du citoyen sur la question constitutionnelle 1326

Guide on the audit of federal contributions 2309

Guide to Canadian ministries since Confederation: July 1, 1967 - February 1, 1982 3238

Guide to intergovernmental programs 2866

A guide to the Economic Development Agreement in the Northwest Territories: building a better future 1952

Guidelines for an annual air quality index - report by the Federal-Provincial Committee on Air Pollution 2261

Half the constitutional story is still to be told 1108

L'harmonie fédérale-provinciale est-elle toujours essentielle? 2021

Harmonization of business law in Canada 888

The harmonization of federal and provincial environmental policies: the changing legal and policy framework 2706

An "industrial strategy" for Canada 2414

Inequality: essays on the political economy of social welfare 2809

The infested blanket: Canada's Constitution and the genocide of Indian nations 571

Inflation and the taxation of personal investment income: an Ontario Economic Council position paper on the Canadian 1982 reform proposals 2868

The influence of fiscal incentives on interregional migration: Canada 1961-78 2794

The influence of U.S. jurisprudence on the interpretation of the Canadian Charter of Rights 879

Influential models of political association in the western tradition 120

Information pamphlets relating to constitutional development and division of the Northwest Territories 3400

Information paper: statute law (Canadian Charter of Rights and Freedoms) 2246

Initiatives pour un autre développement: le Canada en 1979: un inventaire des initiatives visant un autre type de développement pour le Canada: report 2268

An inquiry into provincial jurisdiction over uranium development in Saskatchewan 2861

Institutional and constitutional arrangements: an overview 143

Institutional conservatism: federalism and pension reform 2149

Institutional reforms for representative government 3211

Institutions, constitutions, and public policies: a public-choice overview 3382

Integration and autonomy in Canada-United States relations, 1963-1972 1618

Intégration et diversité: les dilemmes du fédéralisme canadien 108

The Inter-State Commission and Australian transport 2956

The interaction of federal and territorial income tax rates: the case of the Northwest Territories 1610

Interdepartmental coordination and northern development 2086

Interest groups in the Canadian federal system 211

Interest groups, representation and conflict management in the Standing Committees of the House of Commons 3372

Intergovernmental aspects of major resource projects and their infrastructure 1421

Intergovernmental Canada: government by conference? A fiscal and economic perspective 2074

An intergovernmental commission for economic policy? 2003

Intergovernmental cooperation among the governments of New Brunswick, Nova Scotia and Prince Edward Island 1589

International law and the "patriation" of the Canadian Constitution 1159

The international legal environment 2948

The international legal environment: an overview 2949

Interpreting and applying the limitations clause: an analysis of Section 1 843

Interpreting the Charter - use of the earlier versions as an aid 934

The interprovincial and international impact of federal grants to provincial governments: evidence from the Canadian federation 2410

Interprovincial barriers 2568

Interprovincial barriers to trade in agricultural products 2788

Interprovincial barriers to trade in agriculture products 2227

Interprovincial comparisons of university financing: fifth report of the Tripartite Committee on Interprovincial Comparisons 2876

Interprovincial comparisons of university financing: sixth report of the Tripartite Committee on Interprovincial Comparisons 2875

Interprovincial comparisons of university financing: third report of the Tripartite Committee on Interprovincial Comparisons 2874

Interprovincial comparisons of university financing: fifth report of the Tripartite Committee on Interprovincial Comparisons 3112

Interprovincial comparisons of university financing: fourth report 3111

Interprovincial comparisons of university financing: seventh report of the Tripartite Committee on Interprovincial Comparisons 3114

Interprovincial comparisons: day care facilities, full-day programs: October, 1982 2103

Interprovincial economic co-operation - towards the development of a Canadian common market 2877

Interprovincial migration data: a supplement to "internal migration and fiscal structure" 3179

Interprovincial mobility rights under the Charter 1027

Interprovincial product liability litigation 3033

Interprovincial product liability litigation: jurisdiction, enforcement and choice of law 2229

Interprovincial product liability litigation: jurisdiction, enforcement and choice of law in Quebec - private international law 2230

Interprovincial standards program - a model of flexibility and cooperation 2312

Interprovincial trade and the welfare effects of marketing boards 3096

Interregional economic impacts of the Alberta Alsands project 2460

Intertemporal changes in regional productivity in Canadian manufacturing 2435

The law of Union-state relations and Indian federalism 127

The law of your land: a practical guide to the new Canadian Constitution 1061

Law reform in Canada: diversity or uniformity? 1181

Law reform in Canada: the impact of the provincial law reform agencies on uniformity 1133

Law, policy and statutory interpretation under a constitutionally entrenched Canadian Charter of Rights and Freedoms 670

Law, politics and the Manitoba school question: Supreme Court and Privy Council 662

Lawmaking by the people : referendums and plebiscites in Canada 3228

Leading constitutional decisions: cases on the British North America Act 1289

Lean times: policies and constraints: Economic Council of Canada nineteenth annual review 1982 2481

Lecture du Livre blanc et du Livre beige selon une perspective 'super-fédéraliste' 1469

The legacy of the Articles of Confederation 170

The legacy of the Supreme Court of Canada's approach to the Canadian Bill of Rights 1017

Legal and jurisdictional aspects of interbasin transfers 2901

Legal process and the resolution of Indian claims 344

Legal protection of human rights: the contemporary Canadian experience 1237

Legal rights in the Canadian Charter of Rights and Freedoms: a manual of issues and sources 1144

The legal rights provisions - a new vision or déjà vu? 976

The legal status of the federal administration 1071

Legal theory and the "patriation" debate 1045

Legality, legitimacy and the Supreme Court 1269

La législation linguistique fédérale 2893

Legislative interaction of a Canadian province and an American state: thoughts upon sub-national cross border relations 2009

Less equal than others 1838

Lessons from the National Energy Program 2341

Let Quebec go 391

Letter sent to all Premiers on April 19, 1975 on the patriation of the Constitution 799

Lettre à René Lévesque 575

Liberal democracy and the challenge of nationalism in Canadian politics 453

The Liberal Party and the Canadian state 3405

Liberal priorities 1982: the limits of scheming virtuously 2444

Liberal-democratic society and government in Canada constitutional development in the western Northwest Territories 892

Liberalism or liberty, an assessment of Canada's new Constitution 1404

The Liberals and the opposition: ideas, priorities and the imperatives of governing Canada in the 1980's 2445

The limitation of liberty: a consideration of Section 1 of the Charter of Rights and Freedoms 833

Limitations on legislative override under the Canadian Charter of Rights and Freedoms 651

The limits of consultation: a debate among Ottawa, the provinces and the private sector on industrial strategy: a discussion paper 2200

Limits on western growth 492

Linguistic dispersal in Canada 1951-1976 2664

Linguistic minority educational rights in Canada: an international and comparative perspective 2696

Linking Canada's new solitudes: the executive interchange program and business-government relations 2178

Literacy and economic development in nineteenth-century Newfoundland 2109

Living treaties: lasting agreements. Report of the Task Force to Review Comprehensive Claims Policy 351

Le Livre beige et le pouvoir d'urgence 3221

Local and regional government in the Northwest Territories 3275

Local development - conceptual bases and policy implications 2365

Local fiscal reform in Alberta? - a review and assessment of the report of Alberta's Provincial-Municipal Finance Council 2769

Local fiscal response to intergovernmental transfers 2045

Local government and Canadian federalism 1891

Local government and Canadian federalism: review and assessment 1892

Local government in the Canadian provincial north 3397

Local government systems of Australia 1422

The local state in Canada: theoretical perspectives 1904

La logique du Québec: project de manifeste électoral 540

La Loi constitutionnelle de 1982, droit des autochtones 1215

La loi constitutionnelle de 1982 782

The long road to a fresh start? - the First Ministers' Conference on Aboriginal Rights 2015

Long-run effects of the Canadian national energy agreements 3023

The Lougheed legacy 3412

M. François-Albert Angers et l'indépendance fiscale 1830

M. Trudeau ou le triomphe de l'échec 374

The machinery of government in Canada 3258

The Mackenzie river basin study report - a report under the 1978-81 federal-provincial study agreement respecting the water and related resources of the Mackenzie river basin 2285

Macroeconomic perspectives of Canada-U.S. trade agreements 2157

"Maintaining a Constitution worthy of such a country:" reflections on values in Canadian society 1167

Maitre chez who? The Quebec veto reference 1246

Major Canadian projects: major Canadian opportunities: a report 2226

Major government programs affecting the competitive position of provincial livestock industries in British Columbia, Alberta, Saskatchewan, Manitoba, Ontario, and Quebec, prepared for Alberta Economic Development 2651

Major projects inventory issue 2 2248

A major shift in Canada's energy policy: impact of the National Energy Program 2779

The making of Italy as an experiment in constitutional choice 1293

The management of a common property resource: fisheries policy in Atlantic Canada 2755

Management of federal petroleum lands in Canada 2619

Managing Alberta water: the decision-making process 2661

Managing all our resources: a development plan for Newfoundland and Labrador, 1980-85 2838

Managing Canada's North: challenges and opportunities - rapporteurs summary and comments 2575

Managing community development in the New Federalism 117

Managing diversity: federal-provincial collaboration and the Committee on Extension of Services to Northern and Remote Communities 2820

Managing federalism: evolution and development of the grant-in-aid system 2030

Managing federalism: studies in intergovernmental relations 107

Managing oil and natural gas law, policy and intergovernmental relations in the Canadian and American West 2988

Manifestations of Elazar's political subcultures: state opinion and the content of political campaign advertising 115

Manitoba constitutional reference: re an act for expediting the decision of constitutional and other provincial questions, C.C.S.M., C. C180 and re a reference pursuant thereto by the Lieutenant Governor in Council 1127

Ministry of Intergovernmental Affairs Ontario 1962

Minorities and the Canadian state 525

Minorities and the Canadian visual media 366

Minorities as an attitudinal phenomenon: a comparative analysis of youth elites 524

Minority language education in Quebec and anglophone Canada 2721

Minority language education rights 650

Minute Ottawa. Constitution 1263

Minutes of proceedings and evidence of the Special Committee on the Federal-Provincial Fiscal Arrangements 1548

Minutes of proceedings and evidence of the Special Joint Committee of the Senate and the House of Commons on the Constitution of Canada - 3rd session, 32nd Parliament,1980-81 792

Miracles of survival; Canada and French Canada 2032

Mise à jour 1967-1982 de la Cour suprême et la Constitution 1074

Mixed enterprises in Canada 3261

Mobility of capital in the Canadian economic union 2983

Mobility rights in Canada 1308

Mobility rights under the Charter 1065

Mobility rights: personal mobility and the Canadian economic union 2975

The mobilization of bias in closed systems: environmental regulation in Canada 3012

Modern capitalist planning and Canadian federalism: the case of high-technology industries 2433

Modern federalism: an analytic approach 105

Monitoring migration in the Prairie provinces: administrative data sources and methodologies 3074

More questions than answers 336

More strategy for culture: more proposals for a federal policy for the arts and the cultural industries in Canada 2325

More than a poor majority: the story of Newfoundland's confederation with Canada 3395

More than survival: viewpoints toward a theology of nation 588

Motivations 509

Mr. Justice Rand and Canada's federal Constitution 1080

Mr. Trudeau and the West 615

Mr. Trudeau's Constitution: going in style 654

Les MRC et la décentralisation: conception de l'aménagement et extension des compétences 3279

Multicultural regionalism: toward understanding the Canadian West 373

Multiculturalism and Canadian nation-building 293

Multiculturalism and the metaphysics of pluralism 577

Multiculturalism ideology, policy and reality 449

Multiculturalism in Canada: a muddle 296

Multiculturalism in two countries: the Canadian and Australian experience 432

Municipal finance 3205

Municipal government in a new Canadian federal system: report of the Resource Task Force on Constitutional Reform, Federation of Canadian Municipalities, Ottawa 1995

Municipal government in the new Canadian federal system: second report 1996

The municipal government reform movement and Alberta 3204

Municipal wastewater disinfection in Canada: need and application: a report of the Working Group on Wastewater Dinsinfection to the Federal-Provincial Advisory Committee on Environmental and Occupational Health 2504

Municipalities and the division of powers 1836

Nation, state and territorial unity: a trans-outaouais view 300

Nation-building and the Canadian Charter of Rights and Freedoms 1047

Nation-building as body-building: a comparative study of the personalization of city, province and state by anglophone and francophone Canadians 461

The national accounts budgets by province, 1983 2903

National and regional economic development strategies: perspectives on Canada's problems and prospects: colloquium proceedings 3147

National and regional interests in the North 2824

National consultation: problems and prospects 2415

The national deal: the fight for a Canadian Constitution 1323

The national energy conflict 2600

The National Energy Program 2232, 2263

The National Energy Program and the pursuit of claims under international law 3000

National Energy Program mccts falling world oil prices 2606

The National Energy Program: update 1982 2264

National fisheries policy: the perspective of industry 2808

A national fishery policy for Canada: dream or debacle 2608

National images and national maintenance: the ascendancy of the ethnic idea in North America 597

National policy and agrarian development: a reassessment 2756

National policy and prairie agrarian development: a reassessment 2659

National political parties and regional diversity: notes for the Kenneth R. Mac-Gregor Lecturer, Queen's University, Monday, February 25, 1985 3383

National separatism 633

National standards in public services 1898

Nationalism and federalism in Yugoslavia, 1963-1983 171

Nationalism and independence: an economic problem 610

Nationalism, liberalism, and federalism: elements of Canada's constitutional crisis 1046

Nationalism, nationalization, and social communications: an economic perspective on the Canadian case 2829

Nationalisme et multiculturalisme au Canada: affinités et problèmes 450

Nationalisme et régionalisme dans la crise canadienne: essai d'interprétation géographique 573

Nationalizing oil in the 1970s 2552

Native claims in Rupert's Land and the North-west Territory: Canada's constitutional obligations 504

Native claims: negotiating social contracts for the North 359

Native history, native claims and self-determination 270

The native interface: an emerging role in government-native relations 371

Native people and the Constitution of Canada - the report of the Métis and Non-status Indian Constitutional Review Commission 523

The native peoples of Canada and the Canadian Constitution 814

Native proposals for constitutional reform 520

Native rights and self-determination 271

Natural gas pricing in Canada: an economic analysis 2845

Natural resource jurisdiction and political development in the North: the case of Nunavut 2439

Natural resource prosperity: boon or burden for Canadian federalism? 2772

Natural resource revenues and Canadian federalism: a survey of the issues 2040

Natural resource revenues and federal-provincial fiscal arrangements 1980

Natural resources and national politics: a look at three Canadian resource industries 2758

Natural resources and the Constitution: some recent developments and their implications for the future regulation of the resource industries 991

Natural resources and the new Constitution 1093

The natural resources development debate in Canada 2796

New management initiatives: initial results from the Ministerial Task Force on Program Review 2292

New notions of happiness: nationalism, regionalism and Atlantic Canada 235, 2110

The new oil price scenario and the Chretien - Zaozirny agreement: a comment 3008

A new perspective on environmental rights after the Charter 3071

The new power focus in Ottawa: the Ministry of State for Economic and Regional Development 2416

The new Spanish state structure 155

New stresses on Confederation: diverging regional economies 2336

Newfoundland constitutional reference: re a reference by the Lieutenant-Governor in Council concerning the effect and validity of the amendments to the Constitution of Canada sought in the proposed resolution 1191

Newfoundland continental shelf dispute in the Supreme Court of Canada 2545

Newfoundland groundfishery: some options for renewal 2984

Newfoundland in the nineteenth and twentieth centuries: essays in interpretation 3284

Newfoundland offshore claims 1025

The Newfoundland offshore jurisdictional dispute: a postscript 2729

Newfoundland offshore mineral rights 2546

Newfoundland reference: an update 3047

Newfoundland resources: the Supreme Court strikes again 1180

Newfoundland's position on extension of services 1946

Newfoundland's union with Canada, 1949: conspiracy of choice? 3321

Ni fédéralisme renouvelé ni souveraineté-association 380

Ni l'histoire, ni l'évolution politique redonnent ouverture au scénario de Pierre Trudeau 702

No small measure: the Progressive Conservatives and the Constitution 1214

No to renewed federalism no to sovereignty - association 436

Non-fuel minerals and Canadian foreign policy: negotiating from strength and weakness 2334

Non-majoritarian democracy: a comparison of federal and consociational theories 136

Nontariff barriers to interprovincial trade in swine 2362

Normative tax theory for a federal polity: some public choice preliminaries 2195

The North 1391

North - overview of the land, the people, a guide to early history, recent constitutional and political developments 309

NWT - Canada Resource Management and Revenue Sharing Agreement: a proposal for settlement, draft No. 5 1953

Les objets de négociations fédérales-provinciales dans la révision constitutionnelle 1056

Observations des évêques du Québec sur la question constitutionnelle 656

Of customs and coalitions: the formation of Canadian federal parliamentary alliances 3384

Of judges and rights or should Canada have a constitutional Bill of Rights 1385

L'offensive d'Ottawa se poursuit 2468

Official-language populations in Canada: patterns and contacts 2347

An official-languages policy for Ontario 2348

The offshore jurisdiction of the states of the United States and the provinces of Canada 2357

Offshore petroleum agreements: an analysis of the Nova Scotian and Newfoundland experience 2152

Oil and gas revenue sharing: beyond legal foundations and constraints 2667

Oil and gas under the Constitution 663

Oil and gas: Ottawa, the provinces, and the petroleum industry 2682

Old and new money ("Power shift west: myth or reality?") 236

Old myths and new choices: railway freight rates and western economic development 3026

On interpreting simulations with a macroeconometric model: comment: the impact of higher energy prices in Canada 2644

On mérite mieux que ça (à propos du document Ryan) 471

On the analysis of constitutional change in Canada - comments 1346

On the dangers of bickering in a federal state: some reflections on the failure of the national party system 225

Once more, with feeling: brief to the Ontario Council on University Affairs 2399

One piece of a larger problem: the Economic Council on regulation 2776

One prairie province: historical and political perspectives 3396

Only in Canada: reflections on the Charter's notwithstanding clause 1063

Ontario papers on federal-provincial fiscal arrangements: reprinted and summarized for the meeting of Provincial Ministers of Finance, Victoria, B.C., June 25 and 26, 1981 1960

Ontario universities 1984: issues and alternatives: background data 2369

Ontario universities statistical compendium: 1970-71 to 1979-80. part a: macro-indicators 2387

Ontario universities statistical compendium: 1970-71 to 1980-81. part b: supporting data 2388

Ontario universities statistical compendium: 1970-71 to 1981-82, part a: macro-indicators 2389

Ontario universities statistical compendium : 1970-71 to 1982-83, part a: macro-indicators 2390

Ontario universities: options and future 2188

Ontario's perspective on Canadian federalism today - an address by the Hon. Thomas L. Wells, Minister of Intergovernmental Affairs, Province of Ontario to the Royal Commission Society, London, England 1963

Ontario's smarter idea 3329

Ontario, 1610-1985: a political and economic history 3408

Opportunities for industry and business in Canada; regional development incentives 2249

Opposition to multiculturalism among quebecois and english-canadians 2671

Optimal fiscal balance and provincial-local finance 1456

The optimal provision of public goods in a system of local government 3168

The optimal savings question: an Alberta perspective 3338

An optimal taxation approach to fiscal federalism 2555

Optimality in local debt limitation 3128

Optimality, 'public' goods, and local governments: a general theoretical analysis 2895

Organizational differentiation and integration: the case of regional economic development policy in Canada 2135

Origins and meaning of Section 92a: the 1982 constitutional amendment on resources 1161

The origins of public enterprise in the Canadian mineral sector: three provincial case studies: a study 2929

Origins of the Canadian amendment dilemma 1338

Orthodoxie fédéraliste et relations régionales transfrontières: une menace illusoire 1476

Other sources of financing for post-secondary education and research in Canada 2887

The Ottawa accord and the resolution of the Canadian Parliament: now who has our Constitution? 1131

Ottawa and the provinces: regional perspectives 2004

Ottawa and the provinces: the distribution of money and power 1588

Ottawa's expenditure "envelopes": workable rationality at last? 2182

Ottawa's expenditure process, four systems in search for co-ordination 3392

Perspectives on Canadian health and social services policy: history and emerging trends 2783

Perspectives on economic policy: a discussion paper second draft 2269

Perspectives on regions and regionalism in Canada 629

Perspectives on regions and regionalism in Canada : proceedings of the Annual Conference of the Association for Canadian Studies, held at the University of Ottawa, June 8-10, 1982 251

Perspectives on the Canadian economic union 2662

Perspectives on the harmonization of law in Canada 890

Perspectives pour l'élaboration d'une politique culturelle, stratégie II: nouvelle contribution à la formulation d'une politique fédérale sur les arts et les industries culturelles au Canada 2371

Petro-Canada: tool for energy security or instrument of economic development? 3339

Petroleum taxation and efficiency: the Canadian system in question 3129

Petroleum and natural gas and constitutional change 1091

Peuple sans nom: oui à notre nom de canadiens non au sobriquet de québécois on est canadien ou bien on ne l'est pas 576

Physicians and Medicare: professional ideology and Canadian health care policy 3073

Pierre Elliott Trudeau's imprint on the Charter of Rights and Freedoms 708

The place of the prairie West in the Canadian Confederation 347

Le plaisir de la liberté: entretiens 288

Planning and the economy: building federal-provincial consensus 3102

Plebiscite: essai 278

Plus ça change, plus c'est la même chose: reflections on the Canadian general elections of 1984 3265

Le point sur la situation énergétique: internationale, canadienne, québécoise: rapport au Conseil de planification et de développement du Québec: 30 juin 1982 2375

Polarization and depolarization of Quebec political parties 3286

Policy for Canada's Atlantic Fisheries in the 1980's: a discussion paper 2243

Political and constitutional development in the N.W.T. and Yukon: the issues and the interests 1392

Political authority and crisis in comparative perspective 3222

Political change in the "new West" 407

Political constraints and the province-building objective 2052

Political culture and the quality of urban life 121

Political culture in the West 3378

The political culture of Quebec, 1840-1960 3282

Political culture, interparty competition and political efficacy 95

Political cultures of the American compound republic 122

The political economy of Canadian Constitution-making: the Canadian economic union issue 884

A political economy of continentalism 3319

The political economy of economic adjustment 3106

The political economy of energy 3105

The political economy of federalism 49

The political economy of fishing in Newfoundland 2111

The political economy of oil in Alberta 3032

The political economy of policy instruments: tax expenditures and subsidies in Canada 3414

The political economy of province-building: Alberta's development strategy, 1971-1981 3340

The political economy of Quebec: a selective annotated bibliography 3391

Political economy of the Canadian welfare state 2175

The political economy of urban health policy 2567

Political ideas in Quebec and the evolution of Canadian constitutional law, 1945 to 1985 1059

Political ideology and social policy: expenditure and revenue in three Canadian provinces, 1947-1960 3315

The political implementation of multiculturalism 481

Political parties and the state since 1960 3335

Political parties and the survival of Canada 3380

Political parties, provinces and Canadian foreign policy: Trudeau and beyond 1578

The political purposes of the Canadian Charter of Rights and Freedoms 1286

Political rights: and the legal framework of elections in Canada 3229

Political science 322 (text): Federalism in Canada 43

Political structure and the pursuit of economic objectives 2785

Political support in Canada: the crisis years 3296

The political theory of covenant: biblical origin and modern developments 69

The political wisdom of Sir John A. Macdonald 3341

Politically active minorities: political participation in Canadian democracy 335

Politics and constitutional reform in Canada: a study in political opposition 837

Politics and education: cases from eleven nations 3099

Politics and government of urban Canada 1809

Politics and health: cooperative spirit is essential 2978

Politics in federal states: approaches to the study of comparative federalism 81

The politics of Canada's economic relationship with the United States: an introduction 3066

The politics of Canada's economic relationship with the United-States 3065

The politics of Canadian airport development: lessons for federalism 2507

The politics of Canadian economic policy: an overview 2448

The politics of Canadian public policy 3209

The politics of constitution-making: the experience of the United Kingdom 1035

The politics of constitutional change 1122, 1123

The politics of constitutional conservatism 728

The politics of constitutional renewal in Canada 730

The politics of development in Canada's North 2417

The politics of economic development in Canada 3101

The politics of economic policy 2449

The politics of energy: the development and implementation of the NEP 2455

Politics of federalism: Ontario's relations with the federal government, 1867-1942 1452

The politics of freight rates 2426

The politics of gender, ethnicity and language in Canada 301

The politics of health care in Canada 2377

The politics of official bilingualism in Canada 2490

The politics of positive sum 2059

The politics of provincial resource policy 2355

The politics of subnational governance 2084

The politics of survival: federal states in the third world 148

Politics, policy and federalism: defining the role of the Institute of Intergovernmental Relations 1899

Politics, public administration and Canada's aging population 2652

Politics: Canada 1822

Politique d'assimilation et d'anglicisation 570

La politique énergétique canadienne et les provinces de l'Atlantique 3164

Politiques nationales, conjonctures régionales: la stabilisation économique 2669

Poor persons and poor governments: economic criteria for the distribution function and its performance in the American federation 1834

Public-sector politics, modernization, and federalism - the Canadian and American experiences 197

A pure theory of local expenditures 3104

The purposes of American state Constitutions 1094

The push for reprivatization of health care services in Canada, Britain, and the United State 3151

Pussycat, pussycat or patriation and the new constitutional amendment processes 1315

La qualité de la langue après la loi 101: actes du colloque, Québec, 30 septembre-3 octobre 1979 2942

Quebec alienation and the trend toward centralization 534

Quebec and Canada: past, present, and future 387

Quebec at the hour of choice 253

The Quebec cauldron 3407

The Quebec cauldron: a recent account 3406

Québec d'abord: le PLQ et le projet fédéral de modification constitutionnelle 2012

Le Québec doit être représenté à Ottawa par des députés souverainistes 1941

Le Québec et le "repatriement" de la Constitution canadienne 1247

Le Québec et le Canada: les voies de l'avenir 368

Le Québec et ses pêches maritimes: une analyse des politiques et des programmes 2422

Le Québec et son destin international: les enjeux géopolitiques 620

Le Québec fait-il encore partie du Canada? 1168

Quebec first: the PLQ and the federal proposal to amend the Constitution 2013

Quebec has the right to choose 437

Quebec in isolation 690

The Quebec independence movement 426

Quebec nationalism in a comparative perspective 511

Quebec nationalism in crisis 340

Québec: partenaire majeur ou province minorisée? 974

The Quebec problem: an inquiry into the ethics of sovereignty and secession 529

The Quebec protestant churches and the question of nationalism 486

The Quebec referendum: national or provincial event 599

Quebec state and society 400

Quebec turns to technology 2663

The Quebec veto reference: a constitutional postscript 712

La réforme du Sénat canadien à la lumière d'expériences étrangères 3336

La réforme des institutions centrales: quelques jalons 3216

La réforme des relations fédérales-provinciales: introduction 1577

La réforme municipale du gouvernement du Québec: une analyse de la décentralisation 3220

Reforming Canada's financial institutions 3049

Reforming Canadian federalism 382

Reforming Parliament 3247

Reforming regulation 2482

Reforming taxes: some problems of implementation 3060

Reforming the financing arrangements for post-secondary education in Canada 2847

Le régime d'épargne-actions du Québec: mal réellement nécessaire? 2183

The regime of tolerance 689

Region, class and political culture in Canada 536

Regional and linguistic agenda-setting in Canada: a study of newspaper coverage of issues affecting political integration in 1976 601

Regional aspects of Confederation 631

Regional considerations and Canadian trade policies: summary of the proceedings of a research symposium 2576

The regional decline of a national party: Liberals on the prairies 3379

Regional development and collective intervention 326

Regional development and optimal management of the Prince Edward Island lobster fishery 2532

Regional development and the European Community: a Canadian perspective 2750

Regional development and the local community: planning, politics, and social context 3143

Regional development in Ontario: federal and provincial involvement 2672

Regional development in Quebec; intervention by the federal and provincial governments 2675

Regional development matters 2692

Regional development policy in the next decade 2774

Regional disparities 2912

Regional disparities and economic development 2743

Regional disparities in Canada 2483

Regional disparity, migration and economic adjustment: a reappraisal 2917

Regional economic alienation: Atlantic Canada and the West 2116

The regional economic consequences of tariffs and domestic transportation costs 2784

Regional economic disparities: the challenge to federalism and public policy 2215

A regional economic overview of the West since 1945 2851

The regional economy of Canada: environment, economic adjustment and barriers to interprovincial trade 2795

Regional equity and efficiency: some experiments for Canada 2137

Regional government 3404

Regional grievances: the Quebec case 2491

The regional impact in Canada of free trade 3109

The regional impact of tariffs 2786

The regional impact of the disintegration of the Canadian common market: the case of Quebec 2114

The regional patterns in Canada and Canadian culture 630

Regional planning in Canada: history, practice, issues, and prospects 2973

Regional policies in Canada 2258, 2884

Regional policy in Canada: an urban system perspective 2187

Regional policy in historical perspective: the federal role in regional economic development 2167

Regional policy: a matter of perspectives 2701

Regional policy: the embodiment of contradictions 2704

Regional politics in the wake of the Canada Act 409

Regional preferences: citizens' views of public policy 3369

Regional responsiveness and government organization: the case of regional economic development policy in Canada 2136

Regional responsiveness and the national administrative state 2134

Regional stabilization in Canada 2950

The regional structure of the Canadian economy 595

Regional variation in Canada's cultural mosaic 464

Regional variations in public policy 3371

Regional variations in worksharing: the case of Newfoundland 2673

Regionalism and "unlimited identity" in Western Canada 269

Regionalism and ethnicity 452

Regionalism and international trade policy 3036

Regionalism and supranationalism: challenges and alternatives to the nation-state in Canada and Europe 304

Reshaping Confederation: the 1982 reform of the Canadian constitution 895, 897

The resolution of complaints based on race and origin: the Canadian Human Rights Commission 556

Resolution respecting the Constitution of Canada adopted by the Parliament of Canada in December, 1981.; Canada Act, 1982.; Constitution Act, 1982 783

Resolving the energy conflict: from the National Energy Program to the energy agreements 2601

The resource amendment (Section 92A) and the political economy of Canadian federalism 733

Resource conflict, policy change and practice in Canadian fisheries management 2797

Resource development and inter-government relations 1423

Resource management - Canadian federalism 2354

Resource management boundary problems: a paper prepared for the Western Constitutional Forum 2987

Resource policy: international perspectives 2832

Resource revenues and fiscal equalization: a proposal 1895

Resource-leasing options and the settlement of aboriginal claims 254

Resources and the environment: policy perspectives for Canada 2471

Responsabilité et coopération doivent être les nouvelles prémisses du développement régional 2642

Response to Quebec: the other Provinces and the Constitutional debate 439

Response to regional disparity in the Maritime provinces, 1926-1942: a study in Canadian intergovernmental relations 1887

Response to the report of the Task Force to Review Comprehensive Claims Policy: "Living treaties lasting agreements" 527

Responses to the Royal Commission on the Economic Union and Development Prospects for Canada's recommendations on the North 3402

Responsiveness versus accountability in collaborative federalism: the Canadian experience 34

Les ressources naturelles dans une perspective de changement constitutionnelle: le cas du Québec 829

Restraint in government (federal, provincial, and local government revenue and spending trends, 1965-1981) 2905

Restrictions on access to English language schools in Quebec: an international human rights analysis 592

Restructuring the Atlantic fishery: a case study in business-government relations 2657

The resurgence of Canadian nationalism: attitudes and policy in the 1980's 466

Socialisme et indépendance au Québec: pistes pour le mouvement ouvrier et populaire 386

The socialization of medical insurance in Canada 3174

The sociology of contemporary Quebec nationalism: an annotated bibliography and review 457

Some administrative aspects of federalism in India, Nigeria and Malaysia 209

Some comments on the Charter of Rights and Freedoms 786

Some common issues in provincial-municipal transfer systems 1998

Some economic implications of the projected age structure of Canada: a reply 2958

Some evidence on the effect of the separation of spending and taxing decisions 3177

Some issues in Canada-US trade relations 2566

Some miscellaneous aspects of Section 15 of the Canadian Charter of Rights and Freedoms 957

Some perspectives on the Canadian Charter of Rights and Freedoms 1369

Some political realities in the world of stagflation 1831

Some proposals for adapting federal-provincial financial agreements to current conditions 2802

Some reflections on the role of the Government of Canada in the provision of health services 2960

Some suggestions for improving intergovernmental relations 2041

Some thoughts on Canada-United States sectoral free trade 2587

The sorcerer's apprentices: Canada's super-bureaucrats and the energy mess 2523

Sources for the interpretation of equality rights under the Charter: a background paper 1230

South Africa: federal potentialities in current developments 113

La souveraineté pour aller plus loin 539

La souveraineté-association: est-ce économiquement viable? 392

La souveraineté-association: réalisme économique ou utopie 456

Sovereignty-association "Non"-Parti québécois "oui": trends in political support in Quebec 467

The spacial aspects and regularities of multiple interregional migration within Canada: evidence and implications 2560

Speaking notes for the Honourable John C. Munro, Minister of Indian Affairs and Northern Development, for the constitutional resolution debate, Feb. 20, 1981 1184

Special status in Indian federalism, Jammu and Kashmir 96

Speeches and interviews by Hon. Allan Blakeney, Premier of Saskatchewan, in the course of a trip to Ontario and Quebec 2018

The spending power 922

Spending priorities: the Liberal view 2451

The splintered market: barriers to interprovincial trade in Canadian agriculture 2572

Stabilization, allocation and the 1970s, oil price shocks 2603

Staples and the provincial state 549

Startling facts, sobering truths, and sacred trust: pension policy and the Tories 2926

State administrators' opinions on administrative change, federal aid, federal relationships 1413

State and society: Canada in comparative perspective 3214

The state as entrepreneur: from CDC to CDIC 3231

State corporations and resource based development in Quebec, Canada: 1960-1980 3230

State enterprise and partisanship in provincial politics 3240

The state goes fishing: the emergence of public ownership in the Newfoundland and fishing industry 3044

State governments and Australian tariff policy 3133

State language and society: the vicissitudes of French in Quebec and Canada 623

The state of American federalism: 1979 193

The state of American federalism: 1983 192

The state of American federalism: 1984 166

The state of minority language education in the ten provinces of Canada: a report 2392

State political culture and the attitudes of state senators toward social, economic welfare and corruption issues 221

State, capital, and labour: the introduction of federal provincial insurance for physician care in Canada 3131

State, class and capital: demystifying the westward shift of power 580

State-local relations bodies: state ACIRs and other approaches 1414

State-municipal fiscal relations: a comparative study of Australia and India 1606

Statement by the Hon. T.L. Wells, Minister of Intergovernmental Affairs to the Glendon College symposium "Quebec - year of the referendum", Toronto, Ontario, Saturday, March 8, 1980 1966

Statement by the Honourable Thomas L. Wells, Minister of Intergovernmental Affairs on the report of the Constitutional Committee of the Quebec Liberal Party "a new Canadian federation", Tuesday, January 29, 1980 1227

Statement by the Honourable Thomas L. Wells, Minister of Intergovernmental Affairs, opening the debate on Confederation in the Ontario legislature, May 5, 1980 1226

Statement of Union of Nova Scotia Indians, January 6, 1981 to the Joint Constitutional Committee of Senate and House of Commons of the federal Government 618

Statistical compendium - Federal-provincial Task Force on Student Assistance 2276

The statistical protection of minorities: affirmative action policy in Canada 454

Status language planning in Quebec: an evaluation 2676

Steering the course: twenty-first annual review, 1984 2485

Stereotypes, statistics and slippery slopes: a reply to professors Flanagan and Knopff and other critics of human rights legislation 416

Still living together: recent trends and future directions in Canadian regional development 2364

Strained mercy: the economics of Canadian health care 2495

Strange bedfellows: the state and the arts in Canada 3190

The strange case of a provincial Constitution: the British Columbia Constitution Act 1321

The strategic and economic implications for the United States of a sovereign Quebec 2211

Strategic regional development overview - Atlantic Region 2250

Strategic regional development overview - Canada 2251

Strategic regional development overview - Ontario 2252

Strategic regional development overview - Quebec 2253

Strategic regional development overview - Western region 2254

Stratégie économique et restructuration de l'Etat au Canada 2613

A strategy for culture: proposals for a federal policy for the arts and the cultural industries in Canada 2326

Strengthening growth: options and constraints: Economic Council of Canada twenty-second annual review, 1985 2486

Structural change and industrial policy: the redeployment of Canadian manufacturing, 1960-80 2748

The structural problem of Canadian federalism 200

Structure and process in consociationalism and federalism 203

Structure and process in federal and consociational arrangements 17

The structure of Canadian government 3310

The structure of taxation 2744

Submission to the Special Joint Parliamentary Committee of the Senate and the House of Commons on the Constitution...presented by the Honourable J. Angus Maclean on behalf of the Government of Prince Edward Island 795

Les subventions fédérales à la recherche scientifique et technologique 3195

La Suisse, essai de géographie politique 188

Summaries of federal-provincial General Development Agreements and currently active Subsidiary Agreements 1522, 1523

Summaries of federal-provincial General Development Agreements and currently active Subsidiary Agreements 1521

Summary of briefs and hearings, by Louis Applebaum and Jacques Hébert 2273

Summary of discussions (Municipal government in the intergovernmental maze) 1507

Summary of recommendations and positions on select aspects of Canadian constitutional reform 1221

Summary response to report and recommendation on the integration of the two official languages in New Brunswick: a summary 2835

Summary statement on federal-provincial relations: by the Canadian Labour Congress to the Finance, Trade and Economic Affairs Committee of the House of Commons 1511

Support for technology development: a summary of federal programs and incentives, 1983/84 2301

Support for technology development: a summary of federal programs and incentives, 1984 2302

Support to education by the Government of Canada 2311

Supporting the arts: an international comparative study, Canada, Federal Republic of Germany, France, Italy, Great Britain, Netherlands, Sweden, United States 3021

Supremacy of the Canadian Charter of Rights and Freedoms 1009

The Supreme Court and federal-provincial relations: the political use of legal resources 3359

The Supreme Court and the economy 1166

Supreme Court decisions on the Canadian Constitution 810

Supreme Court of Canada - the Constitution and early beginning of the court 811

The Supreme Court of Canada and "the Bowater's law", 1950 1187

The Supreme Court of Canada and basic constitutional amendment 1082

The Supreme Court of Canada as an instrument of political change 693

The Supreme Court of Canada: final arbiter of political disputes 1376

The Supreme Court of Canada: history of the institution 1344

The Supreme Court of Canada: reform implications for an emerging national institution 1107

The union of Lublin, Polish federalism in the golden age 55

Union of states: the theory and practice of confederation 76

Union Republics in Soviet diplomacy : a study of Soviet federalism in the service of Soviet foreign policy 15

The United Kingdom Parliament and the British North America Acts 1137

The United States Bill of Rights and the Canadian Charter: a socio-political analysis 1389

The United States Bill of Rights: implications for Canada 1149

United States federal government--Indian relationship: trusteeship and local government 563

The universal student grant option in the federal financing of post-secondary education 3152

Universities and government 2654

Universities and the future of Ontario: a foundation on which to build: response of the Council of Ontario Universities to the preliminary report of the Committee on the Future Role of Universities in Ontario 2394

Universities: the sleeper in federal-provincial relations 2395

Unravelling Canada's textile policy 2720

Urban federalism: urban studies in a federal context 1925

Urban indian needs: federal policy responsibility in the context of the talks on aboriginal self-government 383

Urban policy aspects of grants to local government 1477

Use of a regulatory tribunal as an inquiry: the satellite case before the Canadian Radio-Television and Telecommunications Commission 2991

The use of litigation under the Canadian Charter of Rights and Freedoms as a strategy for achieving change 928

Using Canadian oil and gas revenues in the 1980's: provincial and federal perspectives 2599

Vers l'interprétation d'une Constitution bilingue 679

Vers une grande décentralisation du financement gouvernemental au Québec 2345

Views on the Canadian Constitution as it affects Indians of New Brunswick 617

Views on the Council for Canadian Unity on constitutional reform 883

Le virage technologique: bâtir le Québec, phase 2: programme d'action économique 1982-1986 2938

The visible hand: the pricing of Canadian oil resources 3142

A vision beyond reach: a century of images of Canadian destiny 474

The voices of democracy: politics and communications in Canada 3196

Subject Index

Aboriginal Lands 1021

Aboriginal Peoples

Aboriginal Claims 254, 270, 306, 307, 310, 313, 316-8, 322, 344, 351, 359, 370, 444, 504, 533, 584, 626, 2575, 3061

Aboriginal Rights 232, 583, 628, 936, 983, 1023, 1215, 1329

Aboriginal Self-Government 248, 249, 257, 270, 271, 282, 286, 295, 312, 320, 323, 331, 371, 383, 412, 414, 430, 431, 445, 446, 477-9, 489, 494, 495, 514, 515, 518, 522, 528, 532, 563, 578, 579, 583, 584, 586, 612, 626, 627, 1223, 1296, 1401, 1943, 3236, 3401

Alberta 1525

BNA Act 658

British Columbia 295

Canada 495, 548, 2153

Canadian Charter of Rights and Freedoms 283, 285, 583, 983, 1154, 1296, 1329

Conflict, Cultural 294

Conflict, Ethnic 294

Constitution Act, 1982. 936, 1215

Constitutional Conferences 499

Constitutional Development 446, 488, 979, 1124, 1195, 1196, 1198, 1202, 1203, 1207, 1208, 1250, 1823, 2221, 3323, 3325, 3327, 3401

Constitutional History 309, 1294

Constitutional Law 284, 285, 313, 323, 361, 433, 444, 494, 504, 507, 512, 514, 522, 523, 571, 572, 596, 617, 618, 626, 636, 936, 996, 1023, 1031, 1215, 1223, 1294-6, 1328, 2825

Constitutional Law - Amendments 761, 814, 1401

Constitutional Law - Patriation 618, 649, 658, 1401

Constitutional Reform 232, 234, 321, 361, 445, 447, 490, 498-502, 512, 520, 572, 578, 583, 587, 606, 671, 835, 954, 1184, 1295, 1632, 1633, 1635-80, 1751, 1776-87, 1790, 1811, 1813-5, 1951, 3268

Constitutions 311

Dene 231, 232

DIAND 479, 627

Drury Report 498, 3253, 3268

Economic Conditions 1554

Education 2825

Energy Policy 3061

English-French Relations 516

Environment 315

Ethnicity, Political Significance of 515

Federal-Provincial Agreements 1554

Federal-Provincial Development Agreements 1525

Federal-Provincial Fiscal Relations 1539

Federal-Provincial Meetings 954, 1634, 1646, 1751, 1776-84, 1787, 1790, 1803

Federal-Provincial Relations 1823, 1943

Federal-Provincial-Territorial Relations 501

Federal-Territorial Relations 3253

Federalism 671, 835

First Ministers' Conferences 321, 431, 636, 1635, 1647, 1648, 1655, 1665, 1666, 1668-72, 1678-80, 1785, 1786, 1811-5, 1951, 2015

Institutions of Government 3326, 3415

Interprovincial Conferences 1864, 1865

Jurisdiction, Divided 2153

Jurisdiction, Provincial 2153

Land Tenure 322

Land Transfers 322

Law and Legislation 257

Natural Resources 254, 2153

Northern Development 1525, 2575, 3061

Northwest Territories 317, 318, 370, 488, 498, 527, 528, 624, 979, 1124, 1196, 1198, 1202, 1207, 1208, 1250, 1811, 1823, 2575, 2987, 3236, 3253, 3268, 3323, 3325, 3326, 3401

Ontario 532, 1223

Penner Report 414, 612, 627

Quebec 516, 936

Regional Development 2575, 3061

Regionalism 835

Resources Policy 254, 835, 2153, 2987

Rights, Constitutional Protection of 231-4, 237, 247, 284, 285, 314, 361, 447, 490, 523, 531, 571, 572, 596, 606, 756, 761, 1031, 1154, 1198, 1202, 1203, 1223, 1239, 1250, 1295, 1632-45, 1650-67, 1669-80, 1786, 1790, 1812-4, 2825

Saskatchewan 237, 533

Separatism 835

Sovereignty 495

Tripartite Local Government Committee 295

United States 495, 563, 2153

Usufruct 996

Yukon 317, 318, 3415

Acadians 585

Accountability 34

Acid Rain 1841

ACIR (Advisory Commission on Intergovernmental Relations) 1418, 1419, 1426

Administrative Agencies 3373

Administrative Appeal Tribunals 1183

Administrative Courts 959, 1099, 1242

Administrative Dualism 209

Administrative Law 1071, 1279

Administrative Tribunals 2815, 3219

Advertising 3070

Aeronautics Law 1189

Affirmative Action 454

Africa 157

Aging 2436, 2652

Agriculture

Agricultural Development Agreements 2699

Agricultural Marketing Boards 2138

Agricultural Policy 2194, 2580, 3045

Agriculture - Price Supports 2651

Agriculture - Economic Aspects 3172

Alberta 2099

Bill C-55 2106

British Columbia 1490

Canada, Maritime 2699

Canada, Western 2220

Energy Policy 2869

Farm Credit 1732

Farm Products Marketing Agencies Act (FPMAA) 3045

Federal-Provincial Development Agreements 1490, 1569, 2224

Federal-Provincial Meetings 1513, 1728-30, 1732, 1735, 1736, 1769, 1933

Federal-Provincial Relations 2118, 2224, 2659, 3045

Freight Rates 2099, 2100, 2106, 2376, 2426, 2588, 2855, 3119

Government Intervention 2580

Grain Trade 3172

Interprovincial Conferences 1844-50

Interprovincial Trade 2227, 2362, 2572, 2788

Land Ownership and Tenure 2194

Land Regulation 2194

Marketing Boards 2118, 2166, 3045

National Policy 2659

New Brunswick 2224

Ontario 2869

Prairie Provinces 3172

Prince Edward Island 1569

Regional Development 1490, 2659, 2699

Regionalism 2659, 2855

Regulation 2138, 2580, 2688

Regulatory Transfers 2688

Trade Barriers 2788

Transportation 1933, 2099, 2100, 2106, 2376, 2426, 2588, 2855, 3119

Transportation Regulation 2138

Western Transition 2342

Air Traffic Control, Bilingual 2181

Airlines 2955

Airports 2469, 2507

Alberta 641, 642

Alberta Heritage Savings Trust Fund 1599, 2040, 2773, 3248, 3338

Amending Power 1142

American Civil War 183

Anarchism 109

Aquaculture 3163

Arab Nationalism 26

Archives 2351

Articles of Confederation 66, 89, 170

Assam 168

Atlantic Accord 961

Atlantic Provinces 1209, 2053, 2629, 2634, 2778, 3004, 3164

Australia 6-8, 13, 28, 82, 102, 104, 144, 145, 150, 167, 223, 605, 887, 905, 935, 971, 980, 1019, 1029, 1304, 1305, 1352, 1415-8, 1421, 1422, 1425, 1426, 1606, 1829, 1913-6, 1919, 1921, 1922, 1926, 2020, 2028, 2057, 2058, 2076, 2080, 2093, 2427, 2464, 2531, 2583,

2609, 2683, 2739-44, 2956, 3133, 3200, 3300, 3375

Australian Loan Council 1416, 1914

Australian Taxation 1917

Austria 72, 75, 141, 1467, 1974

Autonomy 149, 1618

Backward Linkages 2864

Bank Regulation 2810

Banking Institutions 2356

Banzhaf's Power Index 1164

Barbados 134

Beer's Modernization Theory 197

Beige Paper (Quebec) 429, 707, 1469, 3221

Belgium 32, 50, 54, 886

Bicommunal Polity 133

Bicommunalism 133

Bilateral Relations 2563

Bilateralism 151

Bilingualism 277, 319, 327, 421, 462, 485, 566, 625, 679, 684, 709, 962, 1116, 1120, 1147, 2122, 2181, 2184, 2185, 2235, 2283, 2303, 2306-8, 2310, 2347-9, 2385, 2432, 2456, 2467, 2490, 2517, 2538, 2678, 2718, 2835, 2837, 2952, 2964-9, 3058, 3063, 3086, 3093

Bill 101. 341, 2719, 2942, 3192

Bill 22. 341

Bill 57. 3120

Bill C-55. 2106

Bill C-92. 2073

Bill C-97. 1454, 1616, 1949, 2027

Bill of Economic Rights 987

Bill of Rights 985, 1048, 1148, 1149, 1152, 1266, 1274, 1309, 1389

Bloc populaire canadien 264

Block Funding 2647

Block Grants 118, 1464, 2079

BNA Act 160, 643, 658, 724, 729, 926, 927, 1001, 1034, 1038, 1055, 1057, 1062, 1113, 1134, 1137, 1189, 1253, 1289, 1319, 1321, 1327, 2052, 3217

Bowater's Law 1187

Brazil 2609

British Columbia 295, 635, 687, 716-20, 794, 1277, 1321, 1443, 1490-6, 1553, 1699, 1701, 1706, 1707, 1716, 1927, 2009, 2010, 2054, 2198, 2831, 3199, 3358

British Columbia Constitution Act 1321

Broadcasting 2329, 2330, 2863, 3014, 3116, 3165

Budgets 3162

Budgets, Federal 2236-8, 2242, 2292, 2337, 2521, 2695, 2732

Budgets, Provincial 2553, 2554, 2732, 2906-10, 3108

Bund-Länder Fiscal Relations 1467

Bundesrat 40, 3226, 3417

Bureaucracy 2205, 2653, 3385, 3409

Bureaucratization 3004, 3297

Business Law 1176

Business-Government Relations 2063, 2094, 2168, 2173, 2178, 2200, 2202, 2217, 2361, 2406, 2411, 2415, 2462, 2463, 2480, 2522, 2544, 2655, 2657, 2758, 2762, 2821, 2846, 2879, 2915, 2928, 2959, 2962, 2963, 2979, 2994, 3012, 3038, 3094, 3100, 3182, 3224, 3313

Cabinet 3259, 3297

Cabinet Ministers 3249

Cable Broadcasting 3130

Concentration-Deconcentration 3337

Concurrent Powers 2639

Confederalism 59

Confederation 76, 112, 161, 362, 593, 635, 704, 724, 1339, 1341, 1379, 1399, 1602, 2807, 3217, 3238, 3271, 3308, 3314, 3321, 3341, 3349, 3395, 3411

Conference Freight Rates 2204

Conflict Management 1816, 1905, 3372

Conflict of Laws 706, 889

Conflict, Cultural 294

Conflict, Ethnic 47, 60, 114, 152, 294, 513, 558, 569, 2001

Conflict, Linguistic 277, 292, 302, 341, 343, 358, 419, 505, 513, 567-9, 592, 623, 2001, 2184-6, 2456, 2964-6, 3031, 3058

Conflict, Regional 47, 50, 292, 324

Conseil de la langue française 844

Conseil de planification et de développement du Québec 2536, 2981

Conseil des gens d'affaires du Québec 2806

Conseil du patronat du Québec 2806

Conseil patronat du Québec 2807

Conservation 3089

Conservative Party 3243

Consociational Democracy 47

Consociationalism 17, 47, 58, 59, 67, 109, 114, 126, 136, 203

Constitution 113, 128, 723, 750, 1002, 1293

Constitution Act 753, 764

Constitution Act 1981. 821

Constitution Act, 1867. 661, 959, 1099, 1243

Constitution Act, 1982. 640, 651, 668, 739, 740, 776, 846, 936, 1007-9, 1034, 1039, 1040, 1086, 1132, 1158, 1164, 1179, 1215, 1238, 1267, 1268, 1320, 1334, 1350, 1355

Constitution-making 933, 1035, 1084, 1157, 1383

Constitutional Adjudication 1055

Constitutional Charter 637

Constitutional Conventions 499, 713, 949, 1170, 1398

Constitutional Development 446, 488, 660, 757, 758, 806, 847, 892, 923, 979, 1026, 1124, 1125, 1139, 1195-1208, 1212, 1213, 1250, 1324, 1381, 1392, 1823, 2221, 3323-5, 3327, 3328, 3398-404

Constitutional History 55, 175, 176, 186, 309, 396, 455, 668, 669, 674, 676, 677, 690, 704, 725, 728, 747, 955, 963, 1016, 1020, 1049, 1061, 1069, 1070, 1075, 1082, 1083, 1137, 1163, 1168, 1200, 1214, 1269, 1287, 1292, 1294, 1298, 1323, 1334, 1366, 1390, 1399, 1402, 1577, 2085, 3227, 3235, 3271, 3307, 3310, 3321

Constitutional Law

Aboriginal Peoples, See **Aboriginal Peoples** - Constitutional Law

Administrative Appeal Tribunals 1183

Administrative Courts 959, 1099, 1242

Administrative Law 1279

Aeronautics Law 1189

Aquaculture 3163

Atlantic Accord 961

Australia 28, 167, 887, 905, 971, 980, 1029, 1304, 1305, 1352, 3200

Bank Regulation 2810

Export Policy 2163, 3157

Extra-territoriality 706, 930

Family Law 1174, 1299

Farm Credit 1731, 1732

Farm Products Marketing Agencies Act (FPMAA) 3045

Federal Aid to Higher Education 2289, 2393, 2870

Federal Aid to Public Welfare 2113

Federal Aid to Research 2299, 2324

Federal Aid to Sports 2290

Federal Aid to the Arts 2325, 2326, 2327, 2370, 2371, 3021, 3190

Federal Courts 1318

Federal Economic Development Coordinators (FEDC's) 2135

Federal Government 31, 33, 195, 466, 529, 589, 1471, 2007, 2086, 2138, 2182, 2190, 2195, 2350, 2662, 2999, 3022, 3207, 3213, 3238, 3296, 3330, 3337, 3368

Federal Majoritarianism 1333

Federal Parliament 3208, 3311, 3346, 3413

Federal Reform 141

Federal Relations 492

Federal Republic of Germany 3417

Federal State Fiscal Relations 1915

Federal Theory 229

Federal-Provincial Agreements 1553, 1554

Federal-Provincial Committees 943, 2499

Federal-Provincial Conferences 1533, 1581, 1625, 1827, 1994, 2061, 2074

Federal-Provincial Constitutional Relations

Alberta 641, 642, 2551

BNA Act 643, 927, 1038, 1113, 1137, 1253, 1327

Canada, Western 963

Canadian Charter of Rights and Freedoms 924, 939

Constitution - making 1157

Constitution Act, 1867. 1243

Constitution Act, 1980. 950

Constitutional Convention 949

Constitutional History 669, 955, 963, 1020, 1083, 1137, 1163

Constitutional Law, See **Constitutional Law**

Constitutional Reform, See **Constitutional Reform**

Constitutions, Federal 955

Courts, Structure and Role of 691

Dualism 672

Economic Regulation 1113

Energy 994

Energy Policy 2551

Federal-Provincial Jurisdictional Disputes 1111, 1112

Federal-Provincial Meetings 769

Federal-Provincial Relations 2012, 2013

Federal-Provincial Tax Relations 2813

Federalism 154, 213, 219, 669, 691, 937, 998, 1083, 1173, 1216, 1217, 1327, 1372, 1380

Fisheries 937, 3029

Foreign Affairs Committee (U.K.) 1038

Income Support 2617, 2737

Intergovernmental Fiscal Relations 1480, 1482

Intergovernmental Relations 212, 1838, 2038

Interprovincial Migration 2638, 2717

Interregional Migration 2794

Jurisdiction, Divided 1483, 2737

Macdonald Commission 2780

Manitoba 1549, 1907, 1908, 1910

Matching Grants 2411

Medicare 2592

MSERD (Ministry of State for Economic and Regional Development) 2701

National Energy Program 2772

National Standards 1820, 1898

New Brunswick 1945

Newfoundland 1947, 1973

Nova Scotia 2213, 2557, 2632

Ontario 1958-60, 1967

Parliamentary Committees 1511, 1540-3, 1549, 1947, 1957, 2990

Parliamentary Task Force on Federal-Provincial Fiscal Arrangements 2037

Pension Reform 2148

Pensions 2148, 2437, 2492

Petroleum Industry 1833, 2602

Policies, Regional Impact of 631

Powers, Allocation of 160, 734, 947, 1463, 2038, 2983

Prince Edward Island 1984, 2925

Privatization 3151

Provincial Saving 1500

Provincial-Municipal Fiscal Relations 1478, 2042

Public Services 734

Quebec 1697, 1819, 1990-3, 2976

Quebec Nationalism 1830

Regional Development 631, 1522, 2700, 2701, 2730

Regional Disparities 631, 873, 878, 2410

Regional Policies 2700, 2701, 2730

Regionalism 631

Rent Sharing 1599

Research and Development 2493

Resource Revenues 1599, 1604, 1833, 1893, 1895, 1980, 2162, 2602, 2772

Resources Policy 3256, 3257

Saskatchewan 1691, 1766, 2019

Social Policy 1545, 1550, 1820, 1893, 2048

Social Programs 2647

Social Services 2048

Spending Power 734, 1820

Stabilization Policies 1928

Tax Collection Agreements 1629

Taxation 947, 1458, 1478, 1833, 1893, 2002, 2555, 2602, 2632

Toronto 2790

Federal-Provincial Jurisdictional Disputes 992, 1006, 1092, 1111, 1112, 1180, 1182, 1282, 1360, 1393, 1888, 2386, 2468, 2545, 2546, 2569, 2595, 2796, 2827, 2901, 3125, 3165, 3170, 3250

Federal-Provincial Meetings, See Relevant Policy Areas

Federal-Provincial Programs 1430, 1527-30, 1955, 2498

Quebec Workers' Movement 1140

Redistribution 2040

Regional Development 105, 2215

Regional Discontent 61

Regional Disparities 224, 2215

Regional Government 304

Regionalism 22, 54, 129, 137, 189, 211, 304, 324, 413, 476, 559, 607, 835, 1822

Regulation 5, 118, 3020

Regulation, Provincial 2949

Resource Management Powers 733

Resource Revenues 733, 2040, 2812

Resources 835

Resources Policy 2998

Responsibilities, Allocation of 19, 91, 226

Revenue Sharing 146, 1503

Rights, Constitutional Protection of 731

Secession 63

Senate 201, 3367, 3374

Senate Reform 3202, 3226

Separation of Powers 674, 676, 677

Seperatism 835

Social Policy 139, 1944

Social Security 2150

Social Welfare Policy 2149

Socialism 140

South Africa 77, 113

Soviet Union 15, 32, 85, 103

Spain 32, 155

Special Interest Groups 100

Supreme Court 201, 693, 1006, 1336, 1359, 1360

Switzerland 32, 125, 188

Tax Assignment 2745

Tax Harmonization 2169

Tax Sharing 1918

Taxation 147, 1467, 1837, 2745, 2766, 2767

Taxation Federalism 2049

Territory, Political Significance of 96

Third World 148

Trade Policy 938

Transportation 2507

Treaty-Making Power 24, 143, 2055

Unilateralism 151

Union-State Relations 127

Unitarism 1293

United Kingdom 41

United States, See United States

Vorarlberg (Austria) 141

Welfare State 2150

West Germany 6, 8, 10, 11, 29, 32, 40, 145, 185, 190, 216, 228, 2049, 3226

White Paper 404, 1469

Yugoslavia 85, 152, 171

Finance 1581, 2123, 2128, 2129, 2923

Finance, Public 1627

Financial Institution Reform 3049

Financial Institutions 2125, 2983

Financial Market Deregulation 3132

Financial Markets, Regulation of 885

FIRA (Foreign Review Investment Agency) 2548, 2561, 2707, 2896, 3053, 3118

Fisheries 860, 861, 937, 1092, 1518, 1568, 2111, 2151, 2379-81, 2421-4, 2438, 2508, 2532, 2563, 2608, 2634, 2656, 2657, 2746, 2755, 2796, 2797, 2808, 2817, 2916, 2932, 2984, 3029, 3030, 3044, 3125, 3145, 3146, 3170

Fishery Policy 2225, 2243, 2378, 2422, 2839, 3145, 3146

Food Processing Industry 2202

Foreign Affairs Committee (U.K.) 1038

Foreign Economic Relations 333, 1244, 1462, 1757-9, 1788, 1791, 1835, 2144, 2158, 2211, 2287, 2500, 2511, 2559, 2581, 2585, 2587, 2598, 2684, 2894, 2900, 2947-9, 2951, 3024, 3064-6, 3072, 3101, 3153, 3157, 3169, 3188, 3280, 3301

Foreign Investment 2548, 2561, 2713, 3053, 3080, 3118, 3185

Foreign Policy 15, 1348, 2014, 2024

Foreign Relations 470, 2506, 3330

Forestry 941, 1496, 1512, 1562, 1566, 1903, 2101, 2198, 2222, 2953

Forward Linkages 2864

Fowler Report 423

France 32, 53, 137

Free Trade 1906, 2096, 2115, 2157, 2172, 2223, 2287, 2317, 2318, 2419, 2473, 2474, 2527-9, 2559, 2576, 2582, 2587, 2708, 2709, 2789, 2800, 2803, 2828, 2911, 2954, 3051, 3062, 3065, 3076, 3077, 3109, 3137, 3138, 3153, 3154, 3166, 3183, 3184, 3186-9

Freedom of Speech 1238

Freedom of the Press 918

Freight Rate Reform 2855

Freight Rates 2426, 3026, 3135

French-English Relations, See English-French Relations

Functions of Government 2056

GATT 2707, 3024

General Development Agreements 2700, 2703, 3004

General Elections 3245

General Power 1889

Government Aid to the Arts 2288

Government Aid to Transportation 2294

Government Assistance 1529, 2168, 2300, 2434

Government Co-ordination 223

Government Expenditures 3392

Government Grants 3168

Government Intervention 2564, 2580, 2645, 3030

Government Investments 3338

Government Officials 3381

Government Policy 2281, 2621, 2651, 3355

Government Programs 3292

Government Regulation 2402, 3162

Government Spending Policy 2404, 2614, 2687, 2698, 2923

Government Transfers 2177

Grain Trade 3172

Grants 1406, 1486, 1489, 2025, 2026

Grants, Conditional 1456, 1478, 1920, 1926, 1929

Grants, Unconditional 180, 1456, 1931

Grants-In-Aid 1552, 2030, 2289, 2290

Great Britain 32, 36, 37, 455, 561, 644, 774, 915, 1005, 1135, 1330, 3314

Green Paper 3049

Human Rights 948, 1237, 1805, 1806

Hungary 660

Hydroelectric Power 2193

Immigration Policy 721

Imperial Federation 37

Import Policy 2786, 3133, 3157

Income Distribution 3067, 3121, 3122

Income Maintenance Programs 2150

Income Redistribution 1460, 1834

Income Security 1463, 2518, 2787, 3040

Income Support 2090, 2093, 2127, 2159, 2420, 2519, 2617, 2618, 2623, 2737

Income Tax Act 1185

Incrementalism 42

India 57, 96, 127, 168, 169, 172, 209, 1606, 2043, 2044, 2425, 2914, 3259

Indian Act 1021

Indirect Taxation 2738

Individual Policy 2089

Individual Rights 1363

Industrial Adjustment 3106

Industrial Assistance 2726, 3117

Industrial Development 1558, 1565, 2087, 2095, 2124, 2226, 2233, 2244, 2245, 2249, 2259, 2297, 2333, 2498, 2585, 2720, 2748, 2963, 3024, 3027

Industrial Policy 214, 980, 2063, 2088, 2172, 2173, 2244, 2346, 2406, 2415, 2433, 2525, 2526, 2530, 2581, 2635, 2681, 2707, 2882, 3039, 3106, 3117, 3140

Industrial Productivity 3043

Industrial Relations 3169

Industrial Sector 2959, 3038

Industrial Strategy 2097, 2124, 2170, 2200, 2414, 2961

Industrial Subsidies 3024

Inflation 2979

Institute of Intergovernmental Relations 1899

Institutional Reform 1157, 3211

Institutions of Government 40, 201, 824, 1339, 1402, 2056, 3208, 3237, 3244, 3246, 3264, 3295, 3310, 3311, 3318, 3326, 3348, 3374, 3377, 3384, 3415

Integration-Disintegration 26, 59, 60, 68, 70, 75, 85, 90, 108, 112, 157, 163, 178, 183, 190, 194, 195, 275, 546, 601, 604, 634, 1618, 2083, 2114, 2662, 2900, 3196, 3212, 3341, 3377

Interprovincial Trade 3042

Inter-State Commission 1913

Inter-State Relations 2956

Interdepartmental Coordination 2086

Interest Groups 211, 3372

Intergovernmental Agreements 2080

Intergovernmental Conferences 1841, 1842

Intergovernmental Financial Relations 1915

Intergovernmental Fiscal Relations 6, 93, 116, 118, 146, 218, 220, 229, 230, 1406, 1408-12, 1464, 1465, 1477, 1480, 1482, 1486, 1487, 1489, 1501-3, 1628, 1822, 1832, 1834, 1840, 1892, 1912, 1922, 1942, 1944, 1956, 1971, 2004, 2025, 2026, 2043, 2044, 2057, 2070, 2079, 2082, 2084, 2090, 2137, 2567, 2791, 2860, 3317

Intergovernmental Immunity 1177

Intergovernmental Relations
Accountability 34

2971, 2972, 3074, 3092, 3178, 3179, 3193, 3338

Interprovincial Product Liability 1322, 3033

Interprovincial Relations 214, 236, 439, 440, 517, 664, 1092, 1133, 1136, 1170, 1227, 1313, 1397, 1451, 1469, 1589, 1966, 1981, 2040, 2154

Interprovincial Trade 884, 1791, 1961, 2114, 2115, 2227, 2362, 2403, 2405, 2512, 2562, 2568, 2572, 2684, 2785, 2788, 2795, 2877, 2931, 2989, 3096, 3107, 3155, 3156

Interprovincial Transportation 2352

Interregional Adjustment 2848, 2852, 2854, 3124

Interregional Migration 2560, 2794, 3124

Intervention (Federal Government) 2480

Investment 1724, 2098, 2192

Investment Canada 3053

Investment of Public Funds, Law and legislation 2063

Investments-Taxation 2868

Ireland 37, 52

Italy 88, 132, 194, 1293

Japan 2633

Judges, Appointment and Election of 1107, 1283

Judicial Branch 1283

Judicial Independence 1241

Judicial Review 29, 154, 648, 808, 911, 940, 968, 995, 1028, 1044, 1048, 1063, 1074, 1100, 1106, 1182, 1183, 1269, 1277, 1286, 1336, 1337, 1357, 1385

Juridiction, Divided

Aboriginal Lands 1021

Aboriginal Peoples 2153

Administrative Appeal Tribunals 1183

Administrative Courts 959, 1099, 1242

Aeronautics Law 1189

Airports 2469

Alberta 2040

Alberta Heritage Savings Trust Fund 2040

BNA Act 1189, 2052

Broadcasting 3165

Canada 2153, 2357, 2458

Canada Assistance Plan 2737

Canada, Atlantic 1146

Canada, Northern 2824

Centralization-Decentralization 48

Coastal Zone Management 2584

Communications 2578, 2646, 2775

Confederation 2807

Conflict Management 1816

Conflict, Ethnic 2001

Conflict, Linguistic 2001

Conflict, Regional 324

Conseil du patronat du Québec 2807

Constitution 723

Constitution Act, 1867 959, 1099, 1242

Constitution Act, 1982 1320

Constitutional Amendment, See **Constitutional Law** - Amendment

Constitutional Law, See **Constitutional Law** - Jurisdiction, Divided

Consumer Protection 1188

2367, 2676, 2715, 2719, 2721, 2937, 2940-2, 2970, 3031, 3086, 3090, 3093, 3192

Quebec Nationalism 505, 2210

Regionalism 601

Rights, Constitutional Protection of 657, 710, 1037, 2715

Saskatchewan 2541

Telecommunications 2941

Transportation 2181

Law Creation Power 1113

Law Reform 1071, 1133, 1181, 2189

Law, Harmonization of 888-90, 943, 1188, 1403, 2119

Laws, Conflict of 943

Legislation 1357

Legislative Authority 820

Legislative Committees 1219, 1220

Legislative Override 651, 1313

Legislative Supremacy 1347

Legislatures 1994, 3332, 3367

Legitimacy 727, 823

Legitimacy of Governments 3296, 3342

Liberal Democracy 3294

Liberal Party 2927, 3379, 3380, 3405

Liberalism 1046, 3350

Libraries 2351

Limitation Clause 1169

Linguistic Demography 2940

Linguistic Rights 2696

Lithuania 55

Local Expenditures 3104

Local Government 966, 1420, 1422, 1477, 1579, 1892, 1904, 1930, 2007, 2060, 2084, 2207, 3168, 3225, 3275, 3278, 3279, 3397

Local Government Finance 2197

Local Initiative 1615

Locational Surplus 1473

Macdonald Commission, See **Royal Commission on the Economic Union and Development Prospects for Canada**

Maintenance Orders 2189, 2284

Major Projects 2226

Malaysia 209

Manitoba 419, 567, 568, 662, 1126, 1549, 1556-61, 1704, 1723, 1906-11, 2222, 2456, 2540, 2666, 2723, 2751, 2792, 3242

Manitoba Act 419

Manitoba Schools Question 419, 662

Manpower 1765, 2315

Manufacturing Industries 2435, 2582, 2720

Manufacturing Sector 2962, 3001

Maritime Provinces 1887, 2391, 2421, 2699

Maritime Provinces 2421

Maritime Union 252

Market System 2402

Marketing Agencies 3045

Marketing Boards 2118, 2166, 2562, 3096

Marxist Theory 130

Mass Media 639, 3196

Massey Report 298

Massey-Levesque Commission 423

Matching Grants 2411

Medical Policy 2783

Medicare 2571, 2592, 2759, 3055, 3073, 3134

Mega-projects 2446

Metropolitan Government 1624, 1971

Mexico 181, 3103

Migrational Adjustment 2207

Military policy 3330

Mineral Industries 2928

Mineral Resources 2286, 2334

Mineral Royalties 2666

Mines 1583, 1726, 1727, 1775, 2179, 2286, 2796, 2813, 3197

Mining Industry 2120, 2929, 3182

Ministerial Task Force on Program Review 2288, 2291-4

Ministries of State 3250

Ministry of State for Urban Affairs 1808

Minorities, Status of

  Aboriginal Peoples 231

  Acadians 585

  Affirmative Action 454

  Alberta 2541

  Austria 75

  Bilingualism 277, 319, 327, 421, 462, 485, 625, 1116, 1120, 2517, 2538

  Canada, Western 353

  Canadian Charter of Rights and Freedoms 415, 519, 650, 819, 822, 928, 969, 1116, 1120

  Canadian Human Rights Commission 556

  Centralization-Decentralization 137

  Collective Rights 822

  Conflict, Linguistic 277, 567, 568, 3031

Constitutional Law 259, 710, 822, 1060, 1116, 1120

Constitutional Reform 345, 425

Education 1120, 2392, 2696

Education, Bilingual 2392

English-French Relations 277, 296, 485, 1060, 2517

Ethnicity, Political Significance of 75, 163, 258, 301, 376, 448, 475, 562, 625

Federalism 75, 137, 163, 3222

Fiscal Crisis 3222

Foreign Economic Relations 333

France 137

Integration-Disintegration 75, 163

Language Policy 319, 625, 650, 710, 2517, 2539-41, 2721, 3031

Linguistic Rights 2696

Manitoba 567, 568, 2540

Minorities 260

Minority Language Rights 1060

Multiculturalism 293, 296, 432, 449, 481, 577

Nationalism 562, 3222

New Brunswick 2538

Ontario 2539

Pluralism 577

Political Support 3222

Powers, Allocation of 650

Provincial-International Relations 333

Quebec 333, 462, 710, 2721, 3031

Quebec Nationalism 258

Regionalism 137, 353, 376

Rights, Constitutional Protection of 231, 259, 335, 353, 367, 372, 388,

415, 425, 454, 484, 519, 524, 525, 556, 600, 653, 710, 819, 928, 951, 969

Saskatchewan 2541

Social Policy 475

Sweden 462

United States 333

Minority Language Rights 1060

Mixed Enterprises 3261, 3287

Mobility Rights 695, 1027, 1065, 1308, 2975

Modernization 74, 197

Monetary Policy 885, 2463, 2585, 2586, 2640, 2754, 2935, 2993, 3087

Motor Fuel Tax 2145

MSERD 2416, 2701, 3250

MSUA 3250

Multiculturalism 85, 244, 293, 296, 373, 432, 443, 449, 450, 481, 577, 597, 2186, 2303, 2671

Multilateralism 151

Multinational Corporations 2334

Municipal Government 944, 945, 1471, 1624, 1808-10, 1836, 1856-60, 1878, 1891, 1904, 1995-7, 3204, 3205, 3220, 3317, 3354

Municipal Government Reform 3204, 3220

Nation-Building 2975

National Characteristics 1167

National Energy Policy 2440, 2441, 2551, 2843

National Energy Program 2105, 2143, 2232, 2263, 2264, 2266, 2305, 2341, 2407, 2414, 2455, 2552, 2561, 2600, 2601, 2604, 2606, 2615, 2629, 2668, 2713, 2763, 2772, 2777, 2779, 2974, 2992, 3000, 3078, 3080, 3118, 3129, 3171, 3185, 3412

National Oil Policy 2143

National Parks 2146, 2209

National Policy 546, 2559, 2659, 2756

National Security 1015

National Self-determination 426

National Standards 1820, 1898

National Unity 1286

Nationalism 26, 101, 144, 171, 276, 297, 300, 378, 381, 385, 423, 450, 451, 453, 461, 466, 473, 474, 535, 537, 561, 562, 588, 589, 610, 633, 1046, 1264, 2110, 2829, 3222, 3280

Nationalism and Socialism 436, 437

Nationalism, Cultural 298

Natural Law 925

Natural Resources 254, 647, 663, 664, 1025, 1092, 1093, 1161, 1178-80, 1395, 1749, 1750, 2117, 2120, 2146, 2153, 2154, 2158, 2176, 2190, 2291, 2357, 2386, 2449, 2531, 2537, 2545, 2546, 2619, 2620, 2706, 2758, 2781, 2824, 2844, 2865, 2894, 2897, 2922, 2928, 2997-9, 3028, 3127, 3159, 3199, 3285

Natural Resources, Taxation 2768

Neo-Conservatism 3242

Netherlands 32

New Brunswick 993, 1512, 1518, 1535, 1718, 1903, 1945, 2022, 2224, 2538, 2833-6, 2952

New Democratic Party 3345, 3380

New England Governors and Eastern Canadian Premiers 1436-9

New Federalism 20, 27, 51, 139, 174, 192, 204, 1487, 1503

New Zealand 2464

Newfoundland 920, 961, 1025, 1146, 1180, 1187, 1191-3, 1272, 1519, 1686, 1710, 1946-8, 1972, 1973, 2111, 2152, 2378, 2386, 2508, 2545, 2546, 2673, 2729, 2838-42, 2984, 3011, 3044, 3047, 3081, 3161, 3241, 3284, 3285, 3308, 3309, 3314, 3321, 3395

Nigeria 12, 114, 165, 209, 1030

Non-majoritarian Democracy 136

Non-renewable Resources 991, 2334, 2711

Non-tariff Barriers 2403, 2405, 2785, 2795, 2931, 3107, 3155, 3156

North American Integration 3065

Northern Development 355, 1440-8, 1524, 1525, 1559-61, 1876, 1877, 1911, 1972, 2086, 2267, 2320, 2575, 3061

Northern Ireland 52

Northwest Territories

Aboriginal Peoples 488, 498, 527, 624, 979, 1124, 1195, 1196, 1198, 1202, 1207, 1208, 1250, 1811, 1823, 2221, 2987, 3253, 3268, 3323, 3325-7

Aboriginal Peoples - Claims 317, 318, 370, 2575

Aboriginal Peoples - Self-Government 528, 3201, 3236, 3275, 3401

Bureaucracy 3409

Canada, Northern 758, 892, 1391, 2267

Centralization-Decentralization 3409

Civil Service 3320, 3409

Claims 317, 318, 370

Constitutional Change 806, 3268

Constitutional Development 488, 758, 806, 847, 892, 923, 979, 1026, 1124, 1125, 1139, 1195-1202, 1204-8, 1212, 1213, 1250, 1381, 1823, 2221, 3323-5, 3327, 3328, 3398-404

Constitutional Reform 498, 655, 793, 1194, 1811

Development Policies and Strategies 2417

DIAND 3320

Drury Report 498, 3253, 3268

Economic Development 1952

Environmental Policy 2267

Ethnicity, Political Significance of 378

Federal-Provincial Relations 1823

Federal-Territorial Constitutional Relations 1391

Federal-Territorial Development Agreements 1952

Federal-Territorial Economic Relations 1609

Federal-Territorial Relations 355, 3253, 3320

Federal-Territorial Tax Relations 1610

First Ministers' Meetings 1811

Fiscal Transfers 1609, 1610

Institutions of Government 3326

Jurisdiction, Divided 2439

Local Government 3275

Nationalism 378

Northern Development 355, 2267, 2575

Northwest Territories, Division of 1139, 2575, 3201, 3324, 3399, 3400

Nunavut 1026, 1125, 1195, 2221, 3327, 3328

Parliamentary Committees 793

Aboriginal Peoples - Rights 936

Air Traffic Control, Bilingual 2181

Alberta 1890

Beige Paper 429, 1469, 3221

Bilingualism 462, 2181, 2184, 2185, 2968, 2969, 3086, 3093

Bill 101. 341, 2719, 2942, 3192

Bill 22. 341

Bill 57. 3120

Bi-polar Federalism 1059

Bloc populaire canadien 264

BNA Act 927

Caisse de dépôt et placement du Québec 3274

Caisses d'épargne 2335

Caisses de crédit 2335

Canada 35, 272, 368, 387, 423, 561

Canada Bill 1067

Canadian Charter of Rights and Freedoms 645, 851, 1064, 1168, 1267, 1331, 2940

Canadian Common Market 2114, 2115

Canadian History 3210

Caricatures and Cartoons 375

Catholic Church 656, 825

Centralization-Decentralization 241, 423, 534, 2345, 2477, 2641, 2658, 2686, 3220, 3278, 3279

Centres locaux de services communautaires 2686

Charter of the French Language 592, 2184, 3090

Churches, Protestant 486

Civil Service 3086

Commission permanente de la présidence du conseil, de la constitu-tion et des affaires intergouver-nementales 1576

Communications 854

Confederation 2807, 3349

Conflict, Linguistic 302, 341, 343, 358, 505, 592, 623, 2184-6, 3031

Conseil de planification et de développement du Québec 2536, 2981

Conseil des gens d'affaires du Québec 2806

Conseil du patronat du Québec 2806, 2807

Constitution Act, 1982. 936, 1267

Constitutional Change 691, 829, 941, 1050, 1058, 1068

Constitutional Conferences 1170

Constitutional History 186, 396, 690, 1020, 1069, 1168, 1577

Constitutional Law, See **Constitutional Law** - Quebec

Constitutional Reform, See **Constitutional Reform** - Quebec

Cooperative Movement 2924

Corporatism 3206

Courts, Structure and Role of 691

Covenant 186

Development Policies and Strategies 2536, 2663, 2799, 2805, 2981

Economic Conditions 265, 402, 2466, 3361

Economic Development 2663, 2924

Economic Policy 621, 1692-6, 1698, 1711, 2367, 2530, 2641, 2669, 2749, 2804, 2806, 2938, 3316

Economic Relations 1574

Economic stabilization 2669

Economic Union 1485

Education Policy 592, 3093

Energy Policy 2375

English-French Relations 245, 246, 272, 302, 357, 391, 405, 457, 468, 516, 565, 574, 598, 603, 1826, 2181, 2715, 3361

Environmental Policy 1574

Equalization 1990, 1992, 1993

Ethnicity, Political Significance of 258, 334, 384, 561, 570, 614, 632

Export Policy 2163

Federal Government 31, 529

Federal-Provincial Constitutional Relations, See **Federal-Provincial Constitutional Relations** - Quebec

Federal-Provincial Development Agreements 1989

Federal-Provincial Fiscal Relations 1697, 1819, 1830, 1990-3, 2976

Federal-Provincial Meetings 851, 852, 854, 869, 871, 875

Federal-Provincial Relations, See **Federal-Provincial Relations**-Quebec

Federal-Provincial Tax Relations 1884, 2944

Federal-Provincial-Municipal Fiscal Relations 2174

Federalism, See **Federalism**-Quebec

First Ministers' Meetings 1692-9, 1711

Fiscal Policy 1990, 1991, 2174, 2345, 2801

Fiscal Transfers 1894

Fisheries 2422

Fishery Policy 2422

Foreign Economic Relations 333, 1462, 1835, 2211

Foreign Relations 470

Forestry 941

Fowler Report 423

Free Trade 2115, 2800

French Language 2185

French-English Relations, See English-French Relations

Great Britain 561

Health 2363, 2976

Income Support 2519

Industrial Policy 2530

Integration-Disintegration 2114

Interprovincial Meetings 1444, 1446

Interprovincial Relations 439, 440, 517, 1170, 1227, 1313, 1397, 1451, 1469, 1966

Interprovincial Trade 2114, 2115

Interprovincial Transportation 2352

Jurisdiction, Divided 1172, 2807

Jurisdiction, Legal 1451

Language Policy, See **Language Policy** - Quebec

Languages: political-aspects 1171

Legislative Override 1313

Lévesque, René 240, 255, 472

Liberal Democracy 3294

Linguistic Demography 2940

Local Government 3278, 3279

Marxist Theory 130

Massey-Levesque Commission 423

Minorities, Status of 258, 333, 462, 710, 2721, 3031

Monetary Policy 2640

2358, 2406, 2462, 2470, 2471, 2482,
2509, 2522, 2550, 2562, 2579, 2580,
2633, 2645, 2686, 2710, 2754, 2758,
2776, 2815, 2819, 2846, 2861, 2865,
2880, 2892, 2896, 2957, 2991, 2996,
3014, 3015, 3016, 3018, 3019, 3020,
3029, 3030, 3067-9, 3082, 3083, 3088,
3094, 3095, 3100, 3116, 3126, 3130,
3141, 3145, 3161, 3194, 3219

Regulation of Trade 2684

Regulation, Federal Trade and Commerce Power 1166

Regulation, Provincial 2949

Regulations 2463, 2688, 3013, 3071,
3118

Regulatory Federalism 5

Regulatory Reform 2203, 2482, 2489,
2631, 2776, 2792, 3069, 3095, 3132

Regulatory Transfers 2688

Religion 79, 594, 1368

Rent Sharing 1599

Rental Housing 2123

Representative Bureaucracy 2653

Representative Government 3295,
3318

Research and Development 2493,
2654, 2760, 3054

Research and Technology 1825, 2233,
2299, 2302, 2324, 2359, 2433, 2447,
2938, 2980

Residual Power 1141, 1282

Resource Amendment 1179

Resource Development 1909, 2417,
2446

Resource Economics 2487

Resource Management 3089

Resource Management Powers 733

Resource Rents 3129

Resource Revenue 2383

Resource Revenues 390, 545, 663,
733, 920, 1066, 1179, 1280, 1320,
1395, 1484, 1553, 1599, 1604, 1607,
1833, 1893, 1895, 1923, 1953, 1980,
2031, 2040, 2052, 2162-4, 2212, 2597,
2599, 2602, 2606, 2666, 2667, 2768,
2772, 2773, 2781, 2791, 2811, 2812,
2813, 2823, 2852, 2853, 2861, 2920,
2921, 2992, 3006, 3028, 3161, 3181

Resource Revenues, Regionalism
1311

Resource Taxes 2383

Resources 835

Resources Law 2999

Resources Policy 254, 723, 732, 829,
862-4, 991, 1421, 1423, 1559-61, 2117,
2147, 2152-4, 2158, 2176, 2179, 2320,
2354, 2355, 2382, 2383, 2439, 2441,
2458, 2471, 2584, 2667, 2729, 2764,
2796-8, 2832, 2838, 2844, 2861, 2901,
2987, 2997-9, 3050, 3072, 3081, 3084,
3089, 3127, 3159, 3197, 3230, 3256,
3257

Resources, Offshore 863, 864

Responsibilities, Allocation of 19, 91,
226

Revenue Sharing 146, 1460, 1484,
1503, 2176, 2383, 2768, 2781, 2819,
2843, 3097

Rights, Collective 1240

Riel, Louis 558

Rights, Constitutional Protection of

Aboriginal Peoples, See **Aboriginal
Peoples** - Rights, Constitutional
Protection of

Affirmative Action 454

Bilingualism 684

Bill of Rights 1148, 1149, 1152,
1274

Sectoral Integration 2157, 2474, 2527-9, 2708, 2709, 2789, 3051, 3076, 3077, 3138, 3183

Social Policy 139, 1944

Socialism 140

Sovereignty 495

Soviet Union 32

Spain 32

State Government 3293

Supreme Court 648, 1033

Switzerland 32, 2057

Taxation 2986

Territory, Political Significance of 410

Trade Liberalization 3076

Trade Policy 2474, 3066

United States Bill of Rights 685

University Research 2360

Urban Policy 2683

Vertical Fiscal Adjustment 1840

West Germany 6, 8, 32, 1840, 2057

Universities and Colleges, See Education, Post-Secondary

University Research 2360

Uranium 2861, 2922

Urban Federalism 1925

Urban Policy 2683

User Fees 1999

Usufruct 996

Venture Capital 3273

Vertical Fiscal Adjustment 1840

Vorarlberg (Austria) 141

Voting 3305, 3353

Washington State 2009, 2010

Wastewater Disinfection 2504

Water Management 2154, 2280-2, 2285, 2661, 2897

Wealth, Redistribution of 894

Welfare 2761

Welfare State 2150, 2175

Welfare Theory 2782

West Germany 6, 8, 10, 11, 29, 32, 40, 145, 185, 190, 216, 228, 1840, 2049, 2057, 2860, 3226

Western Accord 1553

Western Alienation 349, 354, 364, 379, 406, 411, 427, 503, 581, 605, 615

Western Nationalism 338

Western Premiers' Conferences 2078

Western Separatism 338, 347-9, 382, 406, 427, 455, 503, 526, 538, 550, 551, 555, 560, 582, 605, 615

Western Transition 2342, 2770, 2771, 3009, 3084, 3085, 3135

Western Transportation Initiative 2849

White Paper 363, 404, 459, 460, 1469

Wildlife 1749, 1750

Wildlife Management 2190

Women's Rights 1049, 1186

Women, Status of 1016, 1533, 1798-1802, 1804

Worksharing 2673

Yugoslavia 85, 152, 171, 722

Yukon 317, 318, 355, 1391, 1392, 2267, 3198, 3352, 3415